OCR
A LEVEL

PSYCHOLOGY
FOR A LEVEL YEAR 2

Louise Ellerby-Jones

Sandra Latham

Nigel Wooldridge

This is an OCR endorsed resource

DYNAMIC
LEARNING

OCR
Oxford Cambridge and RSA

HODDER
EDUCATION
AN HACHETTE UK COMPANY

The Publishers would like to thank the following for permission to reproduce copyright material:

Picture credits: p4 © intheskies – Fotolia; p5 © Mary Evans Picture Library / Alamy; p6 © The Granger Collection, NYC / TopFoto; p7 © liszt collection / Alamy; p8 © dundanim – Fotolia; p10 © Maria Brzostowska – Fotolia; p11 © AF archive / Alamy; p14 © Estudi M6 – Fotolia; p20 © U.S. NATIONAL INSTITUTE OF HEALTH / SCIENCE PHOTO LIBRARY; p33 © WELLCOME DEPT. OF COGNITIVE NEUROLOGY / SCIENCE PHOTO LIBRARY; p36 t © rosinka79 – Fotolia, bl © theartofphoto – Fotolia, c © StockRocket – Fotolia, br © Alexandre Zveiger – Fotolia; p37 © phoenix021 – Fotolia; p38 © Serggod – Fotolia; p39 © Sipa Press / REX Shutterstock; p46 © ep stock – Fotolia; p49 © michaeljung – Fotolia; p50 © jcg_oida – Fotolia; p56 tr © The Image Works / TopFoto, br © SCIENCE SOURCE / SCIENCE PHOTO LIBRARY; p59 © thislife pictures / Alamy; p60 © Jules Selmes; p62 © Jules Selmes; p68 l © Alexandr Vasilyev – Fotolia, r © Mitarart – Fotolia; p69 © Thomas D. McAvoy / The LIFE Images Collection / Getty Images; p73 © Zoonar GmbH / Alamy; p76 © David J. Green / Alamy; p77 © AF archive / Alamy; p78 stokkete – Fotolia; p90 © amana images inc. / Alamy; p92 tl © chrisberic – Fotolia, c © tunedin – Fotolia, tr © Gennadiy Poznyakov – Fotolia, b © valery121283 – Fotolia; p109 © David R. Frazier Photolibrary, Inc. / Alamy; p113 © RF Corbis Value / Alamy; p119 © Afro American Newspapers / Gado / Getty Images; p120 © Robert Nickelsberg / Getty Images; p125 © P. G. Zimbardo Inc.; p130 Magic Car Pics / REX Shutterstock; p131 © kyslynskyy – Fotolia; p132 © Everett Collection Historical / Alamy; p137 © Jafaris Mustafa – Fotolia; p138 © Derrick Neill – Fotolia; p142 © Flirt / Alamy; p152 © Mick Sinclair / Alamy; p153 © Neil Grant / Alamy; p154 © Wavebreakmedia Ltd / Thinkstock; p158 © lawcain – Fotolia; p163 © David A. Barnes / Alamy; p165 © Paul Heinrich / Alamy; p166 t © monkeybusinessimages / iStock / Thinkstock, b © ZUMA Press, Inc / Alamy; p168 © Richard Smith / Alamy; p171 © dolfin / iStock / Thinkstock; p174 © sandy young / Alamy; p176 © monkeybusinessimages / iStock / Thinkstock; p181 © PCN Photography / Alamy; p182 © PCN Photography / Alamy; p187 © Howard Sayer / Alamy; p188 l © dpa picture alliance / Alamy, r © DragonImages – Fotolia; p191 © Fuse / Thinkstock; p192 l © Gino Santa Maria – Fotolia, r © AF archive / Alamy; p194 l © galit seligmann / Alamy, r © DuÅjan KostiÄ / iStock / Thinkstock; p196 © italo – Fotolia; p197 © BlueSkyImages – Fotolia; p198 © Steve Bardens / Actionplus / TopFoto; p199 © Gunter Marx / RE / Alamy; p202 © Mike Powell / Getty Images; p203 © Maridav – Fotolia; p206 © Brocreative – Fotolia; p210 © Annegret Hilse / imago / Photoshot; p211 © Comstock Images / Stockbyte / Thinkstock; p213 © Fuse / Thinkstock; p214 © Brand X Pictures / Stockbyte / Thinkstock; p215 © Zsolnai Gergely – Fotolia; p217 © Gavin Rodgers / Alamy; p218 © gosphotodesign – Fotolia; p220 © Al Bello / Getty Images.

Acknowledgements

Every effort has been made to trace all copyright holders, but if any have been inadvertently overlooked the Publishers will be pleased to make the necessary arrangements at the first opportunity.

Although every effort has been made to ensure that website addresses are correct at time of going to press, Hodder Education cannot be held responsible for the content of any website mentioned in this book. It is sometimes possible to find a relocated web page by typing in the address of the home page for a website in the URL window of your browser.

Hachette UK's policy is to use papers that are natural, renewable and recyclable products and made from wood grown in sustainable forests. The logging and manufacturing processes are expected to conform to the environmental regulations of the country of origin.

Orders: please contact Bookpoint Ltd, 130 Milton Park, Abingdon, Oxon OX14 4SB. Telephone: +44 (0)1235 827720.
Fax: +44 (0)1235 400454. Lines are open 9.00a.m.–5.00p.m., Monday to Saturday, with a 24-hour message answering service. Visit our website at www.hoddereducation.co.uk

© Louise Ellerby-Jones, Sandra Latham, Nigel Wooldridge, 2015

First published in 2015 by

Hodder Education

An Hachette UK Company

50 Victoria Embankment

London EC4Y 0DZ

Impression number   10 9 8 7 6 5 4 3 2

Year   2019 2018 2017 2016

Cover photo © grgroup – Fotolia.com

Illustrations by Aptara, Inc.

Typeset in India by Aptara, Inc.

Printed in Dubai

A catalogue record for this title is available from the British Library

ISBN 9781471836282

Contents

Introduction

In Component 1 of OCR A Level Psychology you looked at the methods used throughout psychological research to a greater or lesser extent. You also gained an understanding of the methodological issues in psychology and how psychology is seen predominantly as a science. Component 2 focused on the key research that has contributed to our understanding of human and animal behaviour, alongside some of the debates that exist in psychology. In addition, you have seen that psychology is not one clear idea about human behaviour but is made up of several different and sometimes overlapping theories about why people behave in the way they do, in any given situation.

Using this knowledge, psychologists can take research findings and use them to predict what might happen if they manipulate variables such as making changes to the environment or manipulate the cognitive processes of people. In other words, how they can apply the research findings to real-life situations. It would be nice to think that this is always for the good of society, but there are some situations when such evidence has been misused to justify atrocities, such as genocide or dictatorships. Generally though, people are helped by the application of psychological research, both theories and studies.

In this book we will look at the application of knowledge in the real-life fields of clinical psychology (mental health), child development, criminal behaviour, environmental psychology, and sport and exercise psychology. There are many other applications of psychology that we could have looked at, but the OCR specification has identified these five. The important thing to remember about the OCR specification is that for the Component 3 exam you will need to know the **compulsory** section – Issues in Mental Health – as well as **two** of the four options: child development, crime, environmental, and sport and exercise psychology.

This component is more concerned with the application of knowledge than with detailed knowledge of research studies, although there will be some research mentioned in the background of each topic on which the psychological concepts and ideas are based. You don't need to know these research studies in detail but, if you use them in your assessment, it will show your understanding of the application. However,

you **must** know the Key Research, which will form an integral part of the exam. The background and the key research will enable you to identify how we might devise strategies and techniques for helping people or changing their behaviour for the better. This is the third part of each topic and you will need to be able to apply your knowledge of psychology in a synoptic way to consider practical applications and the issues around implementing these.

PLEASE NOTE: You will not need to know everything about every topic. For example you don't have to know every change of view in the history of mental illness, but you need show an understanding of how views have changed over time. Don't worry if you get confused between Hippocrates and Homer, you don't need to know both.

In a topic such as intelligence, you will only need how some psychologists define intelligence, not all the definitions. You can learn as much or as little as you can cope with. There will be a depth/breadth trade off where you can write about several definitions in less detail than one or two.

Check the specification and make sure you have a knowledge and understanding of each topic in the background.

You will notice that the areas in psychology, such as biological and cognitive, and perspectives such as behaviourism, are revisited to some extent in the Issues in Mental Health section, with the introduction of new perspectives from Humanistic Psychology and Cognitive Neuroscience, which could not be more different in their approach to explaining human behaviour. In each of the options there are six topics: two with a foundation in the social explanation of behaviour, two from the area of cognitive psychology, and two based on the biological assumptions about human behaviour. These are not definitive however (for example, the whole of the child psychology unit could fit into the Developmental area) so don't get too worried about the focus of each topic. You should know by now that nothing is psychology is clear cut – there are always areas for discussion and overlap.

It is hoped that reading about these topics will show you the wide range of applications of psychological research, together with stimulating a critical interest in the world around you and providing a better understanding about what makes you both similar to other humans and uniquely different from everyone else.

Feel free to look at the options that you are not studying for the exam and read any that strike you as interesting. Remember, reading about the application of psychology is not just about passing the exam (but reading the book will certainly help!).

Find out more

- Look on the website of the British Psychological Society (WWW.BPS.ORG.UK) to find out what careers studying psychology can lead to.

Applied Psychology

Chapter 1

Issues in Mental Health

Mental health problems are not necessarily viewed as an illness, sometimes they are disorders or a disturbance of the usual mental functions we expect. They can be relatively minor and short lived, such as worries we all have, or can be serious and/or long-term conditions. There are common symptoms within mental disorders which allow for diagnosis but individual differences mean that no two people will experience a disorder in the same way, just the same as the way people have different pain thresholds and will therefore experience physical discomfort differently.

Mental health disorders are diagnosed by medical practitioners – either by psychiatrists, who are medical doctors who have specialised in mental illness, or by psychologists, who are specialists in the mind only. Both can diagnose and treat patients and it is important that people seek help from professionals, as the earlier the treatment often the better the outcome. Mental illness should not be seen as a person's fault or as a weakness, or something that someone can help. Telling a patient suffering from depression to 'pull themselves together' is as useful as saying to a person with a broken leg 'just walk on it'.

The Mental Health Foundation suggests that mental health problems are very common, with about a quarter of the UK population experiencing some kind of mental health problem in any one year. These may not be diagnosed, or may not need treatment. Anxiety and depression are the most common diagnoses, with about one in ten people affected at any one time. Between one and two in every 100 people experience a severe mental illness, such as bipolar disorder or schizophrenia;

these disorders are known as psychotic disorders during which people may have periods when they lose touch with reality.

Figure 1.1

There is still a stigma attached to mental illness, although legislation and changes in society are, hopefully, slowly eradicating these.

 **Stop and ask yourself...**

- How do you think people with mental illness might be discriminated against?

Links to
- Ethics

The historical context of mental health

The specification requires you to know historical views of mental illness, to know how abnormality can be defined, and how mental disorders are categorised. The key research, 'On being sane in insane places', is by Rosenhan (1973), and the application considers how the categorisation is applied in terms of the characteristics of any one affective disorder, any one psychotic disorder and any one anxiety disorder.

Historical views of mental health

Views on the causes or reasons for mental illness vary according to the culture and the age in which they occur. This in turn influences the 'treatment' of these disorders. Some of them may seem barbaric to us now, but maybe we will look back at the twenty-first century in amazement that some mental illnesses were treated with chemicals!

There is some evidence that prehistoric people believed that madness was caused by possession of devils and the way to release these was to practise trepanation. This is where holes are drilled in the skull to let the 'demons' out; skulls dating back to 6500BC have been found that show this. It can also be seen from the skulls that some of these have healed, suggesting that the patient survived this treatment. Trepanation was also used later and Hippocrates (c. 460–377BC) also gives directions on how to carry out this procedure. During the Middle Ages and the Renaissance, trepanation was seen as a cure for various ailments, including seizures and skull fractures. Much later in the nineteenth century, prefrontal leucotomy treatment was used, which was a precursor to lobotomy used in the twentieth century to cure many disorders such as depression, mania and schizophrenia. This involved cutting a trephine hole into the skull, inserting an instrument and destroying parts of the brain.

If we go back to the times of the Old Testament (around 1000BC) the use of the term 'madness' was an all-encompassing term for psychotic and neurotic illnesses, and it was perceived as a punishment from God. Saul became mad, which was evidenced by his slaughter of 85 priests for no reason, after he had angered God. Interestingly, it is recorded in the Bible that music calmed Saul, perhaps the first documented treatment for 'madness'.

Early civilisations such as the Chinese and Egyptian civilisations viewed mental illness as a result of possession by demons and treatment consisted of exorcism techniques

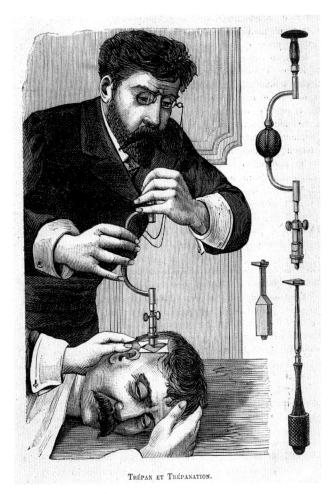

Figure 1.2 Trepanning

(such as beatings, restraint and starvation) designed to drive demons out of the afflicted person's body.

When Homer was writing in ancient Greece (800–700BC) it was still considered that madness was a punishment from the gods. The myth that Hera punished Hercules by 'sending madness upon him' illustrates this view. However, the Greek physician Hippocrates first identified mental illness as a scientific phenomenon. He thought that madness resulted from an imbalance of four bodily humours and could be cured by balancing these four humours.

Man's body has blood, phlegm, yellow bile and black bile. These make up his body and through them he feels illness or enjoys health. When all the humours are properly balanced and mingled, he feels the most perfect health. Illness occurs when one of the humors is in excess, or is reduced in amount, or is entirely missing from the body. (Hippocrates, On the Constitution of Man (c. 500BC), in Jones, 1931)

5

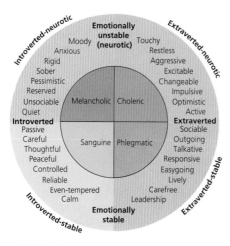

Figure 1.3 The four humours and how they might affect moods

Figure 1.4 Bloodletting, a cure for 'madness'

Depression was thought to be a result of an excess of black bile (melaina chole) and diets, purgatives (laxatives) and bloodlettings would rebalance this excess. Although this seems ridiculous in modernity, it is a significant advance on the theory of religion or mythology as it actually suggests mental illness is a response to physical changes. This founded the medical model of medicine in Europe.

In Ancient Rome, Hippocrates' theory of unbalanced humours was rejected by some (c. 100BC) and replaced with the belief that melancholy resulted from emotions such as rage, fear and grief. Anxiety-prone people had excessive perturbations (disturbances) of the mind. Cicero's questionnaire for the assessment of mental disorders is very similar to the tools used today to assess a patient's psychiatric history and mental state. Following the growth of the Christian church around AD300, it promoted the idea of madness as a punishment from God or demonic (devil) possession. It followed that religion was central to any treatment within medieval asylums such as the Bethlem Hospital in London. Some monasteries also became centres for the treatment of mental disorders. However, older treatments such as bloodletting and purgatives continued alongside prayer and confession.

During the Middle Ages, Eastern cultures that hadn't adopted Christian ideas focused on the separation of the soul with ideas based on science rather than the metaphysical concepts of Christianity.

Mental illness in the Middle Ages had potentially fatal consequences. The burning of witches, who were deemed to be mad, reached its peak in the fourteenth and fifteenth centuries. However, in 1563 *De Praestigiis Daemonum* (The Deception of Demons) was written by Johann Weyer, which argued that the madness of heretics was not divine punishment or demonic possession, but resulted from natural causes. Hysteria and epilepsy were the two illnesses that were most frequently confused with witchcraft or demonic possession and, as these were more prevalent in women, more women were burned as witches than men. The burning of witches began to fade out towards the end of the 1700s as people gained a greater understanding of hysteria and epilepsy.

Hippocrates' humoural theories persisted into the seventeenth and eighteenth centuries even though other theories were contributing to the 'treatment' of madness. More enlightened thinkers began to suggest that disorders of the psyche or mind arose from reasons and emotions, and exposure to stressors was also considered to be a factor in madness, with the beginning of the idea of inheritance of disorders and physical damage. This resulted in a 'moral treatment', which incorporated respect for the patient, a trusting and confiding doctor–patient relationship, a calm environment and routine, and which removed treatments such as diets, purgatives and bloodlettings. In 1796 the Tukes (father and son) in England founded the York Retreat, the first institution 'for the humane care of the insane' in the British Isles.

In the nineteenth century, mental hospitals in North America, Britain and many countries of continental Europe treated the 'insane poor' according to the principles of moral treatment. Psychiatry became a recognised medical speciality, although medical views on the origins of mental illness had not changed much.

Figure 1.5 Bethlem Hospital

Modern psychology began in the 1890s and is responsible for the acceptance that mental illness is a result of influences on the mind, which can vary from biological influences, such as the disease syphilis, to the unconscious conflicts of Freud's theory, and the humanistic beliefs of self-worth, with the behaviourists believing in the idea of learning being involved in the acquisition of disorders. However, the predominant approach to mental illness is the medical model, with mental health now more often than not being diagnosed and treated according to the biological explanation.

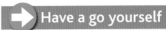 **Have a go yourself**

- Make a timeline to show how attitudes to mental illness have changed over time. This will help with your revision.

Defining abnormality

There is more than one way to define abnormal or atypical behaviour. These each have their flaws, and it is often a problem that labelling a person as abnormal can have a major impact on how they see themselves and how society sees them. Criminals who are diagnosed as insane may find that they are sentenced to a secure hospital instead of prison, or they may be given lesser sentences. People with mental illness may be discriminated against by doctors – residents in mental hospitals who are deemed unable to understand the voting procedure are unable to vote in the UK. There is also evidence of more widespread discrimination against people with a label of mental illness. Examples include higher insurance premiums, as the insurance company may believe that the person is a higher risk, or employers perceiving mental illness as a negative, even though discrimination against people simply because of a diagnosis of a mental disorder is illegal in the UK.

IN THE NEWS

In February 2015 the Commons Home Affairs Select Committee reported that 236 children under the age of 18 with mental health issues were detained in police custody in England and Wales from 2013 to 2014. Keith Vaz, the chairman of the committee, said that this scandal is unacceptable. Over 6000 adults were also detained in police cells under the Mental Health Act; they were not necessarily criminals, just mentally ill. Patients were sometimes restrained by handcuffs and leg restraints, and two patients who were detained due to mental health died in police custody. Even being released from police custody didn't solve the problem: 45 out of the 68 people who were released from police custody and committed suicide within two days of their release, had mental health issues.

So if, as a society, we are going to define abnormality it should be as accurate and fair as possible because, as we shall see in the key research by Rosenhan, this labelling can have short- and long-term consequences.

Rosenhan and Seligman (1984) suggested four definitions that would identify abnormality, not saying that every criteria would necessarily have to be fulfilled: statistical infrequency, failure to function adequately, acting against social norms and deviation from ideal mental health.

Statistical infrequency

Any behaviour that is shown less often than the normal amount for that society is, by its very nature, abnormal. According to the Report of the National Audit of Schizophrenia (NAS) in 2012, 220,000 of the UK population of 63.7 million (3.45 per cent) suffered from schizophrenia. Schizophrenia can therefore be classed as an abnormality. An analysis of NHS data in 2012 showed that depression is one of the most frequently occurring disorders, being diagnosed in 4.7 million people (7.38 per cent of the population). It is still infrequent enough to be classified as abnormal under this criteria.

However, to simply be abnormal does not actually mean that there must be a diagnosis of a psychological disorder. For example, highly gifted individuals in sport, art or intelligence may be abnormal but do not actually have a psychological disorder.

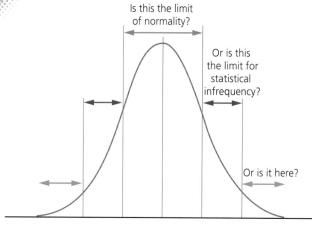

Figure 1.6 Where would you put the cut off point for statistical infrequency?

Failure to function adequately

If a person is unable to live a normal life adequately – for example, is unable to hold down a job, maintain a relationship, look after themselves or interact in society effectively – then they could, under Rosenhan and Seligman's definition, be considered abnormal. Again, it is important that this definition of abnormality does not automatically confer the label of mental illness on that person. Someone may, for many reasons (such as lack of education), not be able to get employment, and lack of money could then foster the lack of relationship and self-care. However, it is fair to say that often such failure to function adequately is a result of a psychological disorder, such as addiction – when all financial resources go on the addictive substance, such as alcohol – or depression, where a person is unable to take care of him or herself due to the lethargy associated with this disorder.

Deviation from social norms

Every society has social norms (normal behaviours) that it maintains through laws, guidelines or societal pressure. In the UK it is illegal to possess or take Class A drugs such as heroin and cocaine; there are also guidelines about how much it is 'safe' to drink per week. Society also pressures people to go to work, and frowns upon people talking to themselves in the middle of the street. So a person who doesn't abide by these acceptable or normal social behaviours expected by society may be considered abnormal. These abnormalities may actually be the result of disorders such as obsessive–compulsive disorder (OCD) where people are driven to extreme behaviours such as excessive double-checking of things like locks, appliances and switches, or repeating certain words to reduce anxiety. These behaviours are not seen as normal in society.

However, if someone doesn't follow a society's norms, such as getting a job, this doesn't necessarily indicate a

Figure 1.7 Failure to function adequately or not?

Figure 1.8 Different or abnormal?

Stop and ask yourself...

- Can you make a list of socially acceptable behaviours that you think show mental health?

Links to
- Validity

psychological disorder. Someone may talk to themselves for a variety of reasons – that 'why did I go up the stairs?' moment we all have sometimes. It is difficult to judge someone as abnormal if it is sometimes acceptable to break our social norms.

One good point about this definition is that it can be culturally specific, as any society has its own set of norms against which to judge people's behaviour.

Deviation from ideal mental health

This is a rather ambiguous criteria, as who is to judge what 'ideal mental health' actually is? Psychologists have criteria that are generally believed to represent, to a lesser or greater extent, ideal mental health. These can include:

- feeling positive about yourself and being able to grow psychologically
- having self-discipline and being able to act independently
- having an accurate perception of reality and coping with the demands of that reality
- having positive social interactions with friends and family.

Not all of these criteria have to be present all of the time for someone to be seen as having mental health rather than mental illness. This definition hints at the symptoms of psychological disorders rather than simple abnormality.

In 1989, Rosenhan and Seligman extended their criteria to include:

- suffering – in some way a person has negative consequences of their behaviour
- maladaptiveness – not fitting in with society and maintaining normal social contacts
- unconventional behaviour – something that wouldn't be expected in society
- irrationality in behaviours that others wouldn't be able to understand
- unpredictability/loss of control that may be unpredictable to the observer or the person exhibiting the behaviour and is not what we would expect
- observer discomfort due to the unpredictability and irrationality of the behaviour
- violation of moral standards where behaviour fails to meet the standards set by society.

Again Rosenhan and Seligman thought that 'normal' people might display one of these, but it is when several of these are met that it can indicate abnormality.

Rosenhan and Seligman are not the only psychologists to attempt to define abnormality. Jahoda developed her criteria for ideal mental health in 1958

and suggested that failure to meet these criteria would suggest a mental illness. Her criteria are:

1. Positive attitudes toward the self.
2. Growth, development and self-actualisation (reaching potential).
3. A balance of psychic forces, with resistance to stress and frustration.
4. Independent behaviour, including non-conformity when it is appropriate.
5. A true perception of reality.
6. Adequacy in love, work and play, and the ability to adapt and adjust to problems.

As you can see, Jahoda's criteria are inherent in the later definitions of Rosenhan and Seligman. There are common themes of positive self-image, growth and development, independent thoughts and actions, accurate perceptions of reality and being able to cope with the demands and problems of that reality, and maintaining interpersonal relationships.

There are problems with trying to use these criteria however, as they are vague and can be difficult to quantify. What is a 'balance of psychic forces'? Many, if not all of us, may have periods where we don't exhibit all of these criteria, and so it is difficult to use them to accurately assess abnormality.

As you can see, the terms abnormality and mental illness are not interchangeable. Abnormality may not be due to mental illness, but could mental illness always be regarded as abnormality under these criteria?

Have a go yourself

- Make a chart of the definitions you are going to revise for the exam. In one column give the definition, in the second give an example from mental health, and, in the third, give a strength and weakness of each definition.

Categorising mental disorders

Medical practitioners and psychologists need to make a diagnosis of patients presenting symptoms, which can then allow appropriate treatment or therapy. As mental illness has been predominantly medicalised – in Western cultures particularly – this diagnosis follows much the same logical process of assessing behavioural criteria identified as symptomatic of a disorder. For physical illnesses, such as chicken pox or a stroke, there are lists of symptoms that people – both medical and non-medical – can look out for. The same process is therefore used when diagnosing such diverse psychological disorders as post-traumatic stress disorder (PTSD) and malingering.

There are two main approaches to categorising disorders and identifying specific disorders within those categories. These are the Diagnostic and Statistical Manual of Mental Disorders (DSM) and the International Classification of Disorders (ICD). Both of these comprise of a set of symptoms that are indicative of each disorder but, beyond that, there are some major differences. DSM is used predominantly in the USA and ICD throughout the rest of the world, although this difference is gradually being eroded – it would be more likely that a practitioner would use both of these tools. These two tools diagnose disorders but within each manual are the categories of disorders that practitioners use to group together illnesses with similar symptoms or behaviours.

The ICD and DSM are updated to allow for changes in social attitudes or norms, for example homosexuality was once considered to be a disorder but was removed from DSM in 1986. Internet gaming disorder was included for the first time in DSM-5 (2013).

These tools may offer a starting point to identify a disorder but they are not useful for explanations or treatments for disorders, and may cause harm by labelling an illness something which it isn't. They could be influenced by corporate pressure; for example, there is an argument that identifying a disease allows a pharmaceutical company to provide a drug to treat it, thus increasing its profits, and keeping medical practitioners in lucrative work.

Krimsky and Cosgrove (2012) found that the 69 per cent of the panel working on the new DSM-5 had links with the pharmaceutical industry, which may have biased their work. Also, there is scope for misuse of drugs or using a diagnosis to avoid looking for other causes of a disorder, such as parenting or the environment. Professor L. Alan Sroufe (2012), who has carried out a longitudinal study on children to assess the incidence of ADHD-type disorders, and wrote the

essay *Ritalin Gone Wrong*, suggests that there is no causal link between brain activity and ADHD, but there is a link. However, simply giving drugs such as Ritalin may not be the answer:

Finally, the illusion that children's behavior problems can be cured with drugs prevents us as a society from seeking the more complex solutions that will be necessary. Drugs get everyone – politicians, scientists, teachers and parents – off the hook. Everyone except the children, that is …

This view was countered by others, such as John M. Grohol (2012). In his rebuttal of Sroufe, *Ritalin Gone Right: Children, Medications and ADHD*, he said:

What it [Sroufe's essay] does demonstrate, to me anyways, is someone who will cherry-pick the vast ADHD research literature to find something that supports his point of view, and then suggest this one study characterizes the vast majority of ADHD research. There are a dozen longitudinal studies measuring how ADHD progresses into early adulthood, and many other studies – some that are far more methodologically rigorous – that demonstrate just the opposite of Dr. Sroufe's claims.

This shows the controversy which surrounds the categorisation and diagnosis of dysfunctional behaviours. The fifth version of the Diagnostic and Statistical Manual of Mental Disorders (DSM-5) was ready for use in 2013 and was expected to be used instead of the previous version (DSM-IV) by 2014. It combined the first three axes of DSM-IV and removed Axis Five, where a patient was given a score out of 100 as to their ability to function. It also revised many of its disorders, and added some more contemporary disorders. For example, it now includes childhood-onset fluency disorder (a new name for stuttering) and has specified a new disorder of hoarding. It removed the DSM-IV subtypes of schizophrenia – such as paranoid, disorganised, catatonic – because the ability to identify specific, separate subtypes of schizophrenia from symptoms lacked diagnostic stability, low reliability and poor validity. It has categories such as tic disorders and then these are subdivided (into three in DSM-5), which are:

- Tourette's disorder (also called Tourette Syndrome; TS)
- persistent (also called chronic) motor or vocal tic disorder
- provisional tic disorder.

DSM-5 also lists, where appropriate, the ICD code number to cross reference the two diagnostic manuals.

ICD is now in its 10th edition (ICD-11 is due by 2017) and is used by all member states in the World Health Organization, and has been translated into 43 languages. ICD-10 came into use in 1994. Chapter V(F)

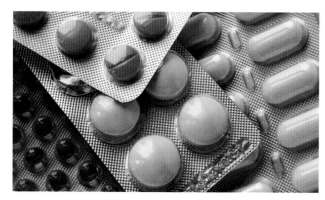

Figure 1.9 What influence does the pharmaceutical industry have over the categorisation of mental disorders?

of ICD-10, which refers to mental disorders rather than physical disorders, has 100 categories of disorder – F00 to F99 – although not all of these are used in ICD-10 (this is to allow for changes and additions when ICD-11 is introduced in 2017).

These categories include, for example, F95 Tic disorders, which is then divided into sub-divisions:

- F95.0 Transient tic disorder
- F95.1 Chronic motor or vocal tic disorder
- F95.2 Combined vocal and multiple motor tic disorder (Tourette's syndrome)
- F95.8 Other tic disorders
- F95.9 Tic disorder, unspecified.

The validity of the diagnostic tools can be questioned, as they are used by practitioners in what could be a subjective or personal way. For example, Ford and Widiger (1989) found that presenting the same symptoms to practitioners but changing the gender of the patient resulted in different diagnosis, with females more likely to be diagnosed with histrionic personality disorder and males with antisocial personality disorder, even when they actually had the other disorder.

The reliability is also questioned by practitioners. Kappa is a measure of the extent of agreement between two clinicians diagnosing the same patients (think of it as a similar concept to inter-rater reliability). The measure ranges from 0 to 1 and considers the probability of the same diagnosis being due to chance – 0 is only chance levels of agreement, 1 is perfect agreement, and 0.50 is an agreement level halfway between the two. Spitzer and Fleiss (1974) looked at the kappa values for each of six prior studies and these values ranged from 0.10 to 0.90 with a mean of 0.52. They concluded that no category of mental disorder has consistently high reliability, but three (mental deficiency, organic brain syndrome (but not its subtypes) and alcoholism) had a satisfactory kappa score:

The level of reliability is no better than fair for psychosis and schizophrenia, and is poor for the remaining categories.

This aspect of validity and reliability is explored further in the key research by Rosenhan below.

Key research: Rosenhan (1973) On being sane in insane places

Background

Rosenhan wanted to see if it was possible to tell the difference between sanity and insanity in a person, and whether hospitals really could tell the difference between someone who is sane and someone who is insane.

Method

Pseudopatients (people pretending to be mentally ill) tried to gain admission to 12 hospitals in five different states on the East and West coasts of the USA. There were old and new facilities, some had good staffing levels and some didn't; 11 of them had some state or university funding, only one was strictly private, relying on patients' fees for their funds.

Each of the eight pseudopatients would call one of the hospitals for an appointment and would pretend to be suffering from symptoms, complaining that they had been hearing voices. These 'voices' were unclear but were saying 'empty', 'hollow' and 'thud'. They were not familiar voices and were the same sex as the pseudopatient. The rest of the pseudopatient's personal details were true, although if they were a medical practitioner, they hid that fact.

Once they were admitted, they immediately acted normally with no mention of the symptoms again. The pseudopatient spoke to people the way he or she would normally behave and speak, for example attempting to engage in conversations. They did everything they were asked, such as going to dinner, but didn't swallow any medication they were given. While on the ward the pseudopatients made notes on what happened, often in public places. They were only able to leave if they were discharged.

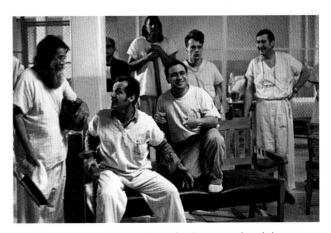

Figure 1.10 *One Flew Over the Cuckoo's Nest* explored the state of mental health hospitals

> **Take it further**
>
> - Read *One Flew Over the Cuckoo's Nest* by Ken Kesey to explore these ideas further.

Participants

The participants were the people in the hospital – not the pseudopatients. Data was collected on the other patients and the medical staff in the hospitals. In all, 12 hospitals were included in the study. Only in one did the hospital administrator and chief psychologist know what Rosenhan (himself the first pseudopatient) was doing.

 Stop and ask yourself ...

- Are there any ways in which the observers could also be seen as participants in this study? What are the strengths and weaknesses of a participant observation? How are these reflected in Rosenhan's study?

Results and discussion

Each pseudopatient (apart from one instance) was admitted with a diagnosis of schizophrenia and released with a diagnosis of schizophrenia in remission. The pseudopatients were never detected as being fake by the medical staff, and their records show this. The time they spent in hospital ranged from 7 to 52 days, with an average of 19 days.

The normal are not detectably sane

It was obviously difficult for the medical staff to identify the sane people who were pseudopatients, although the other patients were less easily fooled. In three hospitals 35 out of 118 patients voiced their suspicions about the 'insanity' of the pseudopatients, saying things like: 'You're not crazy', 'You're a journalist, or a professor', 'You're checking up on the hospital'.

The reason why doctors may have been so ready to misdiagnose could be the bias towards calling a healthy person sick (a false positive, type 2 error), which is better in many ways than misdiagnosing a sick person as healthy (false negative, type 1 error), as then that person would fail to get the treatment they needed. However, while this might work for physical illness it is less clear cut for a diagnosis of medical illness. The stigma of the label of mental illness may override the need to err completely on the side of caution.

Rosenhan then wanted to check if it was just as likely that a doctor could make a type 1 error and misdiagnose a sick person as healthy. He set up a study where staff at a research and teaching hospital who

doubted his findings from the pseudopatients were told that during the next three months one or more pseudopatients would try to get admitted. The staff were told to rate each patient as how likely they were to be a pseudopatient but to treat everyone as if they were a real patient, so that no one would miss out on treatment they needed. A 10-point scale was used, with 1 and 2 reflecting high confidence that the patient was a pseudopatient. For the 193 patients who were admitted:

- at least one staff member rated 41 patients as highly confident they were pseudopatients
- 23 were rated highly confident by at least one psychiatrist and 19 by a psychiatrist plus one other member of staff.

In reality, no genuine pseudopatient had contacted and gone to the hospital.

This shows that it is just as easy to judge the sick as healthy. This may be because staff knew about the research so went too far the other way, and that this wouldn't normally happen, but it does suggest that massive errors in diagnosis can be made when trying to diagnose sanity or insanity.

Experience of psychiatric hospitalisation

Staff and patients were segregated, with staff facilities and work rooms, and the pseudopatients spending time in the ward and dayroom. Staff tended to only come out to administer medication or therapy, to attend a patient conference, or to instruct or reprimand a patient.

Rosenhan suggests this was 'as if the disorder that afflicts their charges is somehow catching'.

To measure the amount of staff and patient interaction, the pseudopatients recorded how much time out of their work room (nicknamed 'the cage') the staff actually spent, even if this time was spent on something other than interacting with patients, such as folding laundry or watching television.

The average amount of time spent by attendants outside of the cage was 11.3 per cent of their shift, and it was rare for a staff member to spend time talking with patients or playing games with them. The actual time nurses spent outside of the cage was so small as to be immeasurable. The number of times they left it was recorded and this averaged 11.5 times per shift; in late and night shifts this reduced to 9.4 times per shift. The range of 4–41 times, suggests that some staff were much more likely to leave the work room than others.

 Stop and ask yourself ...

- Is there scientific proof of this, or is this Rosenhan's subjective interpretation?

Links to
- Psychology as a science

Doctors, especially psychiatrists, were seen even less often – only when they arrived and left – spending the rest of the item in the office. They would leave on average 6.7 times per day (range 1–17).

The 'stickiness' of psychodiagnostic labels

The diagnoses made were in no way influenced by the past 'normal' backgrounds of the pseudopatients, but their case histories were actually interpreted by the label they were given. The label influenced the history. For example, one pseudopatient had a normal background with a close relationship with his mother but was more remote from his father during his early childhood, which is often the case; during adolescence his relationship with his father became more close, while his relationship with his mother cooled. This is what we would expect from many teenagers, but this was interpreted as:

This white 39-year-old male ... manifests a long history of considerable ambivalence in close relationships, which began in early childhood. A warm relationship with his mother cools during his adolescence. A distant relationship to his father is described as becoming very intense.

His relationship with his wife was close and warm, with occasional angry exchanges – again, perfectly normal – and his children had been rarely smacked. This was noted in his case history as:

Affective stability is absent. His attempts to control emotionality with his wife and children are punctuated by angry outbursts and, in the case of the children, spankings. And while he says that he has several good friends, one senses considerable ambivalence embedded in those relationships also.

Behaviours in the hospital were seen and interpreted as being another aspect of their disorder, the label of schizophrenia colouring all the interpretations about what they were doing and why.

Making notes on the behaviour of the medical staff and patients was seen as an aspect of their pathological behaviour – continuous writing must be a behavioural manifestation of their disorder. One nurse asked a pseudopatient who was pacing the hospital corridors: 'Nervous, Mr X?', making the assumption that his pacing was a manifestation of his disorder. 'No, bored,' he said.

Another example was a group of patients sitting outside the entrance to the dining room half an hour before lunchtime. This was labelled as oral acquisitive behaviour in line with what might be expected from schizophrenia, but in fact there was so little to do in the hospital that patients tended to go to the dining room early as it was something to do.

Powerlessness and depersonalisation

Patients were often powerless to influence the interactions with medical staff, and could be punished verbally and physically by staff, although this stopped when other staff (not other patients) came into the room. No one would believe a patient if they complained, but they would believe a staff member. Rosenhan mentions that when he was acting as a pseudopatient a real patient was beaten because he approached an attendant and told him, 'I like you'.

The overwhelming sense of powerlessness was evident. The patients had lost many legal rights, they could not initiate contact with staff, and staff ignored them if they did try to talk to them, more often than not walking straight past. There was no privacy, either in the patient's possessions or case notes, which could be seen by anyone.

The patient was often monitored during bath and toilet times; sometimes there were no doors on the toilets. Physical examinations took place in semi-public places with other staff members there, and staff would point to patients and discuss them as if they weren't there.

The depersonalisation also ran to staff not caring if medication was taken or not; the pseudopatients flushed theirs down the toilet, often finding other patients' medication in there as well.

The sources of depersonalisation

The main concern was the lack of time patients spent with their medical staff, the average daily contact with psychiatrists, psychologists, and doctors combined ranged from 3.9 to 25.1 minutes, with an overall mean of 6.8 minutes. This was over a total of 129 days that the pseudopatients were in hospital and included the time spent during the admissions interview, ward meetings, group and individual psychotherapy sessions, case conferences and discharge meetings.

Avoidance and depersonalisation may also come about as patients are being given medication and staff may feel this is enough, with personal contact not being necessary.

Comparison studies

To consider the data on interpersonal contact, Rosenhan compared the responses to questions from pseudopatients with the responses of people to others who had not been diagnosed with a psychiatric illness.

In four hospitals a pseudopatient approached a staff member with the request, such as: 'Pardon me, Mr [or Dr or Mrs] X, could you tell me when I will be eligible for grounds privileges?', '... when I will be presented at the staff meeting?', or '... when I am likely to be discharged?', always adopting a courteous stance.

Data was also collected from Stanford University; a young female would approach a faculty member who was walking purposefully and asked them the following questions:

1. 'Pardon me, could you direct me to Encina Hall?' ('... to the Clinical Research Center?' was used if the student was at the medical school in Stanford)
2. 'Do you know where Fish Annex is?' (there is no Fish Annex at Stanford)
3. 'Do you teach here?'
4. 'How does one apply for admission to the college?'
5. 'Is it difficult to get in?'
6. 'Is there financial aid?'

Figure 1.11

Data was also collected from a university medical centre with a young female who had six questions. After the first question, however, she remarked to 18 of her respondents: 'I'm looking for a psychiatrist,' and to 15 others: 'I'm looking for an internist.' Ten other respondents received no inserted comment.

Table 1.1 Results of interaction initiated by pseudopatients and young females

Contact	Psychiatric hospitals		University campus (non-medical)	University medical centre (physicians)		
	(1) Psychiatrists	(2) Nurses and attendants	(3) Faculty	(4) 'Looking for a psychiatrist'	(5) 'Looking for an internist'	(6) No additional comment
Responses						
Moves on, head averted (%)	71	88	0	0	0	0
Makes eye contact (%)	23	10	0	11	0	0
Pauses and chats (%)	2	2	0	11	0	10
Stops and talks (%)	4	0.5	100	78	100	90
Mean number of questions answered (out of 6)	*	*	6	3.8	4.8	4.5
Respondents (No.)	13	47	14	18	15	10
Attempts (No.)	185	1283	14	18	15	10

* Not applicable

Table 1.1 shows quite clearly that out of the hospital and on the university campus, all questions were answered, with nobody moving on without stopping. Compare this to the psychiatric hospitals where only 6 per cent of psychiatrists and 2.5 per cent of nurses and attendants stopped or paused to talk.

Similarly, in the medical centre more people stopped, at least pausing, except for when the person said after the first question that she was 'Looking for a psychiatrist' – even the hint of mental illness is enough to reduce the amount of interpersonal contact.

The consequences of labelling and depersonalisation

This research appears to show that we cannot distinguish insanity from sanity, and it is worrying how this type of label, even if it is wrongly applied, can be used.

People can be needlessly stripped of their rights, such as the right to vote or handle their own bank accounts. The stigma attached to labels of mental illness can stick to people and affect their lives forever. Finally, patients might be 'sane' outside the psychiatric hospital but seem insane inside due to the bizarre setting they are responding to.

Summary and conclusions

As we cannot judge the sane from the insane, it makes sense not to admit people to hospital with labels that will stick to them but to have community-based therapy where they are treated as humans without a label, with therapy for specific behaviours rather than a named disorder.

The hospital environment only magnifies the distortion in the behaviour of others towards the patients.

Secondly, the staff in the hospitals were not malicious or stupid but just reacted as directed by the hospital environment. There needs to be some increase in the understanding and sensitivity of mental health workers towards psychiatric patients. This may be achieved by education or through experiencing the impact of hospitalisation.

It must be noted, however, that the experience of pseudopatients may be nothing like that of true patients. While being a very important study, this research was carried out in the 1970s and, as such, may lack validity as, we hope, the situation in mental health facilities would be very different today.

Application: characteristics of an affective disorder, a psychotic disorder and an anxiety disorder

Practitioners can use DSM and ICD to support their diagnoses of mental illness. The categories of disorder in them refer to the disorders that have a similar range of behaviours, not necessarily a similar cause or treatment. There are key facets of behaviour that might indicate one of the categories, which in turn can be investigated in more depth to identify a specific disorder.

The three categories included in the specification are just a sample of the categories in both of the publications. Affective disorders are mood disorders, such as depression or mania; psychotic disorders are disorders where the patient loses touch with reality, such as schizophrenia and bipolar (which has been categorised in ICD as an affective or mood disorder if there are no psychotic symptoms), and anxiety disorders include phobias and post-traumatic stress disorder.

The examples given below are only one such disorder and any other appropriate disorder would be equally acceptable in the exam. You will need to know the characteristics but also wider application issues, such as the problems of applying these categories in diagnosing disorders, or how researchers might investigate the validity or reliability of the characteristics. It is important to recognise that you are not a qualified psychologist and therefore shouldn't attempt to diagnose anyone using the incomplete information below. However, if you have concerns about a person you can always talk to a teacher or MIND for guidance.

To answer a question on this in the exam you would not have to know every one of the characteristics or both ICD and DSM. Look at symptoms that you think define the type of disorder.

Characteristics of an affective disorder: depression

ICD-10

F32.1 Moderate depressive episode

Diagnostic guidelines

At least two of the three most typical symptoms should be present, plus at least three (and preferably four) of the other symptoms.

Several symptoms are likely to be present to a marked degree, but this is not essential if a particularly wide variety of symptoms is present overall.

Minimum duration of the whole episode is about two weeks.

An individual with a moderately severe depressive episode will usually have considerable difficulty in continuing with social, work or domestic activities.

Typical symptoms

Depressed mood, loss of interest and enjoyment, and increased fatiguability.

Other symptoms

(a) Reduced concentration and attention.
(b) Reduced self-esteem and self-confidence.
(c) Ideas of guilt and unworthiness (even in a mild type of episode).
(d) Bleak and pessimistic views of the future.
(e) Ideas or acts of self-harm or suicide.
(f) Disturbed sleep.
(g) Diminished appetite.

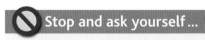

Stop and ask yourself …

- What do you think might be different in today's mental health hospitals?

Links to
- Application

DSM-5

Major depressive episode

Five (or more) symptoms present during the same two-week period including either symptom 1 or symptom 2.

1. Depressed mood most of the day, nearly every day.
2. Markedly diminished interest or pleasure in all or almost all activities most of the day, nearly every day.
3. Body weight loss of more than 5 per cent not due to diet or change to appetite.
4. Insomnia or excessive sleep (hypersonic) nearly every day.
5. Restlessness or less activity nearly every day.
6. Fatigue or loss of energy nearly every day.
7. Feelings of worthlessness or inappropriate/excessive guilt nearly every day.
8. Lack of ability to think, concentrate or make decisions nearly every day.
9. Recurrent thoughts of death or suicide, or suicide attempt.

The symptoms should not be attributable to any other cause, for example another disorder or substance, and must cause clinically significant distress or impairment in functioning.

Characteristics of a psychotic disorder: schizophrenia

ICD-10

F20.0 Paranoid schizophrenia

Diagnostic guidelines

The normal requirement for a diagnosis of schizophrenia must be fulfilled. This is a minimum of one very clear symptom (and usually two or more if less clear-cut) belonging to any one of (a) to (d) **or** symptoms from at least two (e) to (h) should have been clearly present for most of the time during a period of one month or more.

(a) Thought echo, thought insertion or withdrawal, and thought broadcasting.
(b) Delusions of control, influence, or passivity, clearly referred to body or limb movements or specific thoughts, actions, or sensations; delusional perception.
(c) Hallucinatory voices giving a running commentary on the patient's behaviour, or discussing the patient among themselves, or other types of hallucinatory voices coming from some part of the body.
(d) Persistent delusions of other kinds that are culturally inappropriate and completely impossible, such as religious or political identity, or superhuman powers and abilities (for example, being able to control the weather, or being in communication with aliens from another world).
(e) Persistent hallucinations in any modality, when accompanied either by fleeting or half-formed delusions without clear affective content, or by persistent over-valued ideas, or when occurring every day for weeks or months on end.
(f) Breaks or interpolations in the train of thought, resulting in incoherence or irrelevant speech, or neologisms (made up new words).
(g) Catatonic behaviour, such as excitement, posturing, or waxy flexibility, negativism, mutism, and stupor.
(h) 'Negative' symptoms such as marked apathy, paucity of speech, and blunting or incongruity of emotional responses, usually resulting in social withdrawal and lowering of social performance.
(i) A significant and consistent change in the overall quality of some aspects of personal behaviour, manifest as loss of interest, aimlessness, idleness, a self-absorbed attitude, and social withdrawal.

In addition for paranoid schizophrenia, hallucinations and/or delusions must be prominent.

 **Find out more**

Look up the terms you are unfamiliar with and write a summary of the characteristics of the disorder, this will prepare you for an exam question on this topic.

Hallucinations and/or delusions

(a) Delusions of persecution, reference, exalted birth, special mission, bodily change, or jealousy.
(b) Hallucinatory voices that threaten the patient or give commands, or auditory hallucinations without verbal form, such as whistling, humming, or laughing.
(c) Hallucinations of smell or taste, or of sexual or other bodily sensations; visual hallucinations may occur but are rarely predominant.

DSM-5

Schizophrenia

Two of more of the following in one month; at least one must be symptom 1, 2 or 3.

1. Delusions.
2. Hallucinations.
3. Disorganised speech.
4. Grossly disorganised or catatonic behaviour.
5. Negative symptoms such as diminished emotional expression.

Level of functioning should be below that prior to the onset of the symptoms, for example not able to self-care or achieve academic expectations. The disturbance should persist for six months, even if at minor levels, and there should be no other causes such as other disorders or substances.

Characteristics of an anxiety disorder: agoraphobia

ICD-10

F40.0 Agoraphobia

Diagnostic guidelines

All of the following criteria should be fulfilled for a definite diagnosis:

(a) The psychological or autonomic symptoms must be primarily manifestations of anxiety and not secondary to other symptoms, such as delusions or obsessional thoughts.

(b) The anxiety must be restricted to (or occur mainly in) at least two of the following situations: crowds, public places, travelling away from home, and travelling alone.

(c) Avoidance of the phobic situation must be, or have been, a prominent feature.

DSM-5

Agoraphobia

Marked fear or anxiety about two or more of these situations:

- using public transport
- being in open spaces
- being in enclosed places
- standing in line or in a crowd
- being outside of the home alone.

These situations almost always provoke an anxiety attack, and the situations are actively avoided or require a companion. The fear is out of proportion to the danger even if another disorder might induce anxiety, for example irritable bowel syndrome (IBS), the fear is excessive.

The fear/avoidance persists for more than six months and causes significant distress and impairment of normal functioning. There are no other disorders or causes, such as reminders of trauma.

The medical model

The specification requires that you know the biochemical, genetic and brain abnormality explanations of mental illness. The key research is by Gottesman *et al.* (2010) – severe mental disorders in offspring with two psychiatrically ill parents – and the application is the biological treatment of one specific disorder.

The biochemical explanation of mental illness

The biochemical explanation of mental illness, put very simply, is that our bodies have a balance of chemicals that can become unbalanced, which is linked to psychological disorders. You probably have an understanding that a lack of insulin is linked to diabetes, or not enough iron in your body causes a reduction in red blood cells, leading to anaemia. It is the same type of explanation that can be used for some mental illness. It is not always obvious what that causal effect is – which came first, the illness or the chemical imbalance? The role of serotonin in depression has long been held as a theory of depression, and has led to drug treatments of selective serotonin reuptake inhibitors (SSRIs), which are drugs that increase the effect of serotonin in the body.

The effect of neurotransmitters such as serotonin needs to be considered in relation to their role in the nervous system. If the levels of a chemical are out of balance, this can result in the symptoms and diagnosis of mental illness.

Serotonin is a neurotransmitter that moves across the synaptic gap in a neural pathway. Our nervous system is made up of thousands of nerve cells (neurons) which are activated by a stimulus from our senses. This activation is then transferred along the neural pathway to the appropriate area in the central nervous system (spinal cord and brain) for the body to behave in an appropriate way. For example, if we touch something hot the message is sent from the receptors in the skin, via the neurons, to the brain, which interprets the message as 'that is hot', and sends a message back to the muscles to move the hand away. All this happens in microseconds, as the speed of the neural message can be up to 300 mph. Therefore, if we see a stimulus that should make

 Stop and ask yourself…

- What are the problems of using a list of criteria to diagnose a disorder?

Links to

- Validity
- Reliability

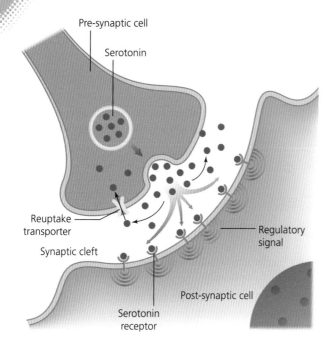

Pre-synaptic cell

Serotonin

Reuptake transporter

Synaptic cleft

Regulatory signal

Post-synaptic cell

Serotonin receptor

Figure 1.12 The synaptic gap between the first (pre-synaptic) nerve cell and the second (post-synaptic) nerve cell is 'bridged' by the serotonin being released from the pre-synaptic cell and floating across to the post-synaptic cell where it will stimulate the electrical charge which will then transmit the message to the next cell and so on

us feel hungry, our brain will ensure we go to find food. However, if this message is interrupted then the body may not behave in an appropriate way. So, seeing a normal, happy stimulus may not make us feel happy as a result of the message not getting to our brains.

The role of serotonin is in transmitting the message across the synaptic gap between two neurons.

Once the post-synaptic cell is stimulated the serotonin is taken back (reuptake) into the pre-synaptic cell, to await further stimulation. However, if the levels of serotonin are low then it would mean the message may not get passed effectively across the gap, before the serotonin is taken back. There is, however, conflicting evidence on this theory. Young and Leyton (2002) found that people given amino acids devoid of tryptophan, which reduced the levels of brain serotonin, resulted in lower mood. Research on mice by Sachs et al. (2015) supported this; they found that in a mouse with a genetic tendency towards serotonin deficiency, low serotonin could be a contributing factor to the development of depressive symptoms when exposed to social stress, however, the common theory is that low serotonin is linked with depression. Other research, such as that by Angoa-Pérez et al. (2014), suggests that there is no such link, again researching mice. This may be an example of when it is very difficult to accurately extrapolate conclusions from animal research to apply to humans.

Another biochemical explanation is the role of dopamine (another neurotransmitter) in schizophrenia. In this disorder an overactive dopamine system is linked to symptoms of schizophrenia, although again it is difficult to derive causal effect, as it may be that the schizophrenia increases the dopamine levels.

The biological treatments for mental illness based on the medical model focus on restoring normal levels of neurotransmitter action. By blocking the reuptake of serotonin, SSRIs increase the effect of serotonin, thereby reducing the symptoms of depression. This therapeutic effect is often taken as evidence which supports the biochemical imbalance theory. Drugs that block dopamine receptors in the post-synaptic receptors can reduce the symptoms of schizophrenia – these antipsychotic drugs bind themselves to the dopamine receptors preventing an overload of dopamine reaching the post-synaptic cell. These antipsychotic drugs are being constantly refined to ensure that they only block the dopamine receptor cells linked with symptoms of schizophrenia, not all cognitive functions. It is interesting to note that drugs such as cocaine increase the amount of dopamine in the synaptic gap, giving rise to the feeling associated with taking the drug, and heroin also acts on dopamine levels indirectly, so it is not surprising then that there is increasing evidence that drug taking can be linked to the onset of psychotic disorders.

Anxiety disorders have been explained by the chemical imbalance of both serotonin and norepinephrine, and drugs used to treat them try to address these imbalances. Again there is a lack of concrete evidence to show the links between the imbalance of serotonin, norepinephrine and anxiety however; it could be that the data on effectiveness published by drug companies is being seen as evidence for the theory.

For example, Effexor (venlafaxine) is an antidepressant that was said to be able to restore the chemical balance linked with anxiety symptoms 'by affecting the levels of two naturally occurring chemicals in the brain – serotonin and norepinephrine. Because Effexor XR affects these two chemicals, it is known as an SNRI, or serotonin-norepinephrine reuptake inhibitor.' (Pfizer, 2014) But remember that this is promotional material from a drug company citing nine years of successful prescription by doctors as evidence for this theory.

The genetic explanation of mental illness

There is some evidence that certain disorders are passed from one parent to a child through genetic transference. In much the same way that children

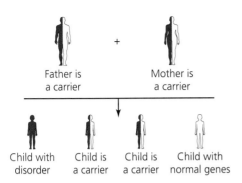

Figure 1.13 Genetic transfer from parents to child can vary

might inherit eye colour or body shape, they could inherit either a disorder or a disposition towards a disorder. There would be no guarantee that they would have that disorder, for example depression, but if the environmental factors are sufficient, the person may be more likely to have that disorder.

Because of the nature of genetics, as only half of the genes come from each parent it is possible for a one child to show such as tendency and a sibling not to. The study of twins who have identical genetic make-up (monozygotic – one egg) with those who are not identical (dizygotic – two eggs) helps us to see the impact of genes and environment. Adoption studies can also show how children with biological parents who have a mental illness and are adopted by parents without such an illness are impacted by their environment and the influence of genes.

Gottesman's key research shows the increased risk if children have two parents with either bipolar or schizophrenia compared to those with one or no parent with this disorder. The findings would support the idea that the greater the genetic influence, the more likely the disorder will be diagnosed, showing an argument for genetic explanations of mental illness. However, the concordance rates (parents and children having the disorder) are not 100 per cent, so there has to be some environmental or individual differences effect that make some people more prone to a diagnosis of mental illness than others.

Gottesman and Shields' research (1976) looked at many studies using both adoption and twin samples, all of which found an increased concordance rate for related pairs, but never 100 per cent concordance rates. For example, their study in 1972 showed a 58 per cent concordance rate for monozygotic twins compared to 12 per cent for dizygotic twins, meaning that if one twin had schizophrenia then there was a 58 per cent chance of an identical twin having it, and only a 12 per cent chance of a non-identical twin having it. It shows that the influence of having identical genetic make-up is higher than for non-identical genetic make-up, but it is still only a 58 per cent chance, not 100 per cent, therefore the environment and/or individual differences must also impact on the occurrence of schizophrenia.

Included in the concept of genetic transference of disorders is the evolutionary theory, which explains that behaviours that have a positive effect on our survival are likely to become traits seen in humans, as the people with these traits initially survived to mate and so passed these on. This is an explanation for phobias, for example of spiders, as if our ancestors didn't have a fear of spiders, or snakes for example, they may have been bitten and died before they could mate. Ohman (1975) showed this in his research where he tried to induce phobias to various objects by presenting images along with an electric shock, and found that people shown images of snakes had a greater response to fear, measured by galvanic skin response (electrical charge carried through sweat on the skin) than those shown houses and faces (as there is no evolutionary need to fear houses or faces).

Obviously treatment of a genetic disorder is difficult – it is hard to 'treat' genetic traits – but more research is being done into embryo manipulation to reduce the inheritance of physical disorders by using genetic material from three parents. It is only a matter of time before this technique is refined and accepted enough before it is used to 'treat' genetic mental disorders. However, it is likely to be a long time before a specific gene can be identified as the carrier of a mental disorder.

Brain abnormality as an explanation of mental illness

Although there has been evidence of a link between brain abnormality and mental illness, in the past it has been difficult to research this.

There is evidence of brain differences post-mortem (after death). Brown *et al.* (1986) studied the brains of 41 patients with schizophrenia and 29 patients with affective disorder. The brains of the patients with schizophrenia were 6 per cent lighter and had

Stop and ask yourself …

● Could social learning theory explain this just as well as genetics? How?

Links to
● Refutability

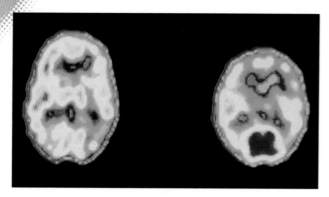

Figure 1.14 Brain scanning techniques can now identify differences in the brain structure of people with schizophrenia (right) compared with a normal brain (left), but can't answer the question of cause and effect

lateral ventricles that were larger in the anterior and particularly in the temporal horn cross section; they also had significantly thinner parahippocampal cortices. This supports previous research into ventricular enlargement, which suggests that such enlargement leads to a loss of matter in the temporal lobe.

Further, a study by Weinberger (1992) into identical twins who were not concordant for schizophrenia (one had it and the other didn't) investigated the brain structures of the nine pairs of twins and found that magnetic resonance imaging (MRI) scans showed differences in the prefrontal cortex and the hippocampus volume in the non-affected twins compared to the affected twins.

It is difficult to actually pin point a specific brain abnormality in patients with any disorder, even using newer brain imaging techniques, but there is evidence that parts of the brain essential to 'normal' functioning may be damaged in patients diagnosed with a disorder such as schizophrenia. There is still the problem of cause and effect, but brain imaging techniques can identify markers of susceptibility to certain disorders. And there is as ever contradictory evidence, along with ethical considerations for this research.

Strakowski et al. (1999) found that patients with bipolar disorder had significant differences in the volumes in the prefrontal, thalamic, hippocampal, amygdala, pallidal and striatal regions compared with a control group. The amygdala was particularly enlarged in these patients. As these areas of the brain deal with moods in humans, it shows that abnormalities in brain structure could be linked to the behavioural symptoms of disorders such as bipolar.

⮞ **Have a go yourself**

- Find a large image of a side view of the brain and mark on the areas of the brain linked to bipolar and what they control. Now write an explanation for mental illness based on brain abnormality.

The volume of brain structures can differ and studies show that patients suffering from depression can show a smaller hippocampus than non-depressed people. There is evidence that cortisol, a chemical released in response to stress, can destroy the hippocampal cells, which may be cells that would normally respond to serotonin. If they are destroyed this would reduce the effect of serotonin in our bodies which, as we saw in the biochemical explanation, is linked with depression.

In a study of elderly women whose depression was in remission, the hippocampus was smaller than in other women of the same age (Sheline et al., 1995).

Positron emission tomography (PET) scans can show the differences in brain activity in people with mental disorders. The image in Figure 1.15 shows how brain activity is different in one person at various stages of the bipolar cycle, from depression to normal to mania. Activity levels are indicated by colour ranging from blue (low activity) through green to yellow and red (high activity).

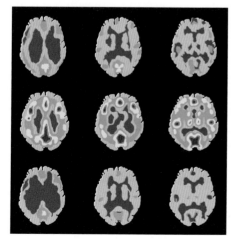

Figure 1.15 Image showing the brain functioning during episodes of depression (top and bottom) and mania (middle)

🚫 **Stop and ask yourself...**

- What are the ethical problems associated with using the medical model to explain and treat mental illness?

Links to
- Ethics

There is a wealth of evidence on many disorders, each having some evidence of brain changes in the patients diagnosed with this disorder. It is difficult to be certain about determinism in terms of a brain abnormality meaning a disorder has to follow. There may be many people walking around with such abnormalities showing no symptoms of a disorder. As brain scanning techniques develop, together with prospective research where people are tracked over time, the changes and subsequent behaviours can be identified and possibly related to specific disorders.

Treatments based on the brain abnormality explanation of mental illness would most likely be by drug therapy, although in some cases surgery may be used, for example in the case of brain tumours that are producing symptoms of disorders.

Baxter et al. (1992) investigated metabolic rates (activity levels) in areas of the brain in patients with obsessive – compulsive disorder before and after drug treatment. The changes in behaviour correlated with a reduction in brain activity in the right caudate nucleus, and there was a trend for the brain activity to also be reduced by behaviour therapy, suggesting that drug therapy might not necessarily be the only way to treat biological differences.

Key research: Gottesman, Laursen and Bertelsen et al. (2010) Severe mental disorders in offspring with two psychiatrically ill parents

Background

If we accept that previous research has found a link between one parent having a mental disorder and an increased incidence of that mental disorder in the child, then it should follow that having two parents with a psychiatric illness would increase the risk (to super-high risk) of the child having this or a similar disorder.

Aim

To investigate in a large sample (previous studies had used very small samples) the probability of a child, with two parents with a psychiatric illness, being diagnosed with a mental disorder, in particular the one that their parents have.

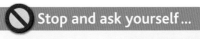

Stop and ask yourself …

● What are the weaknesses of the method Gottesman et al. used?

Participants

The population of Denmark alive in or born after 1968 and with a clear link to their biological parents was established from the Civil Registration System. From these, those aged ten before January 2007 were included with a total of 2,685,301 people and their parents. In all 1,278,977 couples were studied, with some having more than one child.

Anyone who had ever received a diagnosis of schizophrenia, bipolar affective disorder or unipolar depression disorder were identified from the Psychiatric Central Register and couples where both had been admitted to a psychiatric hospital were identified for study (this is a good example of secondary data).

A control group of people with only one parent being admitted was also studied, as was a group of people with neither parent admitted, and a group of 'general public' where there was no data on whether they had had parents with psychiatric illnesses or not. These two groups were representative of the baseline of psychiatric illness in the general population.

Method

Gottesman et al. used data from national statistics to identify people with this diagnosis. As this research was in the public domain and anonymised, they did not need to gain ethical consent from the Danish Ethics Committee. The children of each couple, aged up to 52 years, were checked in the same register for any diagnosis of mental disorder. The diagnosis at discharge from hospital was used to classify the illness using classification from ICD-8 and ICD-10.

Table 1.2 The four groups of participants

Group	Characteristics
Group A	Two parents admitted with a diagnosis of schizophrenia, or two parents admitted with a diagnosis of bipolar, or two parents admitted with a diagnosis of depression
Group B	One parent admitted with a diagnosis of schizophrenia, or one parent admitted with a diagnosis of bipolar, or one parent admitted with a diagnosis of depression
Group C	Neither parent admitted with a diagnosis of a disorder
Group D	No restrictions or data on parental admissions

Links to
● Methodology

Results

Table 1.3 shows the results for offspring admitted with a diagnosis of schizophrenia.

Table 1.3 Results for offspring admitted with a diagnosis of schizophrenia

Group (sample size)	Results
Group A, both parents admitted with schizophrenia (270)	26 (27.3%) admitted with a diagnosis of schizophrenia 40 (39.2%) admitted with a diagnosis of schizophrenia or schizophrenic-related disorders
Group B, one parent admitted with schizophrenia (13,878)	473 (7%) admitted with a diagnosis of schizophrenia
Group C, neither parent admitted with schizophrenia (2,239,551)	9384 (0.86%) admitted with a diagnosis of schizophrenia
Group D, general population (2,701,593)	14,938 (1.12%) admitted with a diagnosis of schizophrenia
Group E, both parents admitted with diagnosis of bipolar disorder	4.8% admitted with a diagnosis of schizophrenia
Group F, one parent admitted with diagnosis of schizophrenia and one with bipolar disorder	15.6% admitted with a diagnosis of schizophrenia

These results show that the risk with two parents diagnosed is 3.9 times higher than with one parent (Group B), (remember that super-high risk Gottesman *et al.* talked about), and 31.7 times higher than neither parent being diagnosed (Group C). Even with a related but not the same disorder being diagnosed in parents (bipolar rather than schizophrenia), the risk of schizophrenia is still 2 times higher than the general population with one parent diagnosed with bipolar, and 4 times higher with two parents diagnosed with bipolar.

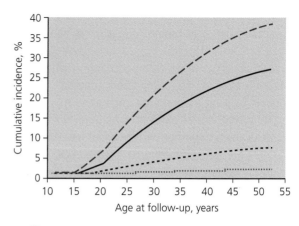

Key

——— Both parents admitted with schizophrenia

– – – Schizophrenia/schizophrenia-like disorder in offspring with both parents admitted with schizophrenia

- - - - Only one parent admitted with schizophrenia

········· Neither parent ever psychiatrically admitted

Figure 1.16 Cumulative incidence of admission with schizophrenia in offspring by age

Table 1.4 shows the results for offspring admitted with a diagnosis bipolar.

The risk of being admitted with a diagnosis of bipolar if both parents were admitted was ratio of 5:7 if there was one parent, and 51.9 times higher than if neither parent had a diagnosis of bipolar. With one parent with a diagnosis of bipolar and one with schizophrenia, the risk was 2–3 times higher than for one parent with bipolar, and with two parents with a diagnosis of schizophrenia the risk was 10 times higher than the general population.

By the age of 52 there was also an increase in the diagnosis of any disorder if patients had been admitted: 67.5 per cent of people with both parents diagnosed with schizophrenia had been admitted with psychiatric disorder, and 44.2 per cent of people with both parents diagnosed with bipolar; this compares to 11.9 per cent with neither parent admitted and 14.1 per cent of the 'general population'.

Table 1.4 Results for offspring admitted with bipolar diagnosis

Group (sample size)	Results
Group A, both parents admitted with bipolar (146)	15 (24.9%) admitted with a diagnosis of bipolar 24 (36%) admitted with a diagnosis of bipolar or unipolar disorder
Group B, one parent admitted with bipolar (23,152)	400 (4.4%) admitted with a diagnosis of bipolar
Group C, neither parent admitted with bipolar (2,239,553)	3452 (0.48%) admitted with a diagnosis of bipolar
Group D, general population (2,701,595)	5534 (0.63%) admitted with a diagnosis of bipolar
Group E, both parents admitted with diagnosis of schizophrenia	10.8% admitted with a diagnosis of bipolar
Group F, one parent admitted with a diagnosis of bipolar and one parent with a diagnosis of schizophrenia	11.7% admitted with a diagnosis of bipolar

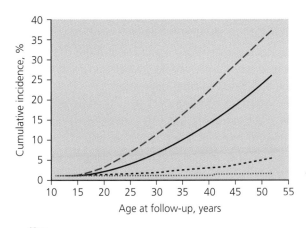

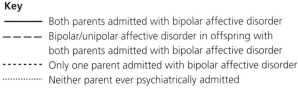

Key

——————— Both parents admitted with bipolar affective disorder
— — — — Bipolar/unipolar affective disorder in offspring with
          both parents admitted with bipolar affective disorder
- - - - - - - Only one parent admitted with bipolar affective disorder
·············· Neither parent ever psychiatrically admitted

Figure 1.17 Cumulative incidence of admission with bipolar affective disorder in offspring by age

One final note: with the age set at 52 years to assess if there had been a diagnosis, it can be seen in Figure 1.16 for schizophrenia that the diagnosis rate is levelling out as the people reach 45 years and beyond, suggesting that this disorder is not often diagnosed in people as they get older. However, in Figure 1.17 for bipolar, the incidence of diagnosis is still increasing, suggesting that this diagnosis is made in older people.

Have a go yourself

- Try to write a 500-word summary of the results from Gottesman *et al.*'s study referring to what it contributes to our understanding of the genetic explanation of mental illness.

Conclusions

Gottesman's study supported the previous smaller studies, and his impressive sample size makes it very robust. He is mindful of the problems of using information for assigning health risks in countries where health care is provided and funded by the public. The data might be different in countries where people have to pay for health care, but Gottesman suggests that this information can help people make decisions about marriage, children, adoption and future planning, although he emphasises the need for well-informed counsellors to help with this. He also mentions the risks involved in this kind of study, citing the Nazi policy of eugenics as an extreme response

to information on the genetic transference of certain characteristics. There are also limitations to the data set, such as people with bipolar and depression being less likely to be admitted and more likely to be treated as outpatients or by GPs. The number of beds in psychiatric wards is reducing but this is not reflected in a drop in admissions; it is rather a trend towards shorter hospital stays. He contends that ICD is a valid measure for diagnosis, but also acknowledges that there needs to be concurrent validity in terms of adoption and twin studies before making any definitive statements about genetic determinism.

Application: biological treatment of one specific disorder

While biological treatments all have the same basic premise that somehow the biological make-up of a person has to be altered in some way, the actual action may have a different effect: consider antidepressants, which increase the effect of serotonin by reducing its reuptake, and antipsychotic drugs that reduce the symptoms of schizophrenia by inhibiting the effect of dopamine.

While drug therapy is not the only biological treatment, it is the most frequently used. It is often quicker than talking therapies such as cognitive behavioural therapy (see page 29) or behaviourist therapies (see page 27). There are considerations such as side effects to consider. These could range from making the condition worse; for example, the antidepressant Prozac (fluoxetine) has been linked to an increase in suicidal thoughts and actions. However research by Kahn *et al.* (2003) failed to support both an increase in suicide risk between patients taking antidepressants and placebos, and between patients taking SRRIs and other antidepressants. Research by Hershal *et al.* (2004) also found that after controlling potential confounding variables – such as age, sex, time and duration of treatment with antidepressants prior to suicidal behaviour – the risk of suicidal behaviour was not significantly different for patients taking any of the four antidepressants amitriptyline, fluoxetine, paroxetine or dothiepin. The research is ongoing.

Other biological treatments include electro-convulsive therapy (ECT). ECT is where electrodes are placed on the patient's head on the temples. The patient is anaesthetised while an electric shock is passed into the patient's brain.

ECT can be a quick fix for reducing severe depression while waiting for drug therapy to become effective. It

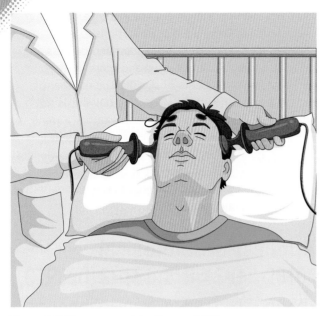

Figure 1.18 Electro-convulsive therapy (ECT)

has risks, however, such as physical trauma and heart problems, although these are not common. It also has psychological risks of short-term confusion and longer-term memory loss.

A milder form of brain stimulation is transcranial magnetic stimulation (TMS) where a magnetic field is created causing a much weaker electrical signal to be applied to the prefrontal cortex. An electromagnetic coil is held against the patient's head, near the forehead, and an electric current creates a magnetic pulse, or field, that travels through your skull. This causes small electrical currents in your brain that stimulate nerve

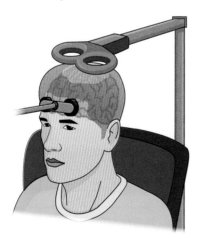

Figure 1.19 Transcranial magnetic stimulation (TMS)

cells in the region of your brain involved in mood regulation and depression.

Biological treatment can comprise of more than one biological therapy, for example drug therapy and ECT could be combined to treat depression.

In the exam for component 3 you could be asked to describe the treatments, but you could also be asked about how to research effectiveness, or any of the methodological or ethical problems in using biological treatments.

Alternatives to the medical model

The specification requires that you know the behaviourist and cognitive explanations for mental illness, plus **one** other from the list of three other explanations (humanistic, psychodynamic or cognitive neuroscience). The key research is Szasz (2011) – The myth of mental illness: 50 years later – and the application is the non-biological treatment of one specific disorder.

The behaviourist explanation of mental illness

You will know from your previous study of the behaviourist perspective that the underlying assumption of this perspective for the cause of all behaviour is learning. So this perspective would suggest that mental disorders are learned and then maintained through either reinforcement (operant conditioning), association (classical conditioning) or imitation (social learning theory).

It is difficult to see how this might explain all psychological disorders but there are clearly many that could be explained this way. In particular, some phobias and other anxiety disorders could be acquired through learned behaviours. To suggest learning is the key to developing a disorder may appear as if we have some say in the matter, but remember the behaviourist perspective is generally deterministic, with us acquiring our behaviours as a result of the environment around us.

🚫 **Stop and ask yourself ...**

- Can you remember the theories of acquisition of behaviour? If not, revisit the terms 'unconditional stimulus', 'unconditional response', 'conditioned stimulus' and 'conditioned response'.

Links to
- Behaviourist perspective

Figure 1.20 Classical conditioning explanation of phobia acquisition

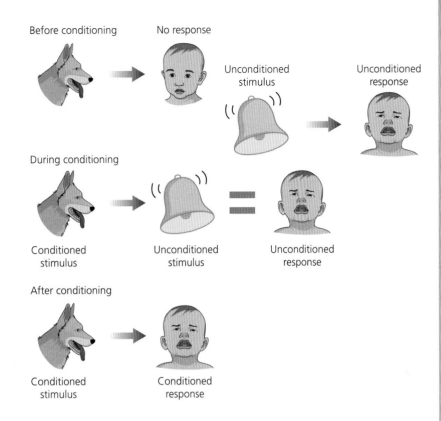

Before conditioning — No response

Unconditioned stimulus — Unconditioned response

During conditioning

Conditioned stimulus — Unconditioned stimulus = Unconditioned response

After conditioning

Conditioned stimulus — Conditioned response

Classical conditioning can be used to explain many anxiety disorders, in particular phobias.

The pairing of one unconditioned stimulus (thunderstorms) with another conditioned stimulus (loud clap of thunder) can lead to the thunderstorm on its own being enough to produce the conditioned response of fear (see figure 1.21 to see how a phobia may be acquired through classical conditioning).

A very famous study for all the wrong reasons was the case of Little Albert (Watson and Rayner, 1920) who acquired a phobia by the researchers pairing a loud noise with a white rat. Previously Albert had shown no fear of the rat but, over the course of a few days, with repeated pairings, the fear brought about by the loud noise was enough to result in a phobia of the rat. This was then generalised to other similar white objects such as a rabbit or a Father Christmas beard.

Take it further

- Have a look on the internet (YouTube is a good place to start) for original footage of the Little Albert experiment. Try using the terms in classical conditioning to explain Albert's fear.

Operant conditioning can explain phobias by linking rewards we get when we show a phobia or other disorder. People with depression caused by a traumatic event may receive attention and so be rewarded for showing signs of a disorder. However, operant conditioning has a stronger role to play in the maintenance of anxiety disorders. Negative reinforcement is the removal of an aversive situation, so if someone with a phobia of lifts gets to a lift door and experiences anxiety, so walks away and takes the stairs, the removal of the anxiety is a reward so they will repeat taking the stairs, thereby reinforcing their phobia of lifts as they are still associated with the fear response.

In terms of social learning theory, behaviours such as depression can be seen in a child who has witnessed symptoms of depression, such as withdrawal and mood swings. Children and teenagers will see many people, including role models, reacting to challenges in unhealthy, ineffective ways and will model what they see, and so will also become frustrated, helpless and depressed.

Treatments based on the behavioural model include those based on the three theories outlined above.

The associations learned through classical conditioning can be removed and positive associations relearned. This can be done through systematic desensitisation, which relies on relaxation techniques being taught to a person who gradually confronts their fear – through a hierarchy of stimuli from least fear provoking to most fear provoking. At each stage the patient uses the relaxation techniques to relearn a feeling of calm associated with the phobic or anxiety-producing stimulus.

McGrath *et al.* (1990) showed this effect in his research with Lucy, a ten-year-old girl who had a fear of loud noises and associated objects such as balloons and party poppers. By teaching her to imagine herself playing with her toys at home, over the course of ten sessions she gradually reduced her fear to a self-rating of 3 out of 10 down from ratings of 7 out of 10 for balloons popping and 9 out of 10 for party poppers.

One way of making this treatment quicker is flooding, where the stimulus is presented directly, for example someone with a fear of spiders (arachnophobia) is presented with a tarantula to hold. The immediate fear response caused by adrenalin on the nervous system is not sustainable for long and eventually the person will calm down (when the spider doesn't actually do anything) and will then associate the feeling of calm with the object rather than a phobic response. One problem with this is that it can actually cause such panic that the phobia is reinforced rather than extinguished.

Aversion therapy is used to produce an unpleasant association, such as nausea in adults with alcohol addiction. A drug is used (sometimes as an implant) that will induce sickness if a person drinks alcohol. Repeated sickness paired with alcohol situations will result in a learned response of aversion to alcohol. Hangovers are nature's aversion therapy! Other negative associations can be produced by giving electric shocks to cause aversion to the stimulus.

Of course it is important that people surrounding the person are able to remove their reinforcement of dysfunctional behaviour by not rewarding the person when they show it. Lewinsohn *et al.* (1990) showed that by training parents to reinforce non-depressed behaviours along with giving cognitive therapy to the their children, the number of teenagers in their study who met the DSM criteria for depression reduced to 52 per cent of the initial group, compared to 57 per cent of the group who had only cognitive therapy. This demonstrates the impact of reinforcing the desired behaviour.

Although it was suggested earlier that psychotic disorders such as schizophrenia were unlikely to be explained through learning, there is some evidence that using behavioural techniques can reduce the symptoms of schizophrenia shown. Paul and Lentz (1977) showed that patients with schizophrenia who were given therapy based on social learning theory together with operant conditioning were twice as likely to be discharged from hospital, and ten times more likely to be living independently than patients who had standard drug treatment.

The cognitive explanation of mental illness

As you will be aware, the cognitive area in psychology is concerned with thinking and, therefore, the assumptions made about mental illness from this area are due to faulty thought processes. For example, people with depression will have different thoughts or cognitions about themselves and the world around them compared to the people without depression. Depressed people tend to have irrational cognitions and distorted thoughts and judgements.

A founding psychologist of the cognitive explanation was Aaron Beck (1961) who suggests there are three main dysfunctional belief themes in people with depression:

- 'I am worthless or flawed.'
- 'Everything I do results in failure.'
- 'The future is hopeless.'

These form the negative cognitive triad and, with these present in someone's beliefs, it is very likely that someone will have a diagnosis of depression. For example, if you have failed an exam and are not depressed then you will work out what you did wrong, you won't doubt your ability to pass, but on that occasion you didn't do what was needed. You won't think the future is ruined (there is always a Plan B!). You would not question your self-worth and would look at other possible career pathways to achieve your goal. However, in a negative cognitive triad you would think: 'I am stupid, I can't even pass an exam, I fail at everything, and there is no point in going on as I have no chance of getting a job or going to university. No one cares about me.'

Beck theorised that, once depressed, a person would select information from their environment to confirm their negative thoughts. Even in the face of a majority of positive evidence, the one small negative point will become the focus of attention. For example, in one day a depressed person might get an A on a maths test, be asked out on a date by someone they like and score a goal in their hockey match, but their whole day will be clouded by one small mistake they made during a driving lesson that for which their driving instructor told

 Stop and ask yourself ...

- What are the ethical problems of using behaviourism to explain and treat mental illness?

Links to
- Ethics

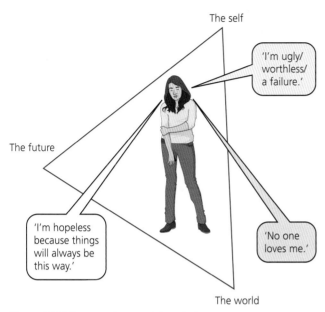

The self

'I'm ugly/ worthless/ a failure.'

The future

'I'm hopeless because things will always be this way.'

'No one loves me.'

The world

Figure 1.21 The negative cognitive triad

them off. This small negative event clouds the rest of their otherwise successful day.

The other main cognitive theorist who influenced the foundations of the cognitive area is Albert Ellis who felt that our irrational thoughts would cause and sustain mental disorders. His understanding of how people with disorders may adopt faulty cognitions can be summarised in three points:

1. 'I must be outstandingly competent, or I am worthless.'
2. 'Others must treat me considerately, or they are absolutely rotten.'
3. 'The world should always give me happiness, or I will die.'

It is easy to see that these are high and unrealistic expectations and so, as they are unattainable, people with this faulty thinking will feel like failures, leading to depression.

Take it further

- If you are interested in the cognitive explanation, look up Beck and Ellis in books and on the internet to get a more in-depth explanation of mental illness.

Psychotic disorders such as schizophrenia are less clear cut in terms of the cognitive explanation. Beck

accepted the biological disposition caused by genes but suggested that the concordance rates of less than 100 per cent would be due to individual cognitive processes. The diathesis–stress model of schizophrenia suggests that genes can create a predisposition for the development this disorder but it actually only develops as a result of a stressor. These stressors may be biological, such as a virus, psychosocial, such as environment, or psychological, such as experiencing trauma. However, there is also a clear link between cognitive deficits and schizophrenia patients. These cognitive deficits can include intelligence, memory, attention and information-processing speed. Patients with bipolar disorder can also show cognitive deficits in processing speed, visual perception and spatial skills. This is where the cognitive neuroscience explanation has aided our understanding of the cognitive tasks that are compromised by disorder.

Treatments based on the cognitive approach aim to change the faulty cognitions of people with disorders, and are sometimes combined with behavioural therapies in cognitive behavioural therapy (CBT).

Ellis worked on rational emotive behavioural therapy (REBT) in the 1950s and his rational therapy (RT) involved the therapist seeking to help the client understand how his or her own beliefs were contributing to their illness. The client then had to act on that understanding by changing his or her self-defeating beliefs and behaviours. The therapist could demonstrate the irrationality, self-defeatism and rigidity of the faulty beliefs and could then reconstruct more rational thoughts. For example, rather than thinking the future is hopeless, the therapist might explore options for the client that are possible, showing the illogical thinking behind 'there is no future', or by looking at what the client can do, which refutes the belief that they are rubbish. For example, a mother with post-natal depression who believes that she is not a good mother could record in her journal all the things she *does* do for the baby; the therapist will review this at therapy sessions, pointing out the illogicality of believing that she is not a good mother in light of the evidence she has provided that she actually is.

According to Beck the aim of cognitive therapy is to help patients modify their distorted thinking, with its consequential dysfunctional behaviour. Therapists

Stop and ask yourself ...

- What behaviours might a mother record that show she is actually a good mother and that would contravene her belief that she is not?

Links to
- Self-report

plan treatment on this basis and work with the patient teaching cognitive and emotional-regulation skills, so the patient becomes their own therapist. Once the skills are taught, often in 6–12 sessions, the patient can use these in future situations without having to continue seeing a therapist. It is a genuinely two-way process, with patients contributing to the agenda of the treatment, discussing specific problems and the goals they want to achieve, using techniques and, for example, keeping journals as feedback.

Cognitive behavioural therapy (CBT)

This non-biological treatment combines the therapeutic strategies of both the cognitive and behavioural explanations. CBT is a talking therapy that has been successful in treating a wide range of disorders, and can be used with children, teenagers and adults. It takes the cognitions of the person and looks at how this affects our behaviour. A faulty belief that no one likes us may make us less likely to seek social situations. The therapist will use the cognitive techniques to change the thinking pattern ('no one likes me') or behavioural techniques to change their behaviour (avoiding social situations) or both of these. It can be used to treat a range of anxiety disorders such as post-traumatic stress disorder, depression and obsessive–compulsive disorder, as well as psychotic disorders such as schizophrenia.

CBT might be done individually or in groups and may take up to 20 weekly sessions. Like cognitive therapy, its focus is on looking at the here and now, which differs from humanistic and psychodynamic therapies, which tend to want to look at the past history and deal with issues left over from previous experiences.

Morrison *et al.* (2014) compared patients who refused antipsychotic drugs for schizophrenia who were either given CBT as well as the usual treatment or a group given just the usual treatment for such patients. Usual treatment for these patients tends to be in the form of more social support and contact with health professionals. They found that CBT plus the usual treatment significantly reduced psychiatric symptoms compared to the usual treatment alone. This would suggest that CBT can actually help people with psychotic disorders such as schizophrenia.

Take it further

- CBT is generally seen as a positive treatment by the NHS. Use textbooks or the internet see if you can find some criticisms or research evidence that it doesn't work. This will help you with your evaluation, but make sure it is valid, objective criticism.

Alternative explanations

You need to know one of the following three explanations for the exam, but you might find it interesting to read the other two, as it might help your evaluation of the one you are studying in depth.

The humanistic explanation of mental illness

The humanist explanation for behaviour is one you haven't come across on this OCR specification, so it is necessary to give a brief outline of its development and underlying assumptions in order to consider its explanation of mental illness.

It developed in the 1960s as a reaction to the scientific, animal-based research of the behaviourist approach and considered the uniqueness of human beings as something that would not allow a scientific approach for studying human behaviour. It is often called the third force of psychology, after the psychodynamic and behaviourist approach. It is concerned more with the person as an individual and believes firmly in self-determination and free will, more so than any other perspective. This makes it more optimistic than behaviourist and psychodynamic perspectives, as these both make the person the 'victim' of their environment and unconscious; it concentrates on the here and now rather than what went before.

As an individual, each person is credited with the potential and the ability to be mentally healthy; they are able to fulfil their potential through psychological growth, reaching the key aim of self-actualisation, which is the ability to be the best one can be. Therefore, anything that prevents this natural ability to grow will cause mental and social problems.

Stop and ask yourself…

- How are your needs met? Can you think of a time you couldn't concentrate in class as one of the lower needs had been compromised, for example you hadn't had breakfast so were hungry?

Links to
- Application

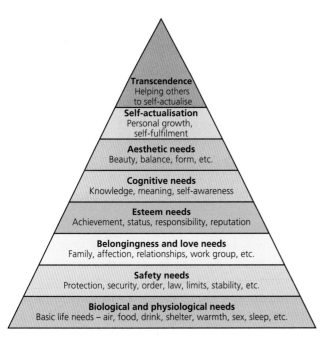

Figure 1.22 Maslow's hierarchy of needs: as each need is met we are motivated to meet the next need until we reach our potential as humans (self-actualisation)

People are innately motivated to achieve. Maslow suggested there is a hierarchy of needs that we strive to meet and, as we meet each one, we progress nearer to the goal of self-actualisation.

The key focus of the humanistic perspective is the self, and concepts such as self-esteem and self-worth are fundamental to this. There are two main founders of humanistic psychology: Carl Rogers and Abraham Maslow.

Maslow, we have seen, believed in the need to self-actualise, but it is possible that we can become fixated at one level of need due to our circumstances. For example, if a person's parents divorce, that person maybe fixated at the esteem needs level, never thinking they are good enough – a common thought of children is that their parents' divorce is their fault, which may manifest itself later in insecurity and jealousy in adult relationships.

Carl Rogers' theory was concerned with the self-image and how this differs from their ideal, self-actualising person. The further one's ideal self is from one's actual self (as seen by the person, not necessarily by others) the lower one's self-esteem (how much a person values his or herself).

Perceived actual self = ideal self → high self-esteem
Perceived actual self < ideal self → low self-esteem

What can influence a person's idea of their actual self are conditions of worth. These are ways in which we behave in order to receive the reward of social (family) acceptability. A child, for example, may 'play quietly' to receive approval from parents. If they play noisily they might not get that approval. So the condition of worth (what makes them a 'good' child) is playing quietly. If the condition of worth is 'pleasing me' or 'loving me more than …' then not meeting that condition of worth can result in withdrawal of approval by others, and can impact negatively on a person's self-esteem.

Other people can influence a person's self-esteem and, if self-esteem is reduced, it can lead to mental health problems. Schizophrenics for instance, don't act in a way that will meet the condition of worth of acting normally and so will not receive societal approval. This estimation of their worthlessness will cause them to suffer even more and be further removed from society; for example, they may not get a job or have a relationship. Not adhering to societal values perpetuates the social stigma.

Rogers believed that anyone imposing conditions for worth is wrong and we should all receive unconditional positive regard, particularly children who should receive this from parents. This is where, whatever you do, you are always valued or loved by them. So no 'I won't love you if you …' but more 'I will always love you, but I don't like your behaviour at the moment …'. We need to know we are loved, and some people will push the boundaries set to see if they really are unconditionally loved, to test their self-worth.

Although we have a natural tendency to self-actualise, with imposed conditions of worth that we don't meet, this tendency to self-actualise can, according to Rogers, become skewed, leading to mental health issues.

Find out more

If you are studying humanistic psychology and are interested in this approach, you can look up Rogers and Maslow on the internet or in any general psychology textbook to read up on their theories in more detail.

The idea that humans have free will is fundamental to the humanistic perspective, as we choose to pursue self-actualisation, making choices that will help us. Therefore, there is little impact from outside sources to determine our behaviour. This is probably naively optimistic because, as

Stop and ask yourself…

- What are the key attributes a therapist needs and what phrases might a counsellor use to show these?

Links to
- Humanistic perspective

we have seen, others can and do influence our self-worth, and although we are motivated to improve our self-worth to meet our ideal self, there are enough people with mental illness to show that people are not always able to choose the path to self-actualisation for themselves.

This leads on to the treatments based on humanistic therapy. If the assumption is to do with low self-esteem, and maybe expectations of the ideal self that are too high, then the therapist has to facilitate the patient to increase the former and reduce the latter. Alongside this, the therapist has to adopt a position of support. The key attributes of the therapist have to be genuine: warm, empathetic (able to put themselves in the other person's shoes), accepting, and providing unconditional positive regard whatever the patient might say, so removing the negative conditions of worth that have brought the person to the therapy couch. This will allow the person to feel valued. Then the therapist has to suggest ideas for the patient to consider in terms of their self-esteem and their ideal self, with the goal of therapy being to reduce the incongruence between these. It is possible that removing conditions of worth for people with schizophrenia may enable them to have a less distorted or skewed actualising tendency.

It is important that the patient is able to lead the dialogue – Rogers called it 'client-centred therapy' – and the patient has to feel that they are being listened to and heard by the therapist. The therapist may have to work hard to understand the patient's perspective on life, which may be very different from 'the norm', but they have to do this to allow the person to resolve their situation. The therapist will not tell the patient what he or she must do, but will give them time and suggestions that will allow them to make their own choices.

The psychodynamic explanation of mental illness

Find out more

If you are studying the psychodynamic explanation and are interested in Freud's research, you can look up his case studies on the internet or in any general psychology textbook. You might be able to purchase some of the books of his case studies very inexpensively online.

Stop and ask yourself…

- Do you remember the case study of Little Hans? If not, reread it to remind yourself (or ask yourself why you have repressed it into your unconscious).

You will recall the case of Little Hans from your study of Component 2, with his phobia of horses and Freud's explanation for this phobia.

Freud's singularly most important view of mental illness is that the unconscious memories and feelings we have will manifest themselves in abnormal behaviour and personality disorders.

These unconscious feelings arise from unresolved conflicts we may have experienced as a child. Conflicts between the id, ego and superego can create anxiety. The id demands gratification, and the superego attempts to put a moral restraint on the id, so that if we do give in to the id we feel guilty. If we don't then our superego may become too strong and cause us to be overwhelmed by guilt and can cause problems such as damaged relationships, acute depression, suicide or even murder as a way to silence the persistently harsh superego. Freud believed that the ego would prevent us from harming ourselves most of the time, so we might turn our need to harm ourselves (and our superego) outwards to harming others, hence the murder.

The ego will employ ego defence mechanisms to prevent our conflicts from damaging ourselves, but the overuse or inappropriate use of these can lead to disturbed behaviour. The ego defence mechanisms include denial, repression and distortion. As a child our defence mechanisms may not be developed enough to fully deal with the trauma of parental bereavement or bullying at school, and so we may find our adult behaviour influenced by these. Also, overuse of the defence mechanisms can cause later mental health problems. Overusing denial, for example, to refuse to acknowledge that a relationship is over, may lead to anxiety and depression. Repression may cause a person to act unconsciously, motivated by the repressed memory. Repressed memories in child abuse cases might influence later adult relationships. Emotions such as anger or betrayal can be turned inwards, away from the true object of the emotion, and this can lead to symptoms of mental illness such as depression.

The role of the ego is important in our understanding of the psychodynamic explanation for schizophrenia. The ego is there to control the demands of the id and the power of the superego, but a cold, rejecting mother can result in a weak, ineffective ego in a child, so the demands of the id can't be controlled, leaving it in charge of the personality. This would lead to a loss of contact

Links to
- Psychodynamic perspective

with reality as a person can no longer identify where their desires and fantasies end and reality begins. The ego would normally manage this. The id would then make us return to a child-like state where imagination and reality mix into one distorted view of life.

The aim of treatments based on the psychodynamic explanation of mental illness is known as psychoanalysis. It is based on the assumption that unconscious conflicts and emotions are the cause of the mental illness and, as by its very nature the unconscious is not available to the person, the therapy has to aid the bringing of the conflicts into the conscious where they can be resolved, removing the cause of the behaviour.

Freud's proposed techniques for accessing the unconscious included dream analysis and free association. He was not, as is often believed, an exponent of hypnosis. Dreams are, according to Freud, the 'royal road to the unconscious' and as such are an ideal way of discovering the real conflicts and desires a person is experiencing. It is not necessarily the actual content of the dream that shows these desires. The actual dream events are called the manifest content; the real underlying meaning of the dream is the latent content. So, dreaming of being chased by a gorilla while running through a shopping centre and wearing a tutu is not a real wish.

Key features of dream analysis

- **Dreamwork** – the process by which latent content becomes manifest content.
- **Condensation** – latent content (unconscious desires) is detailed but has to be condensed into an image to represent many things; the gorilla could represent authority (exams, parents, driving test).
- **Displacement** – the emotions really felt can be attached to a different object; the fear of the gorilla is a fear of failure of exams.
- **Representation** – this is translated into a visual image; running away from the gorilla may represent the unconscious thought that you have not been doing enough revision.
- **Symbolism** – a symbol replaces an actual person or idea. The tutu is your mother who is there at all times to support you; of course, it could be your mother who is there at all times to make you feel foolish. The therapist will help you decide what the image means to you.
- **Secondary revision** – the collection of the images is formed into a logical story.

Figure 1.23 Dreaming of being chased by a gorilla while running through a shopping centre and wearing a tutu is not a real wish!

In dream analysis therapy the therapist will reverse this process with the patient, but always allowing the patient to consider the actual meaning of the dream for themselves, although the therapist might make some suggestions for the patient to consider.

Another way of accessing the unconscious is by the therapist using free association, where a patient will talk out loud about a given topic. When a patient says everything that comes into their head, without processing it or editing it, even the most trivial of comments can be important as the unconscious will dictate what is being said.

Freud felt that 90 per cent of our behaviour is directed by our unconscious so, if we remove the 10 per cent that we are consciously managing, we can access the unconscious. The therapist will identify key points that the patient says to achieve an understanding of the conflicts and repression the patient needs to retrieve from their unconscious and deal with. The therapist will make notes while the patient talks, noting down anything that may help, and then make the suggestions that the patient can choose whether to accept or reject. The technique can work with writing, rather than speaking, and may be more successful as the patient may feel less embarrassed writing something than saying it out loud.

Psychotherapy is not a quick fix and can take many sessions, lasting years, for people to see the benefit. Tschuschke *et al.* (2007) found that in a study of 450 patients there were better outcomes for prolonged psychoanalysis. However, it is not universally thought to be effective.

Unsurprisingly, Szasz' book *Anti-Freud: Karl Kraus's Criticism of Psychoanalysis and Psychiatry* (1990) supports the whole idea that Freud was a myth

 Stop and ask yourself ...

- Think of a recent dream you had. Can you think what your unconscious might have really been thinking?

Links to
- Psychodynamic perspective

Figure 1.24 Free association

maker, and a falsifier of evidence to support a false therapy. Others have questioned the effectiveness of psychotherapy in a more scientific way, in 1952, Eysenck reported that two-thirds of therapy patients improved significantly or recovered on their own within two years, whether or not they received psychotherapy.

In contrast, Leichsenring *et al.* (2004) conducted a meta-analysis of studies and found that short-term psychodynamic psychotherapy gave significant improvements in general psychiatric symptoms and social functioning compared to non-treatment and other non-psychotherapy treatments. However, the use of empirical research into the effectiveness of psychoanalytic therapy compared to other treatments such as CBT is limited. Research has to take a time to see the long-term impact of treatments, and this longitudinal research is still to be published. However, Berin and Garfield (1971) estimated that from 10,000 cases histories 80 per cent benefited if they received psychoanalysis compared to 65 per cent of the patients who had an eclectic therapy (based on several different approaches available at the time).

Take it further

The Freud Museum, Freud's house in London, has some interesting facts about Freud as well as pictures from his life and many of his artefacts. Have a look on their website, or you could visit the museum if you are based in or near London.

The cognitive neuroscience explanation of mental illness

The cognitive neuroscience explanation is a recent (in terms of the development of psychology) discipline which is built on the advances in brain-imaging techniques such as MRI and PET.

Psychologists have previously been interested in facets of behaviour such as memory, but not necessarily in the parts of the brain linked to this. So factors that impact on memory may be studied, such as leading questions on eye-witness testimony. Cognitive neuroscience links these

factors to the areas of the brain linked to these cognitions to see if there are any abnormalities in the brain. If we have an idea of the parts of the memory that are affected we can then, maybe, predict behaviours as we understand which activities that part of the memory deals with. Also, as you saw in the core study by Maguire *et al.* (2000), the brain can be altered by specific use (the increased volume in hippocampus of taxi drivers) and in clinical psychology we could look to use this plasticity of the brain to treat the areas of the brain that are not working effectively.

Using brain-imaging techniques we can see the parts of the brain that are actually altered in people with a diagnosis of mental illness and, from our knowledge of the functions of brain areas, identify the cognitive processes involved in that disorder. For example, we know that language is localised to two main areas – Broca's and Wernicke's – and if these are not working effectively in people with catatonic schizophrenia, then we can suggest that this is why they may be uncommunicative. If it were the areas of the brain associated with memory, then it might be why they are withdrawn – they don't remember basic facts.

So instead of having a simple:

    Biological assumption ↔ disorder

such as:

    Low serotonin levels ↔ depression

there is a cognitive element to our understanding

    Low serotonin levels ↔
    cognitive process impairment ↔ depression

We still don't have evidence of cause and effect, but we do have more understanding of why the symptoms of the disorder occur due to our understanding of the neural deficiencies identified in psychological disorders.

Neurotropic factors are proteins essential in the growth, survival and maintenance of neurons (nerve cells). Brain-derived neurotropic factor (BDNF) is one of the most common of these proteins in the adult brain. Stress, both chronic and acute, is linked to a decrease of the level of BDNF in the hippocampus leading to less than optimal neural cell development. The hippocampus is linked to the hypothalamic–pituitary–adrenal system (HPA), which controls stress and is linked to serotonin levels. As the hippocampus is linked to emotions and memory, neurological malfunction can impact on the cognitive areas of memory and emotion, leading to a behavioural outcome of depression. The HPA may not be able to cope effectively with the stress and serotonin levels may be reduced, which will compound the depression. Research in cognitive neuroscience and mental health is limited due to its recent development,

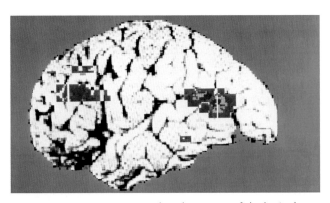

Figure 1.25 Brain imaging can show how areas of the brain do not have optimal neural activity in people with mental disorders

and tends to rely on animal research, but Shrayane (2002) found that increasing BDNF levels in the hippocampus produced an effect that mimicked antidepressants for mice with learned helplessness.

Research shows how poor neural activity in areas of the brain such as the amygdala and the nucleus accumbens (NAc), which are linked to cognitive processes such as feelings of pleasure, motivation and response to reward, as well as sleep and appetite, are linked to symptoms of depression.

De Raedt and Koster (2010) found that decreased activity in neural activity in the prefrontal areas of the brain, which is mediated by serotonin metabolism, controlled by the HPA, is associated with an impaired control of negative schemas (cognitive blueprints), increasing vulnerability to depression.

Barch (2005) suggest that the cognitive deficits associated with schizophrenia, such as disturbances in memory, can be explained by neural deficiency. The lack of control in speech in patients with schizophrenia (disorganised speech is a criteria in both DSM and ICD) could be attributed to neural deficiency in the working memory. This is an area of the brain that controls input and output of stimuli, including visual, spatial, acoustic and language production. Deficits in episodic memory, memory of events that have happened to us, while not directly causing symptoms of schizophrenia, could lead to the confusion seen in schizophrenic patients. If you couldn't remember any previous Christmas seasons, how confusing would the shops, decorations, fancy dress and so on that you see at Christmas be?

While cognitive neuroscience is only just becoming a key psychological area, it clearly adds to our knowledge of the biological explanation and allows for more cognitive-based treatments to be used, focusing on the cognitive skills that are impaired by neural deficiency.

 Find out more

If you are studying the cognitive neuroscience explanation and are interested in this approach, you can look it up on the internet. There will not be many books looking at this explanation of mental illness as it is so new.

Key research: Szasz (2011) The myth of mental illness: 50 years later

Background

Thomas Szasz wrote an essay published in 1960 called 'The Myth of Mental Illness'. This key research is his follow up essay. It is interesting to see how some psychologists who don't follow the scientific beliefs in psychology use non-scientific writings to put across their view point. Szasz uses Shakespeare's *Macbeth* as evidence for the points he is making.

In the original essay Szasz challenged the concept prevalent in the 1950s that mental illness was a medical condition and should be treated as such. He suggested that mental diseases were in fact behaviours that made other people feel uncomfortable and, consequentially, were thought by society to need treating, to make other people feel better rather than to help the person displaying the behaviours. Therefore, they should not be 'treated' in the medical sense, particularly in the light of some of the coercive and unpleasant methods used in the 1950s.

In his follow up essay (delivered as a plenary address at the International Congress of the Royal College of Psychiatrists in 2010 and published in 2011) he aims to reconsider the validity of the points he made in his original essay.

Conclusion

By trying to treat people and preserve life using a medical approach to mental illness as a disease, we are in fact harming the patients that we are trying to help. If, for example, the intention of the schizophrenic patient is to harm him or herself, we should not medicate to prevent this, as this has led to a pseudoscience of 'suicidology'. Mental illness is currently in a 'moral morass'.

 Stop and ask yourself...

- Do you understand the HPA system? If not, look it up in a textbook or on the internet to see how it might impact on cognitive processes.

Links to
- Biological area

Table 1.5 Comparison of points made by Szasz

Points made in 1960	Reconsiderations in 2010
Health care for mental patients consisted of mental hospitals or private non-medical practitioners.	All mental health care is regulated and paid for by public money and the aim is to prevent danger to patients or others.
Mental patients are treated no better than prisoners and are unable to leave, with psychiatrists acting as judge and jury with no ability to appeal.	Political and judicial (legal) decrees and economic criteria have labelled mental illness as a disease and have included non-diseases such as ADHD. This alignment of state and medicine has led to people accepting therapy as a justification for state-sanctioned coercion.
Mental illness is not a disease like a physical disease.	A false belief or 'lying fact' is that all mental illness can be diagnosed accurately and treated successfully.
Mental illness doesn't exist, so it is foolish to look for causes or cures.	Mental illness is seen as a disorder of the brain despite no scientific evidence of the mental illness being caused simply by the brain; physical brain abnormalities may be to blame, in which case it is not a mental illness but a misdiagnosed physical illness.
	Mental illness refers to the judgement of some people about the (bad) behaviour of others, and so will continue to grow with ever more disorders.
	Physicians see the goal as curing the patients. Doctors don't see people as inherently bad; if they do something 'evil', it is due to mental illness.
	If medicine relies on consent for the treatment of physical illness, why is this consent not needed for the treatment of mental illness?
	Mental illness is not caused by bacteria or viruses. People have reasons for behaviours that need to be understood, not treated medically. People need to be helped to overcome their obstacles with respect.

 Take it further

Thomas Szasz has a website (www.szasz.com) which has interesting biographical information and a video clip of his last interview before he died. It's always nice to put a face to a name.

Application: non-biological treatment of one specific disorder

Throughout this section the treatments based on the explanations have been identified along with the explanation. This makes sense as the treatment is always based on the assumption of the explanation. It is important not to use drug therapy as a main therapy in an exam answer on non-biological treatment. This might be fundamental to a cognitive neuroscience explanation but the specification requires a non-biological explanation. Although it is often the case that medication is used alongside some other treatments, make sure that your non-biological treatment is just that.

If you understated the assumptions of the explanation, for example the behaviourist, then it should be fairly easy to apply this to treatment in any scenario. Is it possible to relearn the desired behaviour through association or operant conditioning? Another non-biological treatment could be cognitive therapy, using techniques to change the faulty thinking of a person to a more positive view.

The treatment for the optional explanation if you have studied psychodynamic or humanistic will very clearly be non-biological, but be mindful of the biological element of neuroscience as an explanation for mental illness.

Practice questions

1. Give one explanation that has been used to explain mental illness. [2 marks]
2. How might psychologists categorise psychological disorders? [3 marks]
3. With reference to Rosenhan's (1973) study, discuss the validity of diagnosing mental illness. [5 marks]
4. Outline one non-biological explanation of mental illness. [5 marks]
5. Compare the biological treatment with the non-biological treatment of mental illness. [10 marks]
6. Discuss the issue of determinism in explaining mental illness. [10 marks]

 Stop and ask yourself...

- Can you write for ten minutes on a non-biological treatment for one disorder (you can choose which one)? Think of a scenario that you could refer to, such as a teenager or elderly person.

Links to
- Exam focus

Chapter 2

Child Psychology

Intelligence (Biological)

How clever are you? Would you answer this question in relation to how many GCSE grade A–C you achieved, or how much money you have made from developing Apps, or how many times you have missed lessons without being caught, or how many friends you have? What do you think made you that intelligent? One of the most defined concepts in psychology is intelligence and the definition is often linked to how intelligence is tested. An intelligence test often, but not always, aims to give a quantitative value to a set of skills, which can be based on cognitive skills, such as reasoning, or verbal skills.

What psychologists mean by intelligence

There are many definitions of intelligence. In 1904 Charles Spearman identified that a person's cognitive skills ability tested in one test would show a similar ability in different cognitive skills in another test. He suggested that cognitive skills or 'general cognitive ability' (g) is what we might commonly call intelligence.

Louis Thurston in 1938 considered that we could focus on two specific skills that were indicators of intelligence: verbal comprehension and reasoning. However, one of the issues with defining intelligence simply as cognitive skills is that we know that intelligence scores on different skills, such as verbal or numerical reasoning, can alter over time. Raymond Cattell (1942) suggested there are over 100 skills which someone uses when they are planning what to do and

this might be considered to be intelligence. In which case the definition is not what you know but what you do when you don't know something. He categorised these skills into fluid intelligence (gf), which is a biological or innate ability and is fairly static, not much influenced by environment, and crystallised intelligence (gc), which is what we have learned and assimilated (knowledge taken in and used) and is often tested by intelligence quotient (IQ) tests in terms of knowledge, use of language and acquired skills.

Horn assessed the development of IQ (1967) by researching 14–61 year-old-participants and found that fluid intelligence tended to be higher for younger adults than older adults while crystallised intelligence was generally higher for older adults than younger adults. So, this would suggest that fluid intelligence (innate skills such as problem identifying and memory for reverse lists of number) are lost as we age, but crystallised intelligence (learned skills such as language skills and general knowledge) increases as we age. Horn (1988) and Horn and Noll (1997) suggest that gc can be related to verbal knowledge – following instructions, problem definition and general knowledge about humanities, social and physical science – whereas gf is more linked to concept formation, problem solving, numerical memory and inductive reasoning.

➡ Have a go yourself

- Make a table with the key points of gf and gc to provide a clear comparison for your revision.

🚫 Stop and ask yourself…

- What cognitive skills do you think an IQ test should assess?

Links to
- Cognitive area

Figure 2.1 Fluency is a cognitive skill

Coming more up to date, psychologists now often acknowledge that there is more than one type of intelligence. Sternberg in 1985 developed his triarchic theory of intelligence which, as the name suggests, is based on three skills. He defined intelligence as the mental skills that enable us to be successful. The three skills of his theory are: adapting to, selecting and shaping our environments. The three types of intelligences he identified are:

● analytical intelligence: the skills of analysing, evaluating and judging, for example when problem solving

● practical intelligence: the skills used when actually implementing ideas

● creative intelligence: the skills used when dealing with new or novel ideas and creating.

He changed the name of the theory in the late 1990s to the Theory of Successful Intelligence. His idea was that people would show a profile across the three types of intelligence, which may show one particular strength or may show an integrated profile whereby all three have similar strengths.

The concept of multiple intelligences was further developed by Howard Gardner (1983), who considered that intelligence was not a single entity and so couldn't be measured by simple IQ tests. Gardner looked at a range of research literature for references to intelligence and initially identified seven intelligences. The first two, linguistic intelligence and logical-mathematical intelligence, were traditional intelligences valued in education. He then added three artistic intelligences: musical intelligence, the performance, composition and appreciation of music; bodily kinaesthetic intelligence, using the body to solve problems and using mental abilities to co-ordinate the body; and spatial intelligence, the ability to see and use patterns in spatial activities, either in wide open or confined spaces.

Figure 2.2 There are more than one type of intelligence

Gardner then considered 'personal' intelligences, which reflected the capacity to understand one's own feelings and emotions: intrapersonal intelligence, where the focus is on the self and our feelings and motivation; and interpersonal intelligence, which reflects the capacity to understand the feelings and intentions of other people. Try to remember intra = within (the person) and inter = between (people). This is a very full definition of human cognition, but is still based in the cognitive area. The latter two – inter- and intrapersonal

intelligences – have further been developed by psychologists such as Goleman (1996) who identified two aspects to emotional intelligence (EI):

● understanding yourself, your goals, intentions and behaviour

● understanding others and their feelings.

This is more a behavioural model and is used increasingly in organisational psychology as it can have considerable impact on such features of business as recruitment, management training and customer service.

Stop and ask yourself…

● Are you a thinker, a doer or a creator? Look up the characteristics of these categories on the Internet to see if your initial response was correct.

Links to
● Application

Goleman, however, sees the biology of the brain as a powerful tool in EI. We are hardwired by practice to adopt some behaviours lacking in emotional intelligence, such as not listening to others (too busy thinking of our own response), but if we consciously adopt the habit of listening (or even practising listening, as it has the same biological effect) we can rewire our brain connections to develop the habit of listening. You can see how this would be a powerful tool for employers to develop in their employees.

In conclusion we can see that intelligence is often thought to refer to cognitive skills, either as a general ability (Spearman) or a set of individual skills that reflect the whole of human cognition (Gardner). Increasingly, intelligence is seen as not only cognitive skills but social and behavioural skills with a biological basis.

Biological factors that could affect intelligence

Historically, the biological influence on intelligence was originally limited to the erroneous belief that differing brain size was the contributing factor in the differences in human intelligence. Scholars such as Paul Broca and Francis Galton studied intellectual ability in the nineteenth century and, by measuring head size (sometimes validated by post-mortem information), concluded that brain size indicated intelligence and, therefore, natural gender differences of brain size – with males having larger brains than females – indicated males were inherently more intelligent.

We now have more sophisticated brain scanning techniques and, although more current data indicates a very small correlation between intelligence and head size, this is definitely a correlation and not a causal relationship. There could be a third variable, for example nutrition, which would increase both intelligence and brain size, or it could be that having greater intelligence (for whatever reason) increases the size of the brain. Both of these explanations are at least as plausible than the supposition that a large brain increases intelligence. More recent research has identified that although there

is very little difference in overall intelligence between males and females, there is a difference in the structure and activity within the brain.

Have a go yourself

- Measure the circumference of the heads of a group of people to see if there are gender differences in head size. You could use a statistical test to see if this is significant.

Males have fewer but thicker white matter fibres and more neuron efficiency during spatial tasks, whereas females have more neuron efficiency in task requiring verbal skills. This is reflected in the volume of matter; for example, this is increased in the frontal parietal grey matter for males and more white and grey matter volumes in Broca's area (associated with language) in females. It would appear that males and females can show similar levels of overall intellectual performance by using their differently structured brains in different ways. The performance of the sexes on tasks varies, with men tending to do better on spatial tasks and women on language-based tasks.

Figure 2.3 Men are often better at spatial tasks

Another biological explanation is the genetic transference of intelligence. There is a history of research into genetic transference of intelligence which has found the contribution of genes to intelligence to be between 25 and 50 per cent (Leeuwen *et al.*, 2007). More recent scientific research has been aided by new techniques

Stop and ask yourself ...

- Can you now answer the question: 'What do psychologists mean by intelligence?'

Links to
- Exam focus

Stop and ask yourself ...

- Do you agree that males are better at computer games than females? Why/why not?

Links to
- Individual differences

that have enabled us to identify that individual variation in intelligence is due to many genes, each having a small effect that adds up to a larger difference in overall intelligence (Deary, 2011).

A noticeable difference in intelligence that is linked to the idea of genetic transference is that there are certain cognitive skills that are transferred genetically – these include verbal and organisational skills – whereas there is less genetic transfer of cognitive skills such as memory.

While it must be acknowledged that biology can partially explain inheritance, there has to be some influence from environmental factors, but intelligence does appear to be fairly stable over time. Ian Deary's research (2000) found a correlation of 0.63 in IQ tests for individuals who were tested at 11 and 79 years of age. This would indicate an environmental influence of about 40 per cent.

Environmentally speaking, biology also has a role to play in intelligence, if we consider such factors as the role of prenatal maternal stress, exposure to toxic chemicals and post-natal nutrition.

Research often differs in findings about this. For example, research by Alan Lucas et al. (1998) found that preterm (premature) babies who were breastfed had higher cognitive skills, at age 7½ to 8 years, particularly in the language-based cognitive skills, than bottle-fed preterm babies. However, these were preterm babies and therefore may have been more vulnerable to nutrition that was not in breast milk, and this may have had a negative impact on the cognitive development of those who were bottle-fed. Research by Geoff Der et al. (2006) found that breastfeeding had little or no impact on a child's intelligence in full-term babies, so it would appear that nutrition impacts more on the susceptible individual. For example, if a child has lower than satisfactory levels of nutrition then supplements will help to improve IQ but, for children with healthy diets, a supplement will have little or no impact on his or her IQ. Stephen Schoenthaler et al. (1991) found that when testing the IQs of schoolchildren between the ages of 6 and 12, it was the children who lacked a nutritious diet whose IQ scores were most improved by a daily vitamin and mineral supplement compared to a placebo given on a daily basis.

Figure 2.4 Daily vitamin supplements

The truly impressive finding was that the children who were poorly nourished gained at least 15 IQ points after taking vitamins, but the improvement was only on non-verbal test scores, not verbal tests. This relates to the fluid intelligence identified by Cattell, which appears to be stable in optimum conditions but which can be influenced by suboptimal conditions such as prematurity or poor diet. However, in psychology nothing is black and white. Research by Hanne Mortenson et al. (2002) found that once possible confounding factors, such as mothers' IQ, were controlled there was, in fact, a significant positive correlation between the length of time a baby was breastfed and their later scores on adult intelligence tests. So, there may be longer-term effects of breastfeeding, or it may be the length of time a child is breastfed for that actually impacts on adult IQ.

Having looked at the beneficial effects of nutrition on intelligence test scores, it is also important to consider the effects that toxic substances can have on later cognitive development in children. One such instance is the influence on the later cognitive development of a child when, as a fetus, he or she was exposed to cannabis smoked by the mother during pregnancy. By asking mothers about their cannabis use during pregnancy, Lidush Goldschmidt et al. (2008) found that heavy cannabis use (one or more cigarettes per day) during the first three months of pregnancy was linked to lower verbal reasoning scores on the Stanford-Binet Intelligence Scale in children at the age of 6 years. Heavy use during the second three months had effects on the scores for memory skills and overall scores. Heavy use in the last three months was negatively associated with the overall IQ score. Other factors were also linked to intelligence scores, including maternal IQ, home environment and social support of the mother. There is unlikely to be a direct link between social support of the mother and a child's intelligence, but an unsupported mother may have less inclination and money to provide a stimulating environment that would enhance a child's intelligence.

Of course, it is important to consider other factors when assessing correlational data. Firstly, mothers who smoked cannabis in the first three months (first trimester) most likely smoked it in the second and third trimester as well, so there may be an accumulative effect. Plus the mothers who smoked cannabis may also have been the lower IQ mothers or the mothers with a lack of social support. Or there could be a third factor, such as low income and poor nutrition, or maternal stress that was linked to the cannabis use and lower IQ scores.

It has been widely researched that maternal stress during pregnancy can have a detrimental effect on a child's cognitive development and IQ. The vulnerability of the fetus is seen as making it susceptible to the increase in cortisol (stress hormone) produced by the mother and passed through the placenta to the baby when the mother experiences stress. Susanne King *et al.* (2008) conducted research to investigate the stress caused by a natural disaster (an ice storm) in Quebec.

Figure 2.5 The Great Ice Storm of 1998

She studied 140 children born after the Quebec ice storm of 1998 and found that children aged 5 who had mothers who reported being highly stressed by the storm scored on average 15 IQ points lower than other local children whose mothers experienced less stress. This was also found to be the case in the children at 8½ years old. Vivette Glover (2009) also studied 250 women at 17 weeks of their pregnancy. They completed questionnaires on their anxiety levels and, additionally, the cortisol levels in their blood and the amount in their amniotic fluid was measured. All pregnant mothers have a slightly raised cortisol level but this is usually broken down by an enzyme from the placenta. When the mother is stressed the enzyme works less efficiently, allowing more cortisol into the amniotic fluid. The children exposed to high levels of cortisol tended to have lower a IQ, particularly on verbal and linguistic tests.

Biologically speaking, intelligence could be influenced in an individual by genes in terms of hundreds of differences in DNA, brain structure in terms of volume of white and grey matter, or gender differences in terms of areas of neural efficiency. In addition, any number of environmental factors could influence biological changes that also impact on intelligence, such as nutrition or prenatal maternal stress. This is a simplification of a complex topic however, as we also have to consider the cognitive skills being assessed and which ones are to a greater or lesser extent influenced by genes.

Key research: Van Leeuwen, Van Den Berg and Boomsma (2008) A twin-family study of general IQ

Background

Previous twin studies have looked at both monozygotic (MZ) or identical twins, and dizygotic (DZ) or non-identical twins. These have estimated the contribution of genetics to intelligence to be between 25 and 50 per cent.

Aim

This study aimed to use not only twins but parents and siblings to identify the relationship between family member and IQ, assuming a shared environment and shared genetic material of 100 per cent between monozygotic twins (MZ), 50 per cent between dizygotic twins (DZ) and siblings, and 50 per cent between parents/child.

Participants

A total of 112 families were studied. They had either MZ or DZ twins, plus a sibling aged between 9 and 14 years old and two parents, they had volunteered to take part and passed the screening for disabilities, mental illness and metal materials such as pacemakers (which can interfere with MRI scans). The mean age of the twins was 9.1 years, the sibling 11.9 years, and there were 23 male MZ twins, 23 male DZ twins, 25 female MZ twins and 21 female DZ twins, with 20 DZ twins of opposite sex.

Method

Biological data (to check the MZ status of the twins) plus hormonal and MRI scans was collected. The cognitive testing was based on Raven's Standard Progressive Matrices for the children and Raven's Advanced Progressive Matrices for the parents. This is an IQ test covering a range of cognitive skills. The families arrived between 9 a.m. and 11 a.m. and, with three breaks, the whole testing period was approximately five hours.

A model called the Rasch model was applied, which takes into account the difficulty of each test question and calculates the probability of the person being able to score highly or lowly depending on their individual ability. The IQ score each participant achieved was therefore irrespective of which items were used (as the difficulty was controlled for).

🚫 **Stop and ask yourself ...**

- Can you answer the question: 'Outline the biological factors that might influence intelligence.'?

Links to
- Exam focus

Results

Data analysis showed that there were no sex differences in the group or in any of the three groups (twins, siblings or parents).

Correlations were higher for MZ twins than first-degree relatives (siblings, DZ twins and parent/child pairs). There was quite a high correlation between the IQ of parents. This suggests that the heritability estimate for intelligence (the effect of the genes) was 67 per cent (at 95 per cent confidence level) and the rest was the result of random environmental factors.

For lower IQ groups, the interaction between the genotype (genetic makeup) and environment was higher.

Discussion

It would appear that individual genetic differences can account for individual differences in intelligence. However, important factors such as the environment might have more impact on certain groups of individuals, such as low IQ groups compared to the effect on high IQ groups.

There is no indication that intelligent parents provide stimulating environments to promote intelligence, but rather that children with a predisposed IQ will seek out stimulating (high IQ) or non-stimulating (low IQ) environments.

Application: methods of assessing intelligence

The most usual way of assessing intelligence is to use an IQ test, which comprises of a number of questions that may relate to knowledge and language skills (crystallised intelligence) or problem solving and logic (fluid intelligence). IQ tests have a range of uses: to assess achievement, to diagnose problems or to identify aptitude or potential. One of the first, the Stanford-Binet test, was used originally to identify those who were below average intelligence but was then used to assess all children.

Tests have to be standardised on a group of people and then, to ensure validity, should only be used on people in that group. There would be no point in giving a child an IQ test standardised on adults. One of the most commonly used IQ tests today, particularly in psychological research and practice, is the Wechsler Intelligence Scale for Children or the Wechsler Adult Intelligence Scale. Developed by David Wechsler in 1949, it has been revised to the WISC-IV or WAIS. There are also tests for children aged 3 to 7 years (the Wechsler Preschool and Primary Scale of Intelligence, or WPPSI).

An example of an IQ test question is shown in Figure 2.6.

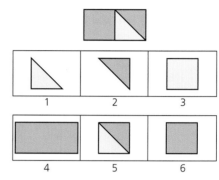

Figure 2.6 Which three of these flat puzzle pieces go together to make this puzzle?

As was suggested at the beginning of this topic the definition and assessment of intelligence often go hand in hand. Sternberg constructed the Sternberg Triarchic Abilities Test (STAT), which consists of multiple-choice questions that assess the three aspects of intelligence he proposed in his triarchic theory: analytic, practical and creative.

Tests have to avoid the ceiling and floor effect. No person should be able to answer all the questions correctly as this would put an artificial ceiling on their test score. Who knows how much higher they could have gone in answering questions? Similarly, if a person could answer no questions then this would not necessarily show the floor of their knowledge (the lowest level). They should also avoid culture bias, and so questions should be 'culture fair'. Yerkes (1919) gave American soldiers IQ tests that had culture bias towards white Americans and found, unsurprisingly, that black Americans were less intelligent than white Americans. The fact that the average mental age of the American soldiers was 13 suggests that this may not have been a valid test of anyone's IQ!

Apart from all of the IQ tests based on questionnaires, and the Wechsler set is only one of many, there are other ways of assessing intelligence. Human figure drawing tests can be used on younger children as well as adults, where a child is asked to draw a number of people (the Goodenough–Harris Drawing Test asks to draw a man, a woman and the child him or her self). Analysis of features of the drawings, such as absence of detail and the proportion of features such as hands and fingers can give an estimation of intelligence. These tests may not be as specific as IQ tests but have shown concurrent validity when assessed alongside standardised IQ tests.

Plubrukam (2003) reviewed the use of the Goodenough–Harris Drawing Test and a standard IQ test administered on the same day and found that the overall correlation across a range of IQ scores was 0.8, which showed the validity of the figure drawing test. It may not be sophisticated enough on its own, but it is a good indicator of intelligence without being invasive or time consuming.

Figure 2.7 Figures drawn by children taking the Goodenough–Harris Drawing Test

Emotional intelligence is often assessed by means of social problems and the answers of the person being compared with those that the majority of a group people from that society gave. There are no right or wrong answers but EI is assessed as traits that society sees as acceptable. This has been criticised as EI is not related to the ability to perform tasks but merely a test of emotions (Brody, 2004).

The use of intelligence tests has to be questioned in terms of the ethics of assessing intelligence. Possible consequences, both negative (for example, the channelling of students into selective schools via the 11+, predicting success, job selection, the inevitable labelling) and positive (for example, being able to teach to ability through streaming, planning interventions for underachievement), should be considered alongside the validity and usefulness of such tests.

Find out more

Research the US Head Start Program online; see if you can find the results regarding IQ.

IN THE NEWS

In 2014 many newspapers reported the findings of research from Kings College in London which studied over 15,000 children who were asked to draw a child. This was based on a test devised in 1920s called Draw-a-Child. Points were given for each correctly presented physical feature, the right number of arms would gain 1 point plus the addition of clothing also scored a point. This assessment of Intelligence, correlated with other IQ tests at the age of 4, showing concurrent validity, but what was more surprising was that when the children were assessed at 14 there was still a strong correlation between their IQ on the Draw-a-Child test and other standard IQ tests, showing the predictive validity of the Draw-a-Child test.

Discussion

Go back to the original question in the introduction: what is intelligence and what affects it? As you have seen, many psychologists disagree as to what intelligence is and how to assess it, and there are a myriad of factors that might influence your intelligence. One consideration is the issues that psychologists might be concerned with when discussing intelligence, in particular the validity of intelligence tests. Are they really measuring what they are supposed to be measuring? What about the effect of social desirability, self report, extraneous variables? All of these can influence test outcomes. Hay fever sufferers taking A Level exams in June will know just what this means!

The ethics of labelling, as highlighted in the application of IQ testing, is another issue. We could also consider the deterministic and reductionist aspect of a biological explanation for intelligence. What about interventions such as Head Start (US Department of Health and Human Services, 2013), which gives intensive support to deprived preschool children and has an impact on later IQ scores.

Can this be explained by biology or environmental factors? An interesting point leading on from the twin studies into IQ is the individual and situational debate, which would be illustrated by twins being raised apart but still having similar IQs, or adopted children who have no correlation with adoptive parents' IQ. Intelligence, and the definition and testing of it, is an inherent part of our education system but needs to be challenged and monitored to avoid some of the stereotyping that has gone on in the past. Even as recently as 2007, Nobel Prize-winner James Watson was expounding that Africans are not as intelligent as white Westerners and, in 2003, suggested that low intelligence should be eliminated through gene therapy. All the more reason to critically analyse the research into intelligence.

Pre-adult brain development (Biological)

Brain development is a complex process comprising development of neurons or nerve cells and the establishment of connections between neurons in different areas of the brain. This development begins at conception and continues throughout childhood until about the age of 25; the brain continues to change during adulthood and old age.

There are various behaviours and changes in cognition that develop alongside these changes in brain structure and function, from which it can be inferred that brain development is linked to behavioural development. Brain imaging techniques now allow us to see the areas of brain at work during specific behaviours and these can be used as a baseline for abnormal development in brain and behaviour. Neuroscience continues to develop techniques as well as our understanding of pre-adult brain development.

While we could look at this from a purely biological viewpoint, psychologists are interested in causes of behaviour and, therefore, the behavioural output is important. As you will see, there are certain areas of the brain that are stimulated more easily in pre-adult brains and these can have an impact on the behaviour of adolescents. In particular, the topic of risk taking is seen as important in helping us understand why young adults are willing to take risks for what would appear to be very little gain. The key research helps us to understand this with specific reference to gambling.

Brain development

There are various ways in which psychologists can study brain development and use their findings to understand the connection between brain development and behaviour. The development of the structure of the nervous system can be studied and this can then be correlated with the emergence of specific behaviours. From this we can infer the two are linked. However, due to individual differences in both brain development and behaviour, this can be flawed. Also there appears to be a biological determinism of brain development but a much less fixed pattern of behavioural development, showing that environmental influences can impact on behaviour rather than it simply being due to brain development.

The inability to actually manipulate brain development restricts the research to merely observing and formulating a theory that cannot easily be tested. Psychologists could turn this method of researching on its head and study behaviour, which in turn is then hypothesised to be linked to neural change. For example, we might consider Kohlberg's moral development to be as a result of specific areas of the brain developing to allow abstract thought.

Another method of studying brain development and behavioural development is to consider the neural structure in areas of the brain in relation to behavioural disorders, trying to identify brain abnormalities that might explain behavioural disorders.

As we have seen from Maguire's core study, the brain can alter in structure depending on stimulation from the environment, and this plasticity suggests the possibility of recovery from some brain injuries. This ability to recover may then support normal brain organisation to enable other areas to develop and overcome the damage. Brain plasticity may, therefore, also result in other brain structures and neurons developing differently.

The plasticity of the immature brain poses another problem to inferring structure–function relations from malfunction in the developing nervous system. Brain damage occurring in infants may produce very different behavioural effects than in adults because early injury has also altered fundamental brain organisation. The trauma does not affect the function of only the brain areas that are damaged directly. It also disrupts other neuroanatomical sites and circuitry appearing later, the subsequent normal development of which was dependent upon the intact structure and function of the regions damaged.

The process of brain growth can be understood by considering the composition of the nervous system. Brain cells or neurons in areas of the brain can become stimulated by sensory input, neurotransmitters or hormones and they will then produce an electrical charge which passes on to the next cell and so on, with areas of the brain being stimulated either in isolation or in connection with other areas. A simple example is the language areas of Wernicke's area and Broca's area. Broca's area is particularly involved in the production of speech. It sends information outside of its area to the motor cortex, to send signals to the larynx, tongue and mouth motor areas of the brain, which then send neural signals to the appropriate muscles, which contract and relax to produce sound. Wernicke's area is involved in the comprehension of language and communication, whatever the language medium (that is, written or vocal) and damage to Wernicke's area can result in muddled and made up language. Broca's area and Wernicke's area are connected so that Wernicke's area produces the language that Broca's area ensures is articulated by controlling speech muscles.

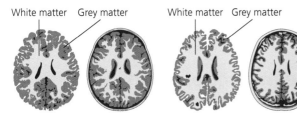

Stop and ask yourself ...

- What are the ways of researching brain development, and what are their strengths and weaknesses?

Links to
- Methodology

After birth the brain develops along a predetermined route, but this is not a linear pattern of growth. During irregular periods of growth the brain will develop much quicker than at other times. For example, Epstein (1978, 1979) found consistent spurts in brain growth at 3–10 months, which lead to an increase in brain weight of 30 per cent by the age of 1½ years. These growth spurts also occur between the ages of 2 and 4, 6 and 8, 10 and 12, and 14 and 16 years. The increments in brain weight were about 5–10 per cent over each two-year period. You can see the link between these ages of growth spurts and the ages at which Piaget suggests children's thinking changes (see page 63).

The various cells of the brain also develop at differing rates. The volumes of grey matter tend to begin to decline around 6–7 years of age and this continues through adolescence, whereas white matter volumes increase over the same time frame.

IN THE NEWS

Research in 2014 into abandoned Romanian children who had suffered from emotional, social, language and mental development neglect found that, compared to children in high-quality care centres or who lived with their families, they had modified white matter, suggesting an interaction between a neglectful and a non-neglectful environment and brain development. Also, some areas in the white matter, such as the corpus callosum, were altered in the neglected children. As white matter is crucial for cognitive development, it is possible to explain cognitive deficits such as impaired language skills in neglected children.

White matter Grey matter   White matter Grey matter

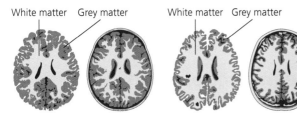

Figure 2.8 Relative amounts of white and grey matter in the brains of adults (left) and children (right)

Grey matter is made up of nerve cell bodies, and makes up about 40 per cent of the adult brain and processes information; white matter is made up of neurons with long axons that carry messages to and from grey matter areas, and between the grey matter and the other parts of the body.

Areas of the brain develop as the neurons become myelinated, that is they get their myelin sheaths that insulate them and allow them to send messages along the appropriate pathways. At birth a baby's nerves will not have a mature myelin sheath, which results in movements that are unco-ordinated and awkward. Multiple sclerosis is an example of a disease in adults where the myelin sheaths have been destroyed. As the child's myelin sheaths develop, movements become smoother and more co-ordinated.

Chugan and Phelps (1986) used positron emission tomography to study glucose metabolism in the brain cells of children. The glucose metabolism would indicate the cells being active. They found that in infants of five weeks of age or younger, glucose utilisation was highest in the sensorimotor cortex. By the age of three months glucose metabolism had increased in most other cortical regions. Further increases were seen in the frontal and posterior association cortex by eight months. So, by eight to nine months the cerebral cortex is active; however, it continues to change as the child continues to develop. Other measures of brain activity, such as the EEG, confirm this cortical activity at birth.

After the development of the primary cortical regions involved in basic sensory and motor functions there is further development in the parietal regions involved in space and language, which mature around puberty (age 11–13 years), and in the prefrontal cortex from late adolescence into adulthood.

Two specific behaviours – motor skills and language – have been considered alongside brain development.

The development of movement in babies is known well. At birth the baby is unable to move about independently, but eventually they learn to crawl at about six months and then to walk at about 15 months, although this is definitely an area of individual difference! Other movement skills, such as reaching out and groping for objects then bringing them to their mouth are another motor skill to be developed. Between one and three months the child can put his or her hand forward and towards an object and he or she will attempt to grip anything it touches. However, between eight and 11 months the child can use a 'pincer grasp' involving the index finger and thumb. Studies have shown a correlation between myelin formation and the ability to grasp. The fine motor neurons become myelinated at about the same time that reaching and grasping with the whole hand develops. The cells of the motor cortex become myelinated at about the time the pincer grasp develops (Kolb and Whishaw, 1996).

Table 2.1 The development of motor and visual skills in relation to brain weight gain

Age	Visual and motor function	Average brain weight (g)
Birth	Reflex sucking, rooting, swallowing and Moro reflexes; infantile grasping; blinks to light	350
6 weeks	Extends and turns neck when prone; regards mother's face, follows objects	410
3 months	Infantile grasp and suck modified by volition; keeps head above horizontal for long periods; turns to objects presented in visual field; may respond to sound	515
6 months	Grasps objects with both hands; will place weight on forearms or hands when prone; rolls from supine to prone; supports almost all weight on legs for very brief periods; sits briefly	660
9 months	Sits well and pulls self to sitting position; thumb–forefinger grasp; crawls	750
12 months	Able to release objects; cruises and walks with one hand held; plantar reflex flexor in 50% of children	925
24 months	Walks up and down stairs (two feet a step); bends over and picks up object without falling; turns knob; can partially dress self; plantar reflex flexor in 100%	1065
36 months	Goes up stairs (one foot a step); pedals tricycle; dresses fully except for shoelaces, belt and buttons; visual acuity 20/20 OU	1140
5 years	Skips, ties shoelaces, copies triangle; gives age correctly	1240
Adult		1400

Language development is a gradual process over the first three years of age. It depends not only on the cognitive skills of perception and memory, but also on motor skills to control mouth and tongue. The temporal and frontal lobes of the child's brain develop in line with linguistic skills and are more variable than some areas in when and how quickly they develop, leading to individual differences in the development of language skills in normal children.

This is only a snapshot of some of the changes in the brain and their impact on behavioural development. The changes continue throughout childhood and adolescence, allowing us to develop motor skills, linguistic competence and cognitive development. Let us move on to the brains of adolescents and the impact of their stage of brain development on risk-taking behaviour.

→ Have a go yourself

- Make a timeline of a child's brain development showing the corresponding motor and linguistic skills.

The impact of brain development on risk-taking behaviour

There has been much speculation about risk taking in adolescents who have a less developed prefrontal cortex. However, there is some contention about this being too simplistic an explanation for risk-taking behaviour. There is no doubt about the fact that brains do tend to develop from back to front, and so the prefrontal cortex does not mature until the mid-20s. It has also been established that a well-developed prefrontal cortex is necessary for high-level reasoning and decision making. It would seem therefore to suggest that the lack of development in adolescents will lead to risk-taking behaviours as they are liable to ignore the negative consequences of the decisions that they make, in light of the lack of high-level reasoning. So, there is a dilemma of wanting to do something now, versus the higher-thinking skill of considering the consequences of an action.

There is also evidence that alcohol reduces social discomfort; adolescents may be more sensitive to this effect due to the feelings of insecurity that are often apparent in puberty, and are therefore likely to drink more to gain the confidence they don't have.

Barkley-Levenson and Galván (2014) in their key research consider it is not only the prefrontal cortex that may be involved in risk-taking behaviours but also areas of the ventral striatum, which mature earlier and can encourage adolescents towards novel, adult-like activities that tend to be risky, such as driving fast or sexual activity. Also, the lack of experience in dealing with these situations may inhibit an adolescent's reasoning and subsequent curtailment of such activities when they become dangerous. The activity is normal but just not handled in the way a more mature adult would.

If we put both of these together we have adolescent brains that tend towards risky behaviour, without the brake of the prefrontal cortex to reasonably assess the consequences. This would result in an inevitable period of risk for adolescents.

However, it is not only adolescents who take risks. Impulsivity in young children aged three has been shown to persist into adolescence, and may be due to inherited traits: so, risk-taking three-year-olds become risk-taking 18-year-olds. As risk taking in adolescence is linked to risk taking preceding adolescence, it is individual differences that result in some adolescents taking risk but some or many not doing so.

We also have to consider the problems with neurochemicals in the brain such as serotonin, a neurotransmitter linked to mood. A reduction in serotonin in the cerebral spinal fluid can lead to impulsivity in rhesus macaque monkeys and this reduction is often seen in situations where the offspring has been subjected to stress as a baby. This would have bearing on children who are abused or neglected and so suffer a stressful infanthood, who have lower levels of serotonin and show more impulsivity. Therefore, risk-taking behaviour may not be entirely down to the underdevelopment of the prefrontal cortex. Neglectful environments are more likely to be seen in low socioeconomic groups, so this suggests that risk-taking behaviour may be seen more in those groups.

Another neurotransmitter, dopamine, is seen in adolescent brains in the ventral striatum and Chambers (2003) suggests that in the animal kingdom this has the effect of encouraging the adolescent to leave the home and, in so doing, taking more risks.

Figure 2.9 Dopamine may have a role in encouraging adolescent animals to leave home

Looking at brain activity in risk-taking adolescents has also identified that individuals with a higher IQ and better memory performance actually have higher levels of sensation seeking, so it would appear that risk-taking behaviours are not always linked to deficits in brain structures.

One important question related to the rise in sensation seeking during adolescence is whether it is associated with a lack of executive control over behaviour as the other forms of impulsivity manifest. Evidence is sparse on this question but, given the small but significant positive correlation between sensation seeking and IQ (Zuckerman, 1994), it would seem that persons who exhibit stronger sensation-seeking drives are no less able to exert executive control over their behaviour. Indeed, in the Philadelphia trajectory study, it was found that differences in sensation seeking are

Stop and ask yourself...

● What are the problems with generalising from research on monkeys to human behaviour?

Links to
● Generalisability

positively correlated with working memory performance (Romer *et al.*, 2009). Adolescents with good memory skills were more sensation seeking.

Thus, it seems that one of the more powerful sources of risk taking in adolescence is not necessarily associated with deficits in executive function. A comprehensive study of brain activation in adolescents and adults (Eshel *et al.*, 2007) looked at the difference in brain activity when adults and adolescents faced a choice between alternatives that had high probabilities of a small financial reward and those that had low probabilities of a higher financial reward. In the research a participant choosing the risky alternative (low probability of high reward) was always worse off than those choosing the less-risky alternative (high probability of low reward). There was more brain activity in the occipital frontal cortex in the adults when they made a risky disadvantageous choice, showing that if the occipital frontal cortex was not developed in the adolescents they would not be able to rely on this area of the brain to control their choices.

Finally, a completely different suggestion based on research into the white matter of the frontal cortex theorises that risk-taking adolescents actually have more mature frontal cortex white matter, giving rise to more adult or mature decisions. Therefore, if they make the choice to partake in risky behaviour, they are doing so after more mature consideration than non-risk-taking adolescents with their immature brains.

> ### ➡ Take it further
>
> - List five types of risk-taking behaviour teenagers are likely to show (use the internet to find out if you're not sure). Can you explain them in terms of lack of development in the frontal cortex? Are there any gender differences? Why do you think this is the case?

Key research: Barkley-Levenson and Galván (2014) Neural representation of expected value in the adolescent brain

Aim

The aim of this study was to identify if there is a difference in neural activity between adolescent and adult brains when given risk-taking scenarios (gambles) with different expected values of the outcomes of those gambles.

Participants

Nineteen right-handed adults, 11 female and 8 male, aged 25 to 30, from the USA were recruited along with 22 right-handed 13 to 17-year-olds, 11 female and 11 male, by a poster and advertisement recruitment campaign at the University of California, as well as a database of participants from previous research.

Because the brain has a dominant hemisphere that is different for left- and right-handed people, all participants were right-handed and therefore had the same (left) dominant hemisphere. This ensured that the dominant hemisphere was not a participant variable.

Consent was gained either from the participants themselves or from parents if they were under 18. It was important that they had no previous diagnoses of mental or neurological illnesses as these might have reflected in different brain patterns of activity, and they had no metal in their bodies (for example, a pacemaker) as this would cause problems with the MRI scans.

After the research had been carried out a total of 20 adolescents and 17 adults were analysed in the final sample, with the others not being able to provide useful data.

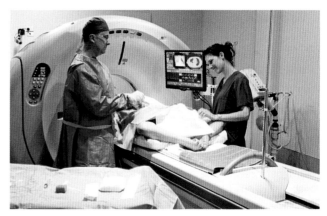

Figure 2.10 An MRI scanner

Method

Once the participants were recruited they were called in to complete some information on their income, both the source and amount of spending money they had per week, as this might have had an influence on their perceptions of winning or losing amounts of money. They were also familiarised with the MRI scanner using a mock version of the scanner. They were each 'given' $20 for taking part and were then told they would be able to gamble and win up to another $20 or lose up to $20. This meant they had ownership of the money and so would have an interest in increasing or keeping it, whereas with 'house' money they wouldn't necessarily worry about the winning or losing of money they didn't actually own.

One week after the intake session, the participants were called back and were then given an fMRI scan while they undertook a decision-making process. Each participant was shown a spinner with the number of dollars that could be lost or gained on each side. They were asked to state if they would be willing to stake their dollars on that gamble. They were told at the end of the experiment that one of the gambles they had said they would be willing to play, would be played, and they would keep the outcome.

There were 144 spinners, with a gain on one side such as 'win $4' and a loss on the other side such as 'lose $2'. In addition there were 24 with win/win and 24 with lose/lose gambles. The participants therefore had to take a risk with the 144 but less of a risk with the win/win or lose/lose gambles. Differences in the brain would show if adolescents and adults considered risk differently. Also, the amount of risk – whether it was a high loss/gain or low loss/gain – which the researchers called the Expected Value (EV) might also affect the amount of the brain activity.

Figure 2.11 Participants were asked whether they were willing to take the risk

Results

In terms of behaviour, both groups accepted the gamble if the expected value was positive rather than zero, win $1/no win or lose; more accepted the gamble if the outcome was zero rather than negative, so no win or lose/lose $2. If there was no real risk – win/win or lose/lose – the adults and adolescents didn't differ in their acceptance or rejection.

However, as shown in the Figure 2.12, the higher the expected value of the win the more likely the adolescent was to accept the gamble compared to the adult.

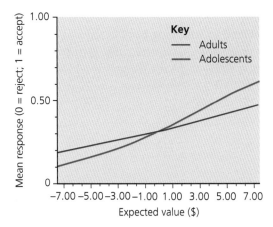

Figure 2.12 The higher the expected value of the win the more likely the adolescent was to accept the gamble compared to the adult

Scan data

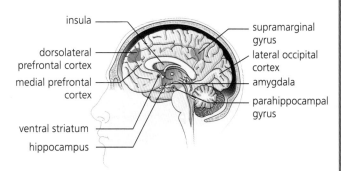

Figure 2.13 Areas of the brain studied in the fMRI scan

Decreased activity in the:
● amygdala – involved in fear response
● parahippocampal gyrus and hippocampus – involved with memory
● insula – involved with turning perceptions into emotions, and preparing for action.

Increased activity in the:
● medial prefrontal cortex – involved in decision making, memory and emotions
● lateral occipital cortex – involved in processing visual stimuli
● supramarginal gyrus – involved in processing linguistic information and meaning, and emotional processing.

There was significantly more activity in the left ventral striatum of the adolescents and this showed greater activity as the EV increased. Of the participants who agreed to gamble on 80 per cent of the highest EV choices, the adolescents showed greater activity in the right ventral striatum. The ventral striatum is involved in some emotional responses, particularly those related to pleasure and behavioural motivation. Higher levels of activity would indicate higher pleasure and motivation.

Discussion

There was clear observed activation of medial prefrontal cortex and dorsolateral prefrontal cortex and adjacent cortical regions during EV computations. The observation of decreased activation in the insula in response to increasing EV is also supported by existing findings. The insula is linked with consciousness, arousal and awareness of self, along with pleasure and emotions. If it's activity is decreased this may result in the adolescent not being aware of what is going on around, but it is a complex area of the cortex and it would be difficult to say exactly how this deactivation influences behaviour.

More importantly, significant developmental differences were observed in the ventral striatum, with adolescents showing significantly greater activation than adults (who showed virtually no activation in this region). The conclusion would be that there are significant maturational changes in the ventral striatum of adolescents. Also, in adults and adolescents who showed the same gambling choices, there was more activation in the adolescent striatum than in the adults. This could reflect more positive emotions and motivation when the adolescent is making risky choices, such a reward could cause the risky behaviours to be maintained through operant conditioning.

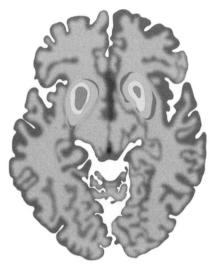

Figure 2.14 Brain scan showing the ventral striatum activated

One possible explanation is that an adolescent brain places greater value on potential rewards than does the adult brain. Barkley-Levenson and Galván suggest this is because adolescents were more influenced by the possibility of winning the larger amount and less focused on the chance of losing the relatively smaller amount. Although adolescents are as astute as adults when presented with a disadvantageous choice, their heightened sensitivity in reward circuitry in the ventral striatum leads to better choices than

adults on advantageous trials. Adolescents appear to be more avoidant of disadvantageous risks than adults are, which shows with their reduced neural activation in response to low EV trials compared to adults in the current study.

In conclusion, the brain undergoes significant maturation during adolescence that influences reward sensitivity and risk-taking behaviour. Adolescents appear to value rewards more than adults, as shown by the higher activation of the ventral striatum, and this value increases gambling behaviour. The heightened reward value tends to lead adolescents to be more likely to gamble in advantageous risk taking compared with adults.

Application: strategies to reduce risk-taking behaviours using knowledge of brain development

The research and explanations for risk taking based on brain development lead to several suggestions for reducing risk-taking behaviours. If we take the theory that stressful childhood results in less serotonin in the cerebral spinal fluid, there is a strong case for intervening with parents who are at risk of neglecting or maltreating their children. Better education or support from practitioners to reduce neglect could prevent risk taking or impulsivity. One such programme was carried out in 1998 (Olds *et al.*, 1998) which involved nurses visiting expectant mothers before the birth and providing training for parents on how to cope with stressors that might otherwise lead to a stressful experience for the child. Results showed that children performed better in school and experienced fewer psychiatric symptoms, and in particular showed lower rates of conduct disorder, which could result in impulsivity.

In addition to educating parents, working with children to provide an age-appropriate curriculum covering risky behaviours to highlight the dangers would also be

Stop and ask yourself ...

- Can you summarise Barkley-Levenson and Galván's research in a page of hand-written text?

Make sure that you explain what this research contributes to our understanding of brain development and risk-taking behaviour.

In an exam you would be expected to do this in about 10 minutes.

Links to
- Exam focus

prudent. One example of a programme that was designed to prevent risk-taking behaviour in novel or new situations was a driving programme that has been adopted in the USA. As adolescent drivers are more likely to drive in a risky manner, and so have more accidents, the programme involved not giving adolescents a full licence until they have completed a probationary period during which their driving rights were restricted, such as not being able to drive at night. This was based on the idea that, in early exposure to new experiences, the learning should be completed in lower risk and supervised conditions, until the skill has been fully mastered. This programme saw a significant reduction in crashes of adolescent drivers, after about six months or about 1000 miles (McCartt, Shabanova & Leaf, 2003).

Figure 2.15 Evidence suggests that learning should be completed in lower risk, supervised conditions, until the skill has been fully mastered

If we assume that adolescents are unable to assess risks, then conversations between parents and their teenage children can help the teenager to learn to assess risk. Talking about behaviour and consequences, such as on films or in the news, pointing out consequences of say, losing a driving licence, which could lead to loss of job, can teach strategies for considering the consequences. Being able to talk to teenagers on a range of subjects can reduce the risky behaviour. For example, if the teenager can always ask parents for a lift then they don't need to risk getting into a car with a driver who has been drinking, making it an easy decision to make regarding risky behaviour.

The social context of the child should also be considered. If peer pressure increases the reward in taking risks, then the resulting brain activity may make the risk seem even more worth taking. Ensuring that teenagers have positive social networks, such as family, peers, school and community, can provide protective factors against risky behaviours.

Summary: The biological area

As there are major biological changes during the development of a child, which will impact on their behaviour, the area of developmental biology obviously has a large part to play in our understanding of behavioural change in childhood. This might be from developing hand–eye co-ordination, which allows children to pick up objects, or more complex brain development which, as we have seen, can impact on risk-taking behaviours.

A person's biology is not static and will be impacted by environmental factors, such as the effect of toxins during pregnancy on the intelligence of a child, or the social rewards gained that can provoke a biological response in the brain in response to a risky stimulus.

The biological explanation of behaviour can include not only chemicals and biological structures but also the effect of genes. It is interesting to note gender differences in risk-taking behaviour, which could be linked to the effect of chromosomes and hormone levels, or could be a direct link to genes, such as the noted link between family members and intelligence, with monozygotic twins having higher concordance rates of IQ than dizygotic twins. It is important to remember that in biopsychology we are not only interested in the biological changes but more focused on the behaviour changes as a consequence of those biological influences.

Stop and ask yourself…

- Can you devise an intervention programme to reduce a risky behaviour such as drug taking in adolescents? What features would you include and why?

Links to
- Application

Perceptual development (Cognitive)

In the cognitive information processing model, it is suggested that information follows a pattern. Firstly, the information has to be paid attention to. You will have seen in Unit 2 that we pay attention to something that is important to us (for example, overhearing our name), something unusual or a strong stimulus, such as a loud noise. We then have to make sense of the incoming stimulus. When we see something, all that happens is the cells in our retina are either stimulated or not. This stimulation is then interpreted by the brain, using our memory, to inform us about what we see. With auditory perception, our ear drums receive vibrations that our brain interprets as sounds, which our memory then clarifies as words or sounds, such as a dog barking.

| Attention is paid | The stimulus is perceived | The stimulus is consigned to memory if necessary | The information in the memory is used to solve a problem |

Figure 2.16 The cognitive information processing model

Psychologists are interested in how we turn physical cell activity into a cognitive perception of the world around us. If you think about it, there appears to be a minor miracle in how we can instantaneously process visual and auditory stimuli – along with tactile, olfactory and gustatory (touch, smell and taste) stimuli – and, using this information, can safely negotiate our way around our environment, often with more than one sense being used. You can probably chew gum (and know it is gum) while walking up stairs (without falling), listening to your friend and texting correctly, a message on your phone.

This is obviously a huge area for psychologists, and we are going to focus on the development of visual perception in this textbook. But the specification stipulates perceptual development, and you are free to use any psychological theory and research on perceptual development you like. However, the key research by Gibson and Walk (discussed below) is about visual perception.

Psychologists are interested in how children develop their perceptual skills, and this is closely linked to the nature–nurture debate. Which skills are we born with and which do we develop over time, as a result of either maturation or interaction with the environment? This can be useful to identify a child who may not be developing at the expected rate, or in the expected way. It can help us to ensure that there are interventions to counteract problems, either physically or environmentally.

There are some cultural differences, in that some cultures will have little experience of certain environments. For example, if you live somewhere that is dense jungle, with little in the way of open landscapes, then the ability to judge distance may be limited if this is a skill learned from interaction with the environment. An often-quoted case is that by Turnbull who studied the BaMbuti pygmies in the 1950s. One of the pygmies, Kenge, who was 22 years old, had (according to Turnbull) never left the Ituri forest before. He went with Turnbull on a drive to the mountains, and in the distance were some buffalo. Without distance perception Kenge thought they were insects. However, as the car got nearer to the buffalo their apparent size increased. Kenge was confused as to how the insects transformed into buffalo. He also made the same mistake on seeing a boat on a lake in the distance. He originally thought it was a small plank of wood that miraculously grew into a boat.

So, there is an ongoing discussion about how perception develops and, importantly, the stages of perceptual development. This development relies on physical maturation, the role of experience and an increased cognitive ability to interpret information from our environment.

Figure 2.17 The ability to judge distance relies on physical maturation, previous experience and our ability to interpret information from our environment

Perceptual development in children

Although the second part of this section looks at how perceptual development is researched, one key point will help you to understand how the following developmental features have been found.

A newborn baby will look at something if it is a new stimulus. If you present the same thing to a baby many times, eventually it will lose interest; if you then present something similar but different in some way, the child will show interest again. For example, if you show a baby a picture of a square and present it again and again, the amount of time the child looks at it will gradually decrease – he or she will become habituated or immune to its effect to stimulate. If you show a series of squares until no interest is shown, and you then show a rectangle, if the child shows an interest in it, we can infer that the child can tell the difference between a square and a rectangle.

Figure 2.18 shows the amount of time a child spends gazing at stimulus.

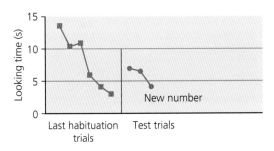

Figure 2.18 Graph showing habituation over number of presentations as the time spent gazing at stimulus reduces; presentation of a different stimulus evokes longer gazes, but eventually this stimulus also becomes habituated. Adapted from Wynn (1995)

Pattern perception

Infants show a preference for certain patterns, showing that they have the visual perceptual skills to perceive the different patterns. Fantz' research (1963) found that babies prefer complex patterns compared to simple patterns, suggesting they can differentiate patterns. He also found that newborn babies preferred patterns that resembled a human face compared to other patterns, again suggesting an innate perceptual ability to recognise faces. In his study in 1963 he looked at children under the age of five days and found that they spent more time looking at faces or patterns than plain colours.

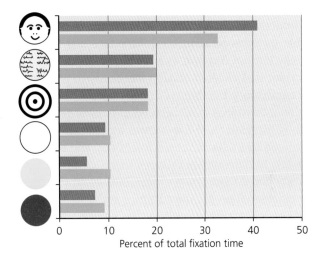

Figure 2.19 Fantz' research showed a higher percentage of fixation time was spent looking at faces, with the least amount looking at the plain grey circle

Face perception

Babies appear to have an innate skill to be able to perceive human faces within a few hours of being born. Newborn babies are able to discriminate their mother's face from other female faces, providing they can see the hair line. They also have a preference for attractive faces over unattractive faces (Slater, 2004) and show a preference for faces of their own ethnicity. They also appear to be able to distinguish faces of ethnicities that are different to their own.

Newborn infants are able to discriminate not only their mother's face, but faces in general from a variety of other images. For example, their preference for a face was shown over a face image such as a smilie, a face with jumbled up features and a check pattern (see Figure 2.20).

Stop and ask yourself…

- What other explanations might there be for a child showing interest or disinterest in an object?

Links to
- Holism

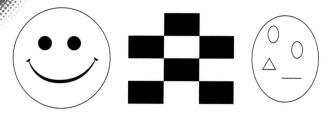

Figure 2.20 Newborn infants are able to discriminate faces from a variety of other images

One-month-old children are able to recognise their mother (or other familiar faces) if the face is shown frontally but not if shown as a full profile. It is important that children develop this ability to recognise with consistency the faces of familiar people. They also develop a constancy in recognition of familiar faces with differing expressions. At five months a child can become habituated to smiles of various intensities, and are then able to differentiate between smiles of different intensity and an expression of fear. This would show not only differentiation but the cognitive ability of the child to group similar expressions together, adding a further example to that category (smiles) and fixing on the different one (fear).

As children develop so their skills at perceiving the characteristics of faces continue to develop. This development may actually cause some apparent perceptual features to diminish. For example, by the time a child is three months old they may 'learn' a face due to repeatedly being shown it, but then fail to pick it out of other faces if it is not the same ethnicity as they are used to. They can do this if it is the same ethnicity as their own environment, however. This suggests that features of faces become more important as the child develops.

By the age of seven months the infant is becoming more familiar with what constitutes a face, and is less likely to prefer an upside down face to one which is the right way up. This could be linked to the child's ability to sit up and therefore see the world up the right way more often.

In relation to gender identification, by the time a child is nine months old they can generally recognise a female face as different from a male face, but not the other way around. This is shown if the face has stereotypical features, such as hair length and clothing. However, this could simply be a child's innate programme to recognise female faces. Research with children who have male primary carers shows that these children can differentiate males from females but not the other way around, suggesting not an innate skill but one that develops due to familiarity with one gender due to care giving.

Constancies

Psychologists have investigated babies' ability to perceive things accurately when they change.

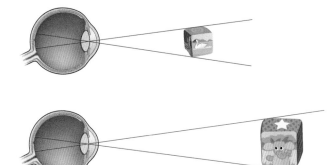

Figure 2.21 The different-sized toys make the same-sized image on the retina of the eye. Having been habituated to the smaller toy, infants are able to perceive that the bigger toy is not the smaller one nearer to them, but a different toy altogether. They therefore have size constancy.

The same can be done for shape constancy. If a cube is rotated does the changing shape of the retinal image mean a baby would see it as a different object or the same one?

Figure 2.22 Despite producing different images on the retina when facing different ways, infants can perceive that they are the same toy

🚫 **Stop and ask yourself ...**

● Can you draw a timeline of perceptual development in terms of face recognition of babies under one year?

Links to
● Developmental area

PART 3 Applied psychology

Size and shape constancies have been found in newborn babies. Children have shown that when they have been habituated to a small cube, then shown the same small cube and a larger cube positioned further away (so that it gives the same-sized image) they will prefer the large cube (the novel object), suggesting that they recognise the small object as one they have seen before.

Take it further

- What other constancies do we develop in our perception?

Depth perception

Children are able to assess depth or distance from an object to themselves. In Gibson and Walk's key research they set up a 'visual cliff' to assess young children and animals in their ability to perceive depth. Another way a child can be assessed for depth perception is shown by their tendency to reach for the nearer of two objects. If they reach for the nearer object a significant number of times, this would indicate some element of depth perception as a skill.

The visual cues that babies and adults use to judge depth perception are varied:

- Height in plane: an object further away will show higher in the image.
- Relative size: the smaller the object appears (if it is the same actual size), the further away it is.
- Superimposition: one object in front of another indicates that the front object is nearer.

Figure 2.23 The higher teddy looks further away; it makes a smaller retinal image and is also behind the front bear

- Texture gradient: the texture of an object gets more open as it gets nearer.
- Linear perspective: as something goes into the distance, the lines of the edge appear to get closer together.

Figure 2.24 The open texture shows the nearness of the track and the smoother texture suggests that part of the track is further away, as does the converging edges of the track

It is a difficult say when babies can perceive depth. They appear to have the ability to see the difference in a surface that is near and one that is far away. Research by Campos and his colleagues showed that six-week-old infants placed on the 'deep end' of the visual cliff had a decreased heart rate, which reflects concentration on the depth. This was obviously before they were old enough to crawl; it would suggest some perceptual skill to differentiate between a close and distant surface, but whether this would be the same as depth perception is debateable. When seven-month-old infants were lowered down on the same 'deep end' illusion, their heart rates accelerated rapidly and they started to whimper, showing a fearful response. The conclusion then is that infants develop the ability to perceive visual depth prior to beginning locomotion and, at some point when the child begins to crawl – at about six months – depth perception, as opposed to perception of a difference, begins to show.

How perceptual development can be studied in babies and animals

We have looked at research into children to try to identify when a perceptual skill is acquired, or whether it is innate. There are problems using young children, in that we have to infer from their behaviour what is happening. This is the same with animals, but we do have the chance to see quicker development when carrying out research on animals, and are able to carry out research that would not be ethical to do with children. Obviously there is the problem of generalisability but seeing a skill across a range of species, including to some extent in humans, gives us some basis for theories of perceptual development.

Researching perceptual development in human children

One of the earliest researchers into perceptual development was Fantz in the 1950s, and he developed a method of recording a child's preference for an object based on how long he or she gazed at it. This preferential looking method involved the child being placed in front of a stimulus or two stimuli and a researcher looking through the apparatus to time how long the child spent looking at a particular stimulus. The longer the gaze, the more the child preferred that stimulus.

Figure 2.25 Example of Fantz' apparatus

As the researcher is behind the stimulus, this should remove some possible experimenter bias, as the researcher would not know which stimulus the baby was looking at. It was also possible to research very small children as they did not need to be able to support themselves in any way.

A video camera could also be used to record the child's gaze, and this would allow for more independent checking in the form of inter-observer reliability.

This is one of the problems with researching very young children, however: we have to assume that what is happening behaviourally reflects the process that we assume is happening. That is why more recent research is introducing the use of brain activity scanning techniques. If researchers think that an infant is processing a novel stimulus differently then they could expect this to be reflected in a different pattern of brain activity.

Another way of measuring perception is to use the behaviourist theory of operant conditioning, where the child receives a reward (often linked with the mother).

Psychologists will often use a dummy or pacifier, as the amount a child sucks on the dummy can indicate interest in a stimulus. When a baby begins to suck faster they are rewarded, maybe with the picture of the mother's face. The child associates the fast sucking with seeing the mother. Gradually, even the most sociable baby will begin to lose interest in the picture of their mother, and so their sucking rate will go back to normal. However, if they are then shown a different picture – say a picture of another person – if they can see the difference they will suck faster to see more of the interesting new stimulus. Having found that a child can tell the difference between two stimuli such as faces, the researcher can use preferential looking to see which stimulus the child prefers.

Figure 2.26 Baby being shown a picture of his mother and of a stranger

Physiological measures

As we saw in the research by Compos, there are physiological measures that can tell us something about a child's perception. Slow heart rates can indicate interest, and fast heart rates fear or excitement. Using preferential looking techniques and conditioning techniques can only tell us about preferences, and that babies can discriminate. It is also an artificial set up and so has low ecological validity. Using electrophysiological measures, such a brain activity, could give us the same information but also an additional insight into whether infants use different processing strategies.

This type of research has its limitations with research into the perceptual development of young children, as it often requires the participant to be still, which is not easy with a baby (it would unethical to restrain them). There are also ethical issues around exposing young babies to the scanning machinery, which might be noisy and frightening. These techniques have been used more with adults, but gradually the improvement in brain scanning techniques will allow this research to become more useful in the study of young infants.

Researching perceptual development in animals

Research into perceptual development on animals has focused on the type of research it would be unethical to carry out on human babies. Psychologists have used a variety of methods to investigate what is truly an innate ability and what develops as a result of interacting with the environment, for example preventing the animal from experiencing any light for a period of time and then testing for perceptual skills, particularly depth perception. As you will see, this is one of the methods used in the key research by Gibson and Walk.

Depriving animals from light is one aspect of the research that could be considered to be unethical. In 1873 one of the first researchers, Spalding, kept chicks in a black sack made from a soft flannel material. They were in the bag when they hatched. When he released them several days later, they could run to their mother, avoiding obstacles, implying that they had the innate skill to identify where objects were and to avoid them. In 1934 Lashley and Russell used rats that were kept in the dark for three months; when tested they used more effort to jump large gaps than small gaps, implying that they 'knew' when something was further away. However, when Nealey and Riley (1963) kept rats in the dark for their first 300 days, they were unable to show depth perception. They concluded that depth perception may be innate but, without interaction with light in the environment, this is a skill that can be lost.

Some of the research, which might be thought even less ethical, involved animals being able to interact with their environment but not being exposed to light; this was achieved by sewing up eyelids, such as on kittens or monkeys. The researchers were adamant that this was done under anaesthetic and caused no harm to the kittens. When their eyelids are unsewn the test for depth perception helped us to understand the conditions necessary for this skill to be shown. Skills shown once the eyes were opened could be considered innate, but skills that had not developed (like the eye–paw co-ordination in Blakemore and Cooper's study) could be considered to be learned as an interaction with the environment.

Other research, such as that by Held and Hein, didn't rely on light restriction but on a 'kitten carousel' in which one kitten in the carousel instigated the movement and the yoked kitten just followed; tests on the kittens with restricted movement showed inferior perceptual skills, such as eye–paw co-ordination.

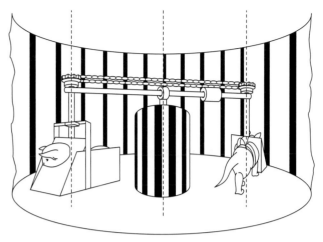

Figure 2.27 The kitten carousel apparatus

One of the pieces of research on chimps by Riesen (1965) compared three chimps – Debi, Kova and Lad – who were kept in experimental conditions from birth to seven months. Debi was kept in darkness; Kova spent 1½ hours a day exposed to unpatterned light and the rest of the time in darkness; Lad was reared in normal light. Debi suffered retinal damage. Lad was no different to any other chimp regarding perceptual development. Kova didn't suffer retinal damage due to the exposure to light, but her perceptual development was underdeveloped.

Blakemore and Cooper (1970) kept kittens in the dark, except for a five-hour period each day when the kitten was in either a vertically striped or horizontally striped environment. At five months old the kittens exposed to vertical strips would only reach out if a vertical pointer was moved in front of them, while kittens exposed to horizontal strips would only reach out if a horizontal pointer was used, demonstrating that the environment has an impact on perceptual development. Using brain activity sensors, they found that the vertical kittens didn't possess cells in the visual cortex of their brain that would respond to horizontal light.

Finally, psychologists can find out about perceptual development by studying animals' ability to learn to perceive if placed in different circumstances. If they can then this would suggest that perceptual skills are learned. Sperry (1943) looked at salamanders and surgically turned their eyes upside down by rotating the optic nerve, to see if they could learn to see the world the right way up. The animals reacted as though the world was upside down, and reversed from right to left, and no amount of training could change their response, suggesting that the skills were innate in the first place.

While we might look in horror at accounts of research that involve surgically moving eyes or sewing up eyelids, there is an advantage to carrying out such research. Obviously it would not be ethical to carry this research out on children. More important is the element of control in such research, which would not be found in studying children – each child's environment would be different, whereas with animals their surroundings can be controlled. It is also easier, as Blakemore and Cooper did, to add neurophysiological data capture to their research. Trying to find out what factors contribute to perceptual development is important work for helping medicine find ways to treat humans.

Key research: Gibson and Walk (1960) The visual cliff

Background

Gibson and Walk were interested in why children and young animals would not fall from high places, i.e., they wouldn't walk over a cliff edge. They wondered if this was learned or innate behaviour. Were young animals and humans born with the ability to perceive depth, or was it learned through their interaction with the environment?

Aim

To see if young animals and human children were able to perceive depth innately and therefore know not to crawl or walk over a visual cliff edge.

Materials

The construction of a visual cliff was necessary to prevent injury, and so a glass pane was placed over a surface that dropped half way across, producing a visual cliff in that there appeared to be a drop, but the child or animal would be supported at all times.

Position A
Position B

Figure 2.28 The visual cliff

Participants

In the first instance Gibson and Walk studied 36 children, aged 6 to 14 months.

Method

Each child was placed individually on a board in the centre of the box, so that the child could crawl off on to the deep or shallow side of the cliff. The mother stood at the shallow end (Position A) or deep end (Position B) of the box and called the child to come to her.

Results

Quantitative data

Of the 36 children, 27 moved off the board:

- 100 per cent of these children moved across the shallow side of the cliff to get to their mother
- only 11 per cent of these children crawled across the deep side of the cliff to get to their mother.

Qualitative data

Children would peep through the glass at the cliff edge and back away. However, many used the glass

Figure 2.29 Child crawling across shallow side

Figure 2.30 Child not willing to cross deep side

to support them as they started to crawl across the shallow edge. Some would test the glass for solidity – which it had - but still didn't cross.

When the mother was in Position B, the most common reaction was to crawl away from the mother or sit and cry because they couldn't get to the mother without crossing the deep side of the cliff.

Conclusion

Children could obviously perceive depth by the time they could crawl, but they appeared not to be cognitively aware of the danger of the cliff edge, shown by the inadvertent use of the glass over the deep side, which, if the glass hadn't been there, would have caused them to fall over the cliff.

By the time children can crawl they have had several months of interacting with the environment and so it is difficult to tell if the ability to perceive depth is innate or learned.

Animal studies

Further research was carried out to test the innateness of depth perception in non-human animals.

Chicks

Chicks less than 24 hours old would never cross the deep side of the cliff.

Goat kids and lambs

As soon as they could stand, which was less than a day old, they would not step on the deep side of the cliff. If they were placed on the deep side they would refuse to put their feet down and, if forced to, would make their legs go limp; they could then be pushed across but would stand as soon as they reached the shallow side.

When the cliff drop was changed to being 30 cm or less, the kids would happily go across, but wouldn't if the drop increased.

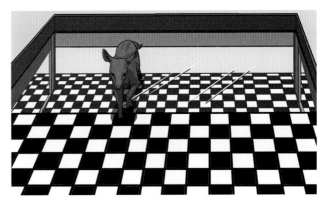

Figure 2.31 Kid placed on deep side (left) leaps to safety across the 'chasm' (right)

Kittens

Cats use their whiskers to perceive space around them but have excellent visual skills. On the first day that they could move freely (at about four weeks old) they would avoid the deep side of the cliff. They wouldn't have had much interaction with the environment to learn depth perception to this degree in the first four weeks of life.

At 27 days, dark-reared kittens had no preference for the shallow or deep side but, once exposed to light, they had developed their depth perception so that within a week it was the same as normally reared kittens.

Rats

Rats appear to rely on the sensitivity of their whiskers to touch and perceive their environments so would happily cross the deep side if they could feel the glass. If the centre board was raised so that they couldn't feel the glass with their whiskers then, on over 95 per cent of the trials, they would not step on the deep side, with some rats never doing so.

Turtles

Gibson and Walk found research by Yerkes in 1904 which showed that turtles appeared to have little preference for the deep or shallow side, which would suggest that there is less need for depth perception in the water as there is less need to fear falling.

Conclusion

It would appear that all animals (including humans) are able to discriminate depth by the time they have independent locomotion, whether it is a day for chicks or six to ten months for humans. This could reflect the evolutionary theory that only those animals that develop this skill survive to breed and so it becomes a genetic trait seen in all of the species.

Controls

To avoid any bias there were some controls of extraneous variables.

Table 2.2 Controlling for extraneous variables

Extraneous variable	Control	Effect
Reflection from the glass may distort the depth	Underlighting to reduce reflection	Rats preferred shallow side
Pattern effect	Grey surface on both sides	Rats showed no preference
Patterned surface	Patterned surface same distance below the glass	Rats showed no preference

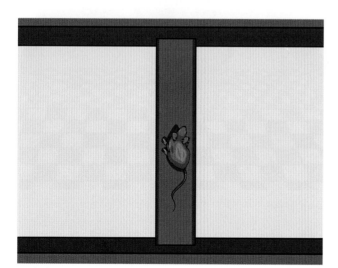

Figure 2.32 Rat shows no preference for grey backgrounds

Testing depth cues

There are two depth cues that animals could use to assess depth: size and motion parallax.

Stop and ask yourself ...

- What are the problems with generalising research on very young animals to humans?

Size

The further away something is, the smaller an image it makes on the eye's retina. Putting a smaller pattern the same distance away from the surface would show if this was the depth cue being used.

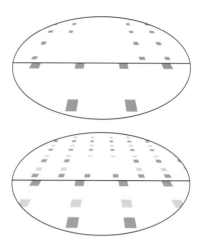

Figure 2.33 a) Image shows the deep side at top of visual field has smaller pattern indicating depth; b) smaller pattern is placed at same distance under glass indicating a shallow surface

Motion parallax

The further something is away from us, the slower it appears to move if we turn our head from side to side.

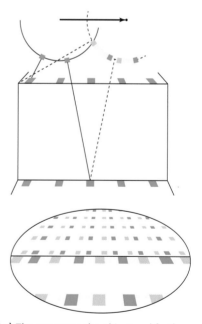

Figure 2.34 a) The eye scans the object and further away appears to move slower; b) motion parallax is tested by putting a smaller pattern at the same distance below the glass

Links to
- Generalisability

Results

Rats prefer the larger size pattern, indicating nearness.

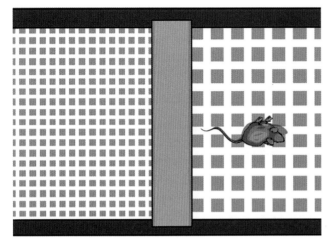

Figure 2.35 Rat prefers larger size pattern, indicating nearness

Infant rats, adult rats and day-old chicks appeared to use motion parallax as their depth cue by preferring the shallow side even when the retinal image size was the same.

Without motion parallax cues, the adult rats and infant rats still showed the same preference for the shallow side, showing that they could also use size cues. Day-old chicks did not show this preference.

Dark-reared rats also preferred the shallow side when they only had motion parallax cues; however, like the day-old chicks, they showed no preference with only the visual cues. This would indicate that motion parallax is the innate depth perception cue and image size is a learned visual cue.

Discussion

Gibson and Walk acknowledge that when using animal research the findings cannot be generalised to humans, but they suggest that there are enough results that would allow us to deduce that humans have a similar pattern of perceptual development. While they realise it is not ethical to raise children in the dark, they suggest that further research on dark-reared kittens, who develop depth perception over the course of a week when they are exposed to light, would help us to understand when each cue is learned.

Application: a play strategy to develop perception in young children

While there may still be some debate of exactly when different perceptual skills develop, what we do know is that interaction with the right environment is essential for normal skills to evolve. Children's play is an essential

part of the child's interaction with their environment and stimulates the development of these skills. While there is no need to have specific play activities, in particular costly educational toys, there are some play strategies that focus on perceptual development.

Of course, there are various senses which need stimulation. Games to develop aural perception skills might include sound bingo: the child has a card with pictures of different animals or everyday objects on and the animal's noise, or noise the object makes, are played in a random order – the child covers the picture if he or she hears the appropriate sound. Tactile baby toys made with different materials, such as a cube with shiny, silky and soft sides, help to develop the perception of touched objects, as would a 'what's in the bag?' game, with objects hidden in a bag and the child identifying them through touch only.

In terms of developing visual constancy skills, toys will aim to help children recognise objects or letters regardless of their orientation. Toys to develop this skill might include shape sorters, where a cube is always a cube even if it doesn't look like a cube, and it will only through the cube-shaped hole.

Figure 2.36 Sorting shapes to go through particular shaped holes can help develop shape constancy

Of course, there are all sorts of toys marketed for perceptual development, and often these skills are only part of the benefit of the toy. The social, cognitive and motor (physical) skills a child develops alongside the perceptual skills are all just as necessary for a child to develop. For example, a baby gym (there are many on the market) allows for motor skills of reaching and grasping; cognitive skills such as cause and effect, categorisation and memory; development of concept of self due to mirrors; in addition to visual skills such as discrimination of shapes and colours and depth perception (how far to reach out to grab a toy).

Cognitive development and education (Cognitive)

By the time you are studying Unit 3 you will be familiar with the concepts of Cognitive psychology and Developmental psychology. In addition to the cognitive processes outlined in the perceptual development topic – attention, perception, memory – problem solving and language development can be considered as cognitive skills that change over time.

The main area of cognitive development as a topic is the change in the way we think about things as we grow from babies into children and from children into adults. You will see this development in Kohlberg's theory of moral development, where a child moves from thinking solely about themselves to an understanding of the needs of humanity. Kohlberg based his work closely on one of the key developmental theories of Piaget, who also believed that children move from an egocentric view of the world (ego = self, centric = centre) in which their view is the only view, to a more abstract thought process that can deal with concepts such as humanity.

Most cognitive development takes place from birth to adolescence and so has a direct link to how children are educated. If you think back to your primary school lessons, where there was a lot of play and hands-on activities, through to your predominantly abstract thinking at A Level, you will see that the changes in your thought processes have been mirrored by more abstract-based education. Psychologists and educators can also build on their knowledge of cognitive processes to develop strategies for learning and revision.

Cognitive development in children

Piaget

Jean Piaget was a Swiss biologist who was originally interested in the biological influences on our thinking. He believed that we were genetically programmed to have the ability to think abstractly and that this is what makes us different to non-human animals. Piaget carried out his clinical interviews on a small number of children, including his own, and he noticed consistencies in thinking across ages, which enabled him to develop a stage theory of cognitive development. This has become the foundation of cognitive developmental theories, although later research has criticised some of his assumptions. He believed the stages were invariant, in that we would have to progress through each stage, and he held firm beliefs about the ages at which these stages would be entered.

The biologist in Piaget first made him consider how an organism (including humans) might adapt to their environment and changes within that environment. He felt that we were born with reflexes, such as moving away from something hot or, as a newborn baby, turning our head towards a bottle or breast for food. He felt that we had mental organisations called 'schema' with which we made sense of the world and which directed our actions. A newborn baby will use its reflex to grasp objects and the schema for holding an object is 'if I can touch it, I can grasp it'. Gradually, however, the baby learns that not everything can be grabbed and must be picked up with finger and thumb, so developing another schema for holding something.

> **Take it further**
>
> - Find out what other reflexes a newborn baby will show.

The process of developing schema is done through assimilation (taking in information), accommodating (changing our schema to fit this new information) and so

Figure 2.37 Learning through play in the early years

producing a state of equilibrium. When you learn to drive you have a schema for changing gear, but this doesn't always work if you change car, so you have to take in the new information – for example, the brakes are sharper – and adapt your schema slightly to push more gently on the pedal, and then you are in a state of equilibrium or balance as you have readjusted your schema. Until you get a totally different car! These processes of assimilation and accommodation occur continuously, from a baby changing its sucking schema from sucking a bottle to sucking a dummy. Your schema of what it means to be a university student may have to change when you actually get to university and find that you have to adjust your expectations to line up with reality and get used to lots of new things, which may cause a temporary state of imbalance while you learn to adapt to a new environment.

More complex schema are called structures (think of the different schema you have for making a cup of tea or coffee).

While this ongoing development of schema continues, Piaget also identified key stages of cognitive development in which the thought processes of children change as they gradually assimilate and accommodate information and change their schema.

These stages with approximate ages are:

- **Sensorimotor** stage (0–2 years) where children base their knowledge of the world on physical experiences and sensory input. To start with children will simply touch, look and taste, and will acquire schema along the way. There are some cognitive milestones, such as acquiring object permanence at about seven months of age: this is where a child understands that something that is out of sight actually still exists. Prior to this, if something is out of sight it is generally forgotten. At this age a child will look over the side of its buggy to look for something it has dropped, a key memory skill. Language development starts towards the end of this stage when some symbols are seen to represent something. A picture of a dog represents a real dog, in the same way that the letters d-o-g come to represent a dog at a later stage.
- **Pre-operational** stage (3–6 years) children continue to develop their use of symbols and language use matures. Memory improves and imagination is shown in play and stories. The child's thinking is not logical, and the egocentric view is shown in believing that what the child sees is what everyone else sees. Piaget

showed this with research in which he sat a child at a table and asked them what someone sitting at another position could see. Children at this age chose the picture that represented what they could see, not what the other person would see.

Figure 2.38 The child is asked what the doll would be able to see from a selection of pictures. If she chooses her own view this shows egocentrism according to Piaget

- **Concrete operational** stage (7–11 years) when the child begins to demonstrate logic and can think beyond what can actually be seen, such as changes in shape not necessarily being accompanied by changes in size or mass (the concept of conservation): one large playdough ball could be the same amount of playdough as four smaller balls. Piaget tested conservation with experiments in which he asked children if two rows with the same number of buttons had the same number if one was longer than the other. Prior to this stage the child would say that the spread out row had more buttons. The child begins to lose its egocentric view.
- **Formal operational** stage (11 years to adult) is the last stage of development. Not everyone reaches this advanced stage. People who do will show the ability to think logically and systematically, such as using symbols to represent abstract concepts (such as ∞ representing proportional it).

Vygotsky

Lev Vygotsky was a Russian psychologist who was interested in the development of thinking and its role in learning. He differed from Piaget in believing that the culture and language of a child would impact on learning, placing an emphasis on social factors that Piaget did not consider in his universal stage theory.

Cognitive development arises out of social interactions in a guided learning environment. This could be at home or school. Vygotsky suggested that children have a zone of proximal development (ZPD), which is

Stop and ask yourself ...

- Can you make a structure for opening a can of drink? What are the stages/schema you need to use for each step?

Links to
- Application

the area of cognitive skills a child can reach with the help of a more-knowledgeable other (who could be a teacher, carer or peer). When a child learns to talk, the first stage would be babbling, which is extended by a carer talking in one or two word utterances. Once a child can talk, saying one or two words, the carer will guide the child to simple sentences, and then onto complex sentences, correcting grammar and extended vocabulary; each time taking the child into the next stage and supporting him or her until those skills are acquired and then moving into the next.

Figure 2.39 A more-knowledgeable other can guide a child on to the next stage

The role of the more-knowledgeable other (a teacher or carer) as being crucial is different from Piaget's view that if you give a child a stimulating environment then he or she will construct knowledge from his or her independent investigations. Another major difference is the emphasis that Vygotsky puts on language as being a precursor for learning, which Piaget again does not suggest. Piaget believed that thinking comes first then the language catches up.

Research by Freund (1990) suggests that Vygotsky's concept of ZPD might be a better explanation of cognitive development and learning than Piaget's discovery learning. Children were given a dolls house and some furniture and had to put the furniture in the right rooms. In one condition children worked alone (discovery learning) and in the other the children played with their mother (more-knowledgeable other, or MKO) in a similar situation. Comparing the first attempt with the attempt after the experimental conditions, those children working with their mother showed greatest improvement, suggesting this would be a more effective way of learning than discovery learning.

Bruner

Jerome Bruner looked at cognitive development in the 1950s and considered that it was not simply understanding concepts or problem solving, but also

Figure 2.40 Children that worked with a more-knowledgeable other showed greatest improvement

the ability to be creative and autonomous, and 'invent' new thoughts (new for the child, if not for society). He agreed with Vygotsky that language was a key tool to enable a child to develop in a stimulating environment.

Bruner formulated a stage theory that, like Piaget, he believed was invariant. These stages are also used as a guide for how to present new information to be learned to present new information to a child. The three stages are:

1. **enactive** stage (0–1 year) where the actual objects need to be touched and played with; the child may have no internalised schema or representation of the object
2. **iconic** stage (1–6 years) where objects are represented by pictures or icons
3. **symbolic** stage (7 years onwards) where words or formulae can represent the object. `

So a child will play with objects in the first stage, look at picture books of objects in the second stage, and then read words or look at symbols that represent these objects in the third stage.

Using these stages in education teachers will go through these stages in the classroom. In a day nursery a child will have toys to play with, in nursery and infant schools objects are used, for example in home corners, dolls represent babies, pictures used for weather charts and in junior schools reading, writing and maths uses symbols to represent objects. In secondary schools we may not always be able to bring in an object – such as a phobia – but we might use everyday examples (remember, at this age you are at the formal operational stage so can deal with abstract concepts) then represent it with pictures and, finally, present it a third time with written words to represent the concept. Even a child who has reached the symbolic stage will be able to function in the iconic and enactive stages, and may need to when learning something new. Hopefully the images in this book (iconic stage) will help you even though you are at the symbolic stage. It would be difficult to learn something, like driving a car, if you didn't actually get in and actually drive it, even if you knew the handbrake represented the braking system and understood the verb 'to brake'.

This highlights another point about cognitive development according to Bruner, and that is that the environment needs to contain objects that stimulate the students' curiosity so that they will be motivated to learn. The role of the more-knowledgeable other in Bruner's theory was to provide an interesting and stimulating environment, and the teacher would guide and support learners to learn for themselves. So, they have less of a role than in Vygotsky's theory but are more important than in Piaget's theory.

Table 2.3 Comparison of the cognitive development theories of Bruner and Piaget

Bruner and Piaget agree	Bruner and Piaget disagree
Children are pre-adapted to learn	Bruner says development is continuous; Piaget suggests a stage theory
Children will naturally explore their environment	Bruner says language precedes learning; Piaget says it comes after learning
Children's cognition develops over time	Bruner believes material represented appropriately with support can presented at any time; Piaget believes it must be stage appropriate
Children are active in their learning	Bruner believes adults and MKO are important; Piaget believes discovery learning is what is important
Symbols can be used when cognition developed	Bruner believes symbols won't replace other forms of representation; Piaget thinks they are the final cognitive skill to acquire

The three cognitive theories of Piaget, Vygotsky and Bruner are the foundation for much of the way that teaching is carried out in schools. However, that is not to say that cognitive development research has ground to a halt. More recently, other psychologists have developed theories of cognition, and applied it to education.

Perry

William Perry (1970) proposed that college students pass through a predictable sequence of stages. His view of cognitive development was a stage theory from dualist to relativist thinking. It has a link to Kohlberg's theory of moral development, as dualist thinking is very much a rigid 'right or wrong' approach, and relativist thinking is understanding multiple points of view that may all be legitimate. His theory has been particularly applied to college and university students rather than younger ages.

Perry's nine-point scheme of student intellectual development operates in a cyclical way. Students move from position one to position nine, but at any point may encounter new areas where they will start again at position one and develop to position nine. Perry gained his data from interviewing Harvard students in the 1950s and used their comments to justify his theory (much like Kohlberg in the Core Study).

Table 2.4 Perry's nine-point scheme of student intellectual development

Position	Type of knowledge	Assumptions	Student's task	Learning methods
Dualism 1 & 2	Received knowledge	'The tutor knows what is right and wrong.' 'My tutor doesn't know what is right and wrong, but others do.'	Learn the right solutions	Repeating Memorising Defining Summarising Reporting
Multiplicity 3 & 4	Subjective knowledge	'My tutors don't know, but somebody out there is trying to find out.' 'Everyone has right to their own opinion.' 'Different tutors think different things.'	Learn how to find the right solution	Examining Investigating Simulating
Relativism 5 & 6	Procedural knowledge	'There are no right and wrong answers, it depends on the situation, but some answers might be better than others.'	Learn to evaluate solutions	Interpreting Differentiating Planning Predicting
Commitment 7, 8 & 9	Constructed knowledge	'What is important is not what the tutor thinks but what I think.' 'I know what I believe in and what I think is valid; others may think differently.'	Student makes a commitment, realises commitment is an on-going, unfolding evolving activity	Incorporating Judging Assessing Criticising

The impact of cognitive development on education

A practical application of Burner's three stages of representation is shown in his concept of the spiral curriculum. Bruner believed that you would first introduce new content to be learned in an enactive mode using physical objects. Later the topic would be revisited (perhaps in the next class in school) but this time using images as an iconic mode. Finally the third time, maybe a year later the topic would be revisited using a symbolic mode of representation. So a teacher introduces a topic, then spirals back and reintroduces the topic in a different mode of representation.

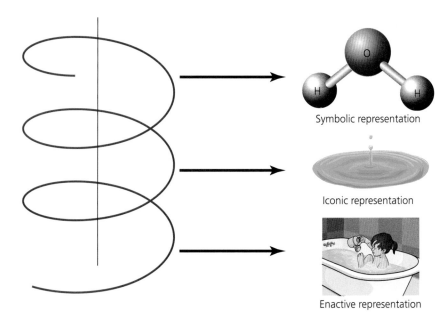

Symbolic representation

Iconic representation

Enactive representation

Figure 2.41 The spiral curriculum, showing the three ways of representing the properties of water

Therefore, Bruner's theory suggests that children can learn quite complex material as long as the presentation is organised appropriately, and they are given enough practice and guidance, as opposed to Piaget's view that a certain stage of thinking is required.

Both Bruner and Vygotsky emphasise a child's environment, especially the social environment, more than Piaget did. Both agree that adults should play an active role in assisting the child's learning.

Bruner, like Vygotsky, emphasised the social nature of learning, citing that other people should help a child develop skills through the process of scaffolding. The concept of scaffolding is very similar to Vygotsky's notion of the zone of proximal development. Scaffolding involves structured support between the more knowledgeable person and a child which aims to help the child learn. Gradually, as the child acquires the knowledge, the support is removed until the child can achieve the task on his or her own.

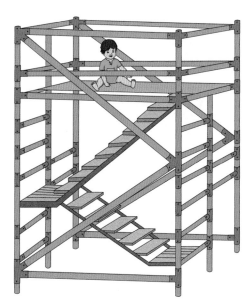

Figure 2.42 Scaffolding involves structured support between the more knowledgeable person and a child

Discovery learning is important according to Piaget and Bruner because it suggests that children will interact with their environment and so construct their own meaning rather than simply memorising something. This type of learning would result in a classroom where children are active, engaged participants in the learning process. Actively engaged children in a discovery learning classroom are less likely to be disruptive or 'problem students' as they will neither be bored nor left behind, as they will be working at an appropriate level for themselves.

Vygotsky believed the role of the teacher should be to facilitate the learning process by designing tasks in the child's ZPD and scaffolding as necessary. Bruner also felt that the teacher was an integral part of learning, primarily to present material in an appropriate manner – enactive, iconic or symbolic – not to lecture, but to let the child discover. Piaget's view was linked to his theory in that a child will learn through discovery and that the teacher should provide an appropriate, stimulating environment with objects to allow the child to discover.

Key research: Wood, Bruner and Ross (1976) The role of tutoring in problem solving

Aim

Wood *et al.* wanted to see if children responded to 'tutoring' when they had a problem to solve, and to look at how this changed with different age groups.

Participants

Thirty children aged three to five years were used, with equal genders and equal numbers in the three years, four years and five years age groups. They all came from Massachusetts and had parents who had volunteered them as a result of adverts. They were predominantly middle class or lower middle-class.

Task

The task was carried out on a one-to-one basis in sessions lasting from 20 minutes to one hour. The task had to be fun, multifaceted (complex) and interesting. It also had to be one that was within the reach of the child but not do-able by the child alone.

The task consisted of a wooden toy pyramid made up of 21 blocks. It was 23 cm high and had a 23 cm square base. There were six layers and each layer consisted of four equal-sized blocks that linked together into two interlocking pairs. These pairs were interlocked with

a rod-and-hole system. The top brick was a cube with one hole in it.

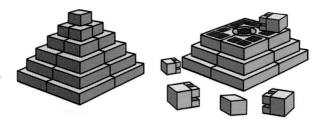

Figure 2.43 Materials for the task. Left the completed pyramid, right the blocks which would link together to make the levels.

Method

Observations were carried out of 'natural' tutorials, not to test a hypothesis about tutoring but to describe how the children responded to a tutor.

The tutor had a standardised set of prescribed actions, which would enable her to work with each child individually but with some comparability across the tasks. She had to try to ensure that the child did as much by his or herself as possible, with some verbal instructions where needed and, only if these failed to help the child, did she physically intervene.

The child came in and was seated at a table with 21 blocks, which he or she was then allowed to play with for five minutes. The tutor would then show the child how to make a pair of blocks and would ask the child to make some more like that one. It took 15 pair constructions to make the pyramid.

The child could respond in one of three ways, as shown in Table 2.5.

Table 2.5 Possible child/tutor responses

Child's response	Tutor's response to child
Ignore the tutor and continue to play	The tutor would again present paired blocks
The child could take the blocks the tutor had just made and play with them	The tutor would again present paired blocks, pairing them in front of the child
The child could take up the blocks and manipulate them in a similar way, such as putting sticks in the holes	The tutor would verbally point out any errors they were making

The child was then left to his or her own devices as much as possible. There was little overt praise by the teacher but an 'atmosphere of approval'. However, understandably some children didn't want to engage in a task when they had enjoyed the imaginative free play with the blocks.

Scoring

If a child was assembling blocks this was noted as either assisted or unassisted by the tutor. If the assembled blocks met the criteria or not, they were labelled as matched or mismatched. If a child rejected the mismatched pair or just put it aside as assembled, it was noted. If the child took apart a wrong pairing or left it, it was noted.

Event sampling was used; whenever a child picked up blocks and put them together or took them apart it was noted.

The interventions by the tutor were noted as:
- direct assistance
- verbal prompt ('Does this look like my one?')
- verbal prompt to carry on ('Can you make some more like this?').

Results

Using two observers with 94 per cent agreement on the events, the researchers observed the following:

Table 2.6 Results observed

	Three-year-olds	Four-year-olds	Five-year-olds
Median number of direct interventions	20	19	10.5
Median number of rejections of tutor assistance	11		< 1
Success rates of showing interventions	40%	63%	80%
Success rates of telling interventions	18%	40%	57%
Median numbers of acts	39	41	32
Ratio of incorrect to correct pairing	9:0	2:8	1:2
Unassisted acts	10%	50%	75%
Median number of no trial and error pairs	< 1	3	7

The numbers of acts was similar for each age group. The composition of the acts was different for each age group.

In general, all age groups would take apart and reassemble correctly constructed pyramids but would take apart and not reconstruct incorrectly constructed pyramids.

This implies that the younger child can comprehend a correctly constructed pyramid before he can produce it. This showed the task was do-able.

Conclusions

The number of tutor interventions was higher for the youngest children, with more showing and less telling. The tutor was ignored more often by the youngest children, and the task of the tutor became one of keeping them engaged in the task. The youngest children made fewer unassisted pairings and a smaller number of these were correct.

The middle age group had more unassisted pairings, with greater accuracy, and began to be able to construct pairings without trial and error, picking up the correct two first time and putting them together correctly. The tutor's role with the four-year-olds was more one of a verbal prodder and corrector, highlighting the problems where there was a mismatch.

The five-year-olds engaged most, with a higher number of acts; more of these were correct, with little assistance and less rejection when assistance was offered. They were able to construct much more without trial and error. The tutor became a confirmer or checker as the child knew what the task was and how to complete it and the role became more and more redundant.

This demonstrates the scaffolding function and how it can be implemented in learning. The task is one in which the child can conceive the problem but can't solve it alone. The tutor lures the child into the task and initially shows and tells them the solution, keeping them on task. The older child no longer needs to be kept on task but needs support in terms of telling more than showing when things go wrong, to enable them to put it right, and finally the role of the scaffolder is to simply confirm that the solution is right with some verbal interventions when necessary.

The role of the tutor was fairly straightforward in the youngest and oldest children, but demanded more individual approaches in the try-it-and-see stage of the middle children, and this was where tutors had to deviate from the standardised interventions more to meet the needs of the child, such as giving the correct piece after several incorrect attempts. This resulted in an individualised approach to learners in the middle stage of learning, where tutors produce effective support by keeping in mind both the task and its solution, plus the performance of the tutee.

Wood *et al.* identified key components of the scaffolding process:

1. Recruitment – engaging learners with the task and keeping them interested is important at first stage of learning.

2. Reduction in degrees of freedom – by reducing the number of possible outcomes the tutor can help learners see the correct solution quicker.

3. Direct maintenance – learners need to be kept motivated, maybe by providing feedback on successful attempts. It is also necessary to move learners on to the next part of the task once the stage has been accomplished.

4. Marking critical features – the tutor can highlight features that are important in the task or which are incorrect in the learner's solution.

5. Frustration control – the tutor should make the task less stressful but has to avoid creating dependency.

6. Demonstration – the tutor can demonstrate or model a solution that the learner has started, and will show the ideal solution, which the learner could then be expected to imitate.

Application: cognitive strategies to improve revision or learning

Cognitive strategies are techniques that help us to learn, understand and remember information from our studies, such as from textbooks or classroom lectures. There are a number of these that students can use, and they are based on our understanding of memory and cognitive development.

Strategies to help learning have been covered in the background and key research. Using scaffolding in any learning situation would appear to be beneficial and would help students of any age and at any stage of cognitive development. Think how much support you had when you first had to learn about research methods and design, and how now you would be able to take exam questions on that topic in your stride.

In terms of memorising, research on memory has shown us that we can use mnemonics to help us. The first letter of a list of features (such as the stages of development) can be used to construct a sentence that is more easily remembered; for example, Piaget's stages of cognitive development are **S**ensorimotor, **P**re-operational, **C**oncrete operational and **F**ormal operational, which could be remembered as **S**mart

People **C**ook **F**ish. You can also link images to help you remember something; so, for example, if you imagine Piaget frying fish on top of a mountain (he was Swiss) you will be able to remember the sentence for his stages.

We also know that rehearsal can help with storing material in the long-term memory, but semantic processing (giving the material meaning) will help store information. So, answering questions and working out where each topic goes on a mind map will ensure that you consider the meaning of the material.

This bring us on to the visual techniques of mind maps, which are cognitive organisers, where categories of information are linked and then links can be made between categories. As this is the way our brain naturally stores information, by categorising and connecting, we are simply using the natural techniques to enhance our understanding and recall.

Summary: The cognitive area

The ability to process information is fundamental to all species; even a primitive animal such as a snail has to process information. If you touch a snail's antennae it will withdraw them as a reflex but, if this is repeated several times, the snail becomes habituated to the touch and doesn't withdraw its antennae (don't try this at home!). It processes the information that the touch doesn't threaten the snail and so it doesn't need to withdraw its antennae. This may be giving cognitive processing to a snail that actually is learning a response rather than thinking about it, but let's give it the benefit of the doubt. A human will also process information and change their behaviour accordingly. We have seen that this cognitive thought can be abstract, such as understanding the concept of conservation, or actual, such as perceiving depth. The information is processed and, using attention, perception and memory skills, the behaviour (or thoughts) will be modified. What psychologists are interested in is how cognitive skills develop in the 'normal' person, so that problems can be identified early and support put in place, or behaviours can be modified if they are not appropriate.

Stop and ask yourself ...

- Can you make a mnemonic for Kohlberg's stages of moral development? Remember, it is better if it can link to the subject matter as well so that you can link the two in your memory.

Links to
- Application

Development of attachment (Social)

What is attachment in babies? A definition from Ainsworth in her key research is:

An attachment may be defined as an affectional tie that one person or animal forms between himself and another specific one.

This would suggest that any relationship, whether reciprocated or not, could be considered an attachment. You might form an attachment with your pet, or a brother or sister, but generally psychologists have been interested in the attachment bond that forms between a baby and his or her main carer. Early research focused on the mother–baby bond where, in our culture at least, it was the norm for mothers to play the main role in child rearing. More recently there has been research into attachment between adults, and it would appear that the type of attachment a child develops with his or her main carer is reflected in the attachment formed in adulthood with a romantic partner.

Figure 2.44 Early attachment research focused on the mother–baby bond

The development of attachment in babies

There are three main areas to consider when looking at the development of attachment:
- theories of attachment – why we form attachments
- types of attachment we form with our main carer
- stages of attachment – how attachments change over time.

Theories of attachment

The theories of attachment often reflect the underlying assumptions about the acquisition of behaviour that psychologists make. For example, a behavioural

psychologist would assume all behaviour is learned, through operant or classical condition, or social learning theory, and therefore the logic is that attachments are learned. On the other hand, evolutionary psychologists would suggest that attachment behaviour has evolved over time to ensure the survival of the species. We could also consider Freudian theories of psychosexual development, or cognitive theories such as Piaget's stages of cognitive development.

The two main theories, which have very different bases, are the behaviourist and evolutionary theories of the development of attachment. The behaviourists believe that babies are born blank slates, with no innate behaviours or characteristics, and they learn everything they become. If this is the case, babies would not be born with innate attachment behaviours and would learn through reinforcement or association to bond with their main carer. The 'cupboard love theory' is based on the behaviourist perspective. You may have heard the expression 'it was only cupboard love' to explain how someone was nice to us only to get something they wanted.

Figure 2.45 When a child cries the main carer will respond and put right whatever the child has wrong with it

A baby will cry when it is uncomfortable; either hungry, tired or lonely; or has a wet nappy. As the child cries the main carer will respond and put right whatever the child has wrong with it. The child then associates (classical conditioning) the carer with the feeling good, and so eventually the carer produces that 'feel good' response even if not providing food, play or a dry nappy. The child is reinforced by crying as the carer appears and removes something unpleasant (negative reinforcement) and so learns to produce the crying again to get the positive response. However, research by Harlow into the behaviour of baby rhesus monkeys found that, given a choice, baby monkeys would choose to spend time with a cuddly surrogate mother made of wire than one which fed them. Also, if the monkey was scared, then it would run to the cuddly 'mother' not the feeding one. This would suggest that the theory of cupboard love may not be correct.

John Bowlby is considered to be the attachment guru. He was originally a psychoanalyst and, as such, was influenced by psychodynamic explanations for parent–infant attachment, such as 'drive theory' in which the driving force for forming attachment derives from gratification of hunger and libidinal drives in the first of the psychosexual stages of development, the oral stage. Bowlby thought this saw attachment simply as an instinct derived from hunger or the libido. He was more influenced by the work of Lorenz who was an ethologist (someone who works with animals in their natural habitat) working with animals, whose studies included one on the attachment behaviour of greylag geese. Lorenz found that these birds would imprint on the first living thing they saw after hatching and, by ensuring he was it, he became their attachment figure.

> **Take it further**
>
> - Search the internet for videos of Lorenz being followed by his attached geese, even to the point of him teaching them to swim.

Figure 2.46 Lorenz and his geese

Bowlby believed that if this was the case with animals, then it would be much the same with human babies. Bowlby's theory was that attachment was an innate behaviour used to ensure the survival of the baby. Concurrent research had shown that babies were able to differentiate their mother's voice and face from other people, and this was a good sign that babies had innate abilities to differentiate their carer. More recent research, such as Bushnell et al. (2011) confirms previous research that the neonate (newborn baby) can recognise its mother's face based on visual stimuli alone. This would support Bowlby's view that there is some innate ability as the basis for baby–carer attachment.

Bowlby suggested that newborn babies of many species, including humans, need to bond quickly with their mother to ensure their survival. This is particularly important when the infant is so dependent on others for its care, as is the case with humans. The human baby will innately show behaviours that are designed to make its carers bond with it. These include smiling and crying, and Bowlby felt that mothers were innately programmed to respond positively to this. This has been tested by MRI scans of mothers' brains, which show certain areas of the mother's brain respond to social releasers from their own baby, but not to other babies who are happy or crying. This supports the idea that the attachment process is innate, as there appear to be specific areas of the brain that facilitate this.

Types of attachment

The term bonding is often used interchangeably with attachment but, strictly speaking, the term bonding refers to skin-to-skin contact and actually is nothing to do with attachment. What is known is that early skin-to-skin contact between mothers and babies after birth can influence breastfeeding duration. Babies who had skin-to-skin contact with their mother for two hours directly after birth showed higher levels of exclusive breastfeeding at both 48 hours and 6 weeks (Thukral, 2012). This fulfils the role of caregiver, but doesn't link to attachment.

There are generally perceived to be four types of parent–infant attachment, each with its own characteristics, which are formed depending on the parenting style and the caregiver's response to the child when he or she feels unsafe. This feeling of being unsafe, i.e. feeling ill, upset, frightened or hungry, activates the baby's attachment system.

Table 2.7 The four types of parent–infant attachment

Type of attachment	Carer's response to child's needs	Key child behaviours
Secure	Sensitive and loving, such as picking up and reassuring a child	Seeks proximity of caregiver
Insecure avoidant	Insensitive and rejecting, such as ridiculing or becoming annoyed	Avoids caregiver in times of need
Insecure resistant	Insensitive and inconsistent, such as overreacting or highlighting carer's own needs	Exaggerates distress and anger to ensure caregiver notices
Insecure disorganised	Insensitive and not normal, such as frightening or frightened, or sexualised, and not always shown when child is distressed (often linked to parent's own traumas)	Bizarre and contradictory behaviours, such as freezing or running away from parent

Ainsworth first identified three of these types, and used her research into the strange situation to characterise the children's behaviours. Main and Solomon (1986) later identified a fourth type, the insecure disorganised type.

This fourth type of attachment is clearly linked to a risk of psychopathological disorders in later life. It is linked to parents' own anxiety as well as social and economic disadvantage.

Table 2.8 Parenting behaviours linked to disorganised attachment

Atypical parenting	Behaviour examples
Withdrawal	Creating physical distance – directing the child away with toys; not greeting on reunion
Fearful behaviours	Frightened/hesitant/uncertain – haunted or high-pitched voice, sudden mood change dissociation/'going through the motions'
Role confusion	Pleading with the child, threatening to cry, hushed tones, speaking as if the child were an adult partner
Affective communication errors	Contradictory signals – inviting approach, then directing child away; using a positive voice, but teasing or putting the child down; laughing at child's distress and/or expressing distressing response to the child's positive affect
Intrusiveness/ negativity	Mocking, teasing, derogating; withholding a toy; pushing the child away; hushing the child

Source: Zeanah *et al.* (2011)

Stages of attachment

While the different types of attachment may be acquired through different parenting styles, and there are contradictory ideas of why attachment occurs, there are clear stages for the development of attachment.

Rudolph Schaffer and Peggy Emerson (1964) carried out a longitudinal study on 60 babies at monthly intervals from birth to 18 months. From the observations of infant–carer interactions, and the behaviours when carers left the child alone, they identified a series of stages for the development of attachments. Of course, there are individual differences within the sample but, as a general rule, these are the stages.

Table 2.9 Schaffer and Emerson's stages of attachment development

Age	Stage of attachment	Typical behaviour
Up to 3 months of age	Indiscriminate attachments	Most babies respond equally to any caregiver
After 4 months	Specific attachments	Infants distinguish between primary and secondary caregivers but accept care from anyone
After 7 months	Single attachment figure	The baby looks to a particular person for security, comfort and protection, and will show fear of strangers and unhappiness when separated from the special person
After 9 months	Multiple attachments	The baby becomes increasingly independent and forms several attachments to adults with whom the child has significant contact

Emerson and Schaffer also found that the main attachment figure was not always the mother; it was the person who responded most accurately to the baby's signals, and this was not necessarily the person they spent the most time with. This is known as sensitive responsiveness. However, by ten months many of the sample had multiple attachments, including attachments to mothers, fathers, grandparents, siblings and neighbours. The mother was the main attachment figure for about half of the children at 18 months old and the father for most of the others.

Bowlby's four stages of attachment mirror those of Emerson and Schaffer.

Table 2.10 Bowlby's four stages of attachment

Age	Stage of attachment	Typical behaviour
Birth to 6 weeks	Pre-attachment	The baby is comfortable being left with an unfamiliar person
6 weeks to 8 months	Attachment in the making	Attachment is beginning to get stronger during this stage; infants respond differently to familiar people than they do to strangers
8 months to 18 months	Clear-cut attachment	Attachment to trusted caregivers continues to strengthen in this stage; separation anxiety is likely in a caregiver's absence
18 months to 2 years	Formation of reciprocal attachment	Children can now understand that a parent returns home from work at a certain time each day, so separation anxiety lessens

These theories of attachment link to the cognitive development of a child. Being able to understand that something exists even when it is not seen (object permanence) develops in children at around nine months, and this is the time at which an attachment is formed with a specific person, as the child now understands that this caregiver still exists even when not in vision. Language development at one to two years is the foundation for the child understanding the routine of, for example, a parent going to work and coming home at a certain time, so separation anxiety is lessened.

Take it further

- Make a timeline of a child's development of attachment using each theory to see if there are similarities and differences between the assumptions of the theories.

The impact of failure to develop attachments

Bowlby's work with delinquent children and his interest in attachment led him to believe that the cause of much delinquent behaviour and adult mental illness was as a result of faulty child–parent attachment. This has been shown in the disorganised type of attachment, which is a strong predictor of vulnerability to mental health disorders in later life. Disorganised attachment has been linked to poor peer relationships (children with this type of attachment were more often rejected by peers at the age of nine); they showed more aggressive behaviours in the classroom; they typically had lower than average maths skills at the age of eight and had low self-esteem.

Children who had been identified as having disorganised attachment in infancy showed higher levels of overall psychopathology at 17 years of age, and tended to exhibit weaker cognitive skills and self-regulation. They were also more vulnerable to psychotic disorders such as dissociation in young adulthood.

Bowlby looked at the lack of attachment as a cause for concern. In 1944 he carried out some research into 44 juvenile thieves who had been referred to the child guidance clinic where Bowlby worked. They lived with their parents and were given several assessments on their intelligence, emotional attitude towards the test and psychiatric history, and were then interviewed by Bowlby. He identified that several displayed what he termed 'affectionless psychopathy'. These were people who showed a lack of affection to others, lack of guilt or shame, and lacked empathy for their victims. He studied a comparison group of teenagers who had emotional problems but had not committed any crime. He was particularly interested in how many teenagers had been separated from their mothers at an early age and therefore had not been able to form an attachment. He found the teenagers who were separated from their mothers in the first two years of life were much more

Stop and ask yourself…

- What are the problems with this kind of retrospective research?

Links to
- Validity

likely to show affectionless psychopathy (14 out of the 44 thieves compared to none of the comparison group, and 12 of these had been separated in the first two years of life).

This showed the problem of lack of attachment and, in keeping with the culture of the time and the common practice of mothers being the main carer for children, Bowlby's maternal deprivation hypothesis proposed that a child who failed to bond with his or her mother, for whatever reason, would be likely to experience mental health problems at a later date. Bowlby's theory was then used to suggest that no child should be separated from its mother, for any reason, and even the best nurseries or day care were still not as good as even the poorest mother.

Bowlby also suggested a critical period when attachments had to be formed or it would be too late to prevent later problems, this being the first two years of life. Research seemed to support this hypothesis. Spitz and Wolfe (1946) found that children who were raised in orphanages and hospitals were less likely to survive beyond one year, and those who did showed more symptoms of depression compared to children who lived in a prison but were cared for by their mothers.

However, some research showed that bonding after the critical period could occur and could alleviate to some extent the effects of maternal deprivation. Hodges and Tizard (1989) carried out a longitudinal study on children who were admitted to a children's home before the age of six months who were then either adopted or returned to their biological mothers at the age of four. This showed that attachment did happen after the critical period, but more often with adoptive parents than biological parents, as adoptive parents were more likely to work hard to form relationships with the children. However, there were still some long-term behavioural effects, with the ex-institutionalised children at the age of 15 having few friends, being more likely to bully, and having less-positive relationships with siblings than two matched control groups.

Rutter (1981) updated Bowlby's idea of deprivation and introduced the idea of privation: deprivation being where a bond had been formed but then broken due to separation, and privation where no bond was formed. This could occur because the child has a series of different carers (which was the case for many of Bowlby's juvenile thieves and Hodges and Tizard's institutionalised children) or family discord that prevented the development of attachment to any figure. Privated children do not show signs of attachment, for example there is no distress when a carer leaves. Rutter felt privation was more likely to lead to the negative

consequences identified by Bowlby and Hodges and Tizard, such as attention-seeking and indiscriminate friendliness, and an inability to keep rules, form lasting relationships or feel guilt. He also found evidence of antisocial behaviour, affectionless psychopathy, disorders of language, intellectual development and physical growth.

➡ Take it further

- Have a look at contemporary or old news items on the internet to see if you can find evidence of criminal behaviour and possible privation/deprivation caused by no bond being formed or an attachment bond being broken.

Research into deprivation where a bond has been broken due to parental separation or death also shows that there are negative effects of deprivation, such as low academic and socio-economic achievement. Bifulco et al. (1987) found that higher rates of depression were found in women whose mothers had died in the first six years of life than in those whose parents separated and the woman had lost their mother through family reordering (divorce). Cockett and Tripp (1994) also looked at these two situations – parental loss due to death or family reordering after divorce – and found that children from the reordered group were more likely to show negative effects in their academic and economic success than those from intact families. Interestingly, intact families with high levels of family discord showed higher levels of negative outcomes than reordered families without discord. This would highlight the effect of discord being part of the consequences of the deprivation. It is not just the breaking of the bonds but the situation before the bond was broken.

Bowlby also considered the short-term effects of breaking an attachment bond, and was supported by the Robertsons who, between 1948 and 1952, filmed what happened when children aged between 17 months and three years were left in hospital or in care when their mother went away for relatively short periods of time, such as two weeks. At this time parents were not allowed to visit their children in hospital for fear of upsetting them, so the child often had no contact with their parent for several days or weeks.

The Robertsons identified three stages of behaviour when a child was separated from his or her carer. The first was distress, with the child protesting, crying and becoming angry. This could last for several days. Eventually, realising that the carer (often the mother) was not going to come back, the child would subside into despair and would not interact with others; they would be quiet, often just sitting, maybe with a cuddly toy. The final stage was detachment, and this showed when the child was reunited with the carer. The child would ignore the carer and try to get away, while still being upset and crying.

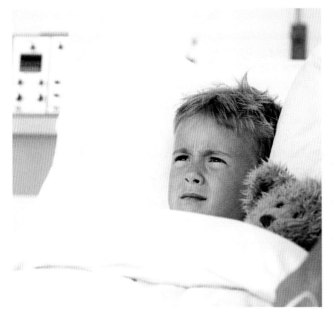

Figure 2.47 Distress in hospital

It would appear that there are short-term and long-term effects of both privation and deprivation, and research from the early period of Bowlby in 1940s to the current date indicate that there are ongoing situations, such as family reordering, which have the same impact as the outdated practices of separating children from parents in care situations. This will obviously have contributed to the current childcare practices we use, which are considered in more detail in the application section of this topic.

Key research: Ainsworth and Bell (1970) Attachment, exploration and separation: Illustrated by the behavior of one-year-olds in a strange situation

Aim

To observe in a laboratory situation the attachment behaviours of a child using the 'strange situation' as an illustration of these behaviours.

Participants

Fifty-six children who had been brought up in a family with white, middle class parents were found through paediatricians in private practice. Twenty-three were observed from birth and were 51 weeks old when put into the strange situation. The other 33 were participants from a different study and were observed when they were 49 weeks old. So, all children were just under one year old.

Procedure

Each child was tested individually in the strange situation episodes. The less-disturbing episodes came first and the whole situation was meant to reflect what might happen in everyday life. The room was 9 feet by 9 feet square, marked into 16 squares for the observers to be able to record the position of the children. At one end of the room was a child's chair surrounded by toys. At the other end was a chair for the mother and, near the door, a chair for the stranger. The child was put in the room and left to move freely. The observers were in an adjoining room with a one way window and recorded narrative accounts that were then analysed at each 15 seconds.

Table 2.11 Different episodes within the strange situation

Episode	Situation
1	Mother carries baby into room, observer follows and then leaves
2	Mother puts child down in specific place and sits down quietly in her chair; only participates if child seeks attention
3	Stranger enters, sits for one minute, talks to mother for one minute and approaches baby with a toy; mother leaves at end of three minutes
4	Stranger sits if baby happy; if baby inactive stranger engages with toys; if baby distressed, stranger tries to distract or comfort, for three minutes unless chid becomes distressed and can't be comforted
5	Mother enters and waits at door for baby to see and respond; stranger leaves; once child is settled with toys mother leaves saying 'bye-bye'
6	Baby left alone for three minutes unless distressed
7	Stranger enters and sits if baby is happy; if baby inactive, stranger engages with toys; if baby distressed, stranger tries to distract or comfort, for three minutes unless chid becomes distressed and can't be comforted
8	Mother returns and stranger leaves

Stranger's chair

Mother

Figure 2.48 The strange situation

Measures of behaviour

- The frequency of exploratory behaviours: locomotor, manipulatory and visual.
- Crying behaviour.

Each 15 seconds was analysed and a score was given for each behaviour seen at that time; as three minutes = 12×15 seconds, the maximum score was 12 per episode.

The following behaviours were rated for strength of behaviour, its frequency and duration, with higher ratings for actual behaviour compared to signalling. These could refer to the baby's interaction with its mother (episodes 2, 3, 5 and 8) or stranger (3, 4 and 7). Some of the examples for each behaviour are given below:

- proximity- and contact-seeking behaviours
  - approaching and clambering up on mother's lap
  - directed cries
- contact-maintaining behaviours
  - clinging, embracing
  - protesting vocally if released
- proximity- and interaction-avoiding behaviours
  - ignoring adult
  - moving away from adult
- contact- and interaction-resisting behaviours
  - pushing away any adult
  - screaming and cranky fussing.

In episodes 4, 6 and 7:

- search behaviour
- following mother to door
- going to mother's empty chair.

▶ **Take it further**

- Have a look at the original study and see what the other behaviours are for each measure.

Results

- **Exploratory behaviour** – this sharply decreased when the child was left with a stranger compared to when left with the mother. When the mother returned the child showed more interest when the mother engaged with the child, but this was not seen when the stranger tried to interact with the child.
- **Crying** – there was minimal crying when the stranger enters the room for the first time, but this rose when the mother left and declined when the mother returned. The child cries when the mother leaves for the second time, and doesn't stop when the stranger enters.
- **Search behaviour** – this was shown by the child moderately when the mother left, but increased slightly when the stranger was present and increased most when the child was left alone.
- **Proximity-seeking and contact-maintaining behaviours** – proximity-seeking behaviour was shown most after the mother returned from being away, and contact-maintaining behaviours were shown most after the second reunion. Occasionally these behaviours were shown to strangers, but much less often than to mothers.
- **Contact-resisting and proximity-avoiding behaviours** – resistant behaviour was generally not shown until the reunion, when some children showed it, but most did not. This behaviour increased with each separation, with half of the children showing it in episode 8. There was less of this behaviour to the stranger. Avoidant behaviours were shown in about half of the children in each reunion and, although one-third showed it to the stranger in episode 3, this reduced in episode 4 and again in episode 7.

Discussion

The children tended to explore in the presence of their mother but, once the situation changed, the child showed attachment behaviours (clinging to mother, less exploring). When the mother had gone there were more proximity- and contact-seeking behaviours; these continued when the mother returned and didn't return to their initial levels at all during the process. The distress, despair and detachment mirror the effects of long-term separation shown in animals, with heightened attachment behaviours on reunion, which can last for longer than the separation.

Resistant and avoidant behaviours tend to be shown together with contact-seeking behaviours, suggesting an ambivalent or rejecting behaviour, and again this reflects other research.

Avoidance of the stranger reduces over the episodes, which would indicate that it is merely a fear of the unknown, whereas avoidance of the mother must have a different cause. This avoidant behaviour has been shown by many researchers, and Bowlby refers to this as 'detachment'.

Propositions for a comprehensive concept of attachment

Ainsworth and Bell suggested that the following points could be formulated based on both this study and previous research, and could apply to both humans and animals. They were formed from an ethological–evolutionary view.

- Attachment can occur with or without attachment behaviours.
- Attachment behaviours are shown more in threatening situations.
- Attachment behaviours are incompatible with exploratory behaviours.
- Attachment behaviours may be shown less after a prolonged absence of the attachment figure, but this doesn't mean the attachment is lessened.
- Individual differences show there are differences in mother–child attachments, but these don't imply differences in strength of attachment.

Application: strategies to develop an attachment-friendly environment

Knowing that separation from the attachment figure can cause short-term (and possibly long-term) detrimental effects means that child practitioners have tried to find ways to reduce the impact of separation, or to prevent it altogether. This enables the child to maintain attachment and therefore minimise the distress to the child.

The Robertsons' rather upsetting films of children who were in hospital, or in care while their mothers were in hospital (a common practise in 1950s), was used as evidence to rethink the visiting restrictions on parents. It was commonplace for parents not to be allowed to visit children in hospital, for fear of upsetting them, or

to restrict visiting to Wednesday and Sunday afternoons. However, the current practice is to enable parents to be on hand, either in accommodation close by so that they can see their child for the whole day, or even to provide beds in the child's room to ensure that the attachment bonds are maintained. Remember, the child may have multiple attachment bonds to other adults and siblings, and there is sometimes room for more than one family member to sleep in the child's room, or close by. Ronald McDonald House Charities, for example, is one of many charities that fund accommodation buildings to enable families to remain close to their children in hospital, thereby maintaining the attachment bonds.

In childcare situations, when a child is going to be spending time in day care, perhaps whole days, while parents go to work, then there need to be supplementary attachment figures. We have seen that young children can make multiple attachments and, with careful planning and a 'key person approach', a day nursery can foster and support attachments between individual children and individual nursery staff.

The key person would be a nursery worker with responsibility for a small number of children. Like sensitive parenting, the key worker will be available and provide comfort to the child, being sensitive to the child's emotional and physical needs. Before the child starts at day care the key person should meet with the child and learn about their likes and dislikes. This will enable them to respond sensitively to the child. The child should be greeted by the key person and be supported to say goodbye to the parent. Also, at the end of the session the key worker would be with the child as they are reunited with the parent, so a link is made. With sensitive handling, the distress of leaving the parent is mitigated. A 'back up' key person can help with staff holidays or absence, and will be on hand to support the child if their key person is not available.

The key person approach is sometimes adopted in hospital, where a child admitted to hospital is linked with a nurse who will take the role of the key person.

Although there has been much research on attachment based on Bowlby's original theories, the focus is still that children need to form secure attachments with a few people, and they are likely to be, but are not exclusively, parents or family members.

Stop and ask yourself ...

- Can you suggest to a nursery owner what strategies he or she might put in place to help children in their care setting and minimise disruption to the child?

Links to
- Application

Attachment between a primary care giver and a baby would appear to be a behaviour that is initiated and maintained through a variety of interactions. Some of these, according to Bowlby, are innate and some, according to behaviourists, learned. The whys and wherefores of attachments being formed may be based on the assumptions of areas; for example, cognitive psychologists suggesting that they are as a result of cognitive changes as young children develop. There is much less discussion about the stages of attachment development and the types of attachment that develop as a result of sensitive, or otherwise, parenting. There is also some evidence that there may be cultural differences in the types of attachment seen in the majority of children; for example, secure attachments are the most frequent in many Western cultures, but not in all.

What there is little doubt about is the effect of attachment bonds not being made or being broken, and this leading to vulnerability in the child's mental health. There is also growing evidence that the attachment style of childhood can be reflected in the attachment style of adult relationships.

One of the problems with research into this area is that much of it is retrospective – asking people to remember what their childhood was like and their relationships with caregivers, asking for subjective information – which is open to social desirability and demand characteristics. There is no disagreement, however, on the benefits to both child and parent of attachment-friendly environments to promote and maintain attachments in situations that might require separation between the child and his or her attachment figures.

Impact of advertising on children (Social)

Do children really copy what they see on television? Bandura's research using the Bobo doll and his subsequent research would indicate that social learning theory is something that has to be considered.

Figure 2.49 It is illegal to rent or sell adult-rated films or games to anyone under the age of 18.

Films and games now have a rating to try to ensure that children don't see inappropriate material, and one criterion for labelling material as inappropriate is that it may be copied and cause harm. However, if it was

the case that every child imitated every bad action, then children everywhere would be acting it the same way, imitating behaviour such as that shown by *Power Rangers*. In 1993 the toddler James Bulger was killed by two young boys, who were said to be imitating the film *Child's Play 3*. While it is possible that the killers had watched the film (there was a copy of it at one of their houses), it is equally possible that they hadn't seen it and that the murder was not influenced by this, or not by this alone.

The nine-o'clock watershed is meant to be the time before which programmes that contain inappropriate material should not be broadcast, as it is assumed that children will be in bed by that time.

The influence of television advertising on children

A survey of children in America found that two-thirds of children under the age of one have watched television, and over one-third do so every day. Nearly one-third have a television in their bedrooms. This would indicate that if television does influence children's behaviour then it is going to start early and have a wide impact (Common Sense Media, 2011).

Stop and ask yourself...

- Is television really to blame for degenerate children's behaviour, as Bandura and subsequent research would suggest?

Links to
- Reductionism

Bandura's research, which showed children learning by observation and imitation, seems to clearly indicate that television programmes and advertising will influence the behaviour of children. However, there is the impact of video or television versus real-life interactions. Troseth and DeLoache (1998) found that two-year-olds who watched a live model through a window learned how to find a toy better than those children who watched a video. Subsequently, research identified that television shows that have an interactive element, such as person talking to the child and waiting for a response, resulted in significantly more learning than simply watching a video with no interaction (Nielsen *et al.*, 2008). Adverts tend to be interactive, asking questions and so on; together with the fact that adverts are presented over and over again, any negative impact would be increased as the behaviour is seen more than once.

The role of advertising on television is obviously to increase sales, and to do this advertisers use all the psychological tricks in the book:
- learning through association – for example, eat this and you will appear young, sexy, fit, attractive, or wear this and have an amazing relationship
- operant conditioning – for example, the reward of having fun friends if you drink a certain alcoholic drink.

Add to this the idea of a role model – think David Beckham in Calvin Klein pants – and you can see that the behaviourist theories have a field day. It is obvious that people are not born with the desire to wear Calvin Klein boxers, and therefore we have to learn the behaviour of wanting to wear them.

Watson (of Watson and Rayner fame, who carried out the Little Albert experiment) went on to make his fortune in advertising using the theory of classical conditioning.

Research by Hanley (2000) was commissioned by the Independent Television Commission (ITC) with the aim of seeing what behaviours will influence both attitudes and behaviour of children, focusing in particular on advertisements. There are many complaints from worried adults about certain adverts that might have a detrimental effect on children. One fizzy drink advert showed an orange man slapping people around the face, behaviour that was repeated in the playground with some children apparently having perforated eardrums after a slap. The advert was subsequently banned by the ITC. Part of the research looked at whether animation, fantasy or humour increased or decreased the effect on behaviour.

There were two particular areas of concern:
- the possibility that very young children might copy the amazing actions they see, such as people climbing out of windows; older children, however, might be tempted to respond to 'dares' based on

material seen in adverts, such as walking along the edge of a high drop
- that a culture of negative or antisocial behaviour might be adopted by young people watching, for example a negative attitude to education or antisocial behaviours such as annoying older people.

Using a mixed sample, the study found that the key influences on children are those people with whom the child has direct contact – parents, teachers, siblings and peers – but that television was also a powerful influence, in particular role models such as celebrities, sports stars and actors. Specific programmes were seen as potentially influencing undesirable behaviour, including *Power Rangers*, which had role models of both genders, and several ethnicities, allowing most children to identify with them and therefore imitate their fights.

Figure 2.50 The Power Rangers

When it came to advertising, the main consequences of children seeing adverts was pester power (trying to persuade adults to buy specific items that had been advertised), copying of behaviour and influencing attitudes.

From showing adverts and a variety of programmes to parents, children and youth workers, the key features of television that seemed to encourage imitation were behaviour that was:
- easy to copy – no special equipment needed
- similar to other acceptable behaviours
- wicked or forbidden
- appealing to a child.

The adverts had specific features that also encouraged imitation, which were:
- simple scenario
- humour and jokes
- people 'getting away with it'
- role models
- shown at appropriate time for age group
- high production values – music, colour, action.

- Watch some children's adverts and see if you can identify examples of each of these features.

Research has been carried out by Buijzen and Valkenburg (2000) to find out if children are actually influenced by the products advertised on television. In December 1997, 50 children were asked to make a list of what they would like for Christmas. These lists were then compared to the television adverts being shown at the same time. Sixty-seven per cent of the seven- and eight-year-olds, 49 per cent of the nine- and ten-year-olds, and 40 per cent of the 11- and 12-year-olds asked for at least one advertised product. Of course, this could be coincidence or the result of other factors, such as peers talking about the products. However, further analysis showed that the amount of time the children watched commercial television (channels that have advertising) was a significant predictor of the products being advertised being on their Christmas lists. Their level of exposure to the network that aired the most commercials was a significant predictor of their requests for advertised products.

Later research by Pine and Nash (2002) compared letters to Father Christmas with the amount of television watched. They found that children who watched more commercial television tended to ask for more from Father Christmas, and also more branded

Figure 2.51 Pine and Nash (2002) found that children who watched more commercial television tended to ask for more from Father Christmas, and also more branded items

items. However, nearly 90 per cent of the toys which had been seen in the adverts were not asked for at all in the children's letters to Father Christmas, which would suggest that children under seven did not recall many specific brand names.

An interesting finding was that children who watched television alone, as opposed to with their family, tended to ask for more toys, showing that being alone might make a child more susceptible to advertising (perhaps because there is nothing to distract them from the full impact of the advert).

This finding was considered by Buijzen and Valkenburg (2005) who found that active mediation, where parents make their opinions known by sharing views about the adverts ('I think that's a lot of money' or 'I don't think that will last very long, it's poorly made'), and concept-orientated communications, where children were encouraged to discuss ideas and challenge others' beliefs ('How many times do you think you would play with that before you got bored?', 'Don't you think you are a bit old for that?'), were able to reduce the impact of advertising.

Stereotyping in advertising

Stereotyping is an attitude which suggests that all people who share one particular characteristic share other similar (usually incorrect) characteristics. A most basic stereotype would be that all women are meek, caring homemakers, while men are strong hunter-gatherers and breadwinners. However much we may disagree with this stereotypical image of the genders, it is interesting to note that this particular myth is perpetuated in much television advertising (although increasingly the man is seen as an incompetent fool with women seen as long-suffering and clever).

You only have to look at television adverts to see the role of women predominantly in cleaning, cooking, and childcare roles, unless it is a 'joke' situation, of men dressed in drag, cleaning, or men who are not as clever as the child. Of course, not all television adverts promote stereotypical gender roles, but there is more subtlety to the portrayal of gender stereotypical products – the use of certain colours, settings, music and voice-overs all tend to follow a particular pattern.

Obviously if children are learning from television, and in particular from adverts, then by promoting

 Stop and ask yourself...

- What are the stereotypes portrayed in a range of adverts over one evening's viewings? Are they all gender related, or can you spot any others?

Links to
- Application

stereotypes we are encouraging children to continue to adopt stereotypical views of gender.

Much research has been carried out into stereotyping in television adverts. In 1998 Beverly Browne carried out a content analysis of adverts aimed at children in the USA and Australia. She supported previous research by finding that boys were shown as being more knowledgeable, active, aggressive and instrumental than girls. Non-verbal behaviours of dominance and control were also shown more by boys. In adverts with both genders she found that the boys tended to be more likely to demonstrate or explain something, showing the boy to be more knowledgeable in both male and non-gender-specific toys. She also found that the genders were never shown using a toy designed for the other, so girls weren't seen playing with cars, and boys weren't seen playing with dolls. Also, the body language gave non-verbal reinforcement of stereotypical behaviour, such as girls being seen as shy and giggly.

Mary Larson (2001) also used a content analysis of 595 adverts aimed at children and featuring children. She found that single-gender commercials portrayed girls in stereotypical domestic settings. Also, the primary activity of children in the commercials analysed was non-creative play, and considerable violence and aggression were portrayed.

Shannon Davis (2003) also found the same gender stereotyping in children's cartoons. Being the main figure, moving within an activity and being in a workplace were all increased if the character was male. Although this is not necessarily reflected in society, it is a quick way for television producers to use cognitive shortcuts to get their message over.

It is not simply the roles of the actors in advertising that portray and maintain gender stereotypes. Renate Welch et al. (1979) looked at 20 toy commercials each being labelled male, female or neutral. From their content analysis of the adverts they found that it was not only the gender of the actors – male in male toys, female for female toys and approximately equal numbers in non-gender-specific adverts – but that a variety of production techniques reinforced gender stereotypes. The voice-overs in neutral and boys' ads were usually male; female voices were generally only used in female commercials. It has been suggested by Welch et al. and elsewhere that this portrays males as authorities in most areas except those toys aimed solely at girls. The editing techniques also showed differences, with the boys' ads and the neutral ads having higher cutting rates (more 'abrupt, instantaneous shifts in view') compared to the higher level of fades and dissolves in girls' ads. Along with this was the loud

music and sound effects in advertisements for boys' toys, while adverts for girls' toys had soft background music. Welch et al. concluded that the adverts 'at the very subtle level of visual and auditory images' maintained 'stereotypes of females as quiet, soft, gentle, and inactive'.

Griffiths et al. (1998) looked at the production techniques in 117 toy advertisements broadcast on British television. Statistically significant differences were found to support their hypotheses:

- More varied camerawork can be found in advertisements directed at boys than in those directed at girls. The counts for the uses of slow motion, high speed and split screen were highest for the boys.
- The boys' and the girls' ads differed in the use of overhead shots and blurred focus: the boys' ads used both of these features more often. Blurred shots may perhaps be used to make boys feel as if they were there in the scene, seeing it for themselves – actively involved rather than passively watching staged events.
- The 'tilt up' action was used exclusively in the girls' ads: this seems to mimic the action of looking up from a subservient position towards someone or something in a superior position. 'Tilt down' shots occurred only in boys' advertisements (and once in a mixed ad); this seems to mimic the action of looking down upon someone or something lowly from a position of superiority.
- In the ads directed at boys the average duration of each shot was shorter than in the advertisements for girls; the rapid pacing of ads for boys echoes the stereotype of masculinity as action-oriented.
- There are more fades and dissolves in advertisements aimed at girls, which stereotypically reflect the consensus that girls prefer gradual and gentle transitions while boys are assumed to favour more abrupt changes of scene.
- The boys' advertisements employed sound effects more often than the ads aimed at girls. The music in the boys' advertisements was more strident, with more instances of rock music than any other group. Slapstick music was almost exclusively a feature of the ads for a mixed audience. Such music may perhaps be seen as appealing to all children's sense of the absurd and comical, irrespective of sex.
- There were no female voice-overs whatsoever in the advertisements aimed at boys; there were also more male voice-overs in the advertisements for mixed audiences; there were more female than male voice-overs in the advertisements directed at girls.

More contemporary research by Lewin-Jones (2009) shows that gender stereotyping still exists in advertising for children of primary school age in the UK.

Have a go yourself

- Can you identify the features on page 80 in children's television adverts today?

Having seen the stereotyping in advertisements, the key question is: does it actually make any difference to the child's perceptions of the gender appropriateness of toys?

Pike and Jennings (2005) looked at children who were shown adverts for either all boys (traditional condition) or all girls (non-traditional) playing with a gender-neutral toy. When asked to sort toys later, including the two toys in the advert, children who had seen the non-traditional girls playing were more likely to say that the toys were for both girls and boys compared to those who had seen the traditional boys playing with the toys, who said they were boys' toys.

Key research: Johnson and Young (2002) Gendered voices in children's advertising

Research questions

- Do advertisers use different language scripts for males and females in adverts aimed at preschool and early primary school children?
- How is gender used as a code to link products to gender roles?

Aim

To find out the themes and discourse styles that might contribute to what children learn about gender from television commercials.

Sample

Advertisements broadcast on commercial television channels, regional television channels in New England, USA, and Nickelodeon were recorded in 1996, 1997 and 1999. These channels were accessible to all television owners and the programmes either side of the adverts were children's cartoons. This would therefore control extraneous variables of who might watch different types of children's television and, therefore, who might be the target audience. This resulted in 149 adverts in 1996, 133 in 1997 and 196 in 1999, so a total of 478 adverts were analysed. These were only adverts within the programme, not either side of it.

The adverts were classified into five categories:
- food items
- toys
- educational and public service announcements, for example anti-drug messages
- recreational facilities, including fast-food restaurants
- video and film promotions.

There was an additional category of 'other' to accommodate adult-targeted adverts that appeared in the 1999 sample (these included Visa and Ford Trucks). However, that is not to say children wouldn't watch them, and the humour in the Visa card advert was accessible to children.

The toy adverts were the main focus for the analysis. In all 147 different adverts were seen, with the rest (41) being repeats.

Method

The adverts were first categorised according to the gender of the target audience:
- boys' toys in which boys were shown
- girls' toys in which girls were shown
- ads where both genders were shown
- no specific gender targeted.

The researchers decided to ignore the non-specific gender of toys such as Frisbee if only boys were seen in the advert, coding it as boy-orientated; if there was a token view of another gender where the advert was targeted at one specific gender then the token view was ignored. So, even with a boy appearing fleetingly in girl-orientated Friend Link toy, the advert was still categorised as girl-orientated. Sometimes the presence of the other gender was hard to spot; for example, a girl in a Super Soaker water gun advert for only three seconds – with a male voice-over and boys playing central roles, the advert was categorised as boy-orientated.

Results

Names of toys

The names of toys reinforced gender attributes. For example:
- boy-orientated toys
  - Big Time Action Hero
  - Beast Wars Transformers
  - Total Justice Super Heroes

- Tonka Magna Crew
- Super Sonic Power Crash Pit Racers
- girl-orientated toys
  - Take Care of Me Twins
  - Girl Talk
  - Friend Link
  - Fashion Magic Fingernail Fun Salon Set
  - Tea Bunnies.

Use of toys

The toys were categorised according to their type, i.e. dolls, trucks, games. It was noticeable that even categorically similar toys, such as Barbie dolls and action figures, were shown differently, with Barbie dolls being placed in scenes with little or no action, compared to the action figures. This reinforced the play differences of the two genders.

Voice-overs

All of the adverts contained voice-overs. These are the faceless voices that give information about the product, try to persuade the watcher to buy the product, and sometimes give disclaimers about the product. Two factors were considered in the voice-overs: firstly the gender was noted, and then whether the gender of the voice-over was exaggerated in the advert.

In the boy-orientated and the both boy- and girl-orientated adverts a male voice was used. In the girl-orientated adverts 89 per cent of the voice-overs were female voices, but four had male voices alongside the female voice. There appears to be a simple formula for working out the gender of the voice-over – that it should match the gender the toy is aimed at – but male voices may be used for girl-orientated toys and must be used for both boy- and girl-orientated toys.

In terms of gender exaggeration, female voices were assessed by both the researchers and independent raters in terms of exaggerated female features, such as high-pitched or sing-song voices, while male features of aggressiveness, loudness and deepness were noted in male voice-overs. This type of exaggeration was heard in 80 per cent of adverts for boys and 87 per cent of adverts for girls but, possibly unsurprisingly, tended not to be seen in toys aimed at both boys and girls. Young children tend not to see this over exaggeration as abnormal, and it could be one way in which they pick up how men and women are 'meant' to talk. If you see children pretending to be a man or a woman, they will mimic these exaggerations.

Verbs used

The language used can imply certain meanings beyond the actual meaning of the words, based on cultural context. The verbs used in the adverts were categorised into five types that could be said to reflect stereotypical attributes. These were:

- action – relating to physical movement, for example ride, jump, crawl
- competition/destruction – relating to competitive or destructive behaviour, for example crush, slam, fire on
- control – relating to power the consumer might have, for example rule, defeat, control
- limited activity – relating to an emotional state or limited movement activity, for example beware, look, wait
- feeling and nurturing – relating to caring or feeling emotions, for example love, cuddle, take care of.

A tally of the occurrence of these verbs is shown below. While there were approximately three adverts aimed at boys to every two aimed at girls, the occurrence of some of the verbs are much higher than would be expected, even given this ratio.

Table 2.12 Occurrence of verb types in boy- and girl-oriented adverts

Verb type	Occurrence in boy-orientated adverts	Occurrence in girl-orientated adverts
Action	68	51
Competition/destruction	113	9
Control	103	24
Limited activity	151	268
Feeling and nurturing	0	66

The differences are fairly obvious, in terms of stereotypical gender behaviour. The similarity between the occurrences of action verbs is probably because all toys are likely to encourage the children to take some action, whichever gender they are.

Speaking roles of boys and girls

The stereotypical gender belief in Western cultures is that women are talkers and men are doers, and there is much research to support the use of language by females to a greater extent than males, although males can manipulate women's speech in conversations. In the adverts it was questioned whether boys and girls appearing in adverts would talk equally and in similar ways. From the 188 adverts, 78 adverts had children speaking. In the boy-orientated adverts there was speaking in only 26 per cent of the adverts, whereas in the girl-orientated and the boy- and girl-orientated adverts, just over half had speaking. This is reinforcing the stereotypical view that girls prefer talk while boys prefer actions.

However, looking at what is said and how often, the results show that girls will talk less often and affirm the boys' comments in any adverts where there is speaking. The following example is from an advert for a board game called Trouble:

Boy 1:   'Hey, want to get into trouble?'
Boy 2:   'Yeah, it's fun getting into trouble.'
Girl: 'Yeah!' (giggles)
Boy 1:   'Back to start.'

In terms of frequency of speaking, in adverts aimed at both boys and girls, girls spoke in five with six utterances, and boys in nine adverts with 21 utterances, implying from a small sample that boys speak more than girls when both are speaking in one advert, and they have more independent things to say rather than reaffirmation, which is shown by more by girls.

Power discourse

The use of the word 'power' in Western culture, either as a noun ('he has the power'), an adverb ('he is powerful') or an adjective ('he is a powerful leader'), all signify strength and control, and are associated strongly with maleness. In the adverts the use of the word power occurred so frequently as to be noticeable when the adverts were first analysed. It was used in 21 per cent of adverts aimed at boys and in only one advert aimed at girls (and then only as the maker of the Barbie car, Power Wheels). In the adverts aimed at boys 28 occurrences were nouns, for example 'get the power', and 17 as adjectives, for example 'power pack', and was part of the name of two toys, Power Rangers Zeo and Super Sonic Power Crash Pit Racers.

Implications

It is fairly obvious that adverts aimed at children promote the gender polarisation of behaviour through production techniques such as voice-overs, linguistic content and names of toys. The implication is that children will learn from adverts the stereotypical behaviour being promoted and imitate these behaviours,

perpetuating the stereotypical behaviour even if society doesn't aim to reflect these stereotypes. Gendered language is promoted through advertisements, and this gendered voice manipulates children into stereotypical roles by becoming a secondary source of learning for the child.

There are reasons why these differences occur in the adverts:

- Previous marketing that has incorporated these stereotypes has been successful; it therefore makes sense to repeat it until it becomes ineffective.
- It is good to promote gender differences in toys so that there is more profit for producers, who can create separate toys for males and females.
- Early gender stereotyping in adverts prepares children for adverts for gender-biased adult products, which they learn are appropriate and which become part of their culture.

Johnson and Young summarise:

For those concerned about teaching gender sensitivity to children, the messages from toy advertisers are still competition. In our ears we hear a sickeningly sweet voice singing 'Potty Dotty' as girls are instructed to practise mothering and a growling voice-over proclaiming the aggressive power of 'Electronic Karate fighters' who swing at each other in an out-of-control scene that cuts back and forth between humans and toy.

Application: strategies to reduce the impact of advertising that is aimed at children

There are several ways, which follow on from the research described above, in which we can either reduce the impact of advertising *per se* or the stereotyping that is inherent in much advertising aimed at children.

One way would be simply to reduce the amount of television, and in particular advertising, that children watch, perhaps by guiding children to channels without adverts or muting the television during ad breaks. Parents and carers have a role to play here by watching television together and discussing the adverts, rather than leaving children to watch television by themselves and absorb all the messages being sent. This may facilitate a discussion about stereotyping, although probably not using that exact word with young children.

One method of reducing stereotyping would be to ensure that production techniques – including camera shots, sounds and music, gender of actors and voice-overs – are equal regardless of which gender the adverts are aimed at.

But perhaps children already behave in gender-stereotyped ways because of social influencers other than television, and adverts simply reinforce what they already believe to be true. The reduction of gender-stereotyped adverts may not guarantee that children would behave differently.

To reduce the impact of television, we could refer to the list of features that seemed to encourage imitation of behaviour and reduce those elements: we could remove humour and jokes, show fewer people 'getting away with it' and reduce the use of celebrity role models. While as psychologists this would be easy to propose, and it may reduce the impact of adverts, the whole purpose of adverts is to persuade children to want something, and therefore this is not going to happen. If we make adverts less persuasive, why would advertising companies want to screen them? Having said that, there are ethical concerns about showing antisocial behaviour, such as smoking or drinking alcohol, at times when children might be watching and be tempted to copy. In 2006 Ofcom published guidelines about adverts for high fat, salt and sugar (HFSS) foods and children. These stated that:

- adverts for HFSS products must not be shown in or around programmes specifically made for children (which includes pre-school children) and will be removed from dedicated children's channels
- adverts for HFSS products must not be shown in or around programmes of particular appeal to children under 16
- programme sponsorship by HFSS food and drink products will carry the same restriction.

There were also revised content rules that apply to all food and drink advertising to children irrespective of when it is scheduled. Key elements of the content rules include a prohibition on the use of licensed characters, celebrities, promotional offers and health claims in advertisements for HFSS products targeted at pre-school or primary school children.

Discussion

While there is much evidence for media influencing behaviour, some researchers have suggested that the artificiality of much of the research means that the findings are limited in their usefulness. The research tends to be in experimental settings, or with controlled use of content, as the researchers are trying to manipulate independent variables, producing a television-watching scenario that does not reflect what might happen in a child's home.

It could be that television lacks direct interaction between the viewer and action on the screen and, as such, tends to be less influential than we may think. We also have to consider the value of prosocial behaviour being promoted through television. Children's television channels have many examples of prosocial behaviour being seen as positive, with the necessary interaction between presenter and viewer, such as asking questions, pausing for answers and so on. In research by Sprafkin *et al.* (1975) children were either shown an episode of *Lassie* (the amazing dog) in which a boy rescued a dog, an episode of *Lassie* without this incident, or an episode of the family comedy show *The Brady Bunch*. Later children had to choose between continuing with a game or helping puppies in distress. There was significantly more help from the children who saw the first *Lassie* episode.

So, there are conflicting ideas about the impact of television programmes, and advertisements, on children, but it does appear that both positive and negative behavioural change can and does occur when children watch television, depending on the content.

The social area

Society – which consists of immediate family, peers and wider societal groups such as cultures – all have an influence on our behaviour. This is one reason why lab experiments are so artificial; very few of us live our lives in a lab (although Skinner did keep his daughter in a Skinner Box!) and so as social beings we will be influenced to a greater or lesser amount by the people (or implied people) in our surroundings.

Most often the first social influence on a baby will be the parent or parents, and this is shown in the bonding which enables a baby to survive in society. The type of parent can impact on the child's personality or temperament, as can the social situation a child might find him or herself in, such as in a hospital or childcare environment. As the child gets older, certainly in Western cultures, the effect of the media on a child becomes more apparent. The social learning theory is perfectly named – the child learns from the social environment through observation and imitation. There are numerous other theories, such as conditioning or the power of authority, which explain the impact of society on behaviour, and a child's socialisation into a culture is the net result of these influences.

Practice questions

1. Outline the biological factors that might affect intelligence. [10 marks]

2. Discuss the issue of reductionism in relation to intelligence. [15 marks]

3. A teacher is interested in seeing if the students in her class have intelligence levels which match the external exams they have to take.
Outline one way in which the teacher could assess the intelligence of the students in her class. [10 marks]

Chapter 3

Criminal Psychology

What makes a criminal? (Biological)

Are criminals born or made? This is a question that has been addressed by many researchers in the last 150 years. Early explanations focused on biology. For example, in 1876 Cesare Lombroso presented a theory, heavily influenced by Darwin's theory of evolution, that criminals were a subspecies of human and could be identified by their physiological characteristics, such as a narrow sloping brow, or physiological anomalies such as extra nipples, toes or fingers. This theory was discredited, however, and for much of the twentieth century social scientists turned their attention to explanations that focus on the nurture argument, such as upbringing.

Since the 1990s, however, a new interest has been shown in biological factors that may influence crime, and this has been largely pioneered by Professor Adrian Raine and his colleagues. Raine suggests that biology may account for as much 50 per cent of the explanation for some violent criminal behaviours in individuals who have dysfunction in their brains.

Physiological and non-physiological explanations of criminal behaviour

Physiological explanations of criminal behaviour: brain dysfunction

Much of Professor Raine's research has focused on an area of the brain called the prefrontal cortex. This part of the brain is above your eyes and just behind your forehead. Low activity in this area of the brain can be indicated by a low resting heart rate.

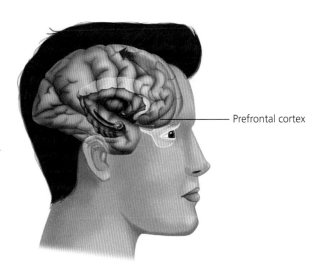

Prefrontal cortex

Figure 3.1 Diagram showing the location of the prefrontal cortex

In normal populations, people with lower than average heart rates tend towards an extravert personality, as they are motivated to increase the arousal that their brain craves. Extraversion is characterised by sensation-seeking or thrill-seeking behaviour. Introverts, on the other hand, have higher than average arousal in their prefrontal cortex and are predisposed to avoid situations that would increase their arousal and cause them undue stress. As with many human characteristics, most of us tend towards the average on the introversion–extraversion scales, with people scoring extremely high and extremely low being the exception rather than the rule.

Have a go yourself

Does a low resting heart rate negatively correlate with extraversion? Design a study to test this. You will need to create a test of extraversion. Create one with ten questions such as 'Would you like to go sky-diving?', 'Do you get bored easily?', and a test of resting heart rate – you can use a heart rate monitor if you can get hold of one, or get your participants to take their pulse and count how many heart beats they have in six seconds. You can then multiply this by ten to get their beats-per-minute resting heart rate. Test 40 participants.

What graphical representation of your data will you need to draw? Which statistical test can you use to analyse your results?

In addition to influencing our personality, the prefrontal cortex performs a number of important cognitive functions:

- It receives incoming information from the nervous system.
- It is involved in planning and regulating behaviour, for example it informs the limbic system, the emotional centre of the brain, when to feel fear based on the consequences an action might have.
- It enables us to focus our attention.
- As you will remember from the core study by Casey *et al.* (2011), the prefrontal cortex plays an important role in our self-control, enabling us to control our impulses.

If there is low arousal in the prefrontal cortex then these abilities are impaired. Raine and his colleagues have investigated the relationship between low activity in the prefrontal cortex and impulsive violent and criminal behaviour. Of the prefrontal cortex, Raine says:

It's the part of the brain involved in regulating and controlling behaviour ... It's a bit like the emergency brake on behaviour. That emergency brake is gone in the violent offender.

Raine and his colleagues published a study that used positron emission tomography (PET) brain scans to investigate the differences between murderers' and non-murderers' brains (Raine *et al.*, 1997a). This research confirmed that impulsive, violent murder may be associated with brain dysfunction in the prefrontal cortex and other areas of the brain known to be associated with aggressive behaviour. This study is the key research for this topic.

Low arousal in the prefrontal cortex is partly heritable but can also occur as a result of birth complications or as a result of a mother drinking alcohol during pregnancy. Children with a low resting heart rate have been shown to be more inclined to be aggressive and display antisocial behaviour than children who do not exhibit low arousal.

In a different study, Raine *et al.* (1997b) showed that in a sample of 1795 children in Mauritius, those children who had been identified as having a low resting heart rate at age three were found to engage in more antisocial and aggressive behaviour than children with high heart rates at age 11. It was concluded that:

... low resting heart rate, a partly heritable trait reflecting fearlessness and stimulation-seeking, is an important, diagnostically specific, well-replicated, early biological marker for later aggressive behaviour.

However, a word of caution. Raine is at pains to point out that biology is not the only factor that influences people's behaviour, and neither does it excuse their behaviour nor exempt people from taking full responsibility for it under the law. Raine stresses that a *biosocial* explanation of crime is essential if a full understanding of the factors that influence people to commit violent and criminal behaviour are to be fully understood. He does, however, emphasise that biology has an important role to play both in furthering our understanding and putting interventions in place to prevent violent and antisocial behaviour:

The dominant model for understanding criminal behaviour has been, for most of the twentieth century, one built almost exclusively on social and sociological models. My main argument is that sole reliance on these social perspectives is fundamentally flawed. Biology is also critically important in understanding violence, and probing through its anatomical underpinnings will be vital for treating the epidemic of violence and crime affecting our societies. (Raine, 2013)

Physiological explanations of criminal behaviour: how do genes influence criminal behaviour?

In 1993 Han Brunner published a research paper that caused a media sensation. A gene for crime had, the newspapers claimed enthusiastically, been discovered. Unfortunately this claim had more to do with wanting to sell newspapers than with accurately reporting the science. Brunner had been cautious in writing about his work. He had emphasised there was no one gene for crime, and had suggested an 'association' rather than a 'cause' between genes and aggressive behaviour.

Stop and ask yourself ...

- What are the functions of the prefrontal cortex in a normal individual?
- Can you explain how dysfunction in the prefrontal cortex might predispose someone to crime?
- List five other factors that might predispose someone to crime other than low activity in their prefrontal cortex

Links to
- Check your understanding

PART 3 Applied psychology

Nonetheless, the word was out that there was a specific gene, which became known as the 'Warrior Gene', that was related to aggressive and violent criminal behaviour, the MAOA gene. The MAOA gene is responsible for the enzyme monoamine oxidase-A (MAOA). The function of MAOA is to breakdown (or metabolise) excess serotonin in the brain, thus helping to control the levels of serotonin available for take-up by the brain.

Brunner's investigation began when, as a doctor in a Netherlands hospital, he was approached by a woman for genetic counselling. In her family there were a number of males who suffered a syndrome of mental retardation that was associated with aggressive, antisocial and violently criminal behaviour. Extensive research by Brunner and his colleagues found 14 such males in the woman's extended family and concluded that they carried a genetic mutation – a point mutation on the X chromosome, so passed down the maternal line. What Brunner discovered was a mutation in the gene that should produce MAOA that meant that those males affected could produce no MAOA at all. This is now known as Brunner syndrome, and only this one family is known to be affected by it.

A case study of five of the affected males included taking five urine samples across a 24-hour period and measuring MAOA activity by measuring metabolites of serotonin in their urine. It was this evidence that revealed the lack of MAOA in the males resulting in high levels of serotonin, which is associated with aggressive behaviour. The types of aggressive and antisocial behaviour the males had engaged in included attempted rape, exhibitionism, arson and assault.

The MAOA low activity variant may increase susceptibility to antisocial traits and aggression, and is therefore a risk factor for criminal behaviour in those who carry this genetic mutation.

Brunner's findings have been used to argue that genetics (a biological explanation), rather than decision-making processes (a cognitive explanation), can influence criminal activity.

Find out more

- What is MAOA-L and how is it related to antisocial and criminal behaviour?

Brunner's findings were supported by a comparative study on mice by Cases et al. (1995) where the MAOA gene was turned off in one group of mice. What was observed in the mice was similar to Brunner's findings in the Dutch family. The MAOA-deficient mice pups had up to nine times the level of serotonin compared to control pups and showed behavioural alterations, including trembling, difficulty in righting (that is, if they fell over they had difficulty getting back into an upright position) and fearfulness – symptoms that could be reversed by giving the pups synthetic serotonin. Adult mice also manifested a distinct behavioural syndrome, including enhanced aggression in males.

A further study on a human population by Caspi et al. (2002), however, showed that in the general population, low MAOA activity alone may not correlate as highly with antisocial and violent behaviour as the combination (interaction) of low MAOA and maltreatment in childhood. In a cohort of 1037 individuals (52 per cent male) born in 1972 in New Zealand, those with the low activity variant of MAOA plus experience of childhood maltreatment accounted for only 12 per cent of the male cohort but accounted for 44 per cent of the cohort's violent convictions.

The findings showed that low MAOA activity alone may not mean a person will become violent or criminal but, when combined with an abusive childhood, it does seem to increase the risk. This finding supports Raine's assertion that a biosocial explanation is needed if we are to explain criminal and violent behaviour, and that neither social nor biological explanations alone are satisfactory. Both Raine and Caspi, then, offer a holistic rather than reductionist explanation of violent criminal behaviour.

Non-physiological explanations of criminal behaviour

Social explanations of criminal behaviour include research into upbringing and the risk factors for crime that children are exposed to in the environment. In the 1960s Farrington and West began the Cambridge study in delinquent development. This was a large-scale study of 411 boys who were aged eight when the study began. The study interviewed them as boys, adolescents and again as adults. In addition, their juvenile and adult criminal records were reported. The study was comprehensive and identified a range of risk factors for offending in boys aged eight to ten.

The most important childhood risk factors were measures of family criminality, daring or risk-taking, low school attainment, poverty and poor parenting. The study suggested that some of these factors could be addressed in similar populations of boys to offer early intervention to reduce the risks of turning to crime. This illustrates the attraction of social explanations of criminality. With the will, expertise and economic backing, we can change a person's environment to try to reduce the likelihood of them turning to crime.

Other social explanations of crime include an early theory by Edwin Sutherland in 1939. Unlike Farrington et al.'s broad and inclusive list of risk factors, Sutherland attributed criminal behaviour solely to learning. He called his theory the differential association hypothesis and, simply put, the theory states that the more contact someone has with attitudes favourable to criminal activity, and the more exposure they have to criminal behaviour in their family and friends, the more criminal behaviour they will themselves come to commit. This is, of course a reductionist and therefore flawed explanation. Nonetheless, it does help to explain some types of crime that perhaps biology may fail to address. An example might be white collar crime, such as stealing office supplies, fiddling expenses or failing to fully disclose earnings for tax purposes. Sutherland's theory suggests how people could be easily integrated into a custom of criminal activity on the basis that 'everybody does it'. In other words, the behaviour has become an accepted social norm.

Figure 3.2 White collar crime such as stealing office supplies from work can be explained by Sutherland's theory

There are also cognitive explanations of crime. For example, one cognitive explanation is that those who commit crime do so because they operate at an immature level of moral reasoning. The Kohlbergian preconventional stage of moral reasoning suggests that behaviour is seen as right or wrong only in terms of the outcome for the individual. In other words, the individual can steal because the outcome is good for him or her ('I didn't have it, and now I do'), and the action will only

be judged by them as bad if the outcome for them is bad (they get caught). They do not see stealing as wrong just because the majority see it as wrong and do not acknowledge any obligation to not steal because of a duty to society.

Palmer and Hollin (1998) conducted a study that compared the pattern of moral development in young offenders and non-offenders to see if moral development was indeed delayed in young offenders. The sample included 126 convicted male offenders aged between 13 and 21 obtained through a Young Offender Institution and at Magistrates' Courts (the offences committed were mainly burglary and car theft) and a comparison group of 332 non-offenders aged 13 to 22 (210 female and 122 male), obtained through schools and a university in the West Midlands, UK. Data was gathered by self-report questionnaire. The questionnaire asked about socioeconomic status and also incorporated two psychometric measures:

- The Sociomoral Reflection Measure – Short Form (SRM-SF), which measures moral reasoning. It is made up of 11 questions that assess the respondents' moral reasoning in relation to contract and truth, affiliation, life, property and law, and legal justice.
- The Self-Reported Delinquency Checklist (SRD) was used to see whether the officially delinquent and non-delinquent were really exhibiting different levels of delinquent behaviour.

Respondents were assured that the questionnaires were entirely confidential.

The SRM-SF showed that the male offenders had the least mature moral reasoning and were predominantly reasoning at Kohlberg's preconventional level. The majority of non-offenders were using conventional reasoning. Palmer and Hollin concluded that young male delinquents seem to have deficits in their moral reasoning, with less mature reasoning exhibited in the value areas relating specifically to delinquent behaviour.

Explanations of criminal behaviour can, as we have seen, be biological or non-biological. Of course, the type of crime that is being described also needs to be taken into account, and perhaps biology has more to offer in explaining violent, impulsive or sensation-seeking criminal behaviour than in explaining acquisitive crime such as stealing, or white collar crime such as fiddling expenses. Perhaps we should be cautious, however, and suggest

🚫 **Stop and ask yourself ...**

- What is the reductionism–holism debate?
- How would you describe the work of (i) Raine, (ii) Brunner, and (iii) Farrington *et al*. in terms of the reductionism–holism debate?

Links to debates
- Reductionism–holism

that whatever the crime being investigated psychologists would be wise to offer a biosocial explanation and avoid simplistic and reductionist explanations.

Key research: Raine, Buchsbaum and La Casse (1997a) Brain abnormalities in murderers indicated by positron emission tomography

Background

Earlier work by Raine and others had demonstrated the relationship between low levels of activity in the prefrontal cortex and violent behaviour. Raine argues that in the violent offender the prefrontal cortex fails to operate its 'emergency brake on violent behaviour' and that this can, in part, explain impulsive and aggressive crimes. The limbic system, including the hippocampus and amygdala, has also been associated with aggressive behaviour. This is part of the 'old brain' and controls our emotion and aggression. Raine suggests that abnormal function in the structures of the limbic system in the different hemispheres may be connected to dysfunction in the corpus callosum. Thanks to the advent of brain-imaging techniques, Raine and his colleagues were able to select a group of violent offenders to study and directly research brain abnormalities in the areas of the brain already known to be associated with violent and aggressive behaviour – to look directly into murderers' brains.

Aims

The aim of the study was to look at direct measures of both cortical and subcortical brain functioning, using PET scans in a group of murderers who were pleading not guilty by reason of insanity (NGRI). Raine *et al.* refer to this group as the 'murderers' in their study for ease of reference and we shall do the same here.

The expectation was that the murderers would show evidence of brain dysfunction in their prefrontal cortex, as well as in other areas that have been linked to violent behaviour, such as the limbic system and corpus callosum. It was also predicted that they would not show dysfunction in areas of the brain not related to violent behaviour.

Method

Subjects

The experimental group (the murderers) consisted of 41 subjects (39 men and 2 women) with a mean age of 34.3 years. They had been charged with either murder or manslaughter and were pleading NGRI. They had been

sent to the University of California imaging centre for the following reasons:

1. To obtain evidence as to whether they were NGRI.
2. To find out if they were competent to understand the judicial process.
3. To see if there was any evidence of diminished mental capacity, which may affect the nature of the sentencing they received.

They were referred for the following reasons:

- six had schizophrenia
- 23 had head injuries or organic brain damage
- three had a history of psychoactive substance abuse
- two had affective disorders
- two had epilepsy
- three had a history of hyperactivity and learning disability
- two had passive–aggressive or paranoid personality disorders.

The control group of 41 people were matched by age and gender and had a mean age of 31.7 years. The six murderers with schizophrenia in the experimental group were matched with six schizophrenic controls. The rest of the control group were thoroughly screened and showed no history of psychiatric illness. None of the controls had committed murder.

The consent forms and procedures for the participation of subjects in the study were approved by the Human Subjects Committee of the University of California.

Controls

- All offenders were in custody and were kept medication-free for two weeks before the brain scanning. Urine tests at the time of scanning confirmed this. The control group were also medication-free.
- Tests were undertaken to make sure that being left-handed or right-handed had no effect on behaviour.
- Fourteen of the murderers were non-white but when they were compared to white murderers on PET measures there were no significant differences between them.
- Twenty-three murderers had a history of head injury, but again they showed no difference from non-head-injured murderers, except in the functioning of their corpus callosum (and the authors accepted that this may have contributed towards a reduction in the murderers' brain activity).

Materials

- Thermoplastic head-holder, individually modelled, to hold the subject's head still while being scanned.
- PET machine to image brain functioning. A 2D colour 'map' of brain activity is generated by the machine.

- Fluorodeoxyglucose (FDG), a tracer injected to trace the metabolism of glucose by the brain. The scanner picks up this radioactive tracer and, by showing the concentration of the tracer, the concentration of glucose metabolism can be shown in different areas of the brain. Glucose metabolism means the brain is using up glucose: the brain 'runs' on glucose in the same way that a car engine runs on fuel. PET scans show where the glucose is being used, indicating the level of activity in those areas. The scans are in colour with the areas of high activity indicated by warm colours, with the highest activity showing up red.
- Continuous performance task (CPT) – this task required the participant to search for targets on a screen and press a button to indicate when the targets were spotted. This is a task that requires concentration and focus so should have employed the prefrontal cortex. This task lasted for 32 minutes.

Figure 3.3 To measure the activity in the prefrontal cortex all participants completed a task that required them to look at a screen and spot targets, indicating with a hand-held button when they saw the target object; this continuous performance task lasted 32 minutes and should have engaged the participant's prefrontal cortex

Procedure

Ten minutes before the injection of the FDG subjects were allowed to practise the CPT task so they knew what to expect. Then, 30 seconds before they began the CPT, they started the actual CPT task. The 30 second delay was to ensure that the novelty of the task did not show up on the scan.

After 32 minutes, the subject was transferred to the adjacent PET scanning room and their brain was scanned ten times at 10 mm intervals to measure brain activity in both the cortical and subcortical regions of the brain.

Results

Although there were no differences in the performance of the task between the two groups, there was evidence of significant differences in brain metabolism in a number of areas.

Find out more

- Search the internet to find out where the areas of the brain are that showed differences in the murderers' and non murderers' brains and draw a diagram of the brain to show these findings.

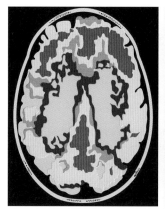
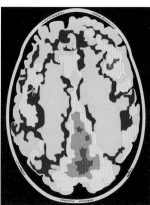

Figure 3.4 Brain scan (PET) of a normal control (left) and a murderer (right), illustrating the lack of activation in the prefrontal cortex in the murderer. The prefrontal region is at the top of the figure, and the occipital cortex (the back part of the brain controlling vision) is at the bottom. Warm colours (e.g. red and yellow) indicate areas of high brain activation; cold colours (e.g. blue and green) indicate low activation

Cerebral cortex

The cerebral cortex has four areas or 'lobes': frontal, parietal, temporal and occipital. Compared with the controls, NGRIs had:
- more activity in their occipital areas
- no difference in their temporal areas

Subcortical areas

Compared with the controls, NGRIs had:
- less activity in the corpus callosum
- less activity in the left side and more activity in the right side in the amygdala and the hippocampus
- more activity in the right side of the thalamus, though no difference in the left side.

What do these results mean? Lower glucose metabolism indicates a lack of activity. Reduced brain activity in the prefrontal areas may explain impulsive behaviour, a loss of self-control, evidence of immaturity, altered emotionality and the inability to modify behaviour. This may make it easier to be aggressive as normal constraints on behaviour may be reduced (Damasio, 1985).

The authors of the study suggest that differences in the limbic system (the amygdala) support theories of violence that suggest violence is due to unusual emotional responses such as a lack of fear. This supports a 'fearlessness theory' of violence – reduced fear enables violence. The authors also say that differences in the corpus callosum correspond to findings in split-brain patients who display inappropriate emotional expression and the inability to grasp the long-term implications of a situation (Sperry, 1974).

Conclusions

The authors suggest that this study provides preliminary but not complete evidence that murderers pleading NGRI have different brain functions compared to non-murdering controls. The study also indicates which brain processes may mean a person is predisposed to violent behaviour. The study shows that the neural processes that underlie violent behaviour can't simply be reduced to pinpoint a single brain mechanism that causes violence. It seems that there are several processes involved and that, if there are deficits in a number of these processes, the likelihood of violent behaviour occurring is much greater.

Typical of Raine's caution in his interpretation of studies into biology and criminal behaviour, the authors are at pains to point out that the findings:

- cannot be taken to show that violence is caused by biology alone
- do not show that NGRIs are not responsible for their actions
- that PET scans cannot be used to 'diagnose' potential murderers
- cannot be generalised from NGRIs to other types of violent offenders
- cannot be generalised to 'crime' in general, as the study did not contain a non-violent criminal control group.

They conclude that what the study does show is that the murderers pleading NGRI had significant differences in glucose metabolism in certain areas of the brain compared to controls. The findings also suggest, but do not conclusively demonstrate, that reduced brain activity in certain areas may be one of the many predispositions towards violence in this particular group of offenders.

Application: biological strategies for preventing criminal behaviour

One approach to stopping violence – one that we see all too often today – is to wait until the child is already kicking down the doors and becoming unmanageable. Unfortunately by then it's often too late to effectively correct course. Why not intervene early in life to prevent future violence? (Raine, 2013)

Primary crime prevention strategies aim to identify children at risk of, or having multiple risk factors for, antisocial and criminal behaviour and to put interventions in place aimed at reducing these risk factors. Developmental crime prevention is a form of crime prevention that can include biological elements as part of a biosocial intervention programme, or indeed be largely biological in nature. Research indicates that the earlier the intervention, the better, since important cognitive growth happens in the womb and in the first two years of life. For some potential offenders, then, prevention needs to begin before they are even born.

Health and nutrition programmes for pregnant women and their infants have been shown to reduce antisocial behaviour in those children. Raine (2013) lists a range of biosocial risk factors for antisocial and criminal behaviour:

- children of mothers who smoke during pregnancy have a three-fold risk of becoming violent offenders compared with children of mothers who don't smoke during pregnancy
- birth complications represent a risk factor for antisocial behaviour and crime
- poor nutrition of a mother during pregnancy doubles the rate of antisocial behaviour
- early maternal care is very important during the prenatal and postnatal periods of brain development.

In a landmark study Olds (1998) conducted trials of a biosocial intervention programme which addressed all of these risk factors. The biological elements of this are related to health and nutrition. A sample of 400 low social class women were randomly allocated to either the intervention or control condition. The intervention comprised of nine home visits from nurse practitioners during the mother's pregnancy, followed by a further 23 visits from nurse practitioners in the first two years of the child's life. The nurses gave mothers advice on reducing smoking and alcohol use, improving their nutrition, and advice on how to meet their child's social, emotional and physical needs. The control group received standard pre- and postnatal care. A 15-year follow up of the study showed an impressive 52.8 per cent reduction in arrests and 63 per cent reduction in convictions in those whose mothers had received the intervention compared to controls. This early intervention, which incorporated biomedical as well as social interventions, had proved highly effective.

Raine and his colleagues have shown that more biologically focused interventions can also be effective. In the Mauritius study discussed earlier, 100 of the 1795 child participants with low resting heart rate were selected and compared with a matched control group. The 100 children received a three-part intervention programme of enrichment:

1. Nutrition – milk, fruit juice and a hot meal a day of fish or chicken or mutton with salad was given.
2. Physical exercise – afternoon sessions of gym, structured games and free play were run.

Figure 3.5 Children undertook a three-part intervention, focused on nutrition, physical exercise and cognitive stimulation

3. Cognitive stimulation – the children went to two specially constructed nursery schools that provided a multimodal curriculum aimed at cognitive stimulation based on toys, art, handicrafts, drama and music.

The control children followed the normal curriculum and had no nutrition or exercise intervention beyond that which was offered in the normal nursery schools in Mauritius at that time. The children were followed up at age 11 and 17.

- At age 11, the children in the intervention:
  - could focus their attention better than controls
  - had more mature brains and the level of arousal in their brains had increased.
- At age 17 the children in the intervention:
  - scored significantly lower on conduct disorder ratings than controls
  - were less cruel to others, less likely to pick fights, not so hot-tempered and less likely to bully other children.

The researchers further investigated the 100 who had experienced the intervention and separated them into two groups, those who had been well nourished at the start of the programme and those who had been poorly nourished. This showed that those who had been initially poorly nourished showed a 52.6 per cent reduction in conduct disorder at age 17 compared to controls, whereas those who had had good nutrition showed just 9.4 per cent reduction compared to controls. This suggests that nutrition has a part to play as a biological intervention to help prevent crime.

Raine does point out that the intervention only reduced adult crime by 35 per cent and did not eradicate it – biology is not the only factor to consider, he explains. He also suggests that it may not be effective for cohorts of children who do not experience poor nutrition.

The study does, however, link to a further possible biological intervention to help prevent antisocial behaviour and crime. In the Mauritius study, could the extra two portions of fish eaten a week have influenced the children's behaviour? Is fish really brain food? Raine

had read research that had suggested that omega-3, a food supplement based on fish oils, had been shown to reduce antisocial and aggressive behaviour. In the Mauritius study, a further 100 children were selected to conduct a trial with omega-3. For six months the children drank a daily juice drink, called Norwegian Smartfish Juice, which contained a whole gram of omega-3, compared with a control group who just drank the juice and received no fish-oil supplement. Measures reported by parents after 12 months (6 months after the daily supplements ended) showed a significant reduction in the aggression, delinquency and attention problems of those taking the omega-3. Why? Raine explains that omega-3:

… enhances brain structure and function by increasing dendritic branching, enhancing synaptic functioning, boosting cell size, protecting the neuron from cell death, and regulating both neurotransmitter functioning and gene expression. (Raine, 2013)

In other words, omega-3 may partly reverse the brain dysfunction that predisposes children to antisocial behaviour and aggression that, unchecked, might lead to adult violence and crime.

Figure 3.6 Omega-3 fish oils have been linked to aggressive and anti-social behaviour

It seems then that we can indeed change the brain to help change behaviour, and that early biological interventions have a part to play. Of course, biology alone is not the cause of the problem and it follows therefore that biological interventions can only be part of the solution. Raine (2013) tells us:

We have promising techniques to block the foundational processes that result in the brain dysfunctions that in turn predispose an individual to violence. That has not been fully recognised within the traditional study of crime – and it really needs to be if we are to be sincere about stopping the suffering and pain associated with violence ... the best investment society can make in stopping violence is to invest in the early years of the growing child – and that investment must be biosocial in nature. You cannot successfully intervene without addressing the brain.

> **Take it further**
>
> - Find out if omega-3 fish oils could help reduce aggression not just in children but in adults too, including prisoners.
> - What other links are there between diet and violence?

The collection and processing of forensic evidence (Biological)

Forensic evidence is information collected, often from a crime scene, which can be presented as evidence in a court of law. The discipline of forensic science collects and analyses a wide range of types of forensic evidence, including ballistics; blood spatter analysis; and analysis of boot, shoe and tyre prints, bite marks, hair and fibre samples, and DNA. The example we will focus on in this chapter, however, is fingerprint analysis.

Fingerprints have been used by the police to identify individuals for over 100 years. The use of fingerprint identification endures as a major method of identification by forensic scientists as it is cost and time effective to collect and relatively easy to analyse. In addition, in all the time that fingerprint analysis has been undertaken, no two people, not even identical twins, have ever been shown to have identical fingerprints. The process of identification of suspects using fingerprint analysis has been greatly assisted by the introduction of digitally stored fingerprints, both national and international databases of people whose fingerprints are on file, and by the computer programs that enable the rapid search of such databases to find a match for a print lifted from a crime scene.

Forensic science, and its supporting technology, instils in us a confidence that such evidence is collected and analysed both systematically and objectively, and provides us with compelling evidence as to the guilt or innocence of suspects.

Motivating factors and bias in the collection of forensic evidence

A high-profile case, however, showed that fingerprint analysis is not as objective and foolproof as both forensic scientists and the general public might believe. On 11 March 2004 a series of bombs went off in a co-ordinated attack on four commuter trains in Madrid, Spain. As a result of these attacks, 191 people were killed and a further 1800 people were wounded. This horrific act led to a full scale international investigation involving the United States Federal Bureau of Investigation (FBI).

Figure 3.7 The FBI's erroneous identification of the Madrid bomber. The latent print from the crime scene (left) and the fingerprint of the innocent suspect who was positively identified by a number of fingerprint experts (right)

A latent fingerprint (a print created by sweat and left behind, without the perpetrator realising) was lifted from a bag believed to have belonged to the bomber and which contained detonating devices. Using the standard FBI fingerprint analysis protocol, a suspect was identified. He was a US suspect, an American Muslim called Brandon Mayfield, who had been a person of interest to the FBI since the 9/11 bombings of the World Trade Center in New York. The FBI protocol included having a number of fingerprint experts examine the fingerprint. All agreed the print was Mayfield's. Mayfield, however, protested his innocence and asked, when he appeared in court, for an expert appointed by the defence to examine the print. This was done and the expert also confirmed that the print was Mayfield's. This evidence would surely have been key in the trial of Brandon Mayfield had it not been for the fact that the Spanish police matched the print to the real bomber, an Algerian national called Ouhnane Daoud. The print was not Mayfield's at all.

Kassin *et al.* (2013) consider the high-profile Mayfield case, and proof that other such errors could be made, as evidence that forensic science is not infallible. For example, they quote research by Hampikian *et al.* (2011) called 'The Genetics of Innocence' which found that several types of forensic science testimony had been found to have wrongly convicted innocent individuals. In the cases where trial transcripts were available to review, Hampikian *et al.* found that:

- 38 per cent contained incorrect serology (blood analysis) testimony
- 22 per cent involved incorrect hair comparisons
- 3 per cent involved incorrect bite mark identifications, and
- 2 per cent involved incorrect fingerprint identifications.

Why do such errors occur?

A cognitive neuroscientist called Itiel Dror had also become interested in fingerprint analysis and, in particular, at what could cause errors of the type that led to the erroneous identification of Mayfield as the Madrid bomber from fingerprint evidence. In an article called 'Cognitive bias in Forensic Evidence' (2012), Dror sums up the problem for forensic science:

… many forensic disciplines that deal with impression and trace evidence lack sufficient instruments and measurements, thereby leaving the decisions to the subjective assessment of the human examiner.

In other words, it is the human expert and not a machine that makes the final judgement of whether forensic evidence is a match or not. It is, therefore, human error that is to blame. Dror considers that the source of such error can be best explained by psychology and cognitive bias.

Such a bias is known as confirmation bias and occurs when people observe more, give extra emphasis to, or intentionally look for evidence that would validate their current beliefs. This bias makes people likely to excuse or completely ignore evidence that would contradict their beliefs.

In forensic science, Dror suggested that cognitive bias could account for the errors that are made. For example, Dror describes two types of processes involved in fingerprint matching. Firstly there are bottom-up processes that are purely data driven and which operate on three levels:

- the examination of the overall pattern of friction ridges
- the examination of the characteristics of specific ridges
- 'zooming in' to examine things such as location and distribution of sweat pores, individual ridge technology and other uniquely identifiable features.

Identifying a fingerprint match using these bottom-up processes might provide compelling, objective evidence. Identifying matches in the real world, however, is hindered by the poor quality of prints. Often they are degraded or contaminated, or are only partial prints. In fact, often there is not enough print evidence to make a match at all. In the real world, the difficult task of pattern recognition in matching prints is further complicated by the top-down processes involved. This refers to how contextual effects mediate how decisions on a match are made. Examples of contextual effects include the expert's prior experience and knowledge, as well as the person's expectations and emotional state. These top-down processes can include biases that override the objective decision making of the bottom-up processes. Examples of cognitive biases that could influence fingerprint analysis include:

- Observer or expectancy bias – this is when the expert anticipates the outcome as a result of information from an initial observer and therefore has preconceived expectations about the outcome (for example, if an officer informs the expert that the suspect has already been identified by an eyewitness and the fingerprint analysis is just needed to confirm their identity).
- Selective attention – prior expectation can lead to the 'filtering out' of ambiguous elements in a partial or ambiguous print where a 'close call' has to be made to create a match.
- Conformity effect – if a fingerprint expert is asked to validate the decision of a peer, or of a superior, this effect may unconsciously bias them to agree with the original decision if they are aware of it.

Stop and ask yourself …

- Can you explain how cognitive bias might account for false positive fingerprint matches such as the error made by the FBI in the case of the Madrid bomber?

Links to

- Check your understanding

- Need-determination perception – this bias arises from a strong desire to solve a particular crime (for example, this could explain why errors were made in the analysis of the Madrid bomber's print, as the motivation to identify the terrorist was high).
- Overconfidence bias – experts may experience overconfidence bias and this may make them believe that they are always right, even in the face of contradictory evidence. The more experienced and intelligent they are, the easier it is for them to defend their biases and beliefs.

The high-profile error made in the case of the Madrid bomber prompted an internal investigation by the FBI and a report from the Office of the Inspector General, which cited 'confirmation bias' as a contributing factor in the case.

Motivating factors and bias in the processing of forensic evidence

Empirical cognitive evidence into the role of context as a cause of cognitive bias in fingerprint analysis was first presented in research by Dror *et al.* (2006). This research suggested that the context could bias their decisions and lead to errors being made. The participants for this study were five volunteer fingerprint experts who consented to being studied in the following 12 months as part of their everyday work. Between them they had a cumulative 85 years of experience as fingerprint experts with a mean experience of 17 years. They were chosen as they were unfamiliar with the fingerprint of Mayfield (who had been wrongly identified by the FBI as the Madrid bomber) and because they could covertly identify a definite match they had made five years earlier in their careers. The archived matches for each of the five participants were each verified by two independent fingerprint experts as definite matches.

The study allowed the fingerprint experts to be studied without knowing when they would be presented with the test material. Each of the five participants were approached by a colleague and asked to examine a pair of fingerprints, as they might be asked to do in their normal working day. They were given a latent print taken from a crime scene and a print exemplar (a print obtained from a suspect). In reality, this was a pair of prints they had recorded as a definite match five years earlier in their career. The context was manipulated by telling them, erroneously, that these two prints were a pair of prints wrongly identified by the FBI as the Madrid bomber, thus the participants were given the expectation that these prints would not be a match.

The results were surprising, as only one of the five (20 per cent) agreed with their original decision that the

pair of prints was a definite match. This means that the other four (80 per cent) contradicted their earlier decision on the prints, with three out of the four (60 per cent) completely contradicting their previous decision by declaring the prints a definite non-match and the fourth judging there to be insufficient evidence to make a match.

The researchers concluded that the failure of the fingerprint experts to give reliable decisions in four of the five cases provided empirical evidence that they had been affected by the contextual information they were given and, in fact, four out of five had been misled by being told these prints were not a match, when in fact they had been verified as matched prints. In other words, their decisions had been affected by cognitive bias, in this case a confirmation bias. This study identified the problem of bias and subjectivity in fingerprint analysis and led to fierce debate between cognitive neuroscientists and fingerprint experts about the influence of cognitive bias as a threat to the objectivity of fingerprint examination as a forensic science.

Forensic evidence is often far from perfect and can be limited in both quantity and quality. It would not be surprising, therefore, that errors may be made where evidence was ambiguous or imperfect, and where top-down processes, including cognitive biases, would be more likely to influence the final decision.

In a further study, Dror *et al.* (2005) manipulated the context as the independent variable in a fingerprint-matching exercise. The participants' emotional state and motivation to find a match were manipulated by providing background information and by using subliminal priming. This was done by providing information about the background of the crime, including showing emotionally provoking photographs. Task difficulty was also manipulated.

Participants were 27 university student volunteers (9 males and 18 females) with a mean age of 23. Ninety-six pairs of fingerprints were selected. Half of these contained obvious bottom-up information so it would be easy to decide if the prints were or were not a match. The remaining 48 pairs were not as clear and were more ambiguous. These would therefore allow top-down processes to have a greater influence on the participants' decisions as to whether they matched or not. These ambiguous prints reflected the types of prints that are often present in real-life cases, thus increasing the study's ecological validity.

Two emotional states, low and high, were introduced by the type of crime (low emotional state included bicycle theft and burglary: cases with no harm to a person; high emotional state included murder and personal attacks: cases where a victim was seriously hurt). Photos were used to reinforce each context.

The dependent variable in the study was the number of matches that were made, and it was predicted that where the emotional context was high and the prints were ambiguous, the most matches would be made.

Participants were each tested on all 96 pairs of prints. Where emotional context was used the description of the crime was given on a computer screen, with the supporting photograph, before the fingerprints to be matched were viewed. In the emotional context plus subliminal priming condition, the words 'same' or 'guilty' were flashed subliminally on to the screen with the information being given. The participant responded by pressing computer keys marked 'same' or 'different' after viewing each pair of prints.

The results of the study showed that in the unambiguous pairs the participants were unaffected by the emotional contexts (top-down processes) manipulated by the study. However, in the ambiguous pairs the top-down processes significantly affected the participants' matches, as shown in Table 3.1.

Table 3.1 Percentage of matches found for the 48 ambiguous fingerprint pairs

Control condition	Low emotional context	High emotional context	High emotional context plus subliminal priming
47%	49%	58%	66%

The study concluded that where the match of the prints was ambiguous, the decisions of the student participants were swayed by emotional context, by the top-down contextual cues provided by the study.

In response to the research by Dror and others, and to the suggestion that fingerprint experts are affected by cognitive bias – in particular by emotional context – Lisa Hall and Emma Player conducted 'in house' research for the Metropolitan Police Service using 70 fingerprint experts. This is our key research for this topic.

Key research: Hall and Player (2008) Will the introduction of an emotional context affect fingerprint analysis and decision making?

Background

Dror's research had suggested that as the clarity of a fingerprint decreases the identification of a match in a pair of prints would be more likely to be affected by top-down processes, such as emotional context.

However, Dror had drawn these conclusions based on research with non-experts (university students). Hall and Player aimed to investigate whether the same effect would be observed in experienced fingerprint experts.

The purpose of this study, then, was to see if the outcome would be the same for trained fingerprint experts – to see if emotional bias could lead to errors in real-life fingerprint identification. The protocol for fingerprint analysis in the Metropolitan Police Service includes providing the fingerprint examiner with a copy of the crime scene report, which details the nature of the crime. No photographic evidence of the crime is provided.

Could the information contained in this report introduce an emotional element that could bias the fingerprint experts' opinions?

Aims

This study aimed to answer two questions:
- Does the written report of a crime, as routinely supplied with fingerprint evidence, affect a fingerprint expert's identification of a poor quality print?
- Are fingerprint experts emotionally affected by the circumstances of a case?

To answer the first question, participants were asked to analyse an artificially obscured fingerprint. To answer the second question, participants completed a specially devised feedback questionnaire.

Method

Participants

Seventy volunteer fingerprint experts working for the Metropolitan Police Fingerprint Bureau took part. Their length of experience ranged from less than three months to more than 30 years, with a mean length of experience of 11 years. The majority (58) were active in teams dealing with a full range of crimes and 12 were in managerial roles (still on the UK National Register of Fingerprint Experts, although not currently active practitioners). They all responded to a request to take part in an experiment but the details of the experiment were not disclosed.

Materials

A fingerprint from a known source was used, from a volunteer whose right forefinger was inked and printed onto paper. This print was scanned into a computer and superimposed on the corner of a £50 note, with the detail of the note obscuring the ridge detail.
Fourteen prints were made for use in the experiment and were compared to ensure consistency. They were also shown to a sample of practitioners with a wide range of experience. This confirmed that the fingerprint was ambiguous.

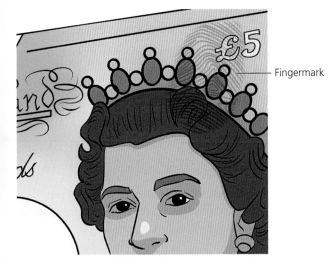

Figure 3.8 A copy of the image used for the experiment showing where the fingerprint was placed, obscured in the top right-hand corner of a £50 note

The materials that each participant was given in the study were:

- one of the 14 printed finger marks
- the relevant ten-print fingerprint form (the suspect's fingerprints)
- the crime scene examiner's report
- a sheet of paper advising participants of the context and including the information that the print was made by the right forefinger.

Procedure

All participants took part in the study as part of their normal working day and were tested in a typical fingerprint analysis room within the New Scotland Yard Fingerprint Bureau. Each was given access to a fingerprint magnifying glass and a Russell Comparator (an optical magnifying unit for comparing two images). They were told to act as they would in a working day, that they could come and go as they pleased, but that they could not discuss the prints they were analysing, nor discuss the details of the experiment. There was no time limit imposed and participants were instructed to treat the experimental material as an ordinary case.

The research was conducted anonymously with each participant identifying themselves on their question sheets using a unique reference number they were given. Using an independent groups design, half of the participants were assigned to a low-emotional context condition and half to high-emotional context condition:

- Low emotional context condition – participants were given an examination report referring to an

allegation of forgery. This was chosen as it is seen as a 'victimless' crime and carries a relatively minor sentence. The modus operandi stated that a 'suspect entered the premises and tried to pay for goods with a forged £50 note. The forgery was spotted by cashier. The suspect then decamped.'

- High-emotional context condition – participants were given an examination report referring to an allegation of murder. This was chosen as there is, inevitably, a victim and it carried the most severe sentence. The final wording of the examination report was altered to read 'suspect then fired two shots at victim before decamping'.

The authors point out that it is usual to refer to the person being investigated as a 'suspect' in the identification of fingerprints but this does not imply any assumption of guilt. Indeed, 'many suspect checks completed by the fingerprint bureau result in no identification'.

The participants filled in a demographic information sheet stating where they worked, their years of experience as an expert, and whether they had ever presented evidence in court. They then completed the examination and were asked to decide if the mark was:

1. Identification (a match).
2. Not an identification (not a match).
3. Insufficient (not enough detail to undertake a comparison).
4. Insufficient detail to establish identity – some detail in agreement but not enough to individualise.

They were also asked to elaborate by providing details of their observations and opinions.

Finally, they filled in the specially designed feedback questionnaire which asked them whether or not they had referred to the crime scene information and, if they had, which part (allegation, modus operandi, date, venue, victim, details of crime scene examination). If they said they had referred to the crime scene report they were also asked if, in their own judgement, the information contained in the report had affected their analysis and, if so, how.

Results

- 57 out of 70 of the participants said they had read the crime scene report, and 30 of these were in the high-emotional context condition.
- 52 per cent of the 30 who reads the report in the high-emotional context condition said they believed it had influenced their decision, compared with 6 per cent in the low-emotional context condition

 Stop and ask yourself ...

- In what way can the ecological validity of this research be challenged?
- In what way can the ecological validity of this research be supported?

Links to research methods
- Ecological validity

The results can be seen in Table 3.2.

Table 3.2 Experts' final opinions of the fingerprint comparison for the low and high contexts

	Number of experts giving final opinion as			
	Identification	Insufficient not suitable for comparison	Some detail in agreement but not sufficient to identify	No identification
High context	6	15	13	1
Low context	7	12	16	0

A chi-squared analysis of the data was conducted which revealed that no significant difference in outcome was observed between the two emotional contexts.

Discussion

In contrast to previous research with non-experts, this research studied fingerprint experts and found that emotional context in the form of knowledge of the type of crime (forgery or murder) did not bias the analysis of ambiguous fingerprints.

Hall and Player suggest that the difference between this study's results and those of research into non-experts could be explained by the experience of the fingerprint experts. The study also showed that 19 per cent of the fingerprint experts did not report reading the crime scene report, suggesting that this information was considered surplus to requirements and was unnecessary for the process of analysing the fingerprints.

The authors also point out that:

... whilst the identifications did not significantly vary between the two groups, 50 per cent of examiners that were given the murder context stated that the severity of the case had an effect on their analysis. Only 6 per cent of the experts given the low-emotional context stated that the examination report had any effect. This shows that even if experts think that a serious crime-type has affected their analysis the final outcome has not been affected. Fingerprint experts appear more adept at dealing with fingerprint analysis in a non-emotional detached manner than non-experts.

Conclusions

The authors conclude that this study suggests that emotional context did not detract from the fingerprint experts' capacity to make a final decision.

Application: strategies for reducing bias in the collection and processing of forensic evidence

The fact that forensic evidence is not totally perfect or totally objective does not mean it is not a powerful ally in the criminal justice system. However, it is important that the integrity and reliability of forensic evidence is maintained and improved, and that it is appropriately presented and perceived in court. (Dror, 2012)

There are a number of strategies that could be used to reduce errors caused by cognitive bias in the analysis of forensic evidence. According to Dror (2012) and Kassin et al. (2013) these might include:

- Educating detectives, judges and juries and the general public as to the strengths and weaknesses of forensic science, portraying a realistic and scientifically based picture of forensic evidence and specifically pointing out its subjective nature and vulnerabilities to bias. For example, in a court case it may be useful for a judge to ask what an examiner knew about the case, and when they knew it.

 Stop and ask yourself ...

- Can you explain why Hall and Player's study did not support the reliability of Dror *et al.*'s (2006) study into emotional context as a biasing factor in the analysis of fingerprints?

Links to research methods
- Reliability

 Stop and ask yourself ...

- Write a paragraph to explain the contribution made by the key research by Hall and Player to our understanding of the impact of psychology on the collection and processing of forensic evidence.

Links to
- Check your understanding

- Training forensic examiners to acknowledge and minimise bias. Awareness of bias is an important step in dealing with it, but it cannot be turned off and on by willpower or awareness alone. Training by cognitive experts could make an important contribution in helping practitioners minimise the influence of cognitive bias on their decisions. For example, forensic science education could include training in basic psychology that is relevant to forensic work, such as aspects of perception, judgement and decision making.
- Proper protocols and procedures are essential if bias is to be avoided. One such protocol is 'sequential unmasking' – a method of controlling examiner bias in forensic analysis by ensuring that irrelevant information that could bias the examiner's decision is filtered out of the process of analysing the evidence. This would mean that the examiner would focus more on bottom-up processing of the evidence, and the process would be more objective as this constitutes a form of 'blind testing'.
- A similar use of a 'blind testing' protocol should be employed in the verification process. That is, when asked to verify a forensic decision the verifier should not be aware of the initial conclusion, and it would be preferable if the verifier was also unaware of the identity of the initial examiner. The examiner should also not be the one to select the verifier. This would avoid conformity bias. A further step might be to conduct cross-laboratory verification if cost and time permitted.
- It is possible that any single item, whether it be a hair sample or a fingerprint, from one suspect might unconsciously lead to a false positive identification from an examiner, as they may be responding to the need-determination perception bias and be highly motivated to find a match. A way to combat this bias is suggested by research by Miller (1987) who presented student subjects with either a hair sample from one suspect to match to evidence or gave them, based on the principle of an identity line-up, a 'line up' of evidence where five hair samples from five suspects were offered for comparison. This has been shown to reduce the number of false positive identifications. This method, which is often called a 'six pack', could be used as a standard protocol in order to reduce bias in the analysis of forensic evidence such as fingerprint matching.

Other suggestions might include searching for the negative; that is, instead of looking for evidence that two fingerprints match, try to find convincing evidence that they do not match. This supports an investigative method whereby falsification of opinions provides a scientific approach to the analysis of forensic evidence.

Experts can also be trained to be more aware of their own biases and seek to minimise their effect, for example limiting the overconfidence bias by always being prepared to consult peers, no matter how experienced and expert they might be in their field.

Even highly qualified experts in forensic science with decades of experience are not infallible – they are subject to the same biases in cognition and psychology in their working life as everyone is. Putting some, or even all, of the suggested strategies in place could help to reduce bias in the collection of forensic evidence.

Have a go yourself

The scientist in charge of a large forensic science laboratory has been made aware of three false positive fingerprint matches from her team in the space of a month.

- How could she educate her team members to try to reduce the incidence of false positive results?
- Suggest **two** other strategies she could use to try to reduce the number of false positive fingerprint matches coming from her laboratory.

Collection of evidence (Cognitive)

An important method used by the police to collect evidence from both witnesses and suspects is the police interview. This topic considers the different techniques used to interview both suspects and eyewitnesses, and their implications.

Collection and use of evidence from witnesses and suspects

Interviewing suspects

At one time it was considered acceptable to extract confessions using physical force under interrogation. Fortunately, we now live in more enlightened times and, therefore, techniques used by the police to elicit confessions from suspects must be more humane. As a result, the techniques that are used in interrogations today are designed not to physically coerce or intimidate but instead to psychologically manipulate the suspect into confessing. An example of this comes from the techniques commonly used in the USA.

Fred Inbau and John Reid were the co-authors of the book *Criminal Interrogation and Confessions*, a police handbook first published in 1962, regularly updated and still used widely in police training in the USA today. This manual includes a number of techniques for interviewing and interrogating suspects, collectively known as the 'Reid Technique', or more correctly the Reid Technique**s**, since a number of different techniques are described; it includes what is known as the Reid Nine Steps of Interrogation. Interrogation differs from interviews primarily in the fact that interrogation is guilt presumptive and accusatory. A summary of the differences between suspect interviews and suspect interrogations as used in the Reid Technique is shown in Table 3.3.

Table 3.3 The differences between suspect interviews and suspect interrogations in the Reid Technique

Interview	Interrogation
Non-accusatory	Accusatory
Dialogue – question and answer format	Monologue – discourage the suspect from talking until ready to tell the truth
Goals: ● Elicit investigative and behavioural information ● Assess the subject's truthfulness ● Profile the subject for possible interrogation	Goals: ● Elicit the truth ● Obtain a court-admissible confession if it is believed that the suspect is guilty
Note taking following each response	No note taking until after the suspect has told the truth

In the Reid Nine Steps, the interrogation is built around active persuasion by moral justification. The interrogator initially presents a monologue and discourages the suspect from denials or explanations. The interrogator progresses the suspect towards an admission by the use of alternative or contrasting questions, offering the suspect two choices, one of which is less morally challenging than the other. A critical part of the process is the development of information that will corroborate and substantiate the suspect's admission of guilt, leading to a written confession being signed in front of witnesses that will be used as evidence against the suspect in court.

Table 3.4 The Reid Nine Steps of Interrogation

Step 1: positive confrontation	Tell the suspect that the evidence all confirms that there is no doubt that he or she is guilty of the crime.
	Following the interview [interrogation often follows on directly from an initial interview] the investigator should step out of the room for a short period of time. Upon returning, he should have in his hand a folder containing the results of the investigation. The investigator should stand directly in front of the suspect and in a confident manner and tone of voice confront the suspect with a statement of guilt.
Step 2: theme development	The interrogator will sit down and then try to shift the blame away from the suspect to some other person or set of circumstances that prompted the suspect to commit the crime. That is, they will try to develop themes containing reasons that will justify or excuse the crime, e.g. you killed your partner, but only after severe provocation, or you robbed your boss but only because you needed the money and they did not pay you well enough. Themes may be developed or changed to find one to which the accused is most responsive. The aim is to provide a moral justification for the crime that the suspect will accept and, in doing so, confess to the crime.
Step 3: handling denials	In the initial stages of an interrogation, the suspect will very rarely sit quietly and listen to the investigator without making some effort to deny the crime. Never allow the suspect to deny guilt:
	If you've let him talk and say the words 'I didn't do it', and the more often a person says 'I didn't do it', the more difficult it is to get a confession. Interrogators need to watch for signals that the suspect is about to make a denial. Guilty suspects often do this by saying 'Can I just say something?' or a similar phrase; interrogators can use these cues to block any denials the suspect might want to offer.
Step 4: overcoming objections	Suspects will attempt to assert their innocence and deny their guilt by offering objections; for example, they may say 'I'd be too scared to do it', or 'I love my wife [and so would not have hurt her]', 'I love my job [so I would not steal from my employer], 'I don't even know him' or 'I don't even own a gun'. The interrogator should not argue with these objections, but instead should acknowledge them and use them, perhaps to develop the theme that the suspect did it but it was out of character:
	I hope that's true – that you do love your job. That just reinforces my point. Now I know you are basically an honest person, a good hard worker, who just made a mistake. The interrogator should try to use this to move towards a confession.

Step 5: procurement and retention of suspect's attention	After their objections have been put down or turned around to imply their guilt, the suspect often tunes out, becomes withdrawn and quiet. It is important for the interrogator to re-engage the attention of the suspect to make sure that the suspect can be directed towards the theme, which is the justification for their guilt, and is stopped from sitting and thinking about the possibility of punishment, as that will reinforce the suspect's resolve to deny the crime. The interrogator should reinforce sincerity (e.g. by keeping good eye contact and using first names) to ensure that the suspect is receptive. Additionally, the interrogator may lean forward and be in closer proximity to the suspect as this will help draw and hold their attention.
Step 6: handling the suspect's passive mood	In this stage the suspect may become passive and may appear defeated, having had their denials and objections rejected. They may have realised that confession to their crime is now inevitable. If the suspect cries at this point, this is due to remorse and should be used to infer their guilt and move towards a confession. If the suspect does not cry, they may adopt a defeated pose, head bowed, slumped shoulders and the interrogator may reinforce sincerity and support, perhaps by putting a hand on their shoulder. The interrogator should use an understanding and sympathetic demeanour to reinforce the theme that infers guilt.
Step 7: presenting an alternative question	An 'alternative question' is presented, giving the suspect two choices for what happened; one more socially acceptable than the other. The suspect is expected to choose the easier option but whichever alternative the suspect chooses, guilt is admitted. The alternative question would develop from the theme, so if it was about stealing money at work, the question might be: 'Did you do it to get back at your boss, or did you do it because were you desperate for the money to pay your bills?' If the theme was based on the crime being out of character, the question might be: 'Is this the first time you have done this, or have you done it lots of times before?' The alternative question should be posed such that the suspect can agree with the interrogator by simply nodding their head or saying a few words, so the question may be followed up with supporting statements that suggest that the more socially acceptable answer can be agreed to, for example: 'I think you did this because you were up to your neck in debt and you were having problems at home and just didn't know what else to do, isn't that why you did it?' The acceptance by the suspect of either of the alternative explanations in the question is a confession of guilt, of course.
Step 8: get the suspect to confess orally and to tell in full the details of their crime	Following an admission of guilt the suspect is encouraged to relate what happened in the crime and the interrogator will ask questions to elicit details and to clarify points.
Step 9: conversion of the oral confession into a written or audio or videotaped confession	In this final stage the suspect writes, or the interrogator writes on their behalf, a full account of their crime, or it is audio or videotaped. This is done in front of a witness brought in, who might be someone else involved in the investigation or a duty solicitor. The suspect, interrogator and witness all sign the confession.

Extracts from Reid Associates

Inbau explains that all nine steps will not always be used and, apart from the initial confrontation step and final admission of guilt/confession step, the order in which the steps are used is not invariant. The Reid Techniques use psychology to manipulate the suspect into a confession. The process is designed to increase anxiety in the suspect and to motivate the suspect to want to get out of the interrogation room, which of course he or she can only do by confessing.

Is this a justifiable way to elicit a confession from a suspect? Inbau argues that these steps are indeed justified since you are interrogating someone whom you believe to be guilty on the basis of your preliminary interview. A confession from the suspect benefits society as if it leads to a guilty plea – time and money is saved as a lengthy trial is not necessary. This can also reduce the anxiety and distress caused to the suspect's victims and can offer them earlier closure on their traumatic experience.

However, the Reid Techniques have been criticised, largely because they too often fail to identify innocent suspects and, as a result, have led to coerced compliant false confessions, where the person falsely confesses to

a crime under the duress of the interrogation. The Reid training manual would suggest that this is not likely and confidently claims that an innocent suspect would not move beyond stage three of the nine steps and assumes, therefore, that any suspect moving into step four must be guilty.

While you might share the opinion of many people, including judges and jury members, that nothing would induce an innocent person to confess to a crime that they did not commit, there is a great deal of evidence to the contrary. Gisli Gudjonsson is a psychologist who is an expert in false confessions. He was involved in a number of high-profile cases in the 1980s which showed that the police had coerced false confessions in the cases of IRA bombings, for example the case of the Birmingham Six. The Birmingham Six were six men who were sentenced to life imprisonment in 1975 but, after a long battle to prove their innocence, eventually had their convictions overturned in 1991 on the grounds that they were 'unsafe and unsatisfactory', despite the fact that signed confessions had been obtained from four of the six men.

Gudjonsson (2003) argues there are four factors surrounding every confession that need to be investigated to find out if a confession has been produced through coercion:

1. **The defendant**: false confessions are more likely from the very young, the very old, those with low IQs and sufferers from mental disorders (for example depression, schizophrenia).
2. **The arrest**: suspects arrested suddenly, violently or in the middle of the night, or interrogated for long periods or at night, are more likely to make false confessions.
3. **Mental/physical state**: confessions are unreliable where the suspect is stressed, anxious, ill or intoxicated.
4. **The interrogation**: coercive, biased or leading interview tactics can encourage vulnerable suspects to make false confessions.

In addition, scoring high on the GSS (Gudjonsson Suggestibility Scale) may identify if a suspect was susceptible to offering a coerced compliant confession. For example, Gudjonsson notes that the four members of the Birmingham Six who did confess scored higher for suggestibility on the GSS than the two who asserted their innocence.

In the UK, procedures have been put in place to try to reduce the likelihood of false confessions. Code E of the Police and Criminal Evidence Act (PACE) (1984) requires all interviews to be recorded in triplicate: a working copy for the police, one for the solicitor and one sealed at the end of the interview and not to be opened until the case is in court, to ensure evidence cannot be tampered with. This ensures that the interview is not coercive and does not lead the suspect, for example by 'feeding' information to them through questions that the suspect later uses to construct a (false) confession. In addition, under the PACE code vulnerable suspects are supposed to be identified and assigned an 'appropriate adult', a role often undertaken by volunteer members of the public, to sit in with them in the interview. Gudjonsson suggests, though, that such vulnerable suspects are still not routinely identified and appropriate adults assigned to them.

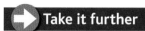 **Take it further**

'You have the right to remain silent …'

Part of the PACE code of conduct includes informing a suspect of their rights, including the right to remain silent and the right to a solicitor. Suspects' rights are given when they are arrested:

You do not have to say anything, but it may harm your defence if you do not mention when questioned something which you later rely on in court. Anything you do say may be given in evidence.

The US equivalent of this is the Miranda Rights, and the right to remain silent is considered to be a constitutional right, known as 'taking the fifth amendment'. The Miranda Rights inform suspects of their right to remain silent, while 'taking the fifth amendment' refers to an amendment to the American Bill of Rights which means that you have the right not to testify if that testimony might implicate you or lead to your conviction for a criminal offence.

The introduction of the Miranda Rights was not welcomed by Fred Inbau. Inbau saw the Miranda Rights as a trend towards putting the rights of the suspect before the rights of society, and he campaigned strongly against this.

What are the implications for the collection of evidence by the police through interview if the suspect upholds their right to silence?

 Find out more

In approximately 30 per cent of the wrongful convictions overturned with DNA evidence, defendants made false confessions, admissions or statements to law enforcement officials or pled guilty.' (The Innocence Project)

Visit the Innocence Project website (www.innocenceproject.org) to read case histories of false confession and to find out more about how the system could be improved to try to reduce false confessions being given in police interviews.

 Stop and ask yourself …

- In the British legal system a defendant is presumed innocent until proven guilty, so accusatory and anxiety-provoking interrogation techniques that, solicitors and suspects may argue, lead suspects to confess under duress are not acceptable police practice in the UK. So the techniques designed by Inbau and Reid should not be used. Nonetheless, false confessions still happen despite the safeguards put in place to try to prevent this. Can you suggest reasons why?

Links to
- Check your understanding

Interviewing witnesses

'Tell me in your own words what you can remember about the person who took your handbag…'

Figure 3.9 Police officers have to be skilful to help witnesses remember events of crimes they have seen happen or been a victim of themselves

From the core study by Loftus and Palmer (1974) into eyewitness testimony, you will be familiar with the idea that witness evidence may not always be accurate. Most witnesses who the police and detectives interview are co-operative witnesses who want to help the investigation with their testimony. However, human memory is fallible and a witness can be led to reconstruct their memory of an event to incorporate information they hear after the event, for example from other witnesses or from media reports of events. It is the task of police interviewers to elicit detailed and accurate information from witnesses. A commonly used technique in which police officers and detectives are trained is the cognitive interview (CI) technique, or the enhanced cognitive interview (ECI) technique.

Ronald Fisher and Edward Geiselman worked together to produce a technique designed to improve the accuracy of witness testimony collected in police interviews. Their work culminated in the development of the original CI technique as a framework for detectives and police to use when interviewing witnesses. Fisher and Geiselman (1984) based the technique on two principles derived directly from empirical research into memory. Firstly, psychological research into context- and cue-dependent memory suggested that recall is better if the cues to recall or context in which recall is taking place match the cues and context in which encoding of the material took place. You will be familiar with the concept of context dependent memory from the core study by Grant *et al*. (1998). Secondly, there may be more than one retrieval path to the to-be-remembered event, and if one retrieval cue does not effectively

trigger recall, other cues may do so. Based on these two principles, the original CI technique was made up of four memory retrieval techniques designed to get as much accurate detail from the witness as possible:

- **Report everything**: witnesses are asked to report everything they can recall from the event, regardless of how trivial or irrelevant it may appear to them. It is hoped that the details will cue and enrich the witness' memory of the central events, increasing the accuracy of their testimony. Even if the details do not prompt further recall it is useful for the police to get details of events as they may help them build up a picture of what happened during the event when used in conjunction with the testimony of other witnesses to the event.

- **Recall in different temporal orders**: witnesses are asked to recall events in different orders, for example starting halfway through a sequence of events and then working backwards, or recalling the whole event in reverse order. It is hoped that varying the temporal order of recall will offer cues to trigger recall of events. It also helps to prevent a person's schemas or scripts from distorting their testimony. In trying to create a beginning-to-end narrative there is a danger that the witness will reconstruct the event, so recalling backwards may help them remember what was happening at the supermarket tills when a robbery was taking place in the to-be-remembered event rather than a version of events that is affected by the witness' script of what usually happens at the supermarket tills.

- **Mental reinstatement of context**: it is not always practical or ethical to interview witnesses at the scene of the crime, so instead witnesses are asked to mentally take themselves back to the scene of the crime and imagine the noise, the smells, whether it was dark or light, who else was there, etc. As well as mentally reinstating the physical context, the witness is encouraged to mentally reinstate their internal state at the time of the to-be-remembered event, including their thoughts and feelings at the time.

- **Recall from a variety of different perspectives**: the witness is encouraged to describe the event as others present may have seen it, for example as other witnesses, the victim or the perpetrator may have seen the incident, although it is important for them to only report things they actually saw themselves to avoid the possibility of reconstruction of their memory of events.

Reporting everything and recalling in different temporal orders are techniques designed to aid cue retrieval using a variety of retrieval paths. Mental reinstatement of context and recalling from a variety of perspectives are designed to prompt memory using the principles of context-dependent or cue-dependent memory.

Fisher *et al.* (1989) conducted research to test the use of the CI technique in a real-life setting, to see if it enhanced memory of both witnesses and victims of real crimes. A field experiment was carried out using interviews with real witnesses by 16 detectives from the robbery division of the Metro-Dade Police Department, Florida. Most of the interviews were with victims of commercial crimes or handbag snatching. Seven of the detectives were trained to use the CI technique in four one-hour sessions. Their interviewing performance was compared with a group of nine detectives not trained in CI techniques. In addition, the performance of the trained detectives before and after training was compared. Both groups of detectives tape recorded their interviews in the four months before the training happened, and a total of 88 interviews were recorded before and 47 in total were recorded in the seven months after the training had taken place, with each of the 16 detectives recording between two and seven interviews each. The tapes were sent to a team at the University of California, who analysed them and quantified the amount of information the interviews had gathered. This team were blind to the condition they were analysing, so did not know whether the tapes were from CI-trained detectives or not. The findings supported the prediction that the detectives using the CI technique obtained more information during the interviews. The seven trained detectives' interviews obtained 63 per cent more information than the interviews by their non-CI-trained colleagues. Similarly, the trained detectives showed a 47 per cent increase in information after CI training than before CI training. The authors concluded that because the CI technique reliably enhances memory and is easily learned and administered, it should be useful for a variety of investigative interviews.

Subsequent research has confirmed the effectiveness of the CI technique in eliciting not only more information from witnesses but also doing so without loss of accuracy.

In 1992 Fisher and Geiselman revised the CI technique to create the enhanced cognitive interview (ECI). They recognised that the memory-retrieval techniques from the CI technique would work more effectively if they were presented within a competent interview framework. The ECI consists of a number of stages (see Table 3.5 below) and training in its use involves training police interviewers not only how to employ memory-retrieval techniques and mnemonic cues, but also how to set up and manage an interview that will put the interviewee at their ease and enable the most detailed and accurate account to be given.

For example, at the beginning of the interview, the interviewer is taught that there is a need to establish rapport with the interviewee. If the interviewee feels relaxed and comfortable they will be able to relax and report their testimony. Establishing a rapport, perhaps by talking for a short while about a neutral topic, may help the interviewee manage their anxiety. Anxiety takes up cognitive processing capacity and can interfere with the retrieval of testimony, so the interviewer has to be skilled in helping the witness relax and feel safe. Anxiety will also be reduced if the interviewer informs the witness before the interview of what is expected. Witnesses have probably never been interviewed before and their experience (from films or television crime programmes) may mean they have a distorted idea of what the interview should be like. For example, they should be told that the interview will encourage focused retrieval on their part, and that this will require them to think hard about what happened, that they should be prepared to report everything, however unimportant it may seem. They should be told that they are the one who will be doing all the mental work and most of the talking in the interview (this is known as transfer of control from the interviewer to the witness).

Following this preparation, the stages move on to context reinstatement and free report, then questioning. The ECI training specifies that leading questions must be avoided and that the most effective questions are open-ended. The ECI also describes a type of questioning designed to enhance a witness' recall. This is called interviewee-compatible or witness-compatible questioning. This means that the interviewer should match their questions to the element of the event that the witness is currently describing; so, if they were describing a getaway car it would be appropriate to ask them questions such as what colour the car was or what type of car, as these would offer prompts to help the witness enhance the mental picture of the car that they are currently thinking of. It would not be appropriate, however, to ask about the perpetrator's clothing at this point as this would require the witness to shift their 'mental image' to a different event.

Another type of retrieval cue used in the ECI might be for the witness to sketch, perhaps a plan of where the event took place, to help cue their memory. Other mnemonic techniques are also used, such as 'memory jogs'. Milne (2004) describes how memory for names could be cued by asking the witness 'Is it a common or unusual name?', 'Is it a short or long name? How many syllables?' or by using the 'first letter technique' where the interviewer goes through the alphabet and asks the witness to stop them at the first letter of the name.

Table 3.5 Structure of the enhanced cognitive interview

Phase 1	Greet and personalise the interview and establish rapport
Phase 2	Explain the aims of the interview • Focused retrieval and concentrate hard • Report everything • Transfer control
Phase 3	Initiate a free report • Context reinstatement • Open-ended questions • Pauses and no interruptions
Phase 4	Questioning • Report everything • Interviewee-compatible questioning • OK to say 'don't know' • OK to say 'don't understand' • Activate and probe an image • Open and appropriate closed questions
Phase 5	Varied and extensive retrieval • Change the temporal order • Change perspectives • Focus on all senses
Phase 6	Investigatively important questions
Phase 7	Summary
Phase 8	Closure
Phase 9	Evaluation

Source: Milne (2004)

In comparison with the original CI, the ECI takes longer to learn and requires more from the interviewer, and to become proficient in the technique requires practice. The level of success of the ECI technique, as with all methods, may depend heavily on the skill and experience of the interviewer.

Critics of both the CI and ECI techniques suggest that they are too time consuming to use fully in an investigation. In order to reduce the amount of time it takes, officers often do not use all the stages. Fisher (2010) suggests that this is likely to be at the expense of establishing a rapport, which is important for the technique to be fully successful. Dando *et al.* (2009) also point out that while the current investigative interview framework for police officers in England and Wales (and many other countries) recommends the use of the CI, research consistently shows that mental reinstatement of context (MRC) is not regularly used or is often poorly applied. Dando *et al.* suggested that this might be because it is time consuming.

Despite these criticisms, when used according to the stages the ECI offers an established, thorough and effective protocol for interviewing witnesses to crime that has a scientific basis in empirical psychological research. In addition, it includes a number of retrieval techniques and mnemonics that can be used separately when time

is limited to assist interviewees in giving full and accurate accounts of the events that they have witnessed.

The key research in this topic by Memon and Higham (1999) offers a review of the CI technique.

Key research: Memon and Higham (1999) A review of the cognitive interview

In this 1999 article, Memon and Higham present the evidence for the CI technique as it stood at that time. The article presents theoretical and methodological issues that they believed needed to be considered in relation to research into the CI technique and its practical use in the field.

The article is in four sections:

1. the effectiveness of various components of the CI technique
2. comparison interviews
3. measures of memory
4. quality of training.

We will summarise these in turn.

The effectiveness of various components of the CI technique

In this section the authors focus on the four main cognitive techniques from the original CI, briefly describing each in turn and noting any evidence or issues related to the technique.

- **Mental context reinstatement**: this is where the witness is instructed to mentally reconstruct the external and internal contexts which existed at the time of the crime.
  - Milne (1997) showed that context reinstatement used alone obtains as much information from witnesses as the complete CI procedure, although other psychological research into the effectiveness of context has produced mixed results.
- **Report everything**: this is where the witness is given the instruction to recall, without 'screening', all the details from the to-be-remembered event, even if they consider them irrelevant or only partially remember them.
- **Recall from a variety of perspectives**: 'This technique tries to encourage the witness to place themselves in the shoes of the victim (if the witness is not a victim) or of another witness to report what they would have seen' (Memon and Highham, 1999).
  - A problem identified with recalling from different perspectives is that there is the possibility that this may lead to the witness fabricating data, or

that the technique might confuse the witness. In practice police interviewers tend not to use this element and some express concern about it misleading a witness.

- In support of this technique, Milne (1997) showed there is some evidence that instructing a witness to recall from a variety of perspectives can produce as much accurate information as the other CI techniques, but does not increase the amount of information recalled compared with the other CI techniques.

- **Make retrieval attempts from different starting points (recall in different temporal orders):** by encouraging witnesses to recall in a variety of orders, for example from the end, the middle or from the most memorable event, the CI technique assumes the witness will be cued to recall extra details.
  - In support of this technique, Geiselman and Callot (1990) found it was more effective to recall in forward order once followed by reverse order, rather than to make two attempts at recall from the beginning.
  - Other researchers, however, have failed to prove that this technique yields more information than a second retrieval attempt when used in the context of a cognitive interview (for example, Memon et al., 1997).

Memon and Higham suggest that in order to fully test the effectiveness of each component of the CI, they need to be studied separately. Memon et al. 1996, for example, tested context reinstatement against recall from a variety of perspectives, recall from a variety of orders and a control group who were given the instruction to 'try harder' in a sample of 5–8-year-olds. This study found no differences between the CI techniques and no difference of any of the techniques compared with the control group. A second study on 5–9-year-olds confirmed these findings. However, the authors point out that these findings may have been caused by the age of those tested – it has been shown that young children have difficulty using the cognitive techniques.

Research by Milne (1997) compared the full CI procedure against each of the four separate cognitive techniques and against a control group who were told simply 'make a second retrieval attempt'. The participants were adults and children who acted as mock witnesses to a filmed event. The results supported the reliability of Memon et al.'s findings as no difference in the number of correct or incorrect details were recorded across the four CI techniques and the control. The results also showed that the full CI technique elicited more information than the single conditions, except for cognitive reinstatement.

Memon and Higham conclude that this suggests that context reinstatement is the most effective cognitive component of the CI technique and that recall from a different perspective and recall in different orders do not appear to be effective technique by themselves, and may introduce problems in terms of confusing the witness or encouraging them to make up information.

The authors do concede, however, that research into this is sparse, and it may be that using the CI technique as a whole has a 'synergising effect on memory retrieval and/or monitoring'.

Comparison interviews

Valid research into the effectiveness of the CI technique should show that it leads to enhanced memory performance in comparison with other police interviewing techniques. But which would offer the best comparison? Memon and Higham consider three other interviewing techniques, the so-called standard interview, the guided memory interview (GMI) and the structured interview (SI):

1. The 'standard interview' is the name given to the type of interview that police officers used prior to the introduction of the CI. While Memon and Higham suggest it was appropriately used as a comparison in early research into the CI technique (for example, in Fisher et al.'s 1989 study of detectives), the fact is that the 'standard' interview was 'somewhat a misnomer given that such interviews are highly variable and far from standard'. Memon and Higham recommend that the standard interview not be used as a comparison in research into the CI since comparisons between the two types of interview would be confounded by:
    - the large individual differences in techniques employed by interviewers using the standard interview, and
    - the motivation of witnesses interviewed using the CI procedure, who may be more highly motivated by the attention they receive in the CI technique compared with a standard interview.

Therefore the standard technique should not be used as it is not an appropriate comparison, especially if the aim of the study is to test the specific effects of the CI techniques on memory.

2. Memon and Higham say that 'the guided memory interview (GMI) draws upon principles of contextual reinstatement as does the CI and by encouraging the witness to mentally reinstate context guides their memory'. This means that the GMI interview would provide a good comparison with the CI technique if the aim of the study was to establish whether the effects of the CI technique on memory

are due to context reinstatement alone or to a combination of its cognitive components.

As pointed out earlier, however, the ECI is more than just the cognitive techniques, and Memon and Higham suggest that for the ECI 'a more appropriate control would be a procedure that achieves good rapport with the witness without using special mnemonic techniques'.

3. They suggest that the structured interview (SI) would be useful here because: 'SI interviewers are persuaded to build rapport with the witness, to allow the witness the opportunity to give narrative descriptions, and to provide ample time for interviewees to respond. Additionally the SI is non-interruptive, expansive, confidence building and fosters the use of good questioning techniques (e.g. active listening, use of open questions, appropriate non-verbal behaviour)'.

The SI, then, is much like the ECI, only minus the cognitive components for enhancing memory performance, and would therefore provide a reasonably good control group if the aim of the research was to measure the effectiveness of the cognitive components within the CI.

Measures of memory

Memon and Higham suggest that research into the CI technique had to this point used fairly simplistic measures of memory performance, including the percentage of correct interview statements elicited or the absolute number of correct/incorrect statements.

These methods do not, for example, allow predictions to be made about how the CI techniques might influence memory monitoring. When a person is asked a question, they search in their long-term memory for possible answers, which are called candidate responses. From these the most likely candidate response is selected and, if it fits the person's response criteria, then they will offer the response. In a standard police interview their response criteria might be quite strict, for example 'I must tell the truth, the whole truth and nothing but the truth', and this might lead them to withhold a response if they are not 100 per cent sure. In the CI technique, the instruction to report everything suggests that a lower response criterion will be set. Memon and Higham suggest that Koriat and Goldsmith's (1994) model raises interesting questions in relation to the CI technique and could be used to inform more sophisticated testing of the impact of elements of the CI technique on memory performance.

Quality of training

Early studies into the CI technique often did not specify the type and quality of training given to interviewers. Sometimes training meant simply reading about the techniques from a brief handout. Sometimes the interviewers simply read out the instructions for the cognitive techniques, so did not require training. However, the ECI is more complex and requires more from the interviewer. In experimental research Memon reports that college student 'interviewers' in the ECI condition found the procedure more demanding and exhausting than their SI-trained counterparts.

A 1994 study by Memon et al. showed that interviewer training was important in encouraging officers to use the CI techniques. Experienced officers received a total of four hours training in the ECI technique. A comparison between CI-trained and SI-trained interviewers showed that the CI-trained officers did not elicit more information from witnesses to a staged event, and both the CI and SI officers demonstrated poor practice in terms of the number and types of questions used. The authors suggest that these results might have been affected by resistance to the training because of the trainer, and that future research using a police sergeant to deliver the training rather than an 'outsider' from a university might show if this was the case. The study also suggested a need for both improved training and more practice to encourage officers to use the CI techniques. Memon and Higham also report that the attitudes, motivation and prior experience of the officers being trained play a big role in determining the kind of results obtained with the CI.

Future research into CI training should obtain baseline measures of these variables, and should provide feedback to the officers on their performance to avoid slipping back into bad habits, and there is also a need to practise the CI technique. It may be that the CI is more efficient at enhancing the witness' memory when officers are able to conduct the interview without having to focus on the procedure.

Although acknowledging that research did not clearly suggest what would be the optimum amount of training to offer, Memon and Higham strongly advised a two-day CI training programme be used.

In order for police forces to benefit most fully from the CI technique they suggest that officers should be identified by potential (shows aptitude to be an excellent interviewer) for the training. While this might help the police to manage their training budgets, Memon and Higham point out that 'the problem with this strategy is that is assumes poor interviewers won't benefit from training and that training individuals who are already good interviewers will make them even better interviewers' and neither of these assumptions may be accurate.

Conclusions

Memon and Higham conclude: 'Although the CI has emerged as one of the most exciting developments over the last ten years, many questions remain unanswered', such as how do the various elements of the CI work? If there are effective components, what are they?

Research into the CI technique needs to establish a suitable control group depending on the aim of the study, and how the CI relates to other techniques could inform the choice of control group. The SI technique is suggested by the authors as a reasonable comparison with the CI.

Other problems to address in both research into the CI and training of officers in the CI technique also need to take into account interviewer variability in terms of attitude, prior interview experience and performance, and motivation.

Solutions to some of these problems will improve our understanding of the conditions under which the CI technique may be most useful as a forensic tool.

 **Have a go yourself**

Design experiments to investigate:

- whether the CI technique only works because of the mental reconstruction of context technique
- which of the four main cognitive techniques, if any, lead to increased amount of information being reported and to more accurate information
- how the use of the individual cognitive techniques compare to the use of the full CI technique
- whether the ECI technique is more effective than the CI at improving memory in witnesses
- whether the length of training in the CI technique affects the effectiveness of police officers' use of the technique.

Application: strategies for police interviews

The CI technique presents a number of suggestions, both as a whole and in terms of its cognitive components and the communications skills it suggests, which could be applied to help the police collect valid evidence from witness interviews.

In terms of interviewing suspects, the Reid Nine Steps offers a range of techniques in which a suspect could be led to confess in a police interview (in the USA).

Take it further

- Create a mind map for revision of all the ways you can think of in which the CI technique or ECI might be used to help police interviewers in the collection of evidence from witnesses.
- Create a mind map for revision of the techniques that a police officer (at least, in the USA) might use the Reid Techniques to help secure a confession from a suspect.

Reducing coerced compliant false confessions in police interviews: the PEACE technique and recording of interviews/interrogations

In the UK an interviewing technique that is based largely on the ECI has been devised. This is known as the PEACE technique and there is a version of this for use with witnesses as well as one for suspects. PEACE is an acronym for the stages of the interview:

- Preparation and planning
- Engage and explain
- Account
- Closure
- Evaluate.

When used with suspects the PEACE interview technique is referred to as an investigative interview and not an interrogation, and is less confrontational and more transparent than the Reid Techniques used in the USA. Kassin *et al.* (2010) suggest that in order to reduce the number of false confessions in the USA:

... that the PEACE approach to investigative interviewing offers a potentially effective alternative to the classic, confrontational style of interrogation.

Kassin also suggests that police and law enforcement agencies in the USA could also adopt a policy of recording police interviews and interrogations, although using video rather than the audio recordings that are used in the UK:

... it is also clear that the videotaping of full interviews and interrogations from a balanced camera perspective will improve the fact finding accuracy of judges, juries, and others who evaluate confessions ... we have reason to believe that many false confessions can be prevented, or at least better identified, thereby reducing the future incidence of wrongful convictions.

Psychology and the courtroom (Cognitive)

Figure 3.10 Under the system of trial by jury, whether or not the defendant (the person who is accused of the crime and is 'on trial') is guilty or not guilty is decided by a jury of his or her peers

Trial by jury

Under the system of trial by jury, whether or not the defendant (the person who is accused of the crime and is 'on trial') is guilty or not guilty is decided by a jury of his or her peers. A jury is usually made up of 12 ordinary members of the public between the ages of 18 and 70. In the UK, the electoral register is used to select people for jury service. It is mandatory for people summoned for jury service to act as jurors and, if they fail to turn up when summoned, they can receive a £1000 fine. While you don't get paid, your employer must release you from work for jury service, and you can claim expenses incurred while on jury service.

In the UK and USA an adversarial system is used in jury trials. The State or, in the UK, the Crown, is represented by the prosecution lawyer or team of lawyers and the defendant is represented by lawyers for the defence, whom they have employed or, if they cannot afford a defence lawyer, will have been appointed by the State to act on their behalf. The court is presided over by a judge. The job of the prosecution is to persuade the 12 jury members that the defendant is guilty as charged, beyond reasonable doubt, and the task for the defence is to persuade the jury that the prosecution has failed to do this. Note that it is not the job of the defence to prove the innocence of the defendant, but the job of the prosecution to prove the defendant guilty. By law, a defendant is considered to be innocent until proven guilty in a court of law.

Firstly the prosecution makes their case against the defendant and witnesses for the prosecution are called to the stand, or witness box, to give evidence against the defendant. The defence lawyer can cross-examine these witnesses. After the prosecution has finished presenting their case, it is the turn of the defence to present their case and witnesses to challenge the prosecution's case and to persuade the jury to return a verdict of not guilty. After the defence rests its case, the prosecution sums up their case for the jury, the defence sums up their case, and finally the judge instructs the jury on their responsibilities in deciding on a verdict. The jury then retires (goes to the jury room) to discuss the case and decide on a verdict. The court is dismissed while the jury is 'out'. Once the jury have decided their verdict the court reconvenes and the judge asks the jury's elected foreman to deliver their verdict. The judge then officially informs the defendant of the ruling and either tells them they are free to leave, or tells them that they have been convicted as charged, which usually leads to sentencing, although in a complicated trial sentencing may be deferred to a later hearing.

How juries can be persuaded by the characteristics of witnesses and defendants

In a jury trial, the jurors listen to both sides of the argument, weigh the evidence, discuss the case and finally they decide on a verdict. Clearly, the role of evidence is important in juridical decision making, but psychological research has revealed that jurors' decisions can be influenced not only by the evidence, but also by other variables, such as the attractiveness of the defendant, or the confidence of a witness. Identifying how extra-legal variables might influence a jury is an important area for research in the psychology of the courtroom as, if we want to ensure that a defendant receives a fair trial, we need to understand how jury members are reaching their verdicts.

As we have said, juries are made up of ordinary people from the general population, and as ordinary people they may have preconceived opinions and beliefs. The way a defendant or witness looks, whether they are male or female, their ethnicity, their age, the way they present themselves in terms of how they dress, their tattoos, how confident they appear to be in their testimony, their perceived status and social class are all factors that have an influence, whether conscious or unconscious, on how a defendant is evaluated by the jury.

Does witness confidence influence jury decision making?

Just because someone appears confident when giving their account of events, it does not mean that what they are saying is true. However, research has suggested that jurors tend to rely heavily on eyewitness factors that are not good indicators of accuracy, and one of these factors is how confident they perceive the witness to be.

While research has consistently shown that the relationship between confidence and accuracy is not a strong one, it seems that jurors mistakenly believe that the confidence of a witness is a strong indicator of whether their account of events is accurate or not. This suggests that the more confident the witness appears to be, the more likely they are to persuade the jury to accept their version of events when reaching their verdict.

Penrod and Cutler (1995) studied witness confidence in a series of studies including one where the confidence of a key female eyewitness was manipulated as the independent variable. In a videotaped mock trial for robbery, the key female eyewitness stated in her evidence that she was either 80 per cent confident about her identification of the suspect or 100 per cent confident. This study used an independent groups design. Participants (the mock jurors) included undergraduate students and experienced jurors. The dependent variable in the study was the percentage of guilty verdicts given in each confidence condition, and a significant difference was shown, with 60 per cent guilty verdicts being given in the 80 per cent confident condition and 67 per cent guilty verdicts being given in the 100 per cent confident condition. The level of confidence reported by the witness clearly influenced the juror's decision when reaching their verdict: the more confident the witness was, the more the jurors were persuaded.

However, since even in the 100 per cent confident condition 33 per cent not guilty verdicts were still given, it shows that witness confidence is only one of a number of factors that jurors can be influenced by. Other research by Penrod and Cutler, for example, showed in a variation of this study that when jurors were educated to assess good and bad witness identifying conditions in a case by an expert psychological witness, then witness confidence had less

influence over the mock juror's decisions. So, perhaps the confidence of the witness is only important to the juror if they have no other criteria on which to effectively judge the accuracy of the witness testimony.

Does the attractiveness of the defendant influence jury decision making?

One common attributional bias researched by Dion *et al.* (1972) is that people believe that 'what is beautiful is good'. We tend to believe that if someone is attractive to look at, then their personalities and behaviour will match. Dion named this bias the 'halo effect' – whereby we tend to assume that if a person displays one good characteristic, then they will have other positive characteristics and attributes as well.

Psychological research has suggested that attractive defendants are treated more leniently and unattractive defendants treated more harshly. For example, research by Stewart (1985) showed a negative correlation between participants' rating of 60 actual criminals' (a range of ages and 56 male, four female) attractiveness and the severity of their actual punishment, suggesting that the less attractive the defendant was, the more harshly they were likely to be punished.

A study that was conducted in 1975 by Sigall and Ostrove suggested a similar effect. However, Sigall and Ostrove also showed that the effect of attractiveness in the defendant on the jury's decision depends on the type of crime that they are on trial for. In a laboratory experiment using a sample of 120 college students (60 male and 60 female), participants read an account of a crime where the defendant was female. The independent variables were whether the crime was a burglary or involved swindling (fraud), and whether the participants read an account that described the female defendant as 'attractive', 'unattractive' or gave no information about her attractiveness (control group). Male and female participants were randomly assigned so that there were ten male and ten female in each attractiveness condition, and then allocated randomly to give five males and five females in each of the crime conditions. Sigall and Ostrove predicted that in a crime where the defendant's beauty would not be relevant, in this study burglary, that she would be treated more leniently by the mock jurors. However, if she was perceived to have used her beauty

---

🚫 **Stop and ask yourself ...**

- Why is it a problem if a juror relies on how confident a witness seems to be when reaching their verdict?
- How do we know from Penrod and Cutler's study that witness confidence is not the only factor that the mock jurors took into account in making their decision?

Links to
- Check your understanding

in her crime, for example swindling, then she would be treated more harshly. After reading the account of the crime, which strongly suggested that the defendant was guilty, the participants were asked to recommend a punishment for her in terms of a prison sentence from 1 to 15 years in jail.

As you can see from Table 3.6, the results support the predictions. The longest mean sentence was given in the attractive/swindling condition and the shortest sentence in the attractive/burglary condition.

Table 3.6 Mean sentence assigned in years to the female defendant in Sigall and Ostrove's (1975) study

Offence	Attractive defendant condition	Unattractive defendant condition	Control condition
Swindling	5.45	4.35	4.35
Burglary	2.8	5.2	5.1

The results support a cognitive explanation of the effect of attractiveness on the juror's decisions. In general, attractive people tend to be treated more generously as they are perceived as less dangerous and more virtuous. However, the jury is more condemning of a defendant who has used their 'gift' of beauty for ill-gotten gain. Attractive people who 'misuse' or take advantage of their beauty (for example, in swindles or confidence tricks) are perceived as being 'beautiful but dangerous'.

A meta-analysis of 80 studies conducted by Mazzella and Feingold in 1994 identified 25 studies into the effects of attractiveness on the judgements of mock jurors. In seven of these studies the mock jurors made a decision about guilt and in 18 they made a decision about sentencing. In each of these studies attractiveness was manipulated visually using photographs. The results of the meta-analysis suggested that mock jurors were generally more lenient towards attractive defendants than to unattractive defendants.

Conducting research into the psychology of the courtroom: the mock trial method

Manipulating variables to see their effects on real juries is neither ethical nor practical, so the method adopted in many psychological studies of jury decision making and persuasion is usually the 'mock trial' method, where participants play the role of jurors. The method used varies: sometimes the trial is presented as a transcript, where the juror participants read an account and then make their judgement, or sometimes as an audio or video recording. These are much shorter in duration than a real trial, naturally, with a study lasting typically from one to three hours in total. The tasks that the 'jurors' are asked to perform vary but commonly involve making their own individual decision on the verdict (guilty/not guilty), but they are also often asked about their level of confidence in the verdict, the reason for their decision or any sentence that might be an appropriate punishment.

The mock trial method provides an ethical way of investigating the variables that can impact on the courtroom and is more cost effective than alternatives, such as the use of a shadow jury in a real court case. Mock trials also allow for more participants to be involved in comparison with studies that use shadow juries. A further advantage of a mock trial is that the same evidence/trial proceedings can be used to test different hypotheses and conditions, providing some experimental control over the study by standardising the content of the trial proceedings. Mock trials also enable researchers to establish the reliability of the findings as the same mock trial method can be used with a different sample to test the consistency of the findings on replication.

A disadvantage of the mock trial method is that the 'jurors' are aware that this is not a real trial and that the freedom or otherwise of the defendant does not rest on their decision, so this lack of a 'high stakes' decision may mean that the studies lack realism (low ecological validity). Similarly, the tasks they are asked to do also lack ecological validity – real trials last longer, real jurors don't give individually assessed verdicts, real juries discuss the case, real juries do not decide on sentencing nor do they have to explain their verdicts, nor give an assessment of their confidence in their decision.

The validity problems with mock trials are compounded by the fact that undergraduate students often make up the sample – this group fails to represent real juries, which represent a broader range of ages and a wide range of educational and socio-economic backgrounds. Students often volunteer to be in these studies, too, and this is a further challenge to the population validity of these studies, as real jurors do not volunteer and can in fact be reluctant to serve on a jury at all and only do so because they have no choice!

 Stop and ask yourself ...

- Suggest four ways in which the tasks that participants were asked to perform in the study by Sigall and Ostrove differ from the tasks that jurors have to perform in a real trial.

Links to methodological issues
- Ecological validity

As we have seen, juridical decisions are affected not only by consideration of the evidence, but also by extra-legal factors such as witness confidence and the attractiveness of the defendant.

The key research for this topic by Dixon *et al.* (2002) investigated whether a further characteristic of the defendant – having a specific UK regional accent – would affect juror's decisions.

Key research: Dixon, Mahoney and Cocks (2002) Accents of guilt? Effects of regional accent, race, and crime type on attributions of guilt

Dixon *et al.* point out that psychological research has shown that people's accents have an effect on the impression that other people form of them, with standard accents being rated more positively than non-standard accents on traits such as competence or intelligence.

In a legal context, the effect of accent had been investigated in a 1983 study by Seggie in Australia where the effect of three accents – British received pronunciation (RP), broad Australian and Asian – were tested. Participants listened to a taped conversation where the alleged suspect pleaded his innocence, then made an assessment of his guilt.

Seggie's research showed that the effect of accent depended on the type of crime, with the broad Australian accent receiving higher guilt ratings for assault (a blue collar crime) and the RP accent receiving higher guilt ratings for theft (a white collar crime).

In this study, Dixon *et al.* aimed to further research the effect of accent in a legal context, in particular the Birmingham, or Brummie, accent. The Brummie accent had received generally more negative evaluations in studies compared with rural regional British accents or RP accents. Following on from this research, Dixon *et al.* predicted that a Brummie-accented suspect would receive a higher rating of guilt than a standard British-accented suspect.

Aims

The main aim of this study was to test the hypothesis that a Brummie-accented suspect would receive a higher rating of guilt than a suspect with a standard accent. It also aimed to see whether race or type of crime would make any difference to how the Brummie or standard speaking suspect was judged.

Method

Design

This study used a 2 × 2 × 2 factorial design, comparing a Brummie-accented suspect with a standard-accented suspect, and comparing black versus white suspects, and blue collar versus white collar crime.

Participants

The study was conducted in the psychology department at University College Worcester (now the University of Worcester). A sample of 119 white undergraduate students (24 male, 95 female, mean age 25.2) participated as part of their course requirements.

Participants who grew up in Birmingham were excluded. This control was used because it was assumed that those people who had a Brummie accent themselves or had grown up used to hearing the accent in a variety of contexts would not have the same negative biases against the accent.

Procedure

Participants listened to a two-minute recorded conversation based on a transcript of an interview that took place in a Birmingham police station in 1995. A standard-accented student in his 40s played the role of a middle-aged police inspector. The role of the suspect was played by a student in his 20s who was a 'natural code switcher', meaning he could speak in either a Brummie accent or a standard accent, having grown up

Stop and ask yourself ...

- What is meant by the mock trial method? Give examples from two psychological studies to support your answer.
- Outline two strengths of the mock trial method, giving examples from psychological studies to support your answer.
- Suggest four challenges to the validity of the mock trial method, giving examples from psychological research to support your answer.
- How might the use of the mock trial method be a challenge to the reliability of psychological research into how juries can be persuaded by the characteristics of witnesses and defendants?

Links to methodological issues
- Validity
- Reliability

near Birmingham but also having lived in other parts of England. He played both the Brummie- and standard-accented suspect on the tapes.

On the tape the police officer was interrogating the young man who was pleading innocence of the crime of which he was accused. The different types of crime were manipulated by creating one tape version where the crime he was accused of was armed robbery (blue collar crime) and another version where he was accused of cheque fraud (white collar crime). The race of the suspect, black or white, was manipulated by altering the inspector's description of the suspect in the script to describe either a white or black suspect. The following excerpt from the tape transcript shows how the type of crime and race of suspect were varied:

Excerpt from the transcript of the taped exchange between suspect (S) and police officer (PO).

PO: OK, would you like to just briefly tell me what your understanding is of the arrest?

S: Well, eh, I was told last night that I was arrested on suspicion of armed robbery/cheque fraud.

PO: OK. Are you involved in that robbery/fraud?

S: No, I'm not.

PO: In any way are you involved in that robbery/fraud?

S: Not in any way whatsoever. It's absolutely not true, not true at all. I speak only for myself and I am not involved in any armed robbery/fraud, in any way, whatsoever.

PO: Well the person that carried out this crime is described as male, white/black, put at 5'9' tall ...'

After listening to their version of the tape, participants completed a rating scale where they rated the suspect on a 7-point bipolar scale from innocent to guilty.

Results

Analysis of the results showed a significant effect of the suspect's accent on the attribution of guilt by the participants, with the Brummie-accented suspect being rated higher on guilt than the standard-accented suspect.

In addition, the results also showed that there was a three way interaction of accent, race and crime type with the Brummie-accented, black suspect and blue collar crime condition receiving significantly higher guilt ratings than the other five conditions.

Conclusions

The authors cautiously point out that this study has problems with external validity:

... attributions of guilt are generally made in a far richer evidential context than we have provided here and it is likely that strength of evidence will moderate any effect of accent on legal decision making.

However, the evidence from this study did support previous research by Seggio in Australia which led Dixon *et al.* to ask the question: 'Do some accents sound guiltier than others?'

Application: strategies to influence jury decision making

Figure 3.11 Lawyers use a range of techniques to try to persuade the jury to believe their version of the case and deliver a verdict that supports their side of the argument

From the research outlined above, which suggests that jurors may judge by appearances, a strategy that could

 Stop and ask yourself ...

- Write a paragraph to explain what the research by Dixon *et al.* suggests about how juries can be persuaded by the characteristics of defendants and what this reveals about the psychology of the courtroom.

Links to
- Check your understanding

be used to influence the jury is impression management by the defendant in terms of how they dress and present themselves. It is usual for defendants to be advised to dress formally for court, and to be neatly groomed with no visible tattoos. The aim is to give the jury a good first impression and to avoid being judged negatively on appearance by the jurors.

Lawyers might also help witnesses to increase their confidence in court by using witness familiarisation techniques. Lawyers have to be careful to avoid 'coaching' witnesses, as this would be considered to be perverting the course of justice, but they can help reduce the nerves a witness might have by explaining to them what will happen in court, and describing the roles of all those present. They can also suggest useful strategies for dealing with cross-examination questions, or perhaps run through a mock cross-examination with the witness. Again, the witness could be advised on how to best present themselves to the court.

Using order of presentation of evidence to persuade the jury

Persuasion is an extra-legal variable and techniques to persuade the jury can be employed by both the prosecution and defence in a jury trial. One such technique is based on memory research. As you will remember from the Loftus and Palmer (1974) core study in Component 2, we tend to construct a narrative, or story, of events that makes our memory of an event logical and meaningful to us. Pennington and Hastie (1988) carried out a laboratory experiment to test the hypothesis that jurors are more easily persuaded by 'story order' (presenting evidence in the sequence that events occurred) than 'witness order' (presenting witnesses in the order deemed most likely to persuade the jury), demonstrating that presenting the case in story order is a more persuasive strategy than presenting witnesses in an order that might 'have most impact' on the jury. The story-order presentation enabled the jurors to more easily construct a narrative for themselves. It should be noted, however, that this strategy provides an advantage if only one side uses it. If both prosecution and defence use story order then neither side gains a persuasive advantage over the jury.

Using an expert witness to persuade the jury

As we saw earlier in the study by Penrod and Cutler, jurors are often persuaded by the confidence of a witness. However, this may be because the jurors are not in a position to judge the witness' evidence against any other criteria. In another study, Cutler et al. (1989)

showed that an expert witness can persuade a jury and influence their decision making. In this study, a sample of 538 undergraduate psychology students took part in a laboratory experiment. The aim of the study was to see the effect of an expert psychological witness who informed the student jurors about memory research and specifically what makes for good and poor witness identifying conditions (WIC) and how this could help them decide if an eyewitness was in a good position or not to clearly identify the perpetrator of a crime. This research therefore provides evidence that one strategy that the defence or prosecution could employ would be to call on an expert witness to influence the decisions that jurors make in cases that depend on the testimony of eyewitnesses by educating them about how to identify a 'good' or 'poor' eyewitness from the WIC described in the case. In addition, the descriptive presentation by the expert witness was more persuasive than the statistical presentation, and this suggests that the expert psychological witness should use this style in order to have the strongest influence on the jury's verdict.

 Find out more

If you are interested in law, criminology or forensic psychology as a university course or for a career, then you could further your knowledge and understanding by observing court proceedings from the public gallery. Most Crown Court trials are open to the public. To find your local court visit the HM Courts and Tribunals page of the Ministry of Justice website (www.justice.gov.uk).

Crime prevention (Social)

Crime prevention refers to a wide range of actions and behaviours that are designed to reduce the likelihood of crime by making a crime more difficult for a criminal, or making it less worth their while. For example, simple crime prevention actions we might all take include locking doors and windows, having immobilisers fitted to our cars, and fitting burglar alarms to our homes and vehicles. Some methods of crime prevention, however, involve whole communities and neighbourhoods. In this topic, the OCR specification requires that you be able to exemplify and evaluate how the features of neighbourhoods and what is known as zero-tolerance policing have been, or could be, used to prevent crime.

How the features of neighbourhoods and a zero-tolerance policy can influence crime

Features of neighbourhoods: Newman's theory of defensible space

Oscar Newman was an architect who became interested in how the features of neighbourhoods and, in particular, housing design might have an influence on crime rates. As a result of his work he developed a theory of crime prevention that involved what he referred to as creating 'defensible space'. In the introduction to his book *Creating Personal Space*, he writes:

Law abiding citizens and communities are the biggest untapped resource for crime prevention we have, if only we knew how to use them. If only we could find a way to empower people to control their immediate environments so that they could work with police to contain criminal activity. 'Defensible Space' does just that, without the specter of vigilantism, and without the need for a continuous infusion of money.

'Defensible Space' operates by subdividing large portions of public spaces and assigning them to individuals and small groups to use and control as their own private areas. The criminal is isolated, because his turf is removed. Even those criminals who live within a community, or housing development, will find their movements severely restricted. 'Defensible Space' does not automatically oust the criminal, it just renders him ineffective.

Newman was involved in research in 1972 into two projects in New York. 'Projects' is a term used in America to describe subsidised housing for people on low incomes or dependent on welfare. The two projects were called Van Dyke and Brownsville. Van Dyke was a series of high-rise flats and Brownsville a series of walk-up buildings, each built around courtyards. This was a quasi-experiment and an independent groups design. The projects each housed approximately 288 people per acre and so social density was similar. However, crime rates and vandalism/graffiti were higher in Van Dyke than Brownsville. Newman looked at the differences between them to try to work out why high-rise housing leads to higher crime rates.

- Being built around courtyards and with a common entrance easily visible from the flats, Brownsville gave greater opportunities for surveillance. Strangers were more likely to be recognised and challenged.
- More care was shown for the communal areas in the Brownsville Project, for example putting wallpaper on communal hallways and keeping the gardens nice – this suggests ownership and puts would-be vandals and criminals off.

Figure 3.12 Walk-up apartment buildings, such as those in the Brownsville estate, have greater defensible space than high-rise buildings such as those in Van Dyke

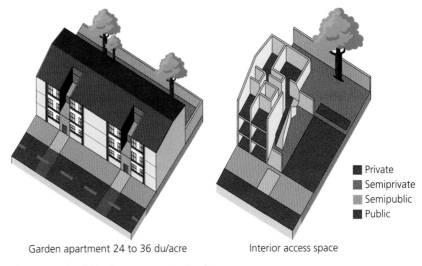

Private
Semiprivate
Semipublic
Public

Garden apartment 24 to 36 du/acre   Interior access space

- Private space is within the apartment unit only.
- The interior lobby, stairs and corridor are semiprivate.
- Grounds can be designated for one family but are usually shared by all the families in the building.
- Only a small number of families (three to six) share the interior circulation areas and grounds.
- The street is within the sphere of influence of the dwellings.

- People in Brownsville were more likely to let their children play out and kept their doors open to keep an eye on them. This means that neighbours were meeting and talking, and so a greater sense of community built up in Brownsville. In high-rise housing parents either did not let their children out or, if they did, had no control over what they were getting up to: the vandalism was often carried out by the children who lived in the project themselves.
- Van Dyke had higher crime rates and more graffiti and vandalism than Brownsville.

While investigating, Newman carried out a short experiment. He tape recorded people having a heated argument and played it in the corridors of Van Dyke and Brownsville. He found that when people heard the noise in Van Dyke they locked their doors and, as the row intensified, they turned up their TVs so they could not hear.

It was very different in Brownsville. Here he and his co-researchers were challenged about what they were doing even before they got into the building to set up their tape player and, once set up, people came out of their flats to see what was going on.

Based on his work in the projects in the USA, Newman developed a theory to reduce crime in low-cost housing

areas. He said that what needed to be established was 'defensible space'. When redesigning the New York projects, he suggested that the community be given control over, and responsibility for, communal areas:

- Since some communal buildings had no semi-private areas that allow social/friendship networks to develop, Newman said these should be incorporated into the design/redesign of such places: semi-private areas should be designed both inside and outside of the building in such a way as to make social interaction inevitable.
- Buildings should be designed so that all space appears to belong to some individual or group – hallways and elevators should be eliminated as far as possible, or put on the outside of the building, or apartments should have windows on to their hallways.
- Interior space, around which the buildings may be built, should be visually accessible from the street.
- Projects should be kept small and the amount of large families that live there should be limited.

Newman suggests that four key factors should be addressed in order to create defensible space, as outlined in Table 3.7.

Table 3.7 Factors to address in order to create defensible space

1. Zone of territorial influence	There should be markers to show that the area is private rather than public, such as fences or hedges
2. Opportunities for surveillance	The physical layout of the building should mean that intruders can be easily spotted – where apartment blocks are built around a courtyard, for example, entrances can be overlooked and people can be seen, so intruders can be spotted Smaller groupings enhance the sense of community and make it easier for residents to work out who is and isn't an intruder
3. Image	High-rise buildings are similar and lack individuality or personalisation. Individuality should be emphasised as it suggests privacy and is linked to the zone of territoriality
4. Milieu	Milieu refers to the surroundings of the building or the setting; buildings set in open spaces often attract vandalism more than those organised round more personal spaces such as courtyards

Newman also emphasises that it is very important when designing/redesigning urban areas that those people who live there already, or who will live there in the future, are involved in the planning so that the residents have a sense of community and ownership of the project.

Features of neighbourhoods: the broken windows theory

In 1982, Wilson and Kelling proposed a situational explanation of crime, which has come to be called the 'broken windows theory'. The basic tenet of this theory

 Stop and ask yourself ...

- If you were going to design a housing estate to house low-income families or families dependent on welfare, what features of Newman's theory of defensible space could you include to help prevent crime? Make sure you can explain *why* these features should help to prevent crime.

Links to
- Check your understanding

is that disorderly neighbourhoods lead to serious crimes. Pratt, Franklin and Gau (2010) define disorder as 'any condition or behavior that fails to conform to traditional standards of decency, cleanliness and proper conduct'. There are two types of disorder:

- physical disorder, such as graffiti, vandalism, littering, abandoned or broken down buildings and uncared for gardens
- social disorder, such as the sale and use of illicit drugs, teenage gangs hanging about and annoying or intimidating people, prostitution, public drinking and intoxication, and panhandling (begging).

The way that a disorderly neighbourhood can influence crime, according to the broken windows theory is that disorder is a trigger for fear in residents, as they see disorder as an indication that serious crime is on the rise, and so their fear of crime increases. The validity of this connection between disorder and fear of crime is well supported by research. What happens next is that, because people fear crime, they spend less time in public places in the community and avoid contact with others when they are out and about. Citizens also fail to challenge minor disorderly behaviour, and this leads to a lack of social cohesion in the community. In communities where citizens feel safe to walk the streets and be in public places, the large number of people present provides 'guardians' for all the others present. This high level of mutual surveillance, and number of people who together might challenge disorderly behaviour or call for support from the police, is a deterrent to those who might engage in disorderly behaviour. If disorderly behaviour escalates and drives people to stay in their homes out of fear of their community then, according to this theory, the scene is set for more crimes, such as drug dealing and prostitution, to take place openly on the streets, which in turn leads to more serious street crimes such as muggings.

However, there are problems with this theory since the validity of the link between increased community disorder and an increase in serious crime is unproven.

In addition, this theory alone cannot account for crime since it is reductionist, focusing purely on social factors.

Wilson and Kelling's work concluded that it is the police, and only the police, who can effectively maintain public order. They suggested that by dealing with minor examples of disorder, foot patrol officers could play a vital role in preventing serious crime, and in this way their theory offers a suggestion for crime prevention.

The work by Wilson and Kelling was well-received by police departments as, unlike most research into policing that criticised police work, the article suggested something positive that the police could actually do. It was also popular as the police were under pressure from the public to improve public order following decades of civil riots, anti-war demonstrations, the rise of gang culture and the increased number of homeless people on the streets, many of whom were unpredictable as a result of suffering from mental health problems.

Zero-tolerance policy

Zero-tolerance policing is a policy that emerged out of the broken windows theory. Under zero tolerance, the priority to crackdown on seemingly minor offences, such as fare dodging or begging (panhandling) increased. Based on broken windows, it was predicted that this crackdown on disorder would reap benefits in the form of reductions in serious crime.

Its use was pioneered by William Bratton. Working with Kelling as an advisor, Bratton was the first to trial the broken windows theory. At first, in his role in the New York City Transit Authority, he made disorder reduction the primary task of the subway police. Bratton had come to New York in 1990 to take up his post and on his first arrival had noticed problems:

... [in the subway] every day over 200 fare evaders jumped over or under the turnstiles and demanded that paying passengers hand over their tokens to them. Beggars were on every train. Every platform seemed to

 Stop and ask yourself ...

- Can you create a flow diagram to illustrate the broken windows theory to show the relationship between disorder, fear of crime, lack of social cohesion and serious crime?

Links to
- Check your understanding

 Stop and ask yourself ...

- What is the reductionism–holism debate?
- Make a list of five other factors, apart from disorderly neighbourhoods, that could explain criminal behaviour.

Links to debates
- Reductionism–holism

have a cardboard city where the homeless had taken up residence. (Bratton, 1995; cited in Dwyer, 2001)

Bratton set about addressing these issues of disorder in the subway. He would send eight to ten officers into the subway and they would arrest 10–20 fare dodgers at a go. This gave the message to would-be fare dodgers that they were not going to get away with it.

When he was appointed as Police Commissioner for the city in 2004, Bratton took his policies to the streets of New York. Since 1990 the New York City Police Department had taken on 7000 extra officers, and apprehending offenders for minor offences such as graffiti or public drinking was emphasised in Bratton's initiatives as one of the police department's priorities.

Bratton called this policy the 'quality of life' initiative, and one of its first target was 'squeegee people', who would, without invitation, wash the windscreen of cars parked at the lights, whether the driver wanted it washed or not, and expect to be paid for this 'service'. Bratton sent officers to carry out 'sweeps' where this was known to happen and they rounded up and arrested all those caught doing it. The policy was described by others as a zero-tolerance policy; Bratton did not like this term, however, as he believed it suggested an overzealous attitude in officers whereas what he said happened in New York in the 1990s was better described as assertive policing, where offences that might have previously been ignored were now paid attention to and dealt with.

In 1992 arrests for serious crimes went down by 25 per cent and Bratton and Kelling were quick to give credit for this statistic to the zero-tolerance policy. They concluded that since the serious crime rate had fallen – with fewer robberies, muggings and murders on the streets of New York – that crime had gone down, and that the public could think the police were responsible! Taken as evidence as being a successful crime-prevention strategy on the tough streets of New York, Bratton's policy was quickly adopted by other police departments across the country. Crime fell in the USA for the five consecutive years up to 1996.

While zero-tolerance policing could be seen as a cause of this, there are other factors that might account for it. For example, it is important to note that police resources increased, for example in New York 7000 new officers had been employed from

1990–94 and these increased resources coupled with increased effort could have played a large part in the drop in the crime statistics. Additionally, the 'quality of life' initiative was only one of a number of policies introduced by Bratton, and this makes it difficult to establish a causal link between the zero-tolerance policy and a reduction in crime.

In addition, the empirical evidence investigating zero tolerance, or 'order-maintenance policing' as it is also known, has presented mixed results. While there are some studies that suggest that such approaches can reduce crime, there are an equal amount of studies that show that order-maintenance policing has no effect at all on crime rates.

Moreover, Pratt, Franklin and Gau (2010) point out that order-maintenance policing can have negative consequences and has been criticised for causing tension and threatening police–community relations. This is especially the case where, as part of order-maintenance policing, the use of stop-and-search means that anyone can be stopped and searched. Overuse of this policy has led to resentment by citizens who object to this intrusive police scrutiny.

Key research: Wilson and Kelling (1982) The police and neighbourhood safety: Broken windows

The main issue in the key research by James Wilson and George Kelling is whether police foot patrols and community policing reduce crime. They begin by describing a programme conducted in the US state of New Jersey in about 28 cities, one of which was Newark. The programme involved the state putting more officers on foot on the street. Although popular with politicians, the initiative was unpopular with police chiefs who saw foot patrols as reducing police mobility and response times to callouts, and also weakened the control of headquarters over the police officers. It was also disliked by many officers as it meant they were outside in all weathers and it was hard work. (Foot patrol had been used as a punishment in some forces.) After five years a review of the programme showed that

 Stop and ask yourself ...

- Can you suggest one way in which a zero-tolerance policy could be considered to be useful?
- What challenges are there to the usefulness of zero-tolerance policies?

Links to debates
- Usefulness of research

PART 3 Applied psychology

118

there was no decrease in crime rates, which Wilson and Kelling suggest was 'to the surprise of hardly anyone'.

However, the review showed there were positive consequences of the programme in that residents in the areas where the foot patrols had operated felt more secure, tended to believe that crime had been reduced and tended not to stay at home behind locked doors as a way of protecting themselves from crime. Officers on foot were also found to have a higher morale and a more positive attitude towards citizens than patrol car officers.

While this could be seen as proof that foot patrol officers do nothing to prevent crime, Wilson and Kelling suggest that the residents in Newark knew that their neighbourhoods were safer as a result of having them. What Wilson and Kelling suggest is that there is a lot of crime in big cities, which causes citizens to have a fear of crime. Citizens may also perceive there to be more crime if they think their neighbourhood is disorderly. In particular, people fear being bothered by disorderly people, and Wilson and Kelling give examples: 'disreputable or obstreperous or unpredictable people: panhandlers, drunks, addicts, rowdy teenagers, prostitutes, loiterers and the mentally disturbed'.

Wilson and Kelling argue that what the foot patrols did was to contribute to the levels of public order, and Kelling had witnessed this first-hand when joining Newark officers on patrol. He noted that officers on patrol knew the regulars, and they knew him, and that part of their job was to make sure that 'disreputable' regulars 'knew their place' and would follow the informal rules established by that officer in that neighbourhood, for example:

- drunks and addicts could sit on the stoops, but could not lie down
- drinking was allowed in side streets but not on the main streets
- bottles had to be in paper bags
- talking to, bothering or begging from people at the bus stop was not allowed
- if customers and business owners argued, the officer assumed the business owner was right, especially if the customer was a stranger
- strangers were moved on if they could not explain satisfactorily what they were doing.

These informal rules were acknowledged by locals and, as a result, the foot patrol officer was able to help maintain order.

Wilson and Kelling suggest that while fear of 'real' crime is important, we should not underestimate the impact of fear of disorder in the community. They also suggest that disorder and crime are linked in a kind of developmental sequence. They use broken windows as an example, suggesting that if a window

Figure 3.13 The rule was that drunks and addicts could sit on the stoops, but could not lie down

in a building is broken and not repaired, that soon all the other windows in that building will be broken, as an unrepaired window signals that no one cares, so breaking the rest of them means nothing.

Disorder, according to Wilson and Kelling, is linked to crime as it leads to the breakdown of community controls, and 'untended' behaviour, such as unrepaired broken windows, can spiral downwards to create public disorder:

A piece of property is abandoned, weeds grow up, a window is smashed. Adults stop scolding rowdy children; the children, emboldened, become more rowdy. Families move out, unattached adults move in. Teenagers gather in front of the corner store. The merchant asks them to move; they refuse. Fights occur. Litter accumulates. People start drinking in front of the grocery; in time an inebriate slumps to the sidewalk and is allowed to sleep it off.

Although this does not mean an increase in violent crime will actually occur, the perceived level of serious crime increases, and residents respond by keeping off the streets, interacting as little as possible with others and, if possible, moving out of the area.

Wilson and Kelling suggest that the lack of public order in such an area makes it much more vulnerable to crime, as it is easy for drug sellers and prostitutes to operate, and that drunks will be robbed by teenagers 'for a lark' and muggings will occur. Policing in these areas is difficult as when complaints are made about disorder, the police explain that they are short-handed and cannot arrest people for petty crimes. The citizens come to see the police as ineffective and stop calling them.

Wilson and Kelling explain that what had happened to policing by the 1980s had evolved over time, with the police role slowly changing from maintaining order to fighting crimes. The role of the police shifted to focus on solving more crimes, and making more arrests.

Wilson and Kelling's broken windows theory suggests then that disorderly neighbourhoods cause fear in the inhabitants and this influences them to keep off the streets, out of public parks, and makes them less likely to challenge disorderly behaviour or to call the police to get them to do something about it. Residents who can afford to do so may leave the area, leaving behind those poorer residents who cannot afford to move; this contributes to urban decay, which in turn increases the likelihood of serious street crime occurring in that area.

The solution to this would appear to be to do more to increase a sense of public order. Wilson and Kelling consider ways in which citizens themselves can achieve this, such as the group of unarmed young people called the Guardian Angels who first patrolled the New York Subway and then set up groups in many other cities, or how groups of 'community watchmen' have been set up, for example to patrol neighbourhoods and challenge strangers. Citizens alone, though, cannot maintain order.

Figure 3.14 Citizens against crime: groups of unarmed young people called the Guardian Angels patrolled the New York Subway in order to reduce crime against passengers

Wilson and Kelling are clear about who needs to be involved if public order is to be maintained – they state that 'the police are plainly the key'. The reason they give for this is the fact that being an officer and wearing a badge makes an officer responsible for stepping in, for example, when someone is attacked, and their uniform makes them easy to identify by citizens as someone who is responsible for helping when called upon to do so.

The barriers to this being identified as a priority for police forces at that time were that:
- police departments' success was judged in terms of their crime fighting and arrest success, so many of their officers were deployed in areas of high crime as a result
- police departments were reducing in size, as a result of economic cutbacks, so would be unable to provide foot patrols everywhere.

Wilson and Kelling suggest that, with limited resources, careful deployment of foot patrols would be needed. They suggest some areas are so badly crime-ridden as to make foot patrol useless, and some so harmonious that foot patrols would be unnecessary. The way forward, they suggest, would be to identify:

... neighbourhoods at the tipping point – where the public order is deteriorating but not unreclaimable, where the streets are used frequently but by apprehensive people, where a window is likely to be broken at any time, and must be quickly fixed if all are not to be shattered.

Finally, and importantly, Wilson and Kelling conclude that the police must not only protect individuals, but also fulfil a role in protecting communities:

Just as physicians now recognise the importance of fostering health rather than simply treating illness, so the police – and the rest of us – ought to recognise the importance of maintaining, intact, communities without broken windows.

Application: strategies for crime prevention

The specification requires that you be able to suggest at least one strategy for crime prevention. From the information on the broken windows theory and zero-tolerance policy you should be able to suggest ways in which order-maintenance policing could be used to prevent crime. From Newman's theory on defensible space you should be also able to suggest how housing and neighbourhoods could be designed, or redesigned, in order to prevent crimes such as vandalism or burglary.

Surveillance is another strategy that can be used to prevent crime. You will have seen that it plays an important part in both Newman's theory of defensible space and in the broken windows theory.

Technology has improved opportunities for surveillance, and the use of CCTV is commonplace today. You can be expected to be observed by cameras in many places, including shops and shopping centres, and in town centres and on the street. Brown (1995) reported on the success of CCTV in town centres in the UK in reducing antisocial and criminal behaviour. Crime report data was collected for three UK cities – Birmingham, Newcastle and Kings Lynn – comparing statistics for before and after the introduction of CCTV systems in each town. Brown concluded that the strategy was very successful in all three cities. Burglaries reduced by 56 per cent in Newcastle and criminal damage reduced by 34 per cent. CCTV seems to be effective in reducing antisocial behaviour and crime where large groups of people congregate.

Other strategies that could be used to prevent crime (Clarke, 1997) include:

- **Target hardening**, which makes the crime more difficult to commit, such as fixing immobilisers on cars, a secure lock on a bike, and installing screens to protect bus drivers from assault from passengers.
- **Access control**, which makes it difficult for would-be criminals to get into places to commit crimes such as theft or vandalism, for example having entry phone access on buildings.
- **Stimulating conscience**, for example by putting up signs such as 'shoplifting is stealing'.
- **Denying benefits** – these are strategies that make the crime less 'worth it' to the offender, for example attaching ink-filled security tags to items of clothing.
- **Facilitating compliance** – to encourage people not to drop litter, bins should be provided; public loos should be available so that people don't urinate in the street.

Effect of imprisonment (Social)

There are a range of punishments that you might expect an offender to receive if they have been tried and found guilty under the British legal system. The one that probably comes to mind most readily is being sent to prison. British prisons house a range of offenders, some of whom have been convicted of offences that caused serious harm or even death to others, and who need to be imprisoned for the protection of the public. These offenders will serve long or even life sentences. At the other end of the scale, and more typical of the prison population in the UK, are offenders guilty of less-serious crimes, such as theft or fraud, with 40 per cent of all offenders serving sentences of four years or less.

Is imprisonment an effective strategy for preventing individuals from committing crime or from reoffending? Are there strategies other than punishment that can be used to prevent reoffending?

Punishment and reform as responses to criminal behaviour

In the specification for OCR you are asked to explain and exemplify the background to this topic on individual crime prevention. Firstly, the specification requires you to consider punishment as a response to criminal behaviour, and the example this book will explore in detail is imprisonment. Secondly, you need to be able to consider methods used to reform and rehabilitate offenders, and the examples in this book are the use of employment-focused programmes and restorative justice.

Imprisonment as an example of punishment

There are a number of features of prison that are designed to be punitive, not least is being locked up in an institution, sometimes hundreds of miles away from home and with the prospect of not seeing family regularly, and then only for short visits. When people are sent to prison they can take very few personal possessions with them and they will usually be expected to share their cell with at least one other inmate. Their movement will be closely monitored and restricted within the prison, for example they may be restricted to their wing or to their landing. They will be locked in their cells at night and sometimes confined to their cells for long periods during the day. Prisons have a strict regime with rules and restrictions on all aspects of behaviour, including what time you wake up, what you wear, how you spend your day, and when and what you eat. Most prisons have work details that might involve working in gardens or workshops, and all prisoners are expected to do their assigned job. Prisoners will usually have some time together out of their cells, called free association.

There are many rules that prisoners have to follow, and clear consequences if they are broken. Although all prisons differ slightly in the way they are operated, the government lays out a set of privileges, punishments and rights for prisoners (see www.gov.uk for further information), including the fact that prisoners who are compliant and obey all the rules can earn privileges such as getting more visits from friends and family, or more spending money each week. However, prisoners who are not compliant can be punished for breaking the rules and can be confined to their cell for up to 21 days, given extra days on their sentence, or have their privileges taken away. Rights include access to health care and legal advice, and from 30 minutes to an hour outside every day.

Is prison effective?

In terms of individual crime prevention, on the one hand we can say that prison is highly effective in the UK for those 85,000 or so inmates currently being held in Her Majesty's prisons. The assumption is that they are not going to be offending while they are locked up.

In addition, prison is a highly effective punishment. Prison takes away an offender's liberty and incarcerates them in a restrictive and adverse environment. This is seen as a way of making the offender 'pay' for their crime, and is seen to be providing justice for both society in general and the victims of crime. Prison provides a restrictive and unpleasant experience for inmates. Apart from the intended restrictions of incarceration, there are also unintended features of prison life that increase the unpleasantness of the experience: overcrowding, boredom and the threat of violence from other inmates, for example.

However, fulfilling the requirement to punish offenders through imprisonment comes at a price. Overcrowding, boredom and the threat of violence from other inmates are all problems that can have a negative psychological effect on inmates, leading to anxiety and depression, especially in the early part of a sentence while the inmate adjusts to their situation. This detrimental effect on the mental health of prisoners leaves them vulnerable to suicidal thoughts and Dooley (1990) reported that the suicide rate of prisoners is four times that of the general population. Young offenders held on remand are at particular risk.

However, despite the potential damage, especially to vulnerable individuals, advocates of the prison system argue that its benefits outweigh the costs because prison functions as a deterrent and puts people off committing crimes. One form of deterrence is individual deterrence, and we can explain this in psychological terms using the principles of behaviourism. If the prisoner has an unpleasant experience (being imprisoned as a result of their crime), operant conditioning would predict that the offender would learn from this consequence and would, on release from prison, be discouraged from committing further offences. In other words, the experience of being released from prison should act as a strong negative reinforcer.

However, rates of recidivism, or reoffending, have remained high in Britain for a decade. If punishment was indeed effective then the offender would not go back to criminal activity, and we would not see high recidivism rates. In 2013 an article in *The Independent* (Jamie Grierson 'Reoffending Rate Increases' 31 January) reported on the rising recidivism figures that were revealed in the statistics in the UK for April 2010 to March 2011:

More than one in four criminals reoffended within a year, according to the most recent Ministry of Justice (MoJ) figures, committing 500,000 offences between them ... Around 280,000 offences were committed by criminals with 11 or more previous offences, while more than 50,000 of these were committed by nearly 11,000 criminals who had previously been jailed at least 11 times.

High recidivism rates suggest a failure in the system to prevent offenders from committing further crime, suggesting that prison does not work well as an individual deterrent and is not effective for individual crime prevention once the offender has completed their sentence and been released.

Prison might also act as a general deterrent through vicarious negative reinforcement. If you see someone else being sent to prison, and you are aware that this is a possible consequence of criminal behaviour, then you might decide that it is not worth the risk and choose not to engage in criminal behaviour yourself. However, prison population statistics suggest that prison is not an entirely effective general deterrent: the UK prison population has been steadily increasing and the system operates close to capacity. The government statistics for July 2014 show this.

Table 3.8 Prison population statistics for the UK, 18 July 2014

Male prison population	81,729
Female prison population	3,932
Total prison population	85,661
Useable operational capacity	86,737

Source: www.gov.uk

Prison as a response to criminal behaviour

It is not the case that most prisoners cannot wait to get out of prison and start reoffending. In fact, the opposite is true. Most believe they have learned their lesson and are determined that they will never be back in prison again. However, leaving prison may mean returning to a situation where the reasons that led a person to crime in the first place may still be likely to influence them.

Indeed, Pakes and Pakes (2009) suggest that prison may have made things worse for them:

... a third [of prisoners] lose their house whilst in prison, two-thirds lose their jobs, and about 40 per cent lose contact with their family.

Additionally, prisoners may have mental health problems or might, ironically have developed problems with drugs, having been introduced to drug use in prison.

Pakes and Pakes also describe prisons as 'the "home" of the excluded and unskilled', citing figures from the government's Social Exclusion Unit (2002) that suggest prisoners are:

- 13 times more likely to have been in care as a child
- 10 times more likely to have truanted from school regularly
- in many cases, poorly educated, lacking basic numeracy and literacy skills, with many not achieving the levels in literacy, numeracy and writing as that expected of an 11-year-old.

With all these factors militating against them, it is easy to see how on release from prison it is not easy for a person to slot into the role of a law-abiding citizen.

This brings us to the final function of prison: rehabilitation or reform of criminal behaviour to non-criminal behaviour. One of the ways that psychologists have been involved in the reform of prisoners is through the design and delivery of programmes to improve the skills and opportunities for prisoners on release with the goal of reducing recidivism.

Some of these programmes focus on training and skills, and preparation for employment on release. Being supported from prison to employment is one way in which social reintegration of prisoners can be assisted. A job is very important in helping someone released from prison as it provides them with a structure to their day, financial security and keeps them away from the activities (and perhaps the people) that might encourage them to reoffend. Having a wage coming

in also makes it easier to secure accommodation, as well as allowing the person to feel that they have some control over their lives and increased self-esteem. Research has suggested that having no prospect of work on release is a high risk factor for returning to crime.

Christa Gillis and Mark Nafekh (2005) investigated a programme operated by the Canadian Correctional Service. The programme involved a planned employment scheme where offenders completed a programme that included techniques on how to look for employment, individual psychometric assessments and on-the-job placements. To investigate the effect on recidivism rates of this community-based employment scheme, Gillis and Nafekh compared two groups of men and women on conditional release (conditional release means that they were released on parole before the end of their sentence).

The researchers carried out a content analysis of data from Canada's Offender Management System. Data was available for 23,525 individuals on conditional release between January 1998 and January 2005, of whom 95 per cent were male and 5 per cent female. This was a quasi-experiment as the independent variable was manipulated by classifying the participants into those who had been on an employment-based programme prior to release and those who had not. The offenders were matched on a number of variables (such as gender, risk level, release year, sentence length, family/marital relations, and substance abuse).

Gillis and Nafekh compared recidivism rates between the two groups of offenders and found that those who were on an employment programme were less likely to return to custody during their period of conditional release, with 70 per cent of those on the employment schemes successfully completing their conditional release period in the community compared with 55 per cent of those who were unemployed. The researchers also compared the median length of time taken to return to prison in the case of the 30 per cent of those on the employment programme and the 45 per cent of those unemployed who were returned to prison during conditional release, and showed that the median time

Stop and ask yourself ...

Using psychological terms and concepts, can you:

- explain why prison as punishment should reduce reoffending
- explain why prison as punishment is not an entirely effective strategy for preventing individuals from reoffending.

Links to debates
- Usefulness of research

Stop and ask yourself ...

- What advantages are there of a prison system that allows for conditional release of prisoners?

Links to
- Check your understanding

before they were sent back to prison for those on the programme was much longer at 37 months compared to just 11 months for those who were unemployed.

The authors concluded that planned employment on release from prison plays an important role in the rehabilitation and social reintegration of prisoners, and suggested that more opportunities for employment-based programmes should be provided for prisoners.

This study provides psychological evidence that a planned programme that enables prisoners to hold down a job is one way of reducing recidivism, and is one possible method of reducing reoffending in individuals.

Key research: Haney, Banks and Zimbardo (1973) Study of prisoners and guards in a simulated prison

Background

If you take a punitive view of prison, you might think that it is desirable for the experience of those incarcerated to be brutal and harsh, teaching them a lesson. However, Haney et al.'s research into prisons, talking to current and ex-inmates and those working as guards, showed that the US prison system went beyond 'brutal but fair' and into the realms of the inhumane, rife with both sexual and physical abuse. This has an impact on prisoners on their release.

The authors suggest there are two explanations for the 'deplorable state' of the US penal system. Firstly there is the dispositional hypothesis, the theory that the brutality in prisons is due to the nature of those who administer it or to the nature of those who populate prisons; in other words, the guards and prisoners are 'brutal types'. This view fits in with our stereotypes of prison guards as sadistic and prisoners as sociopathic. Haney argues that this is a view favoured by the authorities as it allows the status quo to be observed – nothing can be done to

change the way prisons are as people's natures cannot be changed, they can only be contained and dealt with, and brutal guards are needed to deal with brutal prisoners.

A second theory, however, is that it is the way that prisons are organised and operated that leads to their brutality.

Aim

The study aimed to test the dispositional hypothesis; that is, to find out whether it is the individuals or the situation that made prisons brutal.

The researchers wanted to establish a 'new' (albeit mock) prison in which the prison environment would be copied (as far as reasonably and ethically possible) but instead of 'criminals' and 'guard-types', it was to be populated by a group of normal or average men.

A real prison could not be used for both ethical and practical reasons. Ethically it would be unjustifiable to put non-offenders in with real offenders and guards and, practically, in a real prison it would not be possible to see if it was the environment or the people causing the brutality, as both exist there.

The researchers predicted that the allocation to the role of guard or prisoner would dictate participants' behaviour, not their personal dispositions or personalities.

Method

Laboratory emperiment, designed to be as naturalistic as possible.

Location

A mock prison built in the basement of the Stanford University psychology building.

Sample

A newspaper advertisement was placed asking for male volunteers to take part in a study of 'prison life', for $15 a day. Seventy-five potential participants completed questionnaires about family background,

 Stop and ask yourself ...

- Why do you think the US government favoured the dispositional hypothesis? What would be the implications for the US penal system if the dispositional hypothesis was not true?

Links to
- Check your understanding

 Stop and ask yourself ...

- Can you explain how these two theories of what makes prisons brutal places could be used to illustrate the nature–nurture debate in psychology?
- How does the dispositional hypothesis fit in with the debate on individual or situational explanations of behaviour?

Links to debates
- Nature–nurture
- Individual–situational explanations

physical/mental health history, involvement in crime, etc. and each potential subject was interviewed by one of two experimenters.

Finally, 24 were selected who were judged to be the *most stable* (physically and mentally), *most mature*, and *least involved in antisocial behaviours*. The participants were Caucasian, except for one Oriental, and were normal, healthy college students who were in the Stanford area for the summer. They were largely of middle-class socio-economic status.

The participants were initially strangers to each other, for ethical and practical reasons:

- ethical – to prevent damage being caused to participants' existing friendships
- practical – to prevent existing patterns of behaviour or relationships from interfering with the experimental situation.

Participants were allocated randomly to the role of 'prisoner' or 'guard'.

Procedure

What psychological factors/effects can be observed in real prisons?

- Power and powerlessness
- Control and oppression
- Satisfaction and frustration
- Arbitrary rule and resistance to authority
- Status and anonymity
- Machismo and emasculation

The researchers tried to incorporate these experiences into the mock prison.

Instructions to participants

All were told they would be randomly assigned to either the 'guard' or 'prisoner' role and had agreed to play either role for a period of 14 days and nights, for a payment of $15 a day.

Figure 3.15 'Prisoners' and 'guards' playing their role in the Stanford Prison Experiment

They had signed a contract which made it clear that 'prisoners' would be under surveillance (and would therefore have little or no privacy) and that 'prisoners' should expect to have some of their civil rights suspended during the study (excluding physical abuse).

The 'guards' were told that their assigned task was to 'maintain the reasonable degree of order within the prison necessary for its effective functioning'. They were told not to let the prisoners escape. They were to work three-man eight-hour shifts, going home when they were not on duty. They were deliberately given minimal guidelines about their guard role but an explicit and categorical prohibition against the use of physical punishment was emphasised by the experimenters.

Uniforms

The guards:

- wore a khaki shirt and trousers (suggesting a military attitude)
- carried a whistle and police night-stick (symbols of control, power and machismo)
- wore reflective sunglasses, making eye contact impossible.

The prisoners:

- wore loose-fitting muslin smocks with their identification number on the back and front (the use of number and not name was intended to deindividuate and depersonalise the prisoners) – loss of identity
- the smocks were like frocks and made the prisoners adopt 'female' postures, which added to the humiliation of the uniform and rendered them even more emasculating (no underwear was worn)
- a light chain and lock was worn on one ankle (a symbol of oppression and restriction)
- rubber sandals were worn and a cap made from nylon stocking, which was both humiliating and deindividuating (as having hair shaved in some prisons or in the military).

Names

The prisoners were called by their number by the guards and other prisoners.

Guards' orientation day

The day before the study was to start, the guards were brought to the prison where they helped set it up, were briefed on their roles, given their uniforms and established a set of rights and rules for the prisoners.

Procedure for bringing 'prisoners' to the mock prison

- Prisoners were 'arrested' at home by the real Palo Alto Police (this was not part of the experimental contract but was probably very entertaining for the neighbours!).

- They were handcuffed, informed of their rights and taken to the police station where they were fingerprinted and put in a detention cell. The police officers evaded answering questions about whether the arrest was part of the study.
- The prisoner was then collected from the detention cell by one of the guards and an experimenter, blindfolded and taken to the mock prison.
- At the prison, he was made to strip, was sprayed with a 'delousing preparation' (deodorant spray) and made to stand naked in the 'yard' for a while.
- He was then given his uniform, a 'mug shot' was taken, and he was taken to his cell and ordered to remain silent.

> ### → Take it further
>
> Using the information about the guards' and prisoners' uniforms, and the information about the set up of the study for both the guards and the prisoners, write 500 words to explain how these elements of the study might give the participants in the study first-hand experience of the psychological effects that Haney had observed in real prisons.

Results

The study was stopped after six days because of the zeal of the 'guards' and the deterioration of some of the 'prisoners'. 'Guards' were verbally abusive to 'prisoners' – commands were the most common form of verbal behaviour.

After an initial 'revolt' on day two (which was quickly put down by the 'guards'), as the days went on the prisoners' behaviour was that of a 'model prisoner', showing passivity, dependence and flattened mood. Half the 'prisoners' coped in the oppressive atmosphere but the study had a dramatic effect on some prisoners.

Five had to be 'released' because of extreme emotional depression, crying, rage and acute anxiety. The pattern of symptoms was similar in four of them and began as early as day two. The researchers referred to this as 'pathological prisoner syndrome'. The fifth prisoner developed a psychosomatic rash on his body and was subsequently released.

At this point the remaining prisoners were asked if they would be willing to forfeit the money they had earned so far and be 'paroled' (set free). Only two were *not* willing.

When the superintendent (Zimbardo) said he'd have to consider this, the prisoners went meekly back to their cells, showing how tied-in to their roles they had become. They had *internalised* the prison (come to believe in it).

When the experiment was over, the prisoners were delighted; by contrast, guards seemed distressed at the decision to stop the study. None of the guards had failed to turn up on time for their shift, and on several occasions guards stayed on duty, voluntarily and uncomplaining, for several hours and without additional pay.

Note, however, that not all guards and prisoners reacted in the same way: not all guards indulged in cruelty, and prisoners showed individual differences in successful adaptation to the situation.

Conclusions

The study shows how social roles (which are situational or environmental factors) influence behaviour. It implies that it is the structure and organisation of the prison environment which leads to brutal behaviour, as 'normal-average' young men behaved brutally to fit in with their role as guard.

Explaining the guards' behaviour

Haney *et al.* claim that power led to the deterioration in the guards' behaviour, and described this as the *pathology of power* (the syndrome of oppressive behaviour that develops in people given the opportunity to exert power over others).

Another factor which led to the deterioration of the guards' behaviour described by Haney *et al.* was *deindividuation*, where a person undergoes a change of awareness, a change of personal identity, which leads to a reduced sense of personal agency (you do not feel responsible for your behaviour). This often leads to a sense of group identity and is commonly found in military units (in action) and mobs. In this study, Haney *et al.* argued that the behaviour of the guards became dictated by their role.

Explaining the deterioration of some of the prisoners

A number of factors contributed to the deterioration of the prisoners, including:
- the loss of personal identity
- the arbitrary control exerted by the guards (learned helplessness)
- dependency and emasculation.

> ### ⊘ Stop and ask yourself ...
>
> - What contribution does the study by Haney, Banks and Zimbardo make to our understanding of the effects of imprisonment?
>
> **Links to**
> - Check your understanding

In follow-up studies, the guards were perceived as being physically bigger but, in fact, guards and prisoners had the same average height.

Take it further

Visit the excellent website on the Stanford Prison Experiment (www.prisonexp.org) to find out more and watch video clips from the study.

Application: strategies for reducing reoffending

The specification requires that you be able to suggest at least one strategy for reducing reoffending.

From the information on prisons as punishment and deterrent you should be able to suggest how imprisonment might be used as one strategy to reduce reoffending, and why this strategy should work.

Similarly, you might suggest that, based on Gillis and Nafekh's findings, a community-based employment scheme should be offered to prisoners to prevent them reoffending, and be able to explain why this should work.

A further strategy that could be used to prevent reoffending is the use of restorative justice (RJ).

Restorative justice

RJ is a process that tries to recognise the needs of the actual victim. For the victims it is hoped that the outcome of the process will be peace of mind and that it will help them regain a sense of control over their lives. The process often operates alongside the criminal justice system and is not an alternative to prosecution. Offenders who take part in RJ should still expect to be punished to the full extent of the law. However, the idea of RJ is that the victim and the offender are brought together and the victim is able to explain the impact of the crime against them to the person who did it; they can also try to gain an understanding of why they were targeted. This is a common question that victims have. In terms of 'restoration', the offender is expected to agree to actions suggested during the process; so, in the case of vandalism, the offender may agree to be involved in helping to fix or clean somewhere after a similar offence has been committed.

The trained officials will invite both the victim and offender to participate in the RJ process. The process and its purpose are clearly explained, and the process can only go ahead if both sides are in full agreement and voluntarily enter into the RJ process. A meeting is then set up, often at a police station, although this can also be done where the offender is being held in custody. This meeting is commonly known as an RJ conference. Both sides will bring supportive people, possibly friends or family members.

Face-to-face RJ has to be managed sensitively as there is a potential for harm to both the victim, who is meeting face-to-face with the person who caused them harm and anxiety, and the offender, who is agreeing to meet face-to-face with the person against whom they have committed a crime. This could be potentially humiliating for them if not handled correctly, which would be counter-productive.

The structure of the RJ interview usually involves introductions from both sides. The person managing the conference does not take a lead role but sets the agenda for the meeting. This usually begins by asking the offender about the crime and what they think about it. They may also ask them to explain why they have agreed to take part in this meeting. The offender often apologises and offers ways to make amends at this stage. Then their supporters and family members are asked about the offence and its impact on them. Following this, the victim is invited to talk about the offence and to explain how they feel it has impacted upon them. This gives them the chance to have the harm caused to them acknowledged in a way that is not always possible in the criminal justice system, and again those who are there to support them also talk about what they feel the impact has been.

Victims are often less interested in apologies than explanations, and they wonder if 'whatever they did' to cause them to be a victim is something they will do again. It can be very reassuring to find out if the selection of them as victim was purely opportunistic or random, as this can help victims overcome fear of being victims of similar crimes.

The victim is usually keen that the outcome of the meeting should be that the offender should not commit the same offence against anyone else. If there are factors that could help to explain the crime, such as drug abuse or alcoholism, then one of the outcomes of the conference might be that the offender agrees to undertake a drug rehabilitation programme as part of their making amends for what happened.

The discussion is then led by the trained official to agree a 'contract' that is then drawn up and signed by all parties, in which the actions to be taken by the offender are agreed.

While this document is prepared, to relieve the stress and tension of the discussions – which can be highly emotionally charged – tea and biscuits might be served and shared by both sides.

- A young offender has been caught stealing some high-price items from a supermarket. The local police have officers trained to deliver RJ. Explain how an RJ conference between the offender and the manager of the supermarket might be set up and run.
- A burglar has been apprehended following a series of night-time burglaries in a village. He was caught after a dog in a house he was attempting to burgle barked the alert and the householder was able to call the police with a clear description. Three of the householders who were burgled have suffered sleepless nights and anxiety attacks after the robberies, and one woman is devastated by the loss of her mother's antique jewellery. The burglar confesses to the crimes and agrees to take part in an RJ conference as suggested to him by the police and his lawyer. Explain how the conference might be set up and run.

Research by Lawrence Sherman and Heather Strang (2007) used an internet search to identify academic research articles into RJ. Analysis of their 424 search hits allowed 36 papers to be identified where offenders who participated in an RJ programme were compared with offenders who were not.

They suggest that RJ works in property and violence crimes as it is possible to identify a personal victim with whom an RJ conference can be set up. The results suggested that RJ was most effective for violent crime, with the exception of burglary, where RJ was shown to reduce victims' post-traumatic stress symptoms, and reduced repeat offending where RJ was used instead of a prison sentence.

This extensive review suggested that, at least for crimes where a personal victim can be identified, there is convincing empirical evidence that RJ is effective in preventing reoffending in individual offenders.

 Find out more

There are a number of individual treatment programmes that have been and are currently being delivered in prisons in the UK. Many of these take a cognitive behavioural approach based on the assumption that a change in attitude or thinking is required in order for criminals to change their behaviour. Examples of this include the CALM anger management scheme, and cognitive skills programmes such as Enhanced Thinking Skills and Reasoning and Rehabilitation.

- Use the internet to research these programmes. What do they involve?
- What has psychology found out about the effectiveness of these programmes?

📑 Practice questions

1. Outline the influence on crime that the features of neighbourhoods might have. [10 marks]

2. Evaluate the validity of the study by Wilson and Kelling (1982) The police and neighbourhood safety: Broken windows. [15 marks]

3. A report in a national newspaper suggests that the government should focus on crime prevention rather than punishment for criminals as a way to make neighbourhoods safer.

   Suggest how crime could be prevented by changes to the environment. [10 marks]

Chapter 4

Environmental Psychology

Stressors in the environment (Biological)

We all talk about being 'stressed out' from time to time, but what do we mean by this phrase? A distinction can be made between the cause of stress (i.e. the stressor) and the way in which we react to it (i.e. the stress response). A stressor can be defined as a stimulus of some kind that requires an organism to adapt its behaviour to be able to cope with it, while the stress response refers to the organism's biological and psychological reactions to the stressor. Evans and Cohen (1987) identified four types of stressor:

- daily hassles, such as losing your keys
- life events, such as getting married
- ambient stressors, such as wind, pollution, noise and overcrowding
- cataclysmic stressors, such as war and natural disasters.

However, not everyone will respond to a particular stressor in the same way: for some people it will, indeed, cause a stress response, but for other people it may not. Because of such individual differences in how people respond to a given stressor, it has been suggested by Lazarus and Folkman (1984) that there is a cognitive aspect to stress – namely, it involves us making a couple of appraisals, firstly about the level of threat that a particular event poses to us, and secondly about whether we have the resources to cope with it. If we feel that we do *not* have the necessary resources (for example, time, money, social support, relevant ability) then we will experience feelings of stress; if we feel that we *do* have the necessary resources to respond to the threat, then we won't experience feelings of stress.

Given this individual aspect to stress, it cannot be assumed that all environmental stressors will affect everyone in the same way. That said, it is worth investigating which aspects of the environment have the capacity to cause a stress response in people, and which aspects of the environment cause people the highest levels of stress.

Environmental stressors

There are many different aspects of the environment that can cause people to have a stress response. Some of these will be explored in other sections of this chapter; for example, we will look at the impact of the way in which housing is designed in the section on the psychological effects of the built environment, and we will look at invasions of personal space in the section on territory and personal space. The aspects that we will explore here are: noise, temperature, overcrowding and environmental catastrophes.

Noise

Noise can be defined as unwanted sound. What this definition recognises is that at different points in time the same sound could be either wanted or unwanted. For example, music may be a wanted sound at a party, but it may be unwanted sound when you are trying hard to concentrate on writing a really difficult essay. When it is unwanted sound, it is noise.

Glass and Singer (1972) investigated the after-effects of exposure to noise in a series of experiments in which they manipulated different features of noise to try to isolate those aspects that cause feelings of stress. During a typical session participants would be given simple cognitive tasks to carry out and, while doing these, they would be exposed to a specially prepared recording designed to simulate the spectrum of complex noises often present in the urban environment. This recording would last for around 25 minutes, and Glass and Singer manipulated three aspects of it:

- volume – it would be played at either 56 decibels or 108 decibels
- predictability – the noise would either come in nine-second bursts at regular intervals on a 'fixed intermittent' cycle or in bursts of irregular length at unpredictable moments on a 'random intermittent' cycle

- perceived control – some participants would be shown a microswitch and told that they could terminate the noise by pressing the button, while others would not.

After this first stage, the noise would then be stopped and participants would typically be given two further tasks to do: one (involving them tracing over the lines of a diagram without tracing any line twice and without lifting the pencil from the figure) that was designed to measure tolerance for frustration, as two of the diagrams were mathematically insoluble; and another (involving them correcting spelling, punctuation and grammar errors that had deliberately been introduced to a passage from Jane Jacobs' book *The Death and Life of Great American Cities*) that was designed to test quality of performance.

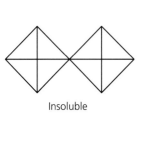
Insoluble

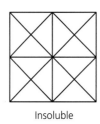
Insoluble

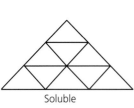
Soluble

Soluble

Figure 4.1 Insoluble and soluble puzzles, as used in Glass and Singer's experiments

Results from Glass and Singer's experiments suggested that, while loudness certainly exerted an effect, nonetheless the greatest effects on the participants' post-noise task performance arose from the noise being unpredictable and the participants perceiving the noise as being something that they couldn't control:

We tentatively conclude ... that perceived uncontrollability and its exacerbation of stress are the mechanisms mediating between unpredictable noise and decrements in frustration tolerance and quality of post-noise task performance.

The key research by Black *et al.* (2007) can be seen as complementing the work of Glass and Singer as, instead of being carried out in laboratory conditions, it relates to noise from a real-life source (that is, aircraft noise). Furthermore, instead of exploring the impact of this on cognitive performance, it investigates whether aircraft noise is related to reductions in people's health-related quality of life and to increases in their blood pressure.

Temperature

In addition to noise, there is evidence that temperature may also be related to stress. Kenrick and MacFarlane (1986) carried out an investigation into how drivers responded when they were trapped behind a stationary car and whether they responded differently in different temperatures. The subjects of their field study were 39 male and 36 female drivers, ranging in estimated age from 16 to 65 years. Sessions were conducted on 15 consecutive Saturdays (between 11 a.m. and 3 p.m.) between April and August, with staff from Arizona State University's Geography Department recording temperature and humidity. For the days sampled in this study, perceived temperatures were calculated to range from 88 °F to 116 °F (31 °C to 46 °C). The site chosen for the study was a traffic light controlling an exit from a residential tract in Phoenix, Arizona. The intersection had a one-lane exit, making it impossible to pass on either the left or right of an obstructing vehicle.

Figure 4.2 A Datsun 200SX – would you mind being stuck behind this car?

The green light was set for a 12-second period. A female confederate, driving a 1980 Datsun 200SX, positioned her car near the target intersection. When the light turned red, she moved her car to the head of the intersection and waited for a subject to pull in behind her. The confederate then waited for the light to turn green and remained stationary throughout the 12-second course of the light. The confederate was instructed to keep still, with her eyes forward, car in neutral, foot off the brake, and her hands on the steering wheel. Once the green light had changed, the confederate made a legal right turn on the red light. An observer, hidden from view, was positioned off to the right and slightly behind the subject's vehicle. At the onset of each trial, the observer counted the number of horn honks delivered by the subject over the 12-second duration of the green light, estimated the duration of each honk, and measured the latency until the first honk. (If no honks were delivered over the course of the green light, subjects were assigned a latency score of 13 seconds.) Only one observer was employed in this study because inter-rater reliabilities for pilot data exceeded r = .90.

Findings supported the contention that heat serves to increase interpersonal hostility. Thus, higher temperatures were associated not only with an increase in the likelihood of using one's horn but also with a significant increase in the amount of time spent leaning on the horn that went well beyond the simple tap needed to communicate the change of light. At temperatures over 100°F (38°C), 34 per cent of the subjects who used their horn leaned on it for over 50 per cent of the total green light interval. In comparison, no subjects below 90°F (32°C) did so. Kenrick and MacFarlane's findings suggest a linear relationship between heat and hostility, and provide evidence that temperature can be an environmental stressor.

Overcrowding

Another environmental stressor seems to be overcrowding. This is related to population density (how many people there are in a given area) but it is not the same thing. Thus, whereas population density can be measured objectively, whether someone experiences an increase in density as a feeling of being overcrowded is a subjective matter that will vary from individual to individual. Investigations of the effects of density on people's perceptions of crowding are typically done by manipulating either spatial density (i.e. the amount of space that a set number of people occupy) or social density (i.e. the number of people in a set amount of space). However, it is difficult to control for extraneous variables in both methods (for example, each extra person added to a manipulation of social density is unique and not just an extra number; if manipulating spatial density, it is unlikely that two rooms will differ only in their size as they will probably also differ in their light levels, temperature, and so on), and they would not enable the researcher to see any long-term effects of changes in population density.

Have a go yourself

- Carry out a two-condition experiment in which for your independent variable you manipulate either social density or spatial density. You could assess the impact of density on concentration levels or cognitive performance for your dependent variable (although you'd need to operationalise how you'd measure these).

Figure 4.3 Sika deer (*Cervus nippon*), as introduced to James Island

As a consequence, animal studies have often been used to investigate the effects of overcrowding, and an example of such research was that reported by Christian *et al.* (1960). In 1916, sika deer (*Cervus nippon*) were introduced to James Island, a 280-acre tract of land in Chesapeake Bay, Maryland, USA. Their numbers grew steadily until, in 1955, a census indicated that the herd numbered 280–300 deer, which meant a density of approximately one deer per acre. Shortly after that, in January–February 1958, 60 per cent of the animals died, with the deaths occurring most commonly among females and the young. As a die-off had been expected, 18 animals were shot and autopsied between 1955 and 1958. Examination

Stop and ask yourself...

- Is it plausible to suppose that there is a linear relationship between heat and hostility, or would there not have to be a point at which it became so hot that people stopped being hostile in the sort of way seen by Kenrick and MacFarlane (such that there was an inverted U relationship between heat and hostility instead)?
- What would be the methodological and ethical problems with trying to get an answer to this question?

Links to
- Extending your understanding

Stop and ask yourself...

- What are the strengths of Christian *et al.*'s study?
- What are the weaknesses of Christian *et al.*'s study?

Links to research methods
- Ecological validity
- Validity
- Generalisability
- Ethics

of their vital organs revealed an increase in the weight of the animals' adrenal glands between 1955 and 1958, with adrenal weight dropping 50 per cent following the die-off. As hepatitis, glomerulonephritis, malnutrition and poisoning were ruled out as causal factors in the die-off, Christian *et al.* suggested that prolonged hyper-stimulation of the cortex as a result of excessive population density and its related social pressures produced the changes in the animals' adrenal glands and their deaths. In short, the increase in population density had caused fatally high levels of arousal in the animals as they experienced the overcrowding as a stressor.

Environmental catastrophes

Environmental catastrophes can also be a cause of stress. These comprise single, powerful events that require considerable adjustment and affect large numbers of people. A distinction can be made between natural disasters (that is, natural events such as volcanic eruptions, earthquakes and tsunamis) and technological catastrophes (artificially caused events such as plane crashes, nuclear accidents and dam bursts). However, it isn't always clear which of these categories to place particular events in, as hurricanes may only have a devastating effect on people because of human activity, such as failure to maintain defences against them, and the reason why a plane could have an accident might relate to environmental events, such as volcanic ash being released into the atmosphere.

An example of an environmental catastrophe was the fire that occurred at the Cocoanut Grove nightclub in Boston, USA, in November 1942. This fire, which resulted in 492 people losing their lives, began in the Melody Lounge in the basement and took hold incredibly quickly, in part as a consequence of all the flammable furnishings in the nightclub, including artificial palm trees.

Approximately 1000 people were crammed into a facility which had a licence for 100 tables, 400 chairs and 30 fixed stools. It had no fire sprinklers and six exits were either locked or impassable. In a study of the survivors, Alexandra Adler (1943) reported that a year after the fire over half were still experiencing nightmares, anxiety and guilt over survival. This was especially the case among those who had remained conscious during the fire, suggesting that loss of

Figure 4.4 The Cocoanut Grove nightclub after the 1942 fire

consciousness can help protect survivors against the development of psychiatric symptoms. Such symptoms would now be likely to attract a diagnosis of post-traumatic stress disorder (PTSD), which is characterised by three clusters of symptoms: persistent re-experiencing of the traumatic event (for example, nightmares and flashbacks), avoidance of stimuli (for example, people or places) that act as reminders of the event, and emotional numbing (for example, losing interest in usual activities).

 Find out more

- Was the Cocoanut Grove nightclub fire a natural disaster or a technological catastrophe, or was it an example of both combined? Use the internet to find out more about both how the fire started and why it caused the loss of so many lives. You could then have a class debate about it.

 Take it further

- Why do some people experience post-traumatic stress disorder in the aftermath of events such as the Cocoanut Grove fire while other people do not? Is it even possible that traumatic events could have positive effects on people? Look up the work of Stephen Joseph in relation to post-traumatic growth.

 Stop and ask yourself...

- How many different types of natural disaster can you identify?
- How many different types of technological catastrophe can you identify?

Links to
- Check your understanding

The impact of environmental stressors on our biological responses

The research we have looked at so far can all be seen as providing evidence of how different features of the environment (noise levels, temperature, crowding, and environmental catastrophes) can cause stress responses. However, what does this mean? How can an environmental event trigger a biological response, and what are the biological responses that they can cause?

The nervous system can be divided into two parts – the central nervous system (CNS), which comprises the brain and spinal cord; and the peripheral nervous system (PNS), which comprises the rest of the body including all our vital organs such as the heart and lungs, kidneys, liver and stomach. Within the PNS, the autonomic nervous system (ANS) controls such processes as respiration, heart rate and salivation; it does this largely automatically, without us needing to pay conscious attention to them. The ANS can itself be divided into two parts – the sympathetic branch and the parasympathetic branch. To a large extent, these two branches of the ANS perform opposite roles, with the sympathetic branch working as the body's accelerator (for example, making the heart beat faster, increasing the rate of breathing, and redirecting blood to the muscles for quick movement), and the parasympathetic branch working as the body's brake (for example, reducing heart rate and respiration, and lowering blood pressure). Essentially, the role of the sympathetic branch of the ANS is to prepare the body for action ('fight or flight'), while the role of the parasympathetic branch is to reverse this and allow homeostatic mechanisms to bring the body back to a normal level of arousal.

In terms of how the sympathetic branch of the ANS prepares the body for action, we need to make reference to the role played by the adrenal glands. They are located on top of each kidney and are approximately 4 cm in height and 7.5 cm in length. The adrenal glands have two parts to them:

- The outer part is known as the adrenal cortex, and this produces essential hormones that we need in order to live, such as cortisol and aldosterone (which help regulate metabolism and blood pressure, respectively).

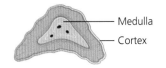

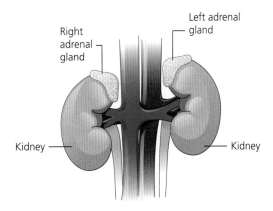

Figure 4.5 The adrenal glands in relation to the kidneys, and the two different parts of the adrenal glands

- The inner part is known as the adrenal medulla, and this produces non-essential hormones such as adrenalin (also known as epinephrine) that are not required for us to be able to live.

It is the role of the adrenal glands in producing these hormones that enables us to respond to stressors. When a threat is encountered, the hypothalamus (a part of the brain responsible for hormone production) sends electrical signals to the adrenal medulla, stimulating the release of adrenalin into the bloodstream. As nerve impulses travel at 150 metres per second, this occurs almost instantly, with the adrenalin preparing the body for action by increasing heart and respiration rates and redirecting blood flow to the muscles.

However, the body can't sustain this level of adrenalin-fuelled arousal for long without becoming exhausted and so, to be able to respond to threats that are more long-lasting, the body has a second way of responding. As this second response is triggered hormonally (rather than electrically), it takes several minutes to kick in but it lasts longer. Essentially, the hypothalamus releases a hormone called CRH (corticotrophin-releasing hormone), which sends a message to the pituitary gland (which lies just below the hypothalamus in the brain) to secrete ACTH (adrenocorticotrophic hormone), which then in turn

---

🚫 **Stop and ask yourself ...**

- Can you describe the different parts of the nervous system?
- Can you describe the two parts of the adrenal glands and how they work?

Test yourself on this material and consider making up a poster to illustrate it all.

Links to debates
- Usefulness

sends a message to the adrenal cortex to release cortisol. As noted before, cortisol helps to regulate metabolism, but it also helps the body respond to stress through its role in converting fats, proteins and carbohydrates into energy.

Hans Selye (1956) divided the physiological changes that the body goes through in response to stress into three stages. As the body responds in the same way whatever the stimulus might be, he called the body's response the general adaptation syndrome (GAS). The three stages are as follows:

1. The alarm reaction stage – after an initial phase of lowered resistance (for example, in which blood pressure momentarily drops below normal), the sympathetic branch of the ANS quickly mobilises the body for action, stimulating the adrenal medulla to release adrenalin and noradrenalin and equipping the body for 'fight or flight'.

2. The resistance stage – if the stressor is not removed, the body enters a stage in which the adrenal cortex effectively takes over from the adrenal medulla. Production of adrenalin and noradrenalin decline, but the body remains primed for action through the release of cortisol, aldosterone and thyroxine (which increases the rate at which energy can be extracted from food).

3. The exhaustion stage – if the stress situation continues, the body's supplies of energy and hormones will become depleted. Selye identified a number of 'diseases of adaptation' that can develop, such as high blood pressure, coronary heart disease and stomach ulcers. In extreme cases, these can result in collapse or even death.

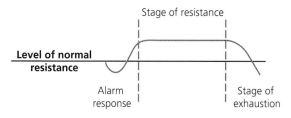

Figure 4.6 The three stages of Selye's general adaptation syndrome

While Selye's work has been very influential, it has not escaped criticism. In particular, it has been suggested that individuals will differ in the ways in which they respond to stressors as a consequence of various mediating factors. At the start of this section, we referred to the cognitive appraisal model of stress by Lazarus and Folkman (1984) which proposes that stress arises from an appraisal of an event as a threat and then a perception that we lack the resources required to respond to the threat. It can be

expected that individuals will differ in their appraisals, and there are a number of factors that will influence this.

One of these may be self-efficacy, which is the belief that we can succeed at something we want to do (Bandura, 1986). Self-efficacy can be influenced by many factors, one of which – enactive influence – is an individual's previous experiences of success or failure. In the context of stress, this might mean that a person who has encountered a stressful situation previously and coped with it may be less likely now to perceive it as threatening than someone who has not encountered it before.

Another factor that might influence a person's appraisals of stressors could be the resources they have available to them, including social support. Even if, then, an individual appraises an event as a threat, if they feel they have the resources to respond to it (for example, people they can call on for help, money to hire specialist support that they might need), then they are unlikely to have the same stress response as someone who doesn't have such resources available to them.

Can ongoing environmental stressors have a biological effect on people? The key research by Black *et al.* (2007) looked at this question in relation to aircraft noise. While it was not able to establish cause and effect (as you'll see, it was only able to investigate associations), nonetheless its finding that aircraft noise is associated with high blood pressure among those residents exposed to it, will clearly be of concern to anyone who lives with environmental stressors on a daily basis.

Key research: Black and Black (2007) Aircraft noise exposure and residents' stress and hypertension

This study investigates whether there is a relationship between a particular environmental stressor – namely, noise from aircraft – and people's well-being. It was carried out in Australia and involved people in a highly exposed, noise-affected area, and people in a control area with similar demographic and socio-economic characteristics completing self-assessments of their health status through a questionnaire that they then posted back to the researchers.

Background

Studies investigating the relationship between health-related quality of life and aircraft noise have been conducted in the USA (Bronzaft *et al.*, 1998; Meister and Donatelle, 2000) and Japan (Miyakita *et al.*, 2002), but no such study had been conducted in Australia.

Aim

This study sought answers to two core questions:
- Is health-related quality of life worse in a community chronically exposed to aircraft noise than in a community not exposed?
- Is long-term aircraft noise exposure associated with elevated blood pressure in adults via noise stress as a mediating factor?

Sample

Sydney (Kingsford Smith) Airport was selected as a case study. Questionnaires were mailed out to 1500 addresses in two areas. The aircraft noise exposure area comprised those areas which, according to Airservices Australia, experienced on an average annual day more than 50 aircraft noise events with a volume louder than 70 decibels (dB). The suburb of South Penrith, located approximately 55 km from Sydney Airport, was chosen as a control area. This area, in the western suburbs of Sydney, was not exposed to aircraft noise but was matched with the noise exposure area on socio-economic indices.

Every home address in these two areas was sent a questionnaire (excluding apartments, commercial buildings, addresses for sale or lease, and abandoned addresses). The cover letter explained that the study was one of environmental noise (i.e. it didn't make explicit mention of aircraft noise) and, given the ethnic composition of neighbourhoods surrounding Sydney Airport, the questionnaire was translated into Arabic and Greek. The researchers received 796 responses, with 704 respondents filling in the questionnaire completely. The number of responses from residents in the control area was a little bit lower than those from the noise exposure area. Respondents ranged in age from 15 to 87 years of age.

Method

The questionnaires completed by respondents contained a number of sections:
- Health was measured in relation to physical functioning, general health, vitality and mental health, with questions being based on those in the internationally recognised SF-36 instrument.
- Hypertension was assessed through a series of closed-end questions asking about the respondents' medical histories in relation to cholesterol levels and high blood pressure.
- Annoyance from noise was measured in two stages with respondents being required firstly to identify

noise sources while at home and then to rate on a 0–10 scale how annoying they find them (where zero meant not at all annoyed and 10 meant extremely annoyed).
- Factors that could potentially have a confounding effect on the researchers' ability to assess the relationship between aircraft noise and health, such as employment status, exercise activities, smoking status, alcohol consumption, nutrition intake and demographic characteristics, were also asked about.

Results

Participants living in the noise-affected area had a mean aircraft noise annoyance score of 6.27, which was significantly higher than the score of 1.03 reported by the control group (p < 0.001). In relation to Black *et al.*'s two core questions, both null hypotheses were rejected. After controlling for potential confounding effects, the mean score of physical functioning, general health, vitality and mental health for the aircraft noise exposure group was significantly lower than that for the matched control group, implying that health-related quality of life is worse in a community chronically exposed to aircraft noise than in a community not exposed.

In relation to their second core question, (i) long-term aircraft noise exposure was significantly associated with chronic noise stress (respondents who were exposed to high levels of aircraft noise had odds of 2.61 on having chronic noise stress), and (ii) chronic noise stress was significantly associated with prevalence of hypertension (respondents who had chronic noise stress had odds of 2.74 on having hypertension compared with those without chronic noise stress).

Discussion

The findings from this study have implications for public policy. Given the commercial interests of the owners of Sydney Airport, proposals such as extending curfew hours to give the community extra relief from aircraft operations are unlikely to be met sympathetically. Stress from aircraft noise is currently managed on an individual basis through the prescription of anti-hypertensive drugs, but it may be that in future non-chemical interventions, such as mindfulness-based stress reduction (MBSR) programmes could be set up, like the one developed at the University of Massachusetts Medical Centre that involves breathing meditation, walking meditation, eating meditation and hatha yoga.

Application: strategies for managing environmental stress

If you were asked to discuss at least one strategy for managing environmental stress, then it may be helpful to keep in mind the difference between problem-focused and emotion-focused ways of managing stress:

- **Problem-focused strategies** are directed at changing the situation that is causing the problem.
- **Emotion-focused strategies** are directed at managing an individual's distress rather than changing the situation.

If aeroplane noise is an issue then a problem-focused strategy might, for example, involve making aeroplane engines quieter, limiting the times during the day when they are permitted to take off or land at an airport, or banning the building of houses within a specified distance from an airport. By way of contrast, an emotion-focused strategy might – as Black *et al.* suggest – involve stress-reduction programmes for the people affected or the prescription of anti-hypertensive drugs.

Take it further

- How could the distinction between problem-focused and emotion-focused strategies be applied to other environmental stressors, such as those arising from the climate, natural disasters or overcrowding?

Rational emotive therapy could be used as part of a strategy for managing environmental stress. Developed by Albert Ellis (1977), this is essentially an emotion-focused strategy based around his A-B-C-D-E paradigm, where:

- A stands for the activating experience that is causing the distress, such as noise from outside
- B stands for the beliefs that an individual might have about this experience, some of which will be rational while others will be irrational
- C relates to the consequences arising from these beliefs
- D is where a psychologist, like Albert Ellis, can help, as this stands for the process of disputing the beliefs and replacing the irrational ones with more rational ones
- E stands for the effects of the therapy, which should hopefully involve a new set of beliefs about the activating experience, enabling the individual to cope should the stressor recur in the future.

As the injunction in an exam question can be expected to be 'Discuss ...', the expectation is that you will get a discussion going by recognising that there are (at least) two sides to the point under consideration. This is an important point to bear in mind. Counter-arguments could always centre on practical problems with implementing a suggestion (for example, to do with added costs for an organisation) and also individual differences between people (for example, to do with some people needing the suggested change more than others). That said, the focus of these questions is on the application of relevant knowledge to the specific scenario in the question, so this should be the central feature of an answer.

Stop and ask yourself…

- How could rational emotive therapy be of help to someone experiencing environmentally-related stress?

Links to debates
- Usefulness

Biological rhythms (Biological)

While Topic 5 (on the built environment) looks at the impact of *physical* conditions on people, it is also important to look at the impact of *temporal* conditions on people, by which is meant conditions relating to time.

In the modern world, people can find themselves travelling long distances by aeroplane, often crossing many time zones in the process. They will frequently experience jet lag, as when they land at their destination there is a difference between the time their body is saying it is and the time the clocks around them are saying it is. Why, though, is jet lag felt more when people travel in an eastward direction, and is there anything that can be done to reduce feelings of jet lag?

It is estimated that nearly 15 million people in the USA permanently work on night shifts or work on rotating shift schedules that include night shifts. In Britain, the figure is estimated at approximately 3.6 million people. In many ways, we all benefit from this, as it means we don't have to worry about emergency healthcare not being available during the night, and it means that companies are able to produce more goods and distribute them more quickly than would be possible if they were restricted to daytime hours alone. However, such shifts clearly require people to change patterns of behaviour that they would have been used to since childhood (that is, having to get out of the habit of being awake during the day and sleeping during the night), so are there any ways in which people can be helped to adjust to shift work?

Biological rhythms

Most of our bodily functions fluctuate according to a daily cycle. This is true of body temperature, which rises to a peak in the afternoon or early evening and falls to a low in the early hours of the morning. It is also most obviously clear in relation to the daily cycles of sleep and activity exhibited by all animals. Such cycles are known as circadian rhythms, a phrase derived from the Latin words for 'around' (*circa*) and 'a day' (*dies*).

Humans are not alone in being governed by circadian rhythms, as they can also be observed in insects, bacteria and plants. This was first demonstrated by the French astronomer Jean-Jacques d'Ortous de Mairan

in 1729 with the plant *Mimosa pudica*. To investigate whether its daily cycle of opening its leaves in the morning and closing them in the evening was driven by sunlight, he conducted an experiment in which he locked them away in a pitch-black cupboard and then, by candlelight, checked to see what they did. Discovering that their leaves continued to follow the same cycle of opening in the morning and closing in the evening, he was able to conclude that this was not because of sunlight (i.e. an outside source) but was, instead, in response to an internal clock.

Figure 4.7 *Mimosa pudica* (with leaves open)

A similar experiment was carried out on a human over 200 years later when, in 1962, French scientist Michel Siffre lived 400 feet below the surface of the Earth in a cave in the French–Italian Alps for two months. The cave was completely dark apart from a light bulb and, although he was in contact with a team on the surface, this was only so that he could let them know when he woke up, when he ate and when he was about to go to sleep. Conditions were not easy as temperatures were below freezing and humidity was 98 per cent. However, with Siffre able to go to sleep when he wanted to and sleep for as long as he wanted to, what was found was that his body followed a daily sleep–wake cycle in much the same way that *Mimosa pudica* does. Although his body went through the same cycle every 24 hours and 30 minutes, instead of every 24 hours, this suggested that humans have an internal body clock that is independent of the natural terrestrial day/night cycle.

Two parts of the brain seem to be involved in controlling the circadian rhythms of humans and other

Stop and ask yourself...

- Imagine you got a job that required you to work during the night (for example, from midnight to 8 a.m.) every night for a week. How would you cope with this? What might make this difficult to adapt to?

Links to
- Understanding the issues

animals. The first of these is the suprachiasmatic nucleus (SCN), which is located deep in the centre of the brain. This acts as an internal clock and controls our daily rhythms including sleep, physical activity, hormone levels, body temperature and digestive activity. The other part of the brain that seems to be involved in maintaining our sleep–wake cycle is the pineal gland. In response to signals originating in the suprachiasmatic nucleus, this produces melatonin, which is a hormone that makes us feel drowsy and tired.

Although our bodies seem to have their own internal clock, it is important to be aware that the daily cycles we go through do seem to be influenced by the levels of light around us. Thus, the SCN receives information about levels of light through the retina at the back of the eyes, meaning that light acts as a *zeitgeber* (which means 'time giver' in German), bringing our internal circadian rhythms in line with the cycles of light and dark in the external world, triggering increased production of melatonin when it is dark and reduced production of melatonin when it is light. It is in part because of the role that light plays in seemingly moderating our internal rhythms that we find it difficult to sleep when it is light, which is just one reason why trying to sleep during the day to be able to work at night (as many shift workers have to do) is something that our bodies find very challenging.

Evidence of the evolutionary benefits that internal clocks provide was supplied in rather unfortunate circumstances by DeCoursey *et al.* (1997), who reported an experiment that they had carried out on white-tailed antelope ground squirrels. A number of these animals had had their SCN surgically destroyed in research to determine the role of the SCN in their health and survival. After some laboratory-based wheel-running research, the ground squirrels were returned to their desert site of origin and placed in a large outdoor enclosure where monitoring by a motion detector, a microchip transponder detector and video surveillance confirmed that those ground squirrels that had had their SCN destroyed were now much more active at night. Thus, whereas the controls were strongly day-active, making 0 to 1.3 per cent of their visits to the food cache at night, the SCN-destroyed animals now made 16 to 52.1 per cent of their visits to the food cache at night. Unfortunately, the risks that this night-time activity exposed them to became apparent when an unplanned night-time attack by a feral cat occurred, which resulted in the death of 60 per cent of the SCN-destroyed ground squirrels but only 29 per cent of the control animals. It seems that one of the functions of the SCN in mammals may be to reduce the activity of animals during times that are unfavourable for activity.

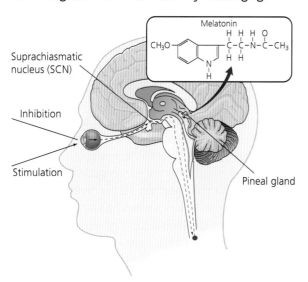

Figure 4.8 The parts of the brain involved in maintaining our sleep–wake cycle

Figure 4.9 A white-tailed antelope ground squirrel (hopefully with its SCN still intact)

Although people's circadian rhythms are remarkably similar – we are currently thought to have an average free-running period of 24 hours and

Stop and ask yourself...

Can you say what the following terms relate to?
- Suprachiasmatic nucleus
- Pineal gland
- Zeitgeber
- Melatonin

Test yourself on these terms and how they relate to each other.

Links to debates
- Check your understanding

11 minutes – nonetheless there are individual differences in the timing of people's circadian rhythms. Broadly speaking, people can be said to have one of two chronotypes, with morning types (people who prefer to go to bed before 11 p.m. and to get up before 8 a.m.) being classified as 'larks', and evening types (people who prefer to go to bed after 11 p.m. and to get up after 8 a.m.) being classified as 'owls'. The lark's body temperature and alertness will peak around mid-afternoon while the owl's will peak hours later.

These traits are difficult to change: as owls find it hard to become larks, so larks find it hard to become owls (Martin, 2003). With working days being orientated more towards early starts, does society favour larks? Preckel *et al.* (2013) investigated this question in the context of children's academic performance. A sample of 272 students attending 9th and 10th grades at five German high schools were given both a chronotype questionnaire (the Lark-Owl Chronotype Indicator) and a standardised cognitive test to complete in class. Parents of 132 of the students also filled in a questionnaire at home rating their child's chronotype. It was found that being an owl was a significant (negative) predictor of overall grade point average (GPA), maths-science GPA, and language GPA after cognitive ability, conscientiousness, need for cognition, achievement motivation and gender were all controlled for. This would offer evidence to support the practice of those educational institutions that choose to experiment with later starts to the school day.

Figure 4.10 Lark or owl – which are you?

 **Have a go yourself**

- Design a questionnaire to investigate people's chronotypes (in particular, whether they are a morning type or an evening type). You could build in an independent variable such as gender or age to find out whether there are differences between males and females or older and younger people in the timing of people's circadian rhythms.

Most of our biological rhythms are circadian, but not all. For instance, there are ultradian (ultra-rapid) rhythms which occur in cycles of less than 24 hours. Examples of ultradian rhythms would include levels of alertness during the day, blood circulation, and the cycle of brain activity during sleep.

In terms of the last of these, it has been known since the 1950s that when we sleep we go through different stages, and studies using the electroencephalogram (EEG), which measures electrical activity in the brain, have revealed that these are characterised by different patterns of brain activity. A sleep cycle will typically last about 90 minutes and will involve progression through various stages of sleep – both the REM (rapid eye movement) and the NREM (non-rapid eye movement) stages. It is the REM stage of sleep that is most closely associated with dreaming, and this stage of sleep is also known as 'paradoxical sleep' because it is simultaneously characterised by physical paralysis and levels of brain activity that are comparable with wakefulness.

As well as ultradian rhythms, which last *less* than 24 hours, there are also infradian rhythms that occur in cycles of *more* than 24 hours. Perhaps the best example of these is the menstrual cycle, which occurs over a period of about 28 days. Infradian rhythms occurring because of seasonal changes are termed circannual rhythms; examples of these include migration (for example, of birds or fish to breeding grounds) and hibernation (for example, of ground squirrels, hedgehogs and bats for the winter).

 Find out more

To find out more about research into sleeping and dreaming, try reading *Night School* by Richard Wiseman. It is highly readable and, as it was only published in 2014, it contains lots of up-to-date insights.

 Stop and ask yourself ...

Can you say what the following terms relate to?
- Ultradian rhythms
- Infradian rhythms
Test yourself on these terms and be able to give examples of each.

Links to
- Check your understanding

The impact of disruption to biological rhythms on our behaviour

One way in which biological rhythms can be disrupted is through sleep deprivation. Many studies have been conducted in this area, mostly (for reasons that will become obvious) on non-human animals. Typical of these is a study by Rechtschaffen and Bergmann (1995) on rats. Using a procedure known as the disk-over-water method, two rats would be placed on either side of a divided 46 cm horizontal disk that was suspended over a tray of water 2–3 cm deep. The brain activity of both rats would be monitored but, in the case of one of them, whenever it was starting to fall asleep or was about to enter a 'forbidden' stage of sleep, the disk would automatically start rotating (at $33\frac{1}{3}$ rpm), forcing the rat to wake up and start walking in the direction opposite to that in which the disk was rotating so as to avoid falling into the water. This would require the other control rat to also start walking, because the control rat was effectively yoked to the sleep-deprived (SD) rat; however, as the control rat could sleep when the SD rat was spontaneously awake and the disk was still, the researchers report that the control rats experienced only modest sleep reduction. Food and water were available to both rats and the cage temperature was kept at 28–29 °C. What was found was that, on average, the rats that experienced total sleep deprivation would die within two to three weeks and, before that, they would show increased food intake and simultaneous weight loss that could both be attributed to excessive loss of body heat, suggesting a role for sleep in thermoregulation.

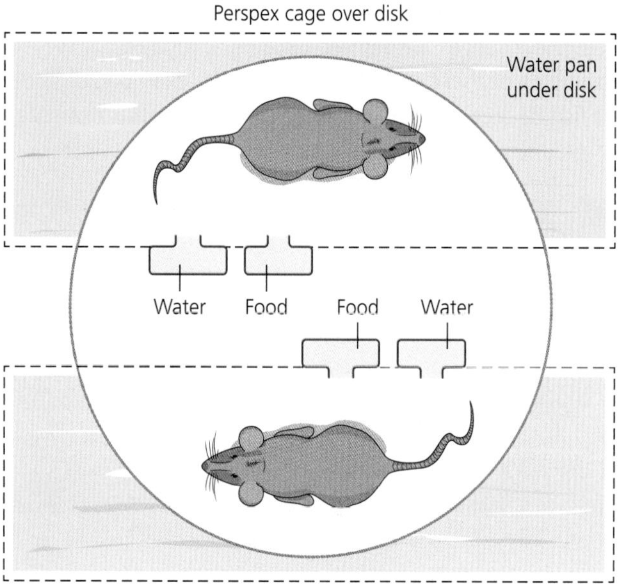

One problem with the study by Rechtschaffen and Bergmann is that we can't be certain that it is sleep deprivation (as opposed to the stress of the procedures used to keep them awake) that caused the rats' deaths. More obviously, it is not clear that we can generalise from the experience of rats to that of humans. How, though, could we do an equivalent study on people? Down the years, there have been individuals who have tried staying awake for significant periods of time, and their experiences are worth reporting. Perhaps the most famous of such attempts was made by American disc jockey Peter Tripp in 1959. He managed to stay awake for a total of 201 hours (more than eight days and nights) and throughout his period of wakefulness he broadcast his daily radio show from a glass-walled portable radio studio that had been set up in Times Square in New York. However, the whole experience took its toll on Tripp, who became abusive three days into the experiment, began hallucinating that his shoes were full of spiders five days into the experiment, and whose body temperature continued to decline as the experiment wore on. After it ended, he fell into a deep sleep that lasted for 24 hours and then declared himself to feel fine. However, those around him felt otherwise, with his wife – who later left him – saying that he had become moody and depressed. Shortly after the stunt, he was found guilty of taking money from record companies to play their records, and all four of his marriages ended in divorce.

➡ Take it further

- Peter Tripp was not the only person to put himself through a sleep-deprivation marathon of this kind. Try looking up Randy Gardner, Toimi Soini, and others.

Clearly, it is difficult to generalise from the experiences of single individuals such as Peter Tripp, and his experience tells us only a limited amount about the impact of sleep deprivation on behaviour. A more controlled experiment by Belenky et al. (2003) suggests that even relatively minor sleep deprivation can adversely affect cognitive performance. Thirty-six healthy volunteers aged 24–62 spent three days sleeping for eight hours (to set a baseline) then seven days sleeping either three, five, seven or nine hours per day before all had a further three (recovery) days in which they again slept for eight hours. During the third day, and on each subsequent day of the experiment, they all underwent a series of psychomotor vigilance tests that measured simple reaction times as they pressed a response button with their preferred thumb

Perspex cage over disk

Water pan under disk

Water   Food   Food   Water

Figure 4.11 The disk-over-water equipment used in the study by Rechtschaffen and Bergmann (1995)

as quickly as possible after the appearance of a visual stimulus. Dependent measures of mean speed, number of lapses (where the participant took over 500 ms to react) and mean speed for the fastest ten per cent of all responses showed that, following even mild to moderate sleep restriction (five or seven hours of daily time in bed), three days of recovery sleep were not enough to restore the performance of participants to baseline levels. Belenky *et al.* suggested that in response to chronic sleep deprivation the brain undergoes adaptive changes maintaining a stable but reduced level of performance.

As well as cognitive performance, sleep deprivation can also affect social behaviour. In a study by Kahn-Greene *et al.* (2006), 26 healthy volunteers completed the Rosenzweig Picture Frustration (P-F) Study before experiencing 55 hours of continuous wakefulness; they then completed the P-F a second time. The Rosenzweig Picture-Frustration (P-F) Study is a projective test consisting of 24 cartoon pictures. In each picture, there are two characters in a frustrating situation and participants are instructed to enter a comment in a 'speech balloon' for the character that is experiencing frustration in the particular scenario. Responses are then assessed for the extent to which the participant is showing aggression in what they write, as opposed to either taking the blame for the feelings of frustration or minimising the feelings of frustration. Compared against their responses before being sleep deprived, participants developed an increased tendency to blame others for problems and a reduced willingness to accept blame themselves. The findings from this study suggest that sleep deprivation significantly weakens the inhibition of aggression and willingness to behave in ways that facilitate effective social interaction (for example, accepting some of the blame oneself).

Aside from sleep deprivation, other ways in which biological rhythms can be disrupted are by jet lag and shift work. Recht *et al.* (1995) investigated the impact of travel across time zones on baseball performance by studying the complete season records for the last three seasons available at the time of their research (1991–1993). They looked at the records for the 19 North American major league baseball teams based in cities of the Eastern and Pacific time zones and (keeping in mind the conventional rule of thumb that resynchronisation from jet lag requires about one day for each time zone passed) collected data for the two games immediately before and after each uninterrupted transcontinental trip made by these teams. They found that the home team could expect to score 1.24 more runs than usual when the visitor had just completed eastward travel. This effect could help to explain why a team travelling from east to west would win 43.8 per cent of their

away games, but a team travelling from west to east would win only 37.1 per cent of their away games.

Why, though, was the effect reported by Recht *et al.* loaded against teams travelling to an away game in an eastward direction? To answer this question, we need to refer to the concepts of 'phase delay' and 'phase advance'. Richard Wiseman (2014) uses the example of trans-Atlantic flights to illustrate these concepts. Imagine you are travelling from London to New York (that is, going from east to west). You depart from London at midday and your flight takes six hours. When you land in New York, your internal clock is telling you that it is 6 p.m. but, with the difference in time zones, the clocks are saying it is only 1 p.m. The obvious thing for you to do will be to try staying awake until, say, 10.30 p.m. local time, which will be 3.30 a.m. on your internal clock. You will feel tired by the time you go to sleep but, assuming that you get up at 8 a.m. local time the following day, you will have had nine and a half hours of sleep and should feel refreshed enough to make the most of your time in 'the Big Apple'. Because you have had to hold back when you go to sleep (i.e. delay moving into a sleep phase) this is known as phase delay.

Now, imagine that you are coming back from New York to London (so, going from west to east). Again, your flight sets off at midday local time and, again, it takes six hours to cross the Atlantic and reach its destination. Unfortunately, the problem you will have this time is that when you arrive in London your internal clock will be saying that it is 6 p.m. but it will be dark outside and the clocks you see at Heathrow will be saying it is 11 p.m. What do you do? Because we find it harder to go to sleep when we are wide awake than to stay awake when we are tired, you are likely to find it harder to make the adjustment to the new time zone and are likely to experience circadian dysrhythmia (more commonly known as jet lag) to a greater degree. Because you have been challenged to bring forward when you go to sleep (i.e. advance into a sleep phase) this is known as phase advance.

Figure 4.12 It is harder to adjust your internal clock when experiencing jet lag

Take it further

- Do you know people who have flown across a number of time zones from east to west and/or from west to east? Ask them about their experiences of this. Which direction of flight left them feeling the most jet lagged? Can they pass on any tips for how to reduce feelings of jet lag?

Why, though, do we find phase advances harder to adapt to than phase delays? To answer this question, we need to return to the research of Michel Siffre and others like him. If it is indeed the case that, free from the influence of light sources (exogenous zeitgebers) that help to reset our circadian rhythms and bring them in line with local conditions, our internal (endogenous) body clocks run on cycles that are longer than 24 hours, then by staying awake longer we will be behaving in a way that is in line with what our bodies would naturally do anyway. It is this thought that lies at the heart of the key research by Czeisler *et al.* (1982) into shift work.

Key research: Czeisler, Moore-Ede and Coleman (1982) Rotating shift work schedules that disrupt sleep are improved by applying circadian principles

The following study describes an intervention that was made in a workplace setting to try to bring the needs of an employer for round-the-clock operations more in line with the biological rhythms of the company's employees. Central to understanding this study was the belief at the time of the research that the human biological clock has a 25-hour cycle. As a consequence of this, Czeisler *et al.* suggested that a schedule in which shifts were rotated forward in a clockwise direction (e.g. after a series of shifts from 8 a.m. to 4 p.m., workers should move to a series of 4 p.m. to midnight shifts) would harmonise better with people's circadian rhythms than the current schedule in which shifts were moved backwards in an anticlockwise direction (e.g. after a series of shifts from 8 a.m. to 4 p.m., workers would be moved to a series of midnight to 8 a.m. shifts). The reason for this suggestion was that, assuming an endogenous free-running sleep–wake cycle averaging 25 hours, each change in shift patterns in a forward direction (i.e. in a phase delay pattern) would

be experienced as a seven-hour change, whereas each change in shift patterns in a backwards direction (i.e. in a phase advance pattern) would be experienced as a nine-hour change.

Background

The human sleep–wake cycle has evolved to fit in with our planet's 24-hour alternation between day and night. However, employers are increasingly running round-the-clock operations that require employees to work shifts which – by rotating between night, evening and daytime duties – violate circadian principles.

Aim

To investigate the effects of taking the properties of the human circadian system into account in the design of work schedules, specifically in relation to the *direction* in which shifts are rotated and also the *interval* between changes in the shifts that people work.

Sample

The study took place at the Great Salt Lake Minerals and Chemicals Corporation in Ogden, Utah. This facility, which was involved in potash production, had for ten years been operating a rotating shift system whereby during the potash harvesting season of September to May crews would work a given eight-hour shift for seven days before rotating to the preceding eight-hour shift. This meant that the scheduled work time would rotate in a 'phase advancing' direction from night shift (midnight to 8 a.m.) to swing shift (4 p.m. to midnight) to day shift (8 a.m. to 4 p.m.).

Figure 4.13 Evaporation ponds in Utah, USA

Czeisler *et al.* studied a sample of 153 male employees. Within this sample, there were 85 workers on rotating shifts who were aged 19 to 68 (mean age 31.4 years). These men were compared against a control group of 68 employees aged 19 to 56 (mean age 27.3 years) whose shifts did not rotate and who either worked day shifts or swing shifts. Both groups of men did comparable jobs.

Method

Initial self-reports indicated that those employees on rotating shifts experienced significantly more problems with insomnia than those on non-rotating shifts. In addition, 29 per cent of the rotators reported that they had fallen asleep at work at least once during the previous three months, and 90 per cent of rotators complained that the schedule changed too often. On top of this, 81 per cent of rotators reported that it took two to four days or more for their sleep schedule to adjust after each phase advance.

Czeisler et al. gave all workers and managers an audio-visual presentation on the basic properties of the circadian sleep–wake cycle that contained suggestions for how they could adjust their sleep time to their work schedule; they were also given an educational booklet designed specifically for the workers at this facility. Czeisler et al. then divided the 85 workers on rotating shifts into two groups: all were moved to a phase delay schedule (as opposed to their previous phase advance schedule) but, whereas 33 workers continued to rotate shifts every seven days, the other 52 workers rotated their shifts every 21 days.

The impact of introducing these new schedules was assessed in several ways. After three months the workers were given questionnaires to fill in about their preferences. After nine months personnel turnover and plant productivity were analysed.

Results

Significantly more workers preferred the new phase delay schedules of rotating their shifts over the old phase advance schedule of rotating their shifts. Complaints that the schedule changed too often dropped to 20 per cent among the workers on the 21-day phase delay rotation schedule, and those on this schedule were significantly more satisfied with their schedule than those on the seven-day rotation schedule. They also reported significantly increased scores on a health index.

With regard to the measures taken after nine months of the new rotation schedules, staff turnover on the 21-day phase delay schedule was reduced to the same range as a comparable control group of non-rotating shift workers. There was also a significant increase in the rates of both potash harvesting and processed potash production after the introduction of the new 21-day phase delay rotation schedule.

Discussion

The results of this field study indicate that work schedules that rotate by phase delay with an extended interval between each rotation are most compatible with the properties of the human circadian timing system. However, the design of any specific work schedule must take into consideration both the nature of the work and the specific needs of the workers.

Application: strategies for reducing the effects of jet lag or shift work

If you were asked to discuss at least one strategy for reducing the effects of jet lag or shift work then there are many that you could refer to. In relation to jet lag Richard Wiseman (2014) lists a series of 'Top tips' to help overcome this. A biological strategy might be to take melatonin supplements in an attempt to try and control sleeping patterns. Alternatively, a behavioural strategy could include beginning to adjust to the new time zones in the days before flying by getting up slightly earlier (if flying in an eastward direction) or getting up slightly later (if travelling in a westward direction). An even more basic behavioural strategy might involve taking a nap on the plane. However, if this is going to be part of the strategy then it is important to plan ahead and bear in mind which side of the plane the sun is likely to be shining on during the flight, and this will depend on whether the plane is flying in the northern or southern hemisphere as well as the direction in which the plane is flying.

Strategies to reduce the effects of shift work include, as Czeisler et al.'s study suggests, moving shift patterns in a forward direction (that is, from early to later) to apply phase delay principles. It is worth noting that, ideally, Czeisler et al. would have moved to the new shift by one to two hours per day over five days until the new shift time was attained; however, this was abandoned because it proved inconvenient for the workers' family lives and also their car pooling arrangements.

Stop and ask yourself...
- Which of the above strategies can be regarded as situational and which can be regarded as individual?
- How does this debate relate to the distinction between emotion-focused and problem-focused strategies for managing stress?

Links to
- Individual and situational explanations for behaviour

Beyond shifting the body's circadian rhythms in this way, the effects of shift work can also be reduced by workers taking stimulants such as caffeine during the night and then, during the day, taking sedatives that will help them to sleep. A more radical strategy to reduce the effects of shift work could be to expand the size of a business so that all staff can work during the daytime (albeit maybe a slightly longer daytime – for example, shifts of 6 a.m. to 1.30 p.m. or 1.30 p.m. to 9 p.m.), meaning that no one has to work night shifts. If this really can't be done, then it would be important to ensure that demanding or dangerous work is avoided during the night shifts.

Take it further

- Look up the Three Mile Island, Exxon Valdez, Challenger and Chernobyl disasters. To what extent was shift work involved in these? What do these disasters suggest about the sort of work that should be done during night shifts?

The Biological area

You have now looked at two topics – stressors in the environment, and biological rhythms – that both take a biological approach. As we have seen, investigations have often involved use of tightly controlled experiments. Some of these have been conducted in laboratory conditions, such as the studies by Glass and Singer (1972), Rechtschaffen and Bergmann (1995) and Belenky et al. (2003). However, many have been conducted in the field, such as the key studies by Czeisler et al. (1982) and Black et al. (2007). Field experiments can be expected to be less tightly controlled but to have higher ecological validity.

Although research in these two topic areas has involved the assumption that environmental factors can affect us physiologically, many of the dependent variables have not entailed direct physiological measures. That said, within the two key studies questionnaires collected data about the health of participants, so it was physiological effects that were being focused on. This will have given the researchers quantitative data that is relatively easy to analyse, but the validity of self-reported data can always be questioned.

As the impact of environmental factors on biology has been central to these two topics, we have been able to review not just research based on non-human animals such as rats, ground squirrels and sika deer, but even research based on plants (*Mimosa pudica*).

Research on animals often benefits from shorter life cycles and from different ethical guidelines, but the extent to which it can be generalised to humans is always questionable.

In terms of the relevance of biological research to debates in psychology, many of the studies suggest that a scientific approach be taken. In spite of many assuming biological determinism, they invariably strive to be useful, suggesting ways to work with our bodies rather than against them.

Recycling and other conservation behaviours (Cognitive)

You are, no doubt, aware of the anxieties that most people have regarding the impact of human beings on the planet and its ability to sustain human life. Specific concerns relate to the speed with which we are changing our climate by increasing the concentration of so-called 'greenhouse gases' in the atmosphere and also depleting the planet of its resources (for example, fossil fuels such as oil and gas, and also animals such as fish).

Why is human activity so problematic? In many ways, the answer is simple: the planet is a finite resource and, as a species, there are now so many human beings that the impact of our collective actions upon the planet has become enormous. To put it bluntly, when there were less of us, we had less of an impact. Of course, we could choose to 'tread lightly' and consume fewer goods (eat less food, not use electricity-hungry mobile phones, not travel by aeroplane and so on), but which of us is going to do this? After all, if we deny ourselves these pleasures then it's not as if the planet will benefit, as someone else will just consume these goods instead of us.

This way of thinking is what sits behind the theory of the 'tragedy of the commons' (Hardin, 1968), in which it was argued that an individual farmer will always be likely to add an extra cow to common grazing land to add to his or her profits but, because this will be true of other farmers too, the individual actions that they each take will eventually lead to the overgrazing and ruination of the common land. None of them would be intending this to happen, but the consequence of all their separate, individual, short-term actions (none of which in themselves would be enough to cause catastrophe) would be a collective disaster for which they would all pay the price.

Is there any way in which we can avoid our own tragedy of the commons? Short of adopting Hardin's dramatic solution – seeing overpopulation as the problem, he argued that 'the only way we can preserve and nurture other and more precious freedoms is by relinquishing the freedom to breed' – we will undoubtedly require 'technical solutions' (for example, ways of generating electricity that have minimal impact on the planet) but, in addition, it will also be important that as many people as possible 'tread lightly' in their consumption of resources by reducing, reusing and recycling to the greatest extent possible. They will need to do this even though other people may not behave in the same way. What 'conservation behaviours' should people adopt though, and how can we encourage people to adopt them?

Conservation behaviours

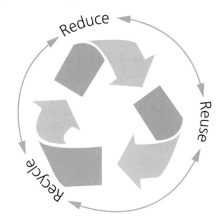

Figure 4.14 Reduce, reuse, recycle

Conservation behaviours can be seen as including all behaviours that help to minimise damage to the environment. These include reducing consumption of resources, reusing rather than disposing of resources wherever possible, and recycling whatever we cannot reuse. However, the definition of conservation behaviours can be extended beyond simply the *amount* of resources that we use. As our environment can also be damaged aesthetically, prevention and control of litter can also be included. Furthermore, as the environment can be

damaged by the release of particular chemicals into the atmosphere, soil or water, so controls on pollution need to be included as well. Is this list exhaustive? Many of you may want to argue that 'the environment' refers to non-human animals as well as the physical environment (land, oceans, and so on) and, as such, we should include actions to protect wildlife within our list of conservation behaviours. Is this going too far? On the one hand, it would seem strange to have more concern for a mountain that can't feel pain than a non-human animal that can but, on the other hand, we may struggle to reconcile conservation of wildlife with a need or desire to eat meat. What this should demonstrate is that the question of what counts as a 'conservation behaviour' is not as simple as it might initially appear.

A distinction that can be made in relation to conservation behaviours is between 'light greens' and 'dark greens'. Both are environmentalists but the difference in thinking is as follows:

- **Light greens** tend to be concerned with actions at the level of the individual. They focus on actions such as recycling waste products, insulating homes more effectively, car sharing and buying produce that is in season and locally sourced. Light greens believe that through such actions as these it is possible to send out signals to producers that they will get more custom if they are environmentally responsible. Essentially, light greens believe that the aim of environmentalism should be to make the current economic model (of globalised capitalism) more sustainable. They would like to live their lives in essentially the same sort of way as they currently do (for example, still using cars and aeroplanes), but just in a less environmentally damaging way.
- **Dark greens** tend to be concerned with actions at the level of society as a whole. They believe in the need for collective action to create whole communities that are more sustainable and in which (for example) people work in the same town in which they live and communities are made more self-sufficient by growing the food that local people eat and generating the electricity that they need (for example, through solar panels and wind turbines on their houses). Dark greens are more inclined to believe that the current economic model needs to be

Stop and ask yourself...

- What conservation behaviours do you engage in? Are there more that you could undertake? What stops you from becoming involved in these? What could get you to take part in them?

Links to
- Understanding the issues

fundamentally changed. They tend to be prepared to change the way they live their lives to make them more environmentally sustainable.

Keeping this distinction in mind, it should be clear that what counts as a conservation behaviour to a light green won't always be the same as what counts as a conservation behaviour to a dark green. It is also important to bear in mind that, in different places around the world, there are different priorities in relation to conservation behaviours. Thus, in the Middle East conservation of freshwater supplies is much more of an issue than it is for those of us living in rainier parts of the world, while in many parts of China air quality has become the most significant environmental concern. That said, with regard to conserving and recycling, it is possible to identify a number of relevant behaviours.

The focus of conservation is on slowing down the rate at which we are using up the planet's resources. One of the key areas of focus is on reducing our reliance on fossil fuels (especially coal, oil and gas), both because supplies of fossil fuels are finite and also because the burning of them seems to be contributing to the increased concentrations of carbon dioxide and other greenhouse gases in the atmosphere and, in turn, to climate change. While we still live in an economy where most of our electricity is created by the burning of fossil fuels, there are a number of actions that individuals can take to reduce their use of them:

- In relation to people's homes, conservation behaviours would include living in smaller houses, installing more energy-efficient boilers, insulating homes more effectively (with double glazing, loft insulation, cavity wall insulation) and turning down thermostats, as well as reducing the proportion of the year heating is on for.
- In relation to travel, conservation behaviours would include using public transport, walking or cycling; where it is unavoidable to use cars, engines should be small, cars should be driven in a fuel-conscious way and car sharing should be done; air travel should be used as sparingly as possible.
- In relation to general lifestyle, conservation behaviours would include limiting family size to a 'replacement' level of two children, making goods last rather

than constantly 'upgrading' them, avoiding buying takeaway food products in single-use packaging, drinking tap water rather than bottled water, having as many vegetarian meals as possible (on the grounds that plant products require less resources to produce than meat products) and campaigning in support of initiatives (such as wind or solar farms) that seek to reduce our reliance on fossil fuels.

With regard to the conservation of other resources, water can be conserved through such measures as not leaving the tap running when brushing teeth, having a shower rather than a bath (or reusing someone else's bath), not flushing the toilet after every use, and avoiding the purchase of too many water-intensive crops such as rice, cotton or sugar cane. Meanwhile, fish stocks (which are highly vulnerable to the tragedy of the commons) can be conserved by consumers paying attention to the type of fish they buy (not those under threat from overfishing) as well as where it has come from and how it was caught (not as a consequence of bottom trawling).

As to recycling, the extent to which it is possible to do this will clearly relate to the availability of recycling facilities in a given area. It is often possible to recycle glass, paper products, metal products, plastics and WEEE (waste electrical and electronic equipment) products; however, if the recycling plants don't exist then, even if you want to recycle a product, you may not be able to.

Factors that influence the tendency to conserve or recycle

Many factors can be expected to influence the tendency to conserve energy or to recycle waste products. Some of these may be *situational*, such as whether there are any recycling facilities nearby, while others may be *individual* (for example, someone who is physically disabled may find it harder to engage in recycling behaviour than someone who is able-bodied). These individual factors can be separated out further as some may be *cognitive* (for example, a perception of the costs

Stop and ask yourself ...

- This section has just been describing conservation behaviours that people could engage in. Where is the psychology in this? As a student of the subject, try to identify questions that psychologists could ask (and maybe try to answer) in relation to these behaviours.

Links to debates
- Research questions
- Idea for a practical activity

of recycling relative to the benefits; a person's attitude towards recycling) while others may be *social* (such as whether a person's peer group engages in recycling behaviour or not).

Any attempt to influence people to conserve or recycle more needs to start from an awareness of what the obstacles to behaviour change might be. However, even if these can be ascertained, important questions remain to be answered. For example, if it is suspected that people are not engaging in conservation behaviours because of a lack of knowledge about why they should do this, then will an education campaign in itself be enough to change their behaviour? Similarly, if it is believed that the problem is not a lack of information so much as people's attitudes (for example, they don't believe that environmental issues are important, or they don't believe that anything they do will make much difference), then what are the best ways to change such attitudes? If it is believed that the focus should simply be on changing people's behaviour, then are practices such as taxing undesirable behaviours the best way to achieve this?

Sitting behind these questions are some important debates, especially the question of whether changes in thinking are needed for changes in behaviour to occur. Many people would argue that this is, indeed, the case. For example, the theory of planned behaviour put forward by Ajzen and colleagues in the 1980s proposed that behaviours flow from behavioural intentions which, in turn, arise from three influencing factors:

- **attitudes towards the behaviour** – composed of both beliefs about the outcomes of the behaviour and a person's evaluations of these outcomes; for example, 'becoming vegetarian will help to conserve resources, and that would be a good thing'
- **subjective norms** – composed of beliefs about the attitudes of other people to the behaviour and an evaluation of whether the person is motivated to want to comply with their desires; for example, 'the people I respect the most are vegetarian and I would like their approval'
- **perceived behavioural control** – composed of beliefs about how easy or difficult a person thinks it will be for them to achieve desired goals, bearing in mind internal and external control factors and past experiences; for example, 'I have succeeded in changing my diet in the past (when I gave up chocolate for Lent) and the local shop stocks plenty of fruit and veg'.

The theory of planned behaviour would lend support to the idea that it is necessary to change people's attitudes towards conserving or recycling if we hope to change their behaviour. However, is this the

case? Behaviourists would take a different approach, arguing that behaviour change can be achieved more straightforwardly through (for example) the rewards or punishments that are attached to particular behaviours. This suggestion draws on the ideas of operant conditioning, in which Skinner suggested that anything that strengthens a behaviour and makes it more likely to be repeated can be deemed a 'reinforcer' while anything that weakens a behaviour and makes it less likely to be repeated can be deemed a 'punishment'.

As you may remember from the 'Funhaler' study by Chaney *et al.* in Unit 2, a distinction can be made between positive and negative reinforcement: positive reinforcement involves receiving something pleasant (for example, a whistle and spinner) whereas negative reinforcement involves the removal of something unpleasant (for example, the symptoms of asthma). Punishments can also be categorised in this way, with 'positive punishments' involving the presentation of something unpleasant and 'negative punishments' involving the removal of something pleasant. Interestingly, Skinner consistently maintained that punishment was much less effective than reinforcement (particularly positive reinforcement) as a way of changing behaviour, his reason being that it may make certain behaviours less likely to happen but what it doesn't do is teach the new behaviours to replace them.

How can the principles of operant conditioning be applied to conservation behaviours in humans? To answer this question it is necessary to introduce a further distinction – namely, that between primary reinforcers (those things that are naturally reinforcing in themselves, such as food, water or sex) and secondary reinforcers (things that are not reinforcing in themselves but which become reinforcing because of their association with primary reinforcers – the classic example is money, which enables us to buy many of those things that we would like to have). Operant conditioning would suggest that one way to achieve changes in people's behaviour towards the environment might be to offer positive reinforcement – perhaps in the form of secondary reinforcers – for those behaviours that, as a society, we would like to encourage more of. As we are about to see, a range of different approaches tend to be taken in the attempt to influence people's tendency to conserve or recycle, some of which are more successful than others.

Strategies to influence people's environmental behaviour can be categorised as either 'antecedent' or 'consequent':

- **Antecedent strategies** are those that occur *before* the behaviour they are attempting to change – examples might include information campaigns, attempts to change people's attitudes, the use of prompts to behaviour (such as signs), or obtaining pledges from people about ways they intend to behave.

- **Consequent strategies** occur *after* the behaviour has taken place – examples might include the presenting of a deposit for returning a bottle (a positive reinforcement) or a fine for littering (a positive punishment), or the lifting of a ban on entering a park (because someone has cleared the park of litter – a negative reinforcement) or the cancellation of a contract with a company that has been found guilty of mass pollution (a negative punishment); it can also include the use of feedback.

We will now look at examples of these strategies in more detail.

Antecedent strategies

Information campaigns

Attempts to change people's behaviour by providing them with more information are based on a 'knowledge-deficit model' since the assumption behind them is that what is holding people back from acting is a deficit in their knowledge. This lack of knowledge could relate to information about the importance of the issue or the precise actions that individuals can take. However, education alone does not appear to be sufficient to influence people's tendency to conserve or recycle, as was shown in a study by Heberlein (1975) in which people were given one of three things – either a booklet of energy-saving tips, a letter informing them about the costs (both personal and to society) of not conserving energy, or a pamphlet actually encouraging them to use more energy. Irrespective of which educational strategy they received, there were no significant changes in behaviour.

Changing people's attitudes

The Yale Model of Persuasion, first developed by Hovland and colleagues at Yale University in the 1950s, can be used as the basis for attempts to change attitudes towards the environment. This suggests that there are four major factors involved in persuasive communication:

- The source – a message will be seen as more believable if it comes from a source that is credible (for example, is known to have expertise in the area), is attractive and is trustworthy (they have nothing to gain by persuading the audience).
- The message – if the audience is well educated then a two-sided argument (in which the alternative position is acknowledged) will be more effective

but, if they are less well educated, then a one-sided argument will be more persuasive. Messages will have most effect if they are not too fear-arousing, as shown by Janis and Feshbach (1953).

- The recipient – if the audience is already committed to an existing position and extremely resistant to change, then smaller attitude changes should be attempted; if, however, the audience does not have strong views either way, then greater attitude change can be sought.
- The situation – messages are most effective when communicated in informal situations (for example, group discussions) as opposed to formal situations (for example, speeches or lectures), partly because in group contexts participants can more easily be required to make a commitment such as to sign a petition and/or donate some money – cognitive dissonance theory predicts that their attitude is then likely to be brought in line with this behaviour.

The Yale Model also proposes that there are three stages to an effective communication:

- attention to the message – it has to be noticed
- comprehension of the message – it has to be understood
- acceptance of the message – it has to be believed.

Evidence that a message can fail to succeed in the second of these stages comes from Jacoby *et al.* (1980), who found that the information in a 30-second television clip was misunderstood by 30 to 40 per cent of the adults who saw it.

Take it further

- Try applying the Yale Model to an environmental message, for example about adopting a largely vegetarian diet.

Prompts

The use of prompts represents another antecedent strategy. These will typically take the form of signs aimed at triggering desired behaviours that might not take place without the presence of a notice (for example 'please turn off the lights when you leave the room') or nudging people away from undesired behaviours that might occur without the reminder ('don't drop litter – use the bins instead').

Prompts that are attractive or unusual can be very effective, as was demonstrated by a scheme called Gum Target that was introduced in Bournemouth in 2002 to address the problem of chewing gum on the town's streets. The front of the gum target prompted people to dispose of their gum by sticking it on a particular image (for example, the face of an unpopular celebrity) or on a particular message; although the scheme was withdrawn after two years, it was still collecting 1000 pieces of gum a week.

Prompts can also be effective if they are polite. For example, Reich and Robertson (1979) handed out three different flyers at a swimming pool. The messages were either 'Help Keep Your Pool Clean', 'Don't Litter', or 'Don't you DARE litter'. The least littering occurred in response to the first message, while the most littering occurred in response to the last message. It is thought that demanding messages of the third kind here cause psychological reactance (Brehm, 1972) as people react against attempts to place restrictions on how they behave.

Figure 4.15 A Gum Target poster

- Carry out a study of prompts in your area. Do any of them illustrate any of the points being made above? Take photographs of them to show to the other students in your class.

Proximity

Proximity is also relevant as an antecedent strategy. This was illustrated in a study by Luyben and Bailey (1979) carried out in four mobile home parks. Simply increasing the number of newspaper recycling facilities available (that is, making it easier for people to recycle because facilities were nearby) led to a 52 per cent increase in the recycling of newspapers.

Pledges

Another antecedent strategy that can make a difference is securing a commitment from individuals or groups

to change their behaviour. This can be particularly effective if people outwardly signal their commitment, as was shown in a study by Baca-Motes et al. (2013) at a hotel in Orange County, California. The study covered a 31-day period in which, at the end of the check-in process, guests would be presented with a card stating the hotel's commitment to the environment and be invited either to make a general commitment to be environmentally friendly during their stay at the hotel or a specific commitment to reuse towels during their hotel stay. A further variable was then manipulated by the way in which the hotel employee would subsequently give a Friends of the Earth pin badge to some (but not all) of those guests handing in the completed commitment card. It was found that those guests who made the specific commitment at check-in and also received a pin badge to signal their commitment were over 25 per cent more likely to hang at least one towel for reuse during their stay at the hotel, and hung up over 40 per cent more used towels than guests who followed the standard check-in procedure at the hotel. This would suggest that getting people to commit to behave in a particular way – and then socially signal that they have made such a commitment – could be an effective way of getting people undertaking conservation behaviours. That said, as only 83 per cent of those invited to make the specific commitment in Baca-Motes et al.'s study were prepared to do so (against 98 per cent of those invited to make the general commitment), and even then the majority of those who made this specific commitment did not behave in the way that they said they would, clearly it will not be enough in itself to achieve sustained behaviour change.

Consequent strategies
Positive reinforcement

Positive reinforcement can be highly effective as a way of influencing the tendency to conserve or recycle. This was shown as early as 1971 when Oregon became the first state in the USA to pass a 'bottle bill' in which people would be given $0.05 for every can, bottle or drink container that they returned. Following enactment of this law, the rate of return for drinks containers rose to 90 per cent, leading to significant reductions in litter as well as improved resource conservation. A similar law was passed in New York State in 1983, leading to similarly dramatic effects (recycling of glass drinks containers increased from 3 per cent to 77 per cent, while recycling of metal drinks containers increased from 5 per cent to 59 per cent).

Punishment

In spite of the effectiveness of positive reinforcement as a strategy for improving conservation behaviour, governments tend to fall back more on punishment (particularly 'positive punishments', such as fines) as their main consequent strategy. While it is possible to appreciate why this might be attractive to governments (for example, as a way of raising revenue), is this an effective strategy?

An example of how punishments can have effects very different from those that might be expected was reported by Gneezy and Rustichini (2000). The study took place in Haifa, Israel, at ten privately run children's day-care centres. The day-care centres operated from 7.30 a.m. to 4 p.m. each day. For the first four weeks of the study, the researchers monitored the number of parents who arrived late to collect their children. Then, in the fifth week of the study, they introduced to six of the day-care centres a system under which anyone arriving more than ten minutes late to collect their child would be fined ten shekels per child – a sum the researchers describe as relatively small but not insignificant. They monitored what happened before, in the seventeenth week of the study, the system of fines was removed. They then monitored what happened for the three weeks after that. Three facts emerged:

1. The effect of introducing the fine (in week five) was a significant increase in the number of late-coming parents.

2. Removing the fine (in week seventeen) did not affect the number of late-coming parents relative to the time of the fine. In particular, the number remained higher in the treatment group than in the control group.
3. There had been no significant difference between the behaviour of the test group and the control group in the initial four weeks.

How did the researchers explain these results? The clue is contained in the title they gave to their research paper – namely, 'A fine is a price'. Essentially, what seemed to happen was that the parents concerned didn't view the fine as a punishment for undesirable behaviour (i.e. being late) but instead saw it as the price for a service – namely, keeping their children in nursery that bit longer. Worse, once it had been established that it was possible to pay to keep a child in nursery after 4 p.m., even the removal of the fine failed to change the perception that this was a service that could be bought – it just happened now to be free!

The research reported by Gneezy and Rustichini clearly does not relate to conservation behaviours, but it has been included here because it may contain lessons that can be applied to the management of environmentally related behaviour, suggesting that introducing a fine won't necessarily change behaviour in the ways that are intended.

Feedback

There is evidence that providing feedback can increase levels of recycling. De Leon and Fuqua (1995) reported a study in which households either signed a letter making a public commitment to recycle and giving permission to publish their names in a local newspaper (the commitment-only group), received weekly feedback on pounds of recyclable paper generated by their group (the feedback-only group), received a combination of both of these interventions (the combined-intervention group) or received neither intervention (the control group). Relative to baseline, the feedback-only group increased the weight of recyclable paper by 25.47 per cent while for the combined-intervention group the increase was 40 per cent. In contrast, neither of the other two groups showed any substantial change over the same period.

- How easy would it be to provide feedback for people on their conservation behaviours? Identify conservation behaviours for which this would or wouldn't be feasible.
- To what extent do the findings from De Leon and Fuqua's study contradict those from the study by Baca-Motes *et al.* into pledges?

Key research: Lord (1994) Motivating recycling behaviour: A quasi experimental investigation of message and source strategies

This study investigates the effectiveness of different ways of trying to persuade people to recycle their waste. Specifically, it looks at how best to frame messages (i.e. positively, in terms of the benefits to gain from recycling; or negatively, in terms of the consequences of not recycling) and also whether it is best to convey the messages in the form of an advertisement, a newspaper report or a personal message (i.e. who the source should be).

Background

Americans threw out 196 million tons of waste material in 1990, which was more than double the amount thrown out in 1960. To try and improve levels of recycling, studies have shown the benefits of people making a public commitment to environmentally responsible behaviours, people being required to keep a record of their behaviour (in a form of self-monitoring), and financial incentives being provided. However, what are needed are methods for motivating people to participate fully in recycling programmes that are practical and cost-effective on a widespread basis.

Aim

This study aimed to investigate the relative effectiveness of two different message approaches (positively and negatively framed appeals) and three different source strategies (advertising appeals, publicity-generated news items and personal-influence appeals) in enhancing people's beliefs about, attitudes towards and behavioural compliance with community recycling programmes.

Sample

Data was obtained from 140 households (20 per condition) in a north-eastern US metropolitan community served by a kerbside recycling programme. Quota sampling was used to try to ensure that the households selected for involvement in the study matched as closely as possible the community's demographic diversity. However, Lord acknowledges that there was a slight bias towards the inclusion of more upmarket suburban neighbourhoods, reflecting an attempt to avoid sending student assistants into certain inner-city neighbourhoods to collect data for safety reasons. Of questionnaire respondents, 57 per cent were female. Ages ranged from 19 to 65, with a mean of 34.9 years.

Method

Data collection proceeded in the following stages:

1. On kerbside collection day of the first week, student assistants discreetly observed and recorded on an observation form the contents of each test household's recycling bin. The observers recorded both the total number of items put out for recycling and also the categories these fell within (newspapers/magazines, bottles, cans, and so on).
2. On the following day, they left a stimulus message at the front door of each test household, avoiding face-to-face contact. This step was omitted for the 20 households in the control condition, but the other 120 households received one of the messages shown in Table 4.1.

Table 4.1 The different messages sent to 120 test households

Message source	Message approach
Advertisement	Positively framed
Advertisement	Negatively framed
Publicity (news article)	Positively framed
Publicity (news article)	Negatively framed
Personal influence	Positively framed
Personal influence	Negatively framed

Positively framed messages focused on the environmental benefits, savings to the community, and personal and social satisfactions arising from full participation in recycling programmes. Negatively framed messages described the risks – physical, environmental and social – of failing to recycle, as well as some of the possible measures that

- Will Lord be examining the effectiveness of antecedent or consequent strategies?

Links to
- Check your understanding

could be necessitated by such failure. In the advertisement conditions, the message had the appearance of an ad and was attributed to a fictitious company claiming to be a distributor of environmentally friendly products in the region. In the publicity (news article) conditions, it was described as having recently appeared in a local news publication. In the personal influence conditions, it appeared in the form of a letter signed by a student assistant and addressed to a personal acquaintance.

Figure 4.16 An example of a positive recycling poster

On kerbside collection day of the following week, the observation of recycling bin contents was repeated (to assess the *behavioural* impact of the stimulus messages).

On the day after the second observation, the student assistants contacted and delivered a questionnaire to the adult member of each household most involved in sorting and taking out the rubbish. This was to obtain data about the participants' *beliefs* in the arguments raised by the messages (assessed by a series of statements with 7-point Likert scales attached to them), their *attitudes* towards recycling (assessed by four 7-point semantic differential items: good–bad, wise–foolish, harmful–beneficial, favourable–unfavourable) and demographic information (gender and age of person completing the questionnaire, highest level of education attained by any household member, and annual household income). Respondents were assured of anonymity and asked to return the questionnaire in a sealed envelope.

Results

Combined together, the experimental conditions showed a significant increase from the first to the second week in both the number of recycling categories and the total number of items put out for recycling. The control group manifested no significant change with respect to either *behavioural* measure.

With regard to message approaches, those who received a positively framed message expressed significantly more favourable *attitudes* towards recycling and stronger *belief* in statements that constituted that message's rationale for participation in the recycling programme than those who received a negatively framed message.

With regard to source strategies, advertising enjoyed an unexpected advantage relative to the other formats in engendering *belief* in the positively framed claims. With regard to increases in recycling *behaviour*, results supported the expected advantages of personal influence, especially when exerted via negatively framed messages.

Discussion

Lord suggests that combinations of the strategies examined in this study could possibly offer results surpassing those generated by any of the experimental conditions. For example, combinations of positively and negatively framed arguments in a single message could produce some of the *attitudinal* benefits of the former and the *behavioural* benefits of the latter in a single message. Alternatively, parties trying to increase recycling could try employing positively framed messages in the mass media, and at the same time recruit concerned consumers to convey negatively framed personal influence among their acquaintances.

Application: techniques to increase recycling and other conservation behaviour

If asked to discuss at least one technique that could be used to increase recycling or other conservation behaviour, it would be worth keeping in mind the distinction between antecedent and consequent strategies. It might be that a strategy would be primarily behavioural (for example, focusing on antecedent strategies such as prompts and consequent strategies such as reinforcement) or, alternatively, it could be more cognitive (working on changing people's attitudes, obtaining pledges, and then providing them with feedback). Alternatively, an effective strategy could be a combination of both, in recognition of the suggestion (Festinger, 1957) that people whose behaviour contradicts their expressed attitudes will experience cognitive dissonance and, as such, feel a discomfort that will either lead to them bringing their attitudes in line with their behaviour or their behaviour in line with their attitudes.

> **Take it further**
>
> - Find out more about cognitive dissonance theory. Look up Festinger and Carlsmith's $1/$20 experiment from 1959.
> - Investigate ways in which people can reduce feelings of cognitive dissonance. How might these be of relevance to attempts to increase people's conservation behaviours?

Ergonomics – human factors (Cognitive)

When equipment is being designed, should designers bear in mind the people who are going to be using it? This will probably seem like a daft question to you – of course they should! However, it wasn't so long ago that the focus was on training people to use the equipment that was there rather than on designing equipment that would mesh with the people who were going to be using it.

A particularly dramatic example of this occurred during the Second World War (1939–45) when a number of Boeing B-17 'Flying Fortress' aeroplanes were crashing upon landing. Alphonse Chapanis, who was the first psychologist to have been employed at the US Army Air Force Aero Medical Lab in Dayton, Ohio, noticed that not only were the switches for the landing flaps and the landing gear (i.e. the equipment that supports a plane when it is not flying – normally wheels) identical, but that they were placed side by side. What was happening was that tired pilots were accidentally activating the wrong switch and coming into land without their wheels in position.

Figure 4.17 Boeing B-17 'Flying Fortress'

This episode made Chapanis realise the need for research into how humans interact with machines, to make such interactions as efficient and as error-free as possible. In particular, machinery needed to be designed around the people who would be using it. This is what ergonomics (or 'human factors' psychology, as it is known in the USA) is all about. Ergonomics can be defined as 'the study of designing equipment and devices that fit the human body, its movement and cognitive abilities' (Steptoe-Warren, 2013).

Efforts to improve how people interact with equipment (often, but not always, in workplace settings) focus on different areas. One such area relates to people's *physical* characteristics. For instance, it is to avoid health problems such as back pain, eyestrain and musculoskeletal disorders that computers in offices will be positioned at a particular height and a particular angle; it is also because of the size of young children that tables and chairs in primary schools are much smaller than those for students in secondary schools or colleges. Such considerations are important, but of more interest to us is *cognitive* ergonomics, which is focused on ensuring that machinery is designed to fit with how people think.

Our interaction with equipment is a two-way process, with equipment communicating with us and us communicating with equipment. Ways in which equipment could fail to communicate effectively with us could include bombarding the user with too much information, foregrounding relatively unimportant information, and communicating information in confusing ways (for example, way-finding maps not being orientated in a forward-up way, with what is high up on a map corresponding to what is ahead in the environment). Ways in which poor design of equipment could make it difficult for us to communicate with them include the direction (clockwise or anticlockwise) in which to turn dials, the number of pedals to press, or (as with the B-17 bombers) where switches are positioned.

Cognitive overload

Cognitive ergonomics presupposes an understanding of how people think. Over the years, attempts to achieve such an understanding have taken a range of forms including carrying out experiments that focus on mental processes separately (perception, attention and memory) and also developing models to try

 Stop and ask yourself...

Think of your own interactions with equipment – perhaps with your mobile phone, computers or with the instrumentation in cars.

- Are there any ways in which they are designed that make them difficult to interact with?
- Can you think of ways in which they could be made easier to interact with?

Links to
- Understanding the issues

to capture what seems to be going on in people's thought processes. In more recent years, neuroimaging techniques have been used to investigate whether there are particular regions of the brain that correspond to the claims made in cognitive models.

The concept of cognitive overload makes the claim that there are limits to the amount of stimuli that people can handle at any one point in time. Bell *et al.* (1996) suggest that there are four parts to the concept of environmental load:

1. The capacity of humans to process incoming stimuli is limited.
2. Information overload occurs when our capacity to process information is exceeded by the amount of information making a claim on our attention. When this happens, the normal reaction is to block out those inputs that are less relevant or distracting and focus harder on the task at hand in a kind of 'tunnel vision'.
3. We give most attention to stimuli that are intense, unpredictable or uncontrollable and that may require some sort of adaptive response.
4. Our capacity for attention can be temporarily depleted by prolonged demands on it that leave it overloaded.

Figure 4.18 There are limits to the amount of stimuli a person can handle at any one point

This model of cognitive overload can be used to explain a number of different experiences. One such experience would be the feeling of exhaustion that many people feel after spending a day in a large unfamiliar city, given the need to pay attention to all the other people,

traffic, road signs, shops, etc. Similarly, imagine trying to study in an environment that was full of other people and which was noisy, had lots of colourful displays (including a TV screen), and in which you were being bombarded with information through distracting websites, text messages and emails. You would probably find it extremely difficult to focus your attention on the work at hand in such a situation, and the effort that this would require would probably leave you feeling exhausted at the end of the day. In the workplace, it is conceivable that an employee could be faced with information coming at them from a range of different angles and have a limited amount of time in which to process this information and put it to use.

How can we know if people are overloaded in this way? One method is known as *secondary task performance*. Working on the assumption that people who are overloaded may focus on doing their primary tasks well (as suggested in the second part of Bell *et al.*'s model), researchers have sought to assess overload by seeing how much spare 'mental capacity' is left over for subsidiary tasks. An example of this came from Brown and Poulton (1961). In their study, participants drove a car in either an area with a relatively small number of important inputs (i.e. a residential area) or an area with a relatively large number of important inputs (i.e. the car park of a crowded shopping centre). While doing this, they listened to a tape containing a series of pre-recorded numbers and had to identify those numbers that changed from one sequence to the next. Participants made more errors on this numbers task when driving in the shopping centre car park, which cognitive overload theory could explain in terms of the participants needing to give more attention to the stimuli associated with their primary task of driving in this environment and therefore having less mental capacity left over for the stimuli associated with the less important numbers task.

Most secondary task performance studies will not be as ethically problematic as Brown and Poulton's study. For example, a more recent experiment by Scholl *et al.* (2003) investigated the impact of talking on a mobile phone on the ability of participants to notice an unexpected object. In this study, participants were divided into two conditions. In one condition, participants viewed a computerised display containing many moving items with various features and were given a multiple

🚫 **Stop and ask yourself ...**

- Have you ever had any experiences of cognitive overload? If so, describe them to someone else. What did you do to cope with the situation?

Links to
- Understanding the issues

object tracking (MOT) task. They completed three trials before, on the fourth trial, an unexpected event occurred as a new salient object suddenly entered and passed across the display, fully visible and in motion for five seconds. It was found that 30 per cent of participants in this condition failed to notice the unexpected object.

In the other condition, participants completed the same task but this time they also had a mobile phone conversation with a confederate during the experiment. Results showed that participants in this condition were no less accurate at the overt MOT task, but this time 90 per cent of them failed to notice the unexpected object!

IN THE NEWS

Traffic accidents caused by mobile phone distraction could kill more people in the UK than drink-driving. In 2012, 548 people were hurt and 17 died as a result of these accidents, while in-vehicle distraction, some of which also involved mobile phones, caused a further 196 deaths between 2010 and 2012. As this number increases (it was only 27 fewer than drink-driving) and accidents caused by drink-driving decrease, mobile phone distraction is set to be the biggest cause of fatal accidents.

Representatives of the government and evidence from road safety cameras have suggested current legislation is not working and want harsher sentences, such as six-point fixed penalties for mobile phone use while driving or a one-year automatic driving ban. It is hoped that more serious consequences will stop people using mobile phones while driving as, in 2012, 583,686 drivers were fined £60 and had three points added to their licence for this offence. This was over ten times the 55,300 who were convicted of drink-driving offences.

An even more common way of measuring how overloaded people are at work than secondary task performance studies is the use of *self-report*. An example of a self-report tool is Hart and Staveland's NASA-TLX (task load index) which was developed in the aviation/space context and is a subjective workload assessment tool that derives an overall workload score from a weighted average of ratings on six sub-scales. These are as follows:

- Mental demands – how mentally demanding was the task?
- Physical demands – how physically demanding was the task?
- Temporal demands – how hurried or rushed was the pace of the task?
- Own performance – how successful were you in accomplishing what you were asked to do?
- Effort – how hard did you have to work to accomplish your level of performance?
- Frustration – how insecure, discouraged, irritated, stressed and annoyed were you?

Many cognitive processes (for example, perception and attention) can be invoked to explain a person's feelings of cognitive overload, but the area we will focus on

will be research into memory. This is a hypothetical construct that has been developed to describe our ability to retain and recall information. As we will see, greater understanding of memory might help to reduce the dangers of cognitive overload in the workplace. Memory can be seen as involving three processes:

- **encoding** – the process by which we turn information that we have encountered into a form that is memorable
- **storage** – the process by which information is held or retained
- **retrieval** – the process by which stored information is recovered.

Since the earliest days of memory research, it has been suggested that our memory system has different parts to it, and this was expressed in the multi-store model of memory put forward by Atkinson and Shiffrin (1968), in which they suggested the existence of three distinct memory stores:

- **Sensory memory** – this is the first storage system, although it is perhaps more accurately described as an aspect of perception than of memory. It retains an impression of the stimulus that has been encountered, but only for a very short period of time.

🚫 Stop and ask yourself...

- What do you see as the strengths and weaknesses of (i) secondary task performance, and (ii) self-report as ways of measuring if workers are experiencing overload?

Links to research methods
- Validity
- Reliability
- Ethics

If the impression is not processed further in any way then it is forgotten.

- **Short-term memory** (STM) – this holds information on a short-term basis. There are limits to the amount of information that can be held in the STM as well as the length of time it can be held there for. However, Atkinson and Shiffrin argued that STM is the first stage for long-term memory (LTM) storage and that, through a process of rehearsal (repetition of the material to be learned), information can be transferred from STM to LTM.
- **Long-term memory** (LTM) – this holds information on a long-term (perhaps even life-long) basis and seems to have unlimited capacity.

Evidence for the claim that there are distinct structural components to memory has come from many sources. For example, there is the case of HM (reported by Scoville and Milner, 1957) who, at the age of 27, had had his hippocampi removed to control his epilepsy. This led to severe anterograde amnesia as he could no longer form any new memories of events that occurred after the surgery. However, as he retained memories of events from before the surgery (especially from before the age of 16), his case would suggest that LTM is separate from STM.

The Brown-Peterson technique is also of relevance in confirming that there are limits on how long information can be held in STM for. Normally, to try to remember a piece of information held in STM, we might repeat it to ourselves over and over many times. To prevent such rehearsal, the Brown-Peterson technique involves participants who have been presented with a three-letter trigram (such as FTH) being instructed to count down in threes from some specified number. With the possibility of rehearsal being denied them, Peterson and Peterson (1959) found that only about 30 per cent of the trigrams would be correctly recalled after nine seconds while less than 10 per cent would be correctly recalled after 18 seconds (see Figure 4.19).

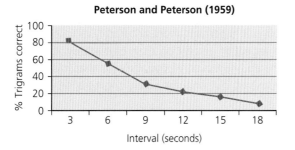

Peterson and Peterson (1959)

Figure 4.19 Results from Peterson and Peterson's study (1959)

Famously, Miller (1956) suggested that there are limits to people's STM spans. In his paper 'The magical number seven, plus or minus two' he suggested, however, that if we 'chunk' information together into units that mean something to us, then the seven chunks of remembered material can actually be quite large. To get a sense of how this works, try remembering the following letters:

OR-GCO-MA-CU-KG-OV

Presented this like this, you may have found these letters quite difficult to remember. However, suppose that the same letters were organised slightly differently, as follows:

ORG-COM-AC-UK-GOV

You may well now recognise that these are all internet domains. If so, the letters should become much easier to hold in your STM as, instead of remembering 13 separate (and probably meaningless) letters, they may now have a (single) meaning. If we can group or organise input sequences into chunks in this way, then the amount of information we can hold in our STM can be increased as, although the memory span remains limited to a fixed number of chunks, the chunks can be made larger and larger.

Have a go yourself

- Try devising a 'chunking' experiment that you can try out on other people. You could use either letters or numbers.

While research such as this would offer support to Atkinson and Shiffrin's multi-store model of memory, the model has not escaped criticism, and one of the most powerful criticisms came from Baddeley and Hitch (2001) who suggested that the way Atkinson and Shiffrin had been viewing STM was too simplistic. Instead of seeing it as a relatively passive structure with just one part to it, they suggested it should be seen as a much more active structure with several parts to it. Recasting it as 'working memory', Baddeley and Hitch's model suggested that STM consists of different subsystems co-ordinated by a central executive that work together to temporarily maintain mental representations of relevance to the performance of a cognitive task in an activated state, as shown in Figure 4.20.

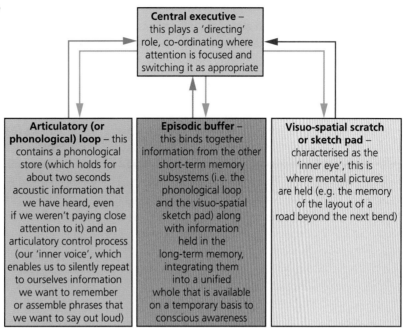

Figure 4.20 Components of 'working memory' (Baddeley and Hitch)

While this remains only a model and the concept of the central executive, in particular, requires more research, nonetheless Baddeley and Hitch's working memory model is of relevance to the concept of cognitive overload because of the way in which problems seem to arise when two or more tasks make use of the same component:

... the use of the sketchpad is interfered with by visual tasks but not by verbal tasks; the phonological loop is interfered with by verbal tasks but not by visual tasks. (*Medin* et al., *2001*)

Drews and Doig's key research can be seen as drawing on this insight by presenting information in different codes (numerical/phonological, and visuo-spatial) and, as such, avoiding overload by utilising different processing mechanisms.

The impact of observation in the workplace environment

As we have seen, ergonomic design necessitates attention being paid to both the physical and the mental requirements of those people who will be employed within a workplace setting. In principle, this sounds fairly straightforward, but in practice it raises difficult questions. For example, lessons learned from experimental research (for example, into short-term memory) could inform the design of workplace equipment, but how confident can we be that such research is ecologically valid and that its findings will apply in 'real-world' settings? Managers in an organisation might be keen to hear suggestions about how their existing equipment could be redesigned either to improve safety or to increase productivity, but how easy will this be to do in practice?

Quite aside from the financial costs that may be entailed by any suggestions that are generated, it would presumably involve relevant experts (such as occupational psychologists) coming into the organisation and observing it as it currently is before making their suggestions and then coming back and observing it again once the suggestions have been implemented. If employees know they are being observed, will this not affect how they behave? Furthermore, how easy will it be to measure the effect of any suggested changes, particularly if a number of changes have been proposed? How can the impact of these changes be measured in isolation from each other to be able to say which have had the most effect? If ergonomics is to be scientific in its approach then questions such as these need answering, but they should serve to illustrate some of the challenges of observation in the workplace environment.

Time studies

One of the people who pioneered the observation of workers was Frederick Winslow Taylor, who believed that by analysing work it would be possible to find the 'one best way' in which to do a given job. Working at the Bethlehem Steel Company in Pennsylvania, USA, he observed shovellers at work. Taylor noticed that first-class shovellers (as he described them) would do their best day's work with a shovel load of about 21 pounds (9.5 kg). He noticed, as well, that workers were allowed to select and own their own shovel. This, Taylor saw, led to great inefficiencies, as the shovellers could find themselves using this shovel to lift loads of approximately 30 pounds (13.6 kg) when shovelling heavy materials such as iron ore but then loads of less than 4 pounds (2 kg) when shovelling light materials such as rice coal. Taylor proposed the construction of a large shovel tool room to accommodate eight to ten different kinds of shovel so that workers could use different shovels for different materials – a small shovel for iron ore, for example, and a much larger one for ashes. This development, which reflected what Taylor called his 'principles of scientific management', was combined with the lessons learned from thousands of stopwatch observations of how quickly the best shovellers could push their shovel into a pile, swing it backwards and then throw their load over a given distance at a given height. Using this information to teach the other shovellers how to use their strength to the very best advantage, Taylor reported (1911) that the Bethlehem Steel Company was able to get the same amount of work out of 140 men that it had previously taken between 400 and 600 men to do.

Motion studies

Figure 4.21 Frank and Lillian Gilbreth observed the physical movements that people made while bricklaying to find the most efficient techniques

Taylor's method of observation in the workplace environment is described as a 'time study' because his main focus was on the length of time it should take to complete a given task; as such, his main tool was the stopwatch. Husband-and-wife team Frank and Lillian Gilbreth took a different view, arguing that the focus should be on the physical movements that people made in the course of their work, with the aim being to improve efficiency by minimising the number of these that need to be made. Such 'motion studies' involved the Gilbreths filming the movements made by workers and then analysing these recordings. Frank Gilbreth's book *Motion Study* (1911) outlines the technique in relation to bricklaying. There are, he explains, three stages to a motion study:

● discovering and classifying the best practice
● deducing the laws
● applying the laws to standardise practice, either for the purpose of increasing output or decreasing hours of labour, or both.

He argues that the variables affecting the amount of work that a worker is able to turn out can be grouped together into categories such as (i) variables of the worker, such as anatomy, health, temperament and training; (ii) variables of the surroundings, equipment and tools, such as heating, lighting, reward and punishment, and tools; and (iii) variables of the motion, such as acceleration, speed, direction, path and length. It is this last category that he was most interested in, and his book includes examples of pictures, charts and diagrams put together to teach apprentice bricklayers standard methods – namely, the pick-and-dip method, and the stringing-mortar method. With standardisation of the trades as the Gilbreths' explicit aim, their claim was that careful observation of the motions made by workers was the key to achieving this, as it was the first step towards guidance about the most efficient movements to make.

Stop and ask yourself…

● The above studies raise the question of *what* to observe (i.e. the length of time it takes someone to do a task, as opposed to the way in which they do it). In what ways might the questions of *when* to observe and *where* to observe also be of relevance here?

Links to
● Methodology

The Hawthorne studies

Perhaps the most famous example of observation in the workplace environment is Elton Mayo's studies at the Hawthorne plant of the Western Electric Company near Chicago in the 1920s and early 1930s. In this research (known as the Hawthorne studies), the aim was to investigate the impact of the physical environment on the productivity levels of the workers. One aspect of the physical environment that was investigated was light levels. Mayo systematically varied the lighting levels for an experimental group (six women assembling electrical relay switching) while keeping the levels of illumination constant for a control group. Not only was it found that both groups increased production, but the gains in productivity made by the experimental group were maintained whether they worked in bright or dull levels of lighting, or even when the researchers only pretended to change the lighting levels.

The results of these studies have been interpreted in many ways. One interpretation (the one that is labelled 'the Hawthorne effect') claims that the performance of the workers improved because of the novelty of the situation and because they knew they were being observed. This interpretation would suggest that an awareness of being observed is enough in itself to lead to improvements in productivity.

Find out more

In the Sport and Exercise chapter, one of the key studies is Zajonc et al.'s 'Social enhancement and impairment of performance in the cockroach' (1969). Within this study, audience effects are investigated.

- How did the presence of an audience affect Zajonc's cockroaches?
- Did the effect vary according to the level of complexity of the task they were carrying out?
- In what ways might this be of relevance to observation of people in the workplace environment?

The Hawthorne studies clearly raise the question of whether knowledge of being observed can affect the behaviour of those who are being observed. The study by Zajonc et al. would suggest that knowledge of being observed increases levels of arousal and, while this may enhance performance on tasks that are simple, familiar or well learned, it may impair performance on tasks that are novel, complex or unfamiliar. As a consequence, workplace studies that collect data through observation may lack validity as they may not be recording people's typical behaviour.

That said, studies such as those described above would suggest beneficial impacts of observation in the workplace environment. Whether carrying out time studies (as Taylor did) or motion studies (like the Gilbreths), it may be possible to identify ways to help less-productive workers perform at the level of the most productive workers. Arguably, the lesson to take from Mayo's Hawthorne studies is that it is less important what specific changes are made than simply running experiments that the workers are involved in. However, it is not clear how time or motion studies could be applied to many modern jobs that require ongoing decision making in dynamic team-based environments, while employees might become suspicious of or annoyed with permanent experimentation that never leads to any settled changes. Perhaps for reasons of this kind, modern ergonomic research – such as the key research we are about to look at – is often more focused on improvements that can be made to the equipment that people work with and obtain information from.

Key research: Drews and Doig (2014) Evaluation of a configural vital signs display for intensive care unit nurses

Drews and Doig assert that 'graphical patient displays provide an enhanced interface between the monitored system (the patient) and the user (the clinician)'. In this study, they investigated the benefits that might be gained by presenting nurses in intensive care units with information about patients in a graphical form rather than numerical.

Background

The intensive care unit (ICU) is a specialised hospital environment where critically ill and injured patients receive continuous physiological monitoring. Standard vital signs acquired and displayed on patient monitors include blood pressure, oxygen saturation, and heart and respiratory rates. Traditional monitoring displays present vital signs data in *numerical* form. Data on trends (such as whether the patient's heart rate is speeding up or slowing down) is generally accessible in a sub-menu but not presented on the main screen.

Aim

The goal of this study was to develop and evaluate a configural vital signs (CVS) display that would help nurses in the rapid detection and identification of physiological deterioration in a patient by presenting vital signs data *graphically* and in context with each other. In particular, instead of nurses just receiving data on a patient's vital signs in numerical form, they would receive:

1. Numerical data on the patient's heart rate, blood oxygen saturation, and systolic, diastolic and mean arterial blood pressures (i.e. the data they would have received anyway).
2. Graphically presented trend data for each of the above measures, positioned immediately to the left of each numerical display.
3. Graphically presented data indicating the degree of variability in the patient's physiology over time and, within this, their current state. A thin grey rectangle indicated normal or customisable thresholds. A solid white rectangle indicated the extent to which the patient's physiology had varied over the previous hour, with its upper boundary representing their maximum systolic blood pressure, the lower

boundary representing their minimum diastolic blood pressure, the left-most boundary representing their lowest heart rate value, and the right-most boundary representing their highest heart rate value. The patient's current state was represented through a current state object (CSO) which, through its spatial position in relation to the white rectangle, indicated how stable the patient currently was. For example, a CSO close to the edges of the white rectangle would indicate ongoing vital signs changes, whereas a centrally located CSO would indicate vital signs stability. The colour of the CSO reflected the blood saturation percentage (100–93 per cent, red; 92–91 per cent, orange; 90–89 per cent, pink; 88–87 per cent, purple; less than 87 per cent, blue).

Within the CVS display, the data was colour co-ordinated from one part of the display to another.

Figure 4.22 Screenshots of (a) the configural vital signs (CVS) display; the centre panel (numerical data) is identical to the control display; (b) current state object (CSO) with low variability (60–85 bpm; left panel) and high variability (60–120 bpm; right panel) of heart rate over the last hour

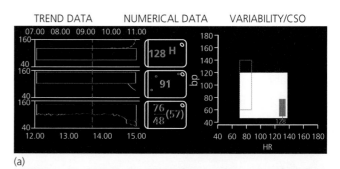
(a)

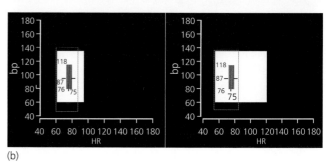
(b)

Sample

A total of 42 registered nurses with critical care training and a minimum of one year of ICU experience took part in this study, with 21 in each condition. Their mean age was 44.59 years (range 25–64), and their mean amount of ICU experience was 8.48 years (range 2–30). Within the sample, 69 per cent were female.

Method

The study involved each participant being presented with four different patient scenarios. Prior to beginning the experiment, they were instructed to verbally evaluate each patient's physiological status, interpret

the data and recommend appropriate interventions as quickly and accurately as possible. Participants were given information about each patient's medical diagnoses, past medical history, and previous and current administered medications. They were then given 300 seconds (five minutes) to complete each scenario.

All participants received information about the vital signs of the patients on a 15-inch desktop computer, but half of the participants (the experimental condition) received information on the patients via a configural vital signs (CVS) display, while the other half (the control condition) received it via a traditional ICU display that consisted of the numerical data section of the CVS display as a primary display with trend information accessible through a single key press.

The dependent measures in this experiment were (i) response time, measured from the start of the scenario to when the nurse verbalised his or her assessment, and (ii) accuracy of data interpretation (i.e. whether the nurse correctly identified the patient's condition).

Scenario presentation order was randomised in the same way for both conditions.

On completion of the four scenarios, all participants completed self-report questionnaires on the tasks, including on the level of mental demand associated with the task.

The four clinical scenarios were as follows:

Table 4.2 Summary of vital sign information required and provided for correct nurse assessment of the patient's state for all scenarios

Clinical scenario	Background information provided	Information required for nursing assessment provided on displays	Information provided in the CVS display
Early sepsis	24 hr following heart valve replacement	BP trending down, yet still WNL; HR trending up and significantly elevated; SpO_2 WNL	Status quo object at edge in lower right corner of variability frame; red colour of CSO, MAB normal; normal shape
Septic shock	48 hr following a small bowel resection, remains mechanically ventilated	BP trending down and critically low; HR trending up and significantly elevated; SpO_2 trending down	Status quo object at edge in lower right corner of variability frame; orange colour of CSO, MAB extremely low; compressed shape
Pulmonary embolus	Advanced age (79 years), 6 days following hip replacement, developed pneumonia, and mechanically ventilated	BP trending down; HR trending up; SpO_2 trending down and critically low	Status quo object at edge in lower right corner of variability frame; blue colour of CSO, MAB lower than normal; compressed shape
Stable scenario	No background information available	BP, HR, SpO_2 WNL; no deterioration of vital signs in trend data	Status quo object centred in variability frame and in normal frame; red colour of CSO, normal shape

BP – arterial blood pressure (systolic/diastolic and mean); CSO – current state object; CVS – configural vital signs; HR – heart rate; MAB – mean arterial blood pressure; SpO_2 – oxygen saturation acquired via pulse oximetry; WNL – within normal limits

Results

With regard to response time, participants in the CVS display condition identified the patient's state 48 per cent quicker than participants in the control display condition in the septic shock scenario and 38 per cent quicker in the pulmonary embolism scenario. They were also significantly quicker to identify the condition of the patient in the stable scenario.

Accuracy of nurses' assessments improved by a third or more when using the CVS display relative to the control display in the septic shock and pulmonary embolism scenarios. The differences in the other two scenarios were not significant, although in the stable scenario it was approaching significance.

The nurses reported significantly lower mental demand in the CVS display condition (mean = 3.95) than in the control condition (mean = 4.71).

Discussion

The authors express frustration that, in spite of empirical evidence demonstrating the benefits of configural

displays, there continues to be a lack of 'bench-to-bedside' translation, meaning that the vast majority of ICU monitoring displays still present clinical data numerically. That said, they acknowledge that future studies are needed to examine a wider range of clinical events as well as a larger number of vital signs, including body temperature. They also accept that, because their CVS display included a number of differences from the traditional display, future studies will be needed to identify the contribution of each design factor to clinical performance.

Application: workplace design based on ergonomic research

If asked to discuss at least one workplace design based on ergonomic research, you may well choose to focus on cognitive ergonomics (in which attempts are made to design equipment that fits with how people think), but you should not forget about more physical aspects of ergonomics, such as ensuring that workplaces are

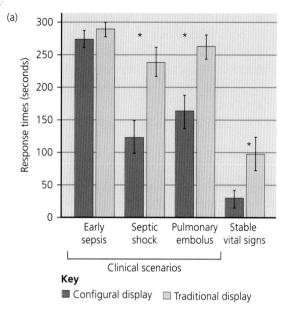
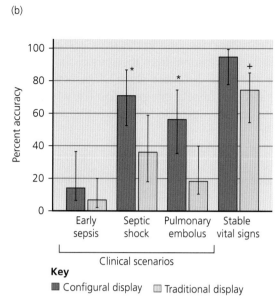

Figure 4.23 (a) Mean response times for individual scenario types and both display conditions; (b) accuracy and confidence internals of data interpretation for individual scenarios between display conditions. *Statistically significant difference; +statistical trend

not too noisy, hot or overcrowded. If exploring these angles, you may find that you can bring in research from other topic areas, such as to do with stressors in the environment, although, equally, you may wish to do additional research of your own in this area. Beyond this, a well-designed workplace could be expected to accommodate people's territorial and personal space needs, particularly as violation of these could lead to people feeling overloaded with too many stimuli.

Take it further

- Have you heard about standing up desks? How/ why could these be justified in terms of ergonomic research?

When talking about the workplace, it is important to keep in mind that for many people (for example, taxi drivers, long-distance lorry drivers, travelling salespeople) their workplace centres on use of a mode of transport. Issues of ergonomics apply to people with mobile workplaces as much as they do to people with static workplaces.

Take it further

- List as many jobs as you can think of where the employee has a workplace that is mobile.
- How many of the above considerations (for example, temperature, territory, the possibility of cognitive overload) will apply to those with mobile workplaces?

The Cognitive area

Research in the last two topic areas – recycling and other conservation behaviours, and ergonomics – has frequently taken a cognitive approach as it has sought to understand the role that thought processes play in environmentally related behaviour. For instance, the key research by Drews and Doig can be seen as drawing on Baddeley and Hitch's working memory model in its attempt to avoid cognitive overload, while a central focus of the key research by Lord was the impact of how messages are framed on people's attitudes.

A general problem with cognitive research is that thought processes cannot be studied directly. Instead, researchers either ask people questions about their thought processes (for example, their attitudes), study how people behave and then make inferences about their thoughts from their behaviour, or generate speculative models to try to capture how people seem to think. The validity of each of these ways of conducting research can, of course, be questioned.

The aim of the key research by Drews and Doig was to propose a development that would fit in with how people think. The aim of the key research by Lord was to find out the best way to change people's thoughts in relation to recycling. Either way, both studies can be seen as useful. Another debate that is raised by research in these areas is the individual–situational explanations debate as, even if the presence of prompts and the proximity of recycling facilities may not guarantee an increase in conservation behaviours, nonetheless they may help to remind people of environmental issues and make such behaviours more likely to happen. This, in turn, raises the free will–determinism debate about the extent to which it is possible to shape people's thoughts about the environment and also whether there are innate limits on people's thinking (for example, in terms of how much material they can hold in their working memories).

Psychological effects of the built environment (Social)

An increasing proportion of the world's population live in urban environments. According to statistics published by the United Nations, 54 per cent of the world's population in 2014 were living in urban environments. This figure was expected to rise to 66 per cent by 2050, with a growing proportion of people living in so-called mega-cities of ten million or more inhabitants, particularly in Asia and Africa. As much of this growth is a consequence of migration from rural to urban areas, it can be assumed that cities are viewed as offering people greater opportunities than the countryside. However, does urban living live up to people's hopes? What are the psychological effects (positive or negative) of living in built-up environments?

Bearing in mind the trend towards growing urbanisation, this is clearly an important question to raise. However, it is actually quite a difficult question to answer. Some of the problems are as follows:

- What counts as a 'built environment'? While it is clear that living in a mega-city such as Tokyo, Shanghai or Delhi would count, what about people living in villages? How urbanised does an environment have to be for it to count as a built environment?
- To what extent can we generalise about the built environment? It should be clear that the challenges facing people living in America's shrinking 'rustbelt' cities (such as Detroit, Cleveland or Pittsburgh) will be very different from those facing people in growing urban centres such as Lagos in Nigeria or Bamako in Mali where the infrastructure (including sanitation) struggles to keep up with population growth.

Figure 4.24 Abandoned housing in America's 'rustbelt'

- What counts as 'psychological effects', and how can we measure these? Reference to statistics for people with mental health needs will clearly be dependent on the extent to which such data is collected and, anyway, could be distorted by any tendency that there might be for people with psychiatric problems to drift towards urban environments. Given these problems, is it appropriate to try measuring psychological effects by looking at levels of prosocial or antisocial behaviour in different environments?
- How should research in this area be conducted? Should before-and-after repeated measures-type investigations be carried out whenever changes to the built environment are being brought in? Alternatively, should people who happen to live in contrasting environments be compared (for example, rural versus urban dwellers)? What about correlation studies (for example, seeing if there is a relationship between the size of a city's population and the number of crimes committed)? As you will no doubt appreciate, there would be problems with all of these different ways of carrying out research.

It will be helpful to keep these issues in mind as we attempt to look further at the psychological effects of the built environment. It will also be worth keeping in mind the question of the extent to which the built environment dictates how people behave. Broadly speaking, there are three positions that have been adopted (Bell *et al.*, 1996):

- **Architectural determinism** holds that the built environment is the main or only cause of the behaviour of the people within it.
- **Architectural possibilism** accepts that the built environment may place potential limits on behaviour (for example, the positioning of walls, buildings, and so on, might mean that I can't get from A to B via the most direct route) but it would still want to claim a large role for individual choice, such that the

built environment is no more than a context in which behaviour occurs.

- **Architectural probabilism** sits in between the two previous positions – it claims that the way the built environment is set up will make some behaviours more likely than others.

The impact of the built environment on our well-being

Many of the environmental stressors we have already looked at (such as noise and overcrowding) will be of relevance when examining the impact of the built environment on our well-being. As we look at these and other features of the urban landscape, it will be worth keeping in mind the sorts of people who will be most likely to be affected by them. Insofar as they are indeed stressors, it can be expected that people will be prepared to pay more to avoid them. As a consequence, it could be those on low incomes (for example, the unemployed, those in low-paying jobs, immigrants and single parents) who would be most exposed to the stressors within urban environments, as they will be the ones left living in those parts of the built environment with the most negative effects.

Noise

Evidence of the negative effects of urban noise came from a study by Cohen et al. (1973) in which a relationship was found between the floor level a child lived on and their reading ability. The study was carried out on 54 children, all of whom lived in the Bridge Apartments in New York City. These consisted of four 32-storey aluminium buildings erected in 1964 on bridges spanning Interstate 95 in the upper part of Manhattan. The children were all in the second, third, fourth or fifth grade, and they all attended the same public elementary school not far from the apartment buildings. Noise level readings confirmed that apartments on the higher floors experienced less traffic noise than those on the lower floors (for instance, the average noise reading on the 32nd floor was 55 decibels, the average for the 20th floor was 60 decibels, and the average for the 8th floor was 66 decibels).

Results from these noise-level readings were then correlated against the children's results on the Metropolitan Achievement Tests (MAT) that are administered annually in New York elementary schools.

As the researchers hypothesised that living in a noisy environment might make the children inattentive to acoustic cues, they first tested the children's auditory discrimination abilities by seeing how many similar-sounding words (for example, 'cope-coke', 'gear-beer') they would recognise as different in a tape-recorded test.

For the 34 children who had lived in the apartments for four years or more, Cohen et al. found that there was a significant correlation between floor level and auditory discrimination (+0.48). They also found that there were significant correlations between auditory discrimination and all three scores within the MAT – namely, for word knowledge (+0.55), reading comprehension (+0.48) and reading total (+0.53). Controlling for socio-economic variables, the researchers claimed to have found an indirect association between noise level and reading deficits as apartment noise level accounted for a substantial proportion of the variance in auditory discrimination, and the latter variable contributed significantly to variance in reading achievement. Since reading ability could affect performance at school generally, this would suggest one aspect of the built environment – noise levels – that is related to well-being.

Overcrowding

Overcrowding can also affect well-being. Evidence of this comes from a number of different studies. For example, Bickman et al. (1973) found that how helpful people are is affected by density of population. Stamped addressed envelopes were dropped in either high-, medium- or low-density student dormitories, and helping behaviour was measured by the percentage of letters that were posted on to the addressee. As results showed that the highest proportion were posted on in the low-density condition (88 per cent, as against 79 per cent in the medium-density condition, and only 58 per cent in the high-density condition), this would suggest that overcrowding can influence helping behaviour.

A study by Newman and McCauley (1977) found comparable results in relation to preparedness to make eye contact with a stranger. This was most likely to occur in the rural Pennsylvania town of Parkesburg but was less likely to occur in the Bryn Mawr suburb of Philadelphia, and was least likely to occur in the centre of Philadelphia itself. For instance, whereas 80 per cent of passers-by would make eye contact with a female stranger at a post office in Parkesburg, this

Stop and ask yourself…

- In what ways could noise levels be reduced in built environments?

Links to debates
- Usefulness

figure dropped to 45 per cent in Bryn Mawr and to only 15 per cent in Philadelphia city centre.

More disturbing results about the impact of overcrowding on well-being came from Huey and McNulty (2005) who analysed data on prison suicides from the fourth and fifth enumerations of the Census of State and Federal Adult Correctional Facilities (CCF), collected in 1990 and 1995 by the US Census Bureau. They found that suicides among prisoners were strongly related to overcrowding as all of the prisons that had at least one suicide in 1990 or 1995 had values on the overcrowding index above the grand mean, with the average (2.67) nearly one standard deviation above, whereas all those that had no suicides fell well below the mean. Huey and McNulty conclude that overcrowding is a critical feature of prison environments that dramatically raises the risk of suicide.

Have a go yourself

- Try carrying out a letter-drop study of your own. You could leave ten stamped and addressed letters on the ground in a town or city and ten stamped and addressed letters on the ground in a village and then see which are more likely to be picked up and posted on. If doing this, think carefully about the controls to try imposing on your study.

Commuting

For most people, another feature of life in built environments is commuting to work. This can often feel very stressful, but what effect does it have on a person's well-being? Research released by the Office for National Statistics (2014) tried to address this question. Drawing largely on data from the Annual Population Survey, in which about 60,200 employed or self-employed people were interviewed either face-to-face or by telephone, comparison was made between commuters (defined as people who spent one minute or more travelling to work) and non-commuters (people who said they worked from home in their main job). After controlling for such factors as the participant's age, presence of dependent and non-dependent children in the household, health/disability, and where in the UK a person was based, it was found that, on average, commuters had lower life satisfaction, a lower sense that their daily activities were worthwhile, lower levels of happiness, and higher anxiety. Respondents had been asked to rate themselves on these four variables

on a scale of 0 to 10, where 0 is 'not at all' and 10 is 'completely', and results revealed that the worst effects of commuting on well-being were associated with journey times lasting between 61 and 90 minutes. Taking the bus or coach to work on a journey lasting more than 30 minutes was the commuting option that had the strongest negative relationship to well-being. Perhaps surprisingly, when commuting times reached three hours or more, the negative effects on personal well-being disappeared.

It is important to note, however, that even the main findings only showed a small difference between commuters and non-commuters of between 0.1 and 0.2 on the four questions about personal well-being.

Figure 4.25 For enhanced well-being, make sure bus journeys don't exceed 30 minutes

Crime and deindividuation

Figure 4.26 Can the anonymity of a costume increase the likelihood of antisocial behaviour taking place?

Something else that can affect our well-being is either becoming a victim of crime or being fearful of

- In what ways could overcrowding be reduced in built environments?

Links to debates
- Usefulness

becoming a victim of crime. Can the design of the built environment have an effect on either of these things? In the next section, we will see that an absence of defensible space – land that is perceived to be owned and controlled by someone else – can be argued to create the conditions for crime to occur. More generally, however, large urban environments can be expected to increase the likelihood of crime as a consequence of deindividuation, which is when an individual's identity is lost among a group of people.

Evidence of this came from a study by Diener *et al*. (1976) of 1352 children taking part in trick-or-treat at Halloween in Seattle. In the entrance to a number of houses, the experimenters left two bowls, with one containing sweets and the other containing money. The householder would greet them and say that they could take one sweet but then rush off, pretending to attend to something out of sight. In reality, what they did was disappear behind a fake wall and observe the behaviour of the children through a peephole. Children who were alone were much less likely to either take an extra sweet or to steal some of the money than children in groups, but what was also of interest was that whereas 20.8 per cent of children in groups would steal or break the (number of sweets) rule if they had been asked their names and addresses, this figure would rise to 57.7 per cent among children who were in a group and had not been asked for their names and addresses. Although this study was based on the behaviour of children, it clearly suggests that anonymity (from wearing a costume, from being in a group, and from not disclosing your name and address) can increase the likelihood of antisocial behaviour taking place. Insofar as features of the built environment make it feasible to achieve such anonymity, they may contribute to a reduction in the well-being of people living there.

> **Take it further**
>
> - Explain how the following features of the built environment could be expected to reduce deindividuation: street lighting, CCTV, cul-de-sacs.
> - Suggest other measures that could be taken to reduce deindividuation.

The impact of urban renewal on our well-being

Porteus (1977) has defined urban renewal as an integrated series of steps taken to maintain and upgrade the environmental, economic and social health of an urban area.

Defensible space

A notorious example of an urban renewal scheme that did not go as planned was the Pruitt-Igoe public housing project in St Louis, USA. Built in 1954, the scheme was designed to house 12,000 people in 43 buildings containing 2740 apartments.

The buildings were designed to give residents a sense of space as they were lifted up off the ground by pillars, leaving the ground level free for a 'river of trees' to flow under the buildings. All buildings were 11 storeys high and, on every third floor, there were communal rooms, a laundry and a garbage room, which also contained a garbage chute. Elsewhere, corridors were narrow and people were discouraged from loitering by an absence of semi-private areas. The design also incorporated wall tiles from which graffiti could easily be removed, light fixtures that were supposedly indestructible, and radiators and elevators that were vandal-resistant.

Figure 4.27 The Pruitt-Igoe housing project in St Louis, Missouri, USA

A great deal of thought had clearly gone into the design of the Pruitt-Igoe project and yet, by 1970, 27 of the 43 buildings were empty, and two years after that the project was demolished. What had gone wrong? Architect Oscar Newman describes how the housing project had become crime-ridden:

The river of trees soon became a sewer of glass and garbage. The mailboxes on the ground floor were vandalized. The corridors, lobbies, elevators and stairs were dangerous places to walk through. They became covered in graffiti, and littered with garbage and human waste. The elevators, laundry and community rooms were vandalized and garbage was stacked high around the choked garbage chutes. Women had to get together in groups to take their children to school and go shopping. (www.defensiblespace.com)

Why had this happened? The temptation might be to point to the fact that the development was occupied by single-parent welfare families and to note that high-rise buildings occupied by middle-income families don't experience the same fate. Newman himself considers this thought before pointing out a crucial difference between the two types of development:

... middle-income apartment buildings have funds available for doormen, porters, elevator operators, and resident superintendents to watch over and maintain the common public areas. But in high-rise public housing, there are barely enough funds for 9 to 5 non-resident maintenance men, let alone for security personnel, elevator operators, or porters. Not surprisingly, therefore, it is within these interior and exterior common public areas that most of the crime in public housing takes place. (www.defensiblespace.com)

Given the limited funds available for public housing projects, the comparison that Newman was more interested in was with Carr Square Village, a row-house development located across the street from Pruitt-Igoe. This was occupied by an identical population but had remained fully occupied and trouble-free throughout the construction, occupancy and decline of Pruitt-Igoe. Furthermore, even within Pruitt-Igoe there were areas that were clean, safe and well-tended. Newman was interested in the characteristics of these areas:

If one could get oneself invited into an apartment, one found it neat and well maintained – modestly furnished perhaps, but with great pride. Why such a difference between the interior of the apartment and the public spaces outside it? One could only conclude that residents maintained and controlled those areas which were clearly defined as their own. Landings shared by only two families were well maintained, whereas corridors shared by 20 families, and lobbies, elevators, and stairs shared by 150 families were a disaster – they evoked no feelings of identity or control. Such anonymous public spaces made it impossible for even neighbouring residents to develop an accord on what was acceptable behaviour in these areas, impossible to feel or exert proprietary feelings, impossible to tell resident from intruder. (www.defensiblespace.com)

This idea – that residents will maintain and control areas that are clearly defined as belonging to them – was termed 'defensible space', and Newman's suggestion was that criminals would be rendered

ineffective by public spaces being subdivided and assigned to individuals and small groups to use and control as their own private areas. As such, well-being can be improved by design that makes areas appear as if they are owned and likely to be defended.

Take it further

- Look up the concept of 'designing out crime'. In what ways is this similar to or different from Newman's concept of defensible space?

Green spaces

Newman's suggestions are clearly of relevance to urban renewal schemes. However, they need balancing against evidence that well-being is enhanced by living close to urban green spaces such as parks. For example, White *et al.* (2013) conducted a longitudinal study based on data collected annually from over 10,000 people between 1991 and 2008. Even after the researchers accounted for changes over time in participants' income, employment, marital status, physical health and housing type, they found that individuals reported less mental distress and higher life satisfaction when living in greener areas. The effects on well-being of living in an urban area with relatively high levels of green space were quite strong, being equivalent to roughly a third of the impact of being married. This would suggest that giving people access to green spaces is an important part of urban renewal, and the key research by Ulrich (1984) would lend further support to the suggestion that green spaces can have a restorative effect on people.

Privacy

If balancing the need for open green spaces against the need for closed 'defensible' spaces is one challenge for urban planners, another centres on balancing the need for privacy against the need for social interaction. According to Irwin Altman (1975), privacy can be defined as 'the selective control of access to the self or to one's group', and we manage interactions between the self and others in order to achieve an optimal level of privacy, which sits somewhere between 'loneliness' on the one hand (that is, too much privacy) and 'crowding' on the other (that is, too little privacy). This

Stop and ask yourself ...

- Are parks undefended spaces that invite crime, or oases of calm in urban environments that enhance our quality of life? What do you think? As social scientists, how could we get a definitive answer to this question?

Links to
- Discussion point
- Idea for a practical activity

can be related to levels of arousal and, to maintain our preferred levels of privacy, we use verbal mechanisms (for example, saying 'I'd prefer to be left alone right now'), non-verbal mechanisms (for example, orientating our bodies away from someone) or environmental mechanisms (for example, the erection of territorial markers such as fences or hedges around our property).

It is in relation to the last of these that urban renewal comes in as it is not obvious that people's apparent need to maintain an optimal level of privacy will be achievable within the kinds of property that developers are building with increasing frequency (such as apartment blocks). Quite aside from the way in which many modern properties provide limited spaces to retreat to if being shared with another person, their close proximity to other flats with consequent noise pollution may affect people's well-being by not enabling the individual living within them to manage their levels of privacy (and arousal) in the way that they need to.

A heterogeneous social mix

Research into prejudice and discrimination can also be seen as of relevance to urban renewal schemes. In his Robber's Cave experiment, Sherif (1956) showed both how conflict between groups can emerge and also – more hopefully – how such conflict can be overcome.

The experiment was based on boys aged 11 to 12 who were all healthy, socially well-adjusted, somewhat above average in intelligence, and from stable, white, Protestant, middle-class homes. They believed that they were joining a regular summer camp but in fact they were taking part in an experiment on group relations. Experiments were conducted in 1949, 1953 and 1954, but it is the 1954 study that we will focus on. In this study, the boys arrived at Robber's Cave in Oklahoma in two separate buses and, during the first phase of the experiment, were kept apart. They each formed their own group identities, with one group calling themselves the Eagles and the other group calling themselves the Rattlers. To produce friction between the groups of boys, a tournament of games was then organised. These included baseball, a tug-of-war and a treasure hunt and, after starting in a spirit of good sportsmanship, they soon descended into ill-feeling, with rivals calling each other 'stinkers', 'sneaks' and 'cheaters'. The depth of antipathy was revealed by the way in which, after one defeat, the Eagles burned a banner left behind by the Rattlers and then the next morning the Rattlers seized the Eagles' flag when they arrived on the athletics field.

The experiment then moved into its next phase as Sherif showed how two groups in conflict can be brought into harmony. Bringing the two groups together for social events, such as going to the movies and eating in the same dining room, only served as opportunities for the two groups to berate and attack each other as they threw food, paper and insults at members of their rival group. Believing that, where harmony between groups has been established, the most decisive factor is the existence of 'superordinate' goals that have a compelling appeal for both but which neither could achieve without the other, Sherif now created a series of situations that required the boys to all work together towards a common end. One of these involved a breakdown in the supply of water to the camp while another involved the truck that was to take the boys on an outing to a lake some distance away not starting. The joint efforts to overcome these crises did not dispel the intergroup hostility immediately but, gradually, the series of co-operative acts reduced friction and conflict, with the boys ending the name calling, having a joint campfire, and even spending prize money on refreshments (malted milks) shared between all.

Figure 4.28 Robber's Cave State Park, Oklahoma, USA

Sherif's conclusion that hostility gives way when groups pull together to achieve over-riding goals that are real and compelling to all concerned can be seen in times of war when whole populations work together to resist a common enemy, but what relevance does this have for urban renewal? At the very least, the first phase of his experiment would suggest that cities in which people live in different districts, whether on the basis of social class or ethnicity, are only likely to become disharmonious as people in these districts view others with suspicion and see those in other districts as in some way different. Such feelings could be expected to increase as all compete with each other for limited resources, such as housing, jobs or places in favoured schools. However, there are hopeful messages to take from Sherif's study. As the final stage of his experiment brought out, if people from all different groups can be brought together to work on achieving common goals, then this can dissipate intergroup hostility. Perhaps more controversially, if people are not separated off into different 'groups' in the first place, then maybe such common endeavours wouldn't be needed. In terms of urban renewal, what this might suggest is town planners taking actions to ensure mixed, heterogeneous communities right from the start.

Key research: Ulrich (1984) View through a window may influence recovery from surgery

The following study looks at whether the view patients have through their hospital window could affect their recovery from surgery. It involved looking, retrospectively, at the medical records of patients who had a view of either trees or a wall.

Background

Previous studies have shown a strong tendency among American and European groups to prefer natural scenes over urban views that lack natural elements such as views of vegetation and, in particular, water. Most natural views seem to elicit positive feelings, reduce fear among people who are stressed, and hold people's interest; they may also block or reduce stressful thoughts.

Aim

This study aimed to find out if the view that hospital patients have through their window might affect their recovery from surgery.

Sample

The sample consisted of 46 patients in a suburban Pennsylvania hospital, all of whom had undergone gall bladder surgery. The patients in the sample were all aged between 20 and 69 years of age, had no history of psychological disturbance, and experienced no serious post-operative complications. The 46 patients consisted of 23 pairs of patients (15 female and 8 male) who were matched on relevant criteria so that, within each pair, they would differ only in the view they had from their hospital bed – one patient within each pair had a

view of trees while the other patient within each pair had a view of a brick wall.

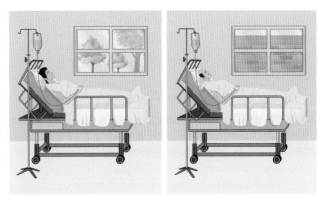

Figure 4.29 Does the view that hospital patients have through their window affect their recovery from surgery?

Method

Records of patients assigned to rooms on the second and third floors of a three-storey wing of the hospital between 1972 and 1981 were obtained. All rooms were double occupancy and were nearly identical in terms of dimensions, window size, arrangement of beds, furniture and other major physical characteristics. The only real difference was the view from the window, as windows on one side of the wing looked out on either a small stand of deciduous trees or a brown brick wall.

The records that were analysed related to those patients occupying these rooms who had undergone a cholecystectomy (gall bladder removal) between 1st May and 20th October in each year (the period of time when the trees had foliage). Patients who had had either a tree-view or a wall-view were matched into pairs on the basis of their sex, age (within five years), whether they were a smoker or non-smoker, whether they were obese or within normal weight limits, the general nature of their previous hospitalisation, their year of surgery (within six years) and floor level. For those on the second floor, patients were also matched on the colour of their room (some rooms were blue while others were green).

A nurse with extensive surgical floor experience but who was blind as to the scene that had been visible from a patient's window then gathered five types

Stop and ask yourself...

- How, in practice, can mixed communities be achieved?
- What would be the obstacles to achieving genuinely mixed communities?
- What kinds of 'superordinate' goals could potentially get different groups of people working together?

Links to
- The challenges of applying psychology

of information from each set of records: length of hospitalisation; number and strength of analgesics each day; number and strength of doses for anxiety each day; minor complications requiring medication (for example, persistent headaches and nausea); and nurses' notes.

Results

In terms of length of hospitalisation, this was measured from day of surgery to day of discharge, and records showed that tree-view patients spent significantly less time in the hospital than wall-view patients (7.96 days compared with 8.70 days). In terms of intake of analgesics during days two through to five after surgery, tree-view patients took significantly fewer moderate and strong pain doses and more doses in the weak category than the wall-view patients did. Nurses' notes were classified as either negative (for example, 'upset and crying' or 'needs much encouragement') or positive (for example, 'in good spirits' or 'moving well'), and significantly more negative notes were made by nurses in relation to the wall-view patients than the tree-view patients (3.96 per patient compared to 1.13 per patient). There was no significant difference between the two groups of patients with respect to either consumption of anti-anxiety drugs or minor post-operative complications.

Discussion

The findings from this study suggest that views of a natural scene can give patients therapeutic benefits as they recover from surgery and, as such, decisions about the design and location of hospitals should take into account the quality of patient window views.

That said, the findings from this study cannot be extended to all built views as the built view in this study was particularly monotonous. Similarly, the conclusions cannot be extended to other patient groups, such as long-term patients for whom low arousal or boredom may be more of an issue than the anxiety issues typically associated with surgeries.

Application: how environmental design can be used to improve health/well-being

Hopefully, all that you have read in this section of the book should give you plenty of ideas for suggestions about how the design of the built environment can affect well-being. However, it may also be worth noting a couple of additional design features. For instance, does the

colour of a room affect the well-being of people within it? Research in this area suggests few reliable conclusions. However, it does seem to be the case that lighter-coloured rooms are seen as more open and spacious (Acking and Kuller, 1972; Baum and Davis, 1976); furthermore, a colour known as Baker-Miller pink seems to have an effect on aggression levels. This was found in a study by Gilliam (1991) in which systolic and diastolic blood pressure levels were lower when emotionally disturbed participants were in a pink room than a white room. Similarly, Bennet et al. (1991) found that prisoners in police cells were less abusive and violent if allocated to a pink cell than a magnolia one. In terms of why Baker-Miller pink might have such an effect, this is unclear; however, studies like these do at least go some way towards telling us about the actual effects of colour on people.

> ### ➡ Have a go yourself
>
> - Try investigating the impact of colour on people's mood. You could carry out an experiment in which different groups of participants do an impossible task (think back to Glass and Singer) on different coloured pieces of paper. You could then ask them to self-report their levels of frustration on a rating scale.

Road layout is also worth keeping in mind, and can be linked in with research that we have already seen into deindividuation and defensible space. Armitage (2011) investigated whether cul-de-sacs are less likely to experience crime than through roads, and also whether some cul-de-sac designs experience more crime than others. Focusing on property developments in Greater Manchester, the West Midlands and Kent, she analysed data for recorded crime from January 2007 through to December 2009 and found that sinuous true cul-de-sacs (curvy cul-de-sacs without 'leaky' footpaths) are the road layout where the lowest levels of crime are likely to occur. However, footpaths can be included within residential developments as long as they are required/ desired (and therefore well used), short, direct, wide, overlooked, well-lit and not running along the side or rear of properties. In general, residential developments should limit connectivity and through-movement in order to reduce crime.

Armitage's study was carried out in the UK and, before we leave this topic area, it is worth emphasising that findings about the built environment that are true for one culture may not be true for all cultures. This was brought out in research by Kent (1991). Over 50 cultural groups were classified on the extent to which they segment their living space for different tasks (having different spaces for sleeping, entertaining and eating) with Europeans, Americans and Saudi Arabians being classed as highly likely to do this (even to the point of having interior walls to delineate the spaces for different functions) while Mbuti pygmy and Navajo people were classed as very unlikely to do this. Kent further reported that Navajo people occupying a Western-style, three-bedroom house used the living room to both sleep and eat in, whereas Euramericans occupying a low-segmentation house created barriers of their own to segment the space.

Territory and personal space (Social)

Do you have a particular place around school or college that you always meet up in with your friends at the start of the day and during breaks? Maybe there are some chairs at the end of the maths corridor that you always gravitate towards, or a particular table in the canteen. How would you feel if you went to this place and found it occupied by some other students?

Imagine you are in a nightclub. You probably don't mind strangers standing or dancing really close beside you. Imagine now that you are standing in the middle of the field at school or college. You are the only person standing there until someone else – a complete stranger – comes and stands right beside you. They are no closer or further away from you than they would be if in a busy nightclub. How would this feel?

These two scenarios relate, respectively, to territory and personal space. We will explore them in more depth as we get into this section but a good way of characterising the difference between them is that territory relates to a particular location, is owned in some way and (unless it's a seat in a car or on a train, etc.) doesn't move anywhere, whereas personal space relates to people and goes everywhere that people go. As the above example demonstrates, another feature of our personal space requirements is that they can vary with the situation we are in. Where territory and personal space are similar is that both are involved in regulating our interactions with others.

Territory in the workplace

Territories tend to be areas that have marked perimeters to them, placing limits on who can enter them. For Sommer (1969), a territory will be visible, relatively stationary, visibly bounded, often home-centred, and regulating who will interact. They may be permanent, exclusive areas, such as your home, with very clear indicators of how far they extend, such as the presence of fences around the edges of them. Alternatively, they may be temporary, such as a seat in a classroom or a seat on a train, which we might indicate our 'ownership' of by leaving items of clothing, stationery or reading material on. Such items can be seen as territorial markers, indicating that although we might leave our territory (for example, to go to the toilet), we expect it to be there for us upon our return and we do not expect anyone else to occupy it in our absence. Territorial markers are effective insofar as they ward off intrusions from what we perceive as our territory, and the fact that we put them down and that (in general) other people interpret them in the way that we intend them to, reflects the sort of cognitions and behaviours that underpin human territoriality.

Figure 4.30 Territorial markers in public spaces – or someone inviting crime?

There are various theories as to why we behave in a territorial way. One socio-biological theory sees territorial behaviour as a relic from our evolutionary past, that we *inherit*. However, other theories see it as *learned*, pointing to nomadic cultures that are relatively unterritorial to suggest that it is unlikely to be biologically driven. Still other theories see it as reflecting our *cognitive* need to simplify the world by categorising

🚫 Stop and ask yourself ...

- Do you have places that you regard as your territory? Do you take actions to indicate to others that these belong to you? If so, why do you think you do this? How could we find out why people behave in territorial ways?

Links to
- Understanding the issues
- Idea for a practical activity

information. Of course, it could also arise from an *interaction* of instinct and learning, and this is a position that has also been advanced.

Take it further

- Investigate the territorial behaviour of non-human animals. Are there particular animals that territory matters to the most? If so, in what ways do they communicate their territorial claims?

Altman (1975) claimed that there are three types of territory that are used by humans. These differ in how *important* they are to the lives of the individuals or groups who perceive them as theirs, and also in the *length of time* they will be occupied for, how the occupant and others *think* about them, the extent to which they will be *personalised* (for example, covered with decorations by the occupier), and how likely it is that they would be *defended* if someone else were to try violating the territory. The three types of territory are primary, secondary and public.

Territorial behaviour in humans is surprisingly difficult to research. As Bell *et al.* (1996) point out, *laboratory experiments* are difficult to perform with humans because territoriality implies a strong attachment between an individual and a place that is not easy to create under artificial laboratory conditions. Consequently, *field experiments* have often been carried out, with experimental manipulations (for example, territorial invasions) being introduced in real-world settings such as student dormitories where people perceive a degree of territorial 'ownership'. Another method that has often been used has been (non-experimental) *field observation* of behaviour in naturally occurring territories.

Table 4.3 Territorial behaviours associated with primary, secondary, and public territory

Territory type	Extent to which territory is occupied/extent of perceived ownership by self and others	Amount of personalisation/likelihood of defence if violated
Primary territory (e.g. home, office)	*High.* Perceived to be owned in a relatively permanent manner by occupant and others	*Extensively personalised*; owner has complete control and intrusion is a serious matter
Secondary territory (e.g. classroom)	*Moderate.* Not owned; occupant perceived by others as one of a number of qualified users	*May be personalised to some extent during period of legitimate occupancy*; some regulatory power when individual is legitimate occupant
Public territory (e.g. area of beach)	*Low.* Not owned; control is very difficult to assert, and occupant is perceived by others as one of a large number of possible users	*Sometimes personalised in a temporary way*; little likelihood of defence

Based on Altman (1975), from Bell *et al.* (1996)

An example of this last method comes from Smith (1981), who compared people from West Germany and France against data gathered by Edney and Jordan-Edney on Americans in terms of how they competed for beach space on holiday. Data was gathered from a beach on the island of Sylt in West Germany, the beach at Pampelonne near St Tropez in France, and a beach in Connecticut state park, USA, with every tenth territory being approached to take part in the study. Short interviews were conducted with the groups they approached (to establish the nationality of the group, the amount of time the group would be on the beach that day, and the size of the group) while data was also collected on the size, depth and width of the occupied space, as well as the numbers and types of items used as territorial markers. While the study suggested that people from West Germany made extremely large territorial claims more often than either the French or the Americans, the study also found that, overall, males claimed more territory than females regardless of their nationality, and that shapes of territory were similar, with groups establishing circular territories and individuals establishing elliptical territories. Interestingly, over a fifth of the West Germans, and only the West Germans, made reference to the English phrase 'A man's home is his castle' while gesturing at the sandcastle

Stop and ask yourself...

- What type of territory would a desk in an office be? Is it primary, secondary or public territory?

Links to
- Check your understanding

boundaries that they had created, and a fifth of the West German sample actually put up signs stating that a particular area was 'reserved' for them between two particular dates. By way of contrast, when French participants were interviewed, they typically could not grasp the concept of territoriality, no matter how much explanation was given.

Figure 4.31 A man's home is his castle

Field observations have also been conducted indoors, particularly in libraries, presumably because of how readily available they are to university-based researchers and because of the central importance they play in the working lives of students and lecturers alike. For example, Sommer (1969) investigated the influence on the likelihood of territorial invasion of how densely occupied the library was. At low levels of density, people tended to respect any kind of marker (for example, a book or an item of clothing, even a sandwich), sitting instead at tables without any personal effects on them. However, when levels of density in the library were higher, it seemed to be the case that some territorial markers had more of an effect than others. Thus, markers that seemed personal and valuable (such as items of clothing or notebooks with names on them) continued to be respected, but items that lacked these characteristics (such as a library book or a newspaper) were less likely to be respected and the desk would often be 'invaded'. People seemed to be taking an attributional

approach, trying to interpret whether a particular marker indicated an attribution of intent to return to the desk on the part of the person who had been occupying it. Studies have also been conducted into the effectiveness of gender-related territorial markers, and it has been found in classroom settings that territories with 'male' markers on them are less likely to be invaded than territories with 'female' markers on them (Haber, 1980).

How does all this relate to the workplace? In office environments, many people will regard their desk as their territory and they may 'mark' their territory with personal items such as photographs, amusing quotes, knick-knacks or certificates. Such 'territorial markers' can be seen as indicating ownership of the space.

The key research for this section, by Meredith Wells (2000), will explore further whether men and women differ in how they personalise their workspaces and also how important doing so is to their well-being; it will also explore whether personalisation of workspaces is associated with (a) the well-being of employees, and (b) the well-being of the organisations that employ them. As you will see, men and women were found to differ in the ways in which they personalised their workspaces. Perhaps more importantly, it was found that being allowed to personalise workspaces was related to both enhanced employee well-being and reduced staff turnover.

Figure 4.32 A personalised desk

Stop and ask yourself...

- What are the benefits and drawbacks of laboratory experiments, field experiments and field observations as methods of measuring people's territorial behaviour?

Links to methodological issues
- Validity
- Reliability
- Ecological validity
- Ethics
- Check your understanding

173

The possibility of office workers personalising their desks depends on what they are allowed to do by their employer. If a system of 'hot-desking' is in place, where workers are permitted to use any desk that happens to be available at a given time, then this will not be compatible with employees being able to claim a territory at work. Such non-territorial arrangements have attractions for office managers as they help to minimise unused or underused space and, in a 2005 survey of workers from eight different countries, the Flexible Working Survey found that 39.6 per cent of the people in their sample worked from a hot-desk.

What impact, though, do hot-desking arrangements have on workers? Through participant-observation and interviewing, Hirst (2011) found that in hot-desking environments a social structure can emerge in which some employees are able to settle in one place, and these are distinguished from others who have to move constantly. She also found that the practice of movement itself generates additional work and a sense of marginalisation for hot-deskers. Ditchburn (2014) has claimed further that hot-desking can contribute to a sense of loss and leads workers to identify less with their organisation. He also notes that keyboards that have multiple users have been found to have five times the levels of bacteria than keyboards with a single user. Perhaps it is for reasons such as these that Wheeler and Almeida (2006) found that just 1 per cent of professionals would choose to hot-desk.

> ### Have a go yourself
>
> - Design a survey to investigate whether office workers have desks of their own or whether their offices have 'hot-desking' arrangements. Build into your survey some attitude scales to find out how satisfied your respondents are with the arrangements. Administer the survey to an opportunity sample of office workers you know.

Personal space in the workplace

Personal space is not the same as territory. We have seen that territory relates to a particular location, which typically remains static (unless it is a seat on a train, plane, etc.) and has visible boundaries; it can also be left behind. By way of contrast, personal space relates to people, is portable and has invisible boundaries.

Often characterised as a kind of mobile bubble that stays with us wherever we go and which helps regulate our interactions with others, our personal space needs to expand and contract in accordance with a wide range of factors. *Individual factors* that may affect a person's personal space needs include:

- their age – young children seem to have fewer personal space requirements than older children (Aiello, 1987; Hayduk, 1983)
- their culture – according to Hall (1966), people from 'contact' cultures (for example, Mediterranean, Arabic, Hispanic) seem to prefer less interpersonal distance than people from 'non-contact' cultures (for example, northern European, white American)
- their personality – introverts maintain more personal space than extroverts (Cook, 1970; Patterson and Holmes, 1966)
- the nature of the relationship between people – females in particular will position themselves closer to people they like (Edwards, 1972; Heshka and Nelson, 1972).

Situational factors that may affect a person's personal space needs include temperature as, if weather conditions were exceptionally cold, people might be expected to huddle together for warmth; light levels also seem to influence personal space needs, as Gergen *et al.* (1973) found that students left alone in a pitch-black room for an hour often touched, hugged or even kissed one another, certainly not suggesting a need to maintain personal space in this situation!

Based on observation of white, middle-class Americans, Edward T. Hall (1963) suggested that personal space can be divided into four zones. The particular zone that might be used will depend on factors such as the nature of our relationship with the other person or people that we are interacting with and also the activity we are engaged in. The four zones are labelled intimate distance, personal distance, social distance and public distance.

Research by Middlemist *et al.* (1976) revealed the impact that invasions of personal space can have on people. Designed to test the theory that invasions of personal space cause physiological arousal such that behavioural responses to personal space invasion (for example, reasserting a distance we feel comfortable with) occur because they reduce the arousal, a field experiment was conducted in a men's lavatory at an American university. Men who entered the three-urinal lavatory to urinate were forced to use the left-most urinal. A confederate was positioned either immediately adjacent to the participant (the close distance condition), one urinal removed from the participant (the moderate distance condition) or was absent from the lavatory (the control condition). An observer stationed in a toilet stall with stopwatches and a periscope embedded in a stack of books lying on

Table 4.4 Hall's four personal space zones

Personal space zone	Appropriate relationships and activities	Sensory qualities
Intimate distance (0 to 1½ feet)	Intimate contacts (e.g. making love, comforting) and physical sports (e.g. wrestling)	Intense awareness of sensory inputs from other person (e.g. smell, radiant heat); touch overtakes vocalisation as primary mode of communication
Personal distance (1½ to 4 feet)	Contacts between close friends, as well as everyday interactions with acquaintances	Less awareness of sensory inputs than intimate distance; vision is normal and provides detailed feedback; verbal channels account for more communication than touch
Social distance (4 to 12 feet)	Impersonal and business-like contacts	Sensory inputs minimal; information provided by visual channels less detailed than in personal distance; normal voice level (audible at 20 feet) maintained; touch not possible
Public distance (more than 12 feet)	Formal contacts between an individual (e.g. actor, politician) and the public	No sensory inputs; no detailed visual input; exaggerated non-verbal behaviours employed to supplement verbal communication since subtle shades of meaning are lost at this distance

Based on Hall (1963), from Bell *et al.* (1996)

the floor of the toilet stall recorded, using visual cues, data for two dependent variables – namely, micturation delay (the time between when a participant unzipped his fly and when urination began) and micturation persistence (the time between the onset and completion of urination).

Results confirmed that closer distances led to increases in micturation delay and decrease in micturation persistence, supporting the arousal model of personal space invasions, which proposes that close interpersonal distances are interpersonally stressful, increasing arousal and discomfort, and that it is this arousal that produces behavioural responses to invasions.

The study by Middlemist *et al.* investigated personal space in an ecologically valid but ethically dubious way. More common methods of measuring personal space include simulations, laboratory stop-distance methods, and naturalistic observation. Simulation methods may

involve reconstructing scenarios using dolls or teddy bears and measuring people's personal space needs through manipulation of their positions. Laboratory stop-distance methods may involve the participant walking towards another person and stopping when they begin to feel uncomfortable or, alternatively, the participant being the person that the researcher walks towards, with the participant indicating their personal space needs by saying when they would like the researcher to stop approaching them. Naturalistic observation may involve photographing or filming people in natural settings and then measuring distance between people by, for example, counting floor tiles of known size between them.

The theory that Middlemist *et al.* were testing is not the only theory as to why we need personal space. Their proposal was that the distances we maintain between ourselves and others are related to our levels of physiological arousal, with people experiencing

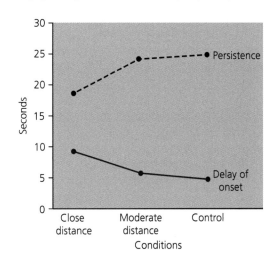

Figure 4.33 Equipment used by Middlemist *et al.* (1976) to observe the effects of personal space invasions in a men's lavatory – do people really take this many books with them to the toilet?

Figure 4.34 Mean persistence and delay of onset for urination at three levels of personal space invasion

arousal when personal space is inadequate and taking actions accordingly. However, this *arousal* theory is not the only conceptual explanation that has been advanced, and Bell *et al.* (1996) suggest three others. Firstly, *overload* theory suggests that we maintain personal space between ourselves and others to avoid being bombarded with too many social or physical stimuli (for example, facial details and smells) that exceed our limited capacity for the processing of stimuli. Secondly, the maintenance of personal space has been explained in terms of *stress*, with the suggestion being that we maintain personal space in order to avoid various stressors associated with too-close proximity. Lastly, the *behavioural constraint* approach has suggested that the reason why we maintain personal space is to prevent our freedom to behave the way we want to from being taken away from us because others are too close.

How does all this relate to the workplace? In office environments, there has been a movement away from closed-plan offices (in which workers either had a room to themselves or shared them with a small number of colleagues) towards open-plan offices, whereby workspaces for a hundred or more colleagues can be put in the same room, separated only by such office furniture as portable screens, shelving, filing cabinets and computer monitors. In itself, this doesn't have to carry implications for people's personal space requirements, but what if the move to open-plan offices is combined with colleagues working in closer proximity to one another in higher-density environments (something which the presence of walls can prevent)? Will this have an impact on workers' performance?

Figure 4.35 An open-plan office

The short answer to this question seems to be that it depends on the tasks that workers are trying to perform. Research from Evans (1979) was fairly typical in finding that participants in high-density conditions demonstrated poorer performance on complex tasks but no impairment on simple tasks. How can this effect be explained?

Referring back to the concept of arousal, the Yerkes-Dodson Law might be of relevance here. This proposes an inverted-U relationship between arousal and task performance, with performance being optimal at intermediate levels of arousal and poorer if levels of arousal are either above or below this optimum point. However, of even greater relevance is the proposal that the inverted-U relationship varies according to the type of task a person is being asked to perform, with the optimal arousal level being lower for tasks that are found to be more complex. This would suggest that in workplace environments employees should be given sufficient space for them to not feel over-aroused, especially if the tasks they are being asked to perform are ones they are likely to find complex.

 Stop and ask yourself...

- What are the benefits and drawbacks of simulation, laboratory stop-distance methods and naturalistic observation as ways of measuring people's personal space needs?

Links to methodological issues
- Validity
- Reliability
- Ecological validity
- Ethics
- Check your understanding

 Stop and ask yourself...

- What do you think might be the reason(s) why we seem to need personal space? How could you obtain empirical evidence to prove your theory?

Links to
- Check your understanding

Figure 4.36 The Yerkes-Dodson Law

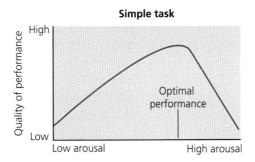

Simple task

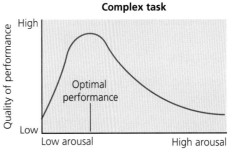

Complex task

Key research: Wells (2000) Office clutter or meaningful personal displays: the role of office personalisation in employee and organisational well-being

The following study investigates employee personalisation of office environments. Personalisation is defined by Wells as 'the deliberate decoration or modification of an environment by its occupants to reflect their identities'. As it is 'generally considered a form of territorial behaviour by which people use their personal belongings to mark and defend their territories and to regulate their social interactions', Wells was interested in its significance in the workplace for the well-being of both employees and organisations as a whole.

Background

Some facilities managers see personalisation by employees of their workspaces as disorder or 'visual chaos', and there is a long-standing assumption (not empirically proven) that an environment that appears orderly promotes efficiency. As a consequence, some offices have adopted policies that restrict the extent to which employees may personalise their workspaces, the types of items employees may display, and the location of personal displays.

Aim

This study was interested in obtaining answers to four questions:

1. Do men and women personalise their workspaces differently?
2. Is personalisation of workspaces associated with enhanced employee well-being?
3. Is personalisation of workspaces more important to women's well-being than to men's?

4. Is a company's personalisation policy associated with organisational well-being?

Sample

The sample comprised the office workers in 20 companies in Orange County, California. All were small businesses (albeit with at least 15 office employees) and all volunteered to take part in the study. The companies included two manufacturing companies, two real estate agencies, a law firm, an automobile dealership and an air conditioning firm. Within these companies, 661 surveys were given out to office workers and 338 surveys were returned. For the follow-up case studies, 23 employees (15 women and 8 men) from five of the companies agreed to participate. Employees who personalised very much or very little and did not appear to be extremely busy were chosen.

Method

Data was collected in two ways – namely, employee surveys and then follow-up case studies:
- The survey instrument was made up of seven sections assessing the following:
  - workspace personalisation
  - satisfaction with the physical work environment
  - job satisfaction
  - well-being (global well-being, physical health and psychological well-being)
  - employee perceptions of organisational well-being (including staff morale, productivity and absenteeism)
  - personality traits (need for affiliation, need for privacy, and creativity)
  - personal demographic information.

- The case studies involved tape-recorded, structured interviews based on open-ended questions. These interviews lasted 10–15 minutes and were followed up with examination of the interviewee's workspace using an observation checklist; a photograph of the workspace was also taken.

Results

Findings in relation to the four hypotheses were as follows:

1. Men and women were found to personalise their workspaces differently. Women personalised their workspaces to a greater *extent* than men (the average number of items displayed by women was 11.12 against 7.68 for men). In terms of the *types of item* displayed, women tended to personalise with symbols of their family, friends and pets, as well as with trinkets and plants, while men tended to personalise with symbols of their achievements (e.g. diplomas) and sports paraphernalia. With regard to the *reasons* for their personalisation, women did this to express their identities and their emotions, and to improve the feel of the workplace, whereas men personalised to show their status within the company.

Figure 4.37 Men and women personalise their workspaces differently

2. In relation to the second research question, personalisation was significantly associated with satisfaction with the work environment; this in turn was positively associated with job satisfaction, which was then positively associated with employee well-being. Thus, the results from this study revealed an indirect relationship between workplace personalisation and employee well-being.

3. The *survey data* suggested that personalisation was *not* significantly more important to the well-being of women than it was to men; however, data from the *interviews* suggested that it might be, with one woman saying: 'When I am away from my kids for so long during the week, just to look up to [pictures of] their faces once in a while makes it all worthwhile. It is a stress reliever.' Another woman said she 'wouldn't work' for a company that prohibited workspace personalisation, adding: 'That would be too strict, and it's none of their [expletive deleted] business.'

4. Companies having more lenient personalisation policies reported a more positive organisational climate, a more positive social climate, greater levels of employee morale, and reduced staff turnover. This suggested support for the hypothesis that a company's personalisation policy might be associated with organisational well-being.

Discussion

This study would appear to have obvious practical implications for business managers and office designers, particularly if they want to avoid the expense involved in hiring and training new employees. However, Wells urges some caution, emphasising that it is unclear whether or not a lenient personalisation policy is the cause of greater levels of organisational well-being (as opposed to other policies the company may be operating). She also points out that the findings may not be generalisable to large companies; that said, as small businesses represent over 99 per cent of all employers in the USA, the findings are applicable to the majority of the American workforce.

> ### ➡ Take it further
>
> - Ask adults you know who work in offices and have a desk of their own if they would be kind enough to take a photograph of their desk. Show these photographs to other people. Can they tell if the person who works at the desk is male or female?

Application: office-design strategies based on research into territory or personal space

If you were asked to discuss at least one office-design strategy based on research into territory or personal space, it would be important not to confuse the two concepts. Territory is distinct from personal space, so it would be vital to ensure that any suggestions about office-design strategies relate to the relevant concept. That said, an important point to note is that there would not be any easy solutions to office-design problems, and that any suggestions you might want to make would be dependent upon a range of different factors.

With regard to territory, Wells' study would suggest that employees should be permitted to personalise their desks as her study found that companies having more lenient policies about staff personalising their desks reported a more positive organisational climate, a more positive social climate, greater levels of employee morale and reduced staff turnover. However, it is noticeable that she did not find that the staff were more productive, which may well be what matters most to senior managers.

Other factors of relevance here might be the gender or nationality of the workers, as employees who are male or German may, as we saw in the beach study by Smith (1981), have a preference for larger territories. That said, it is worth keeping in mind that economic factors may make it impossible for firms to give staff the space they would like (for example, if the business is situated in a city where rents are high) and so they may have to establish hot-desking arrangements in order to minimise unused or underused space. Whether this will matter to staff will, of course, come down to the way in which they perceive their workspaces (as primary, secondary or public territories).

In relation to personal space, the needs of staff will once again vary in line with different factors. For example, if the work that staff are engaged in is complex (for example, computer coding) and members of staff are more often introverted in terms of their personality type, then it might be appropriate to afford them more personal space, possibly even having some closed-plan spaces available within the design. However, even then Hall's research suggests it will depend on the culture they come from, while other studies suggest that the gender of the employees could make a difference as male–male pairs maintain greater distances from each other than female–female pairs (Aiello, 1987).

Of course, all this assumes that employers have a choice about how much personal space they are able to permit their workers and, as noted earlier, if they are in a high-rent area or are in a line of business that does not draw in large amounts of money, their ability to do this may be limited.

The Social area

Research in the last two topic areas – psychological effects of the built environment, and territory and personal space – can be seen as largely taking the Social approach, as the focus has been on the impact of other people on our behaviour. For instance, we have seen how the presence of large numbers of people nearby can affect our likelihood of engaging in either altruistic or affiliative behaviour and we have also seen how, to deter other people from occupying territory we see as ours, we make frequent use of territorial markers.

Given the subject matter of these topics, it is perhaps not surprising that much of the research we have looked at has come from the field. Some of this has involved field experiments, such as the study by Newman and McCauley (1977) but other methods such as correlation studies have been used, as in the study by Cohen et al. (1973). Perhaps more surprising has been the way in which a study such as that by Middlemist et al. (1976) used a physiological measure to assess the effect of other people on their participants.

Research in these areas can adopt a form of environmental determinism as it is assumed that the way the built environment is formed will affect behaviour in predictable ways. Similarly, there is a focus on how situational factors (for example, the colour a room is painted or noise levels) affect behaviour. While individual and cultural differences (for example, regarding personal space needs and even use of internal space) may complicate the picture, much of the research we have looked at can be seen as useful; that said, whether budgets permit office workers being allowed the territory or personal space that they might desire is another matter.

Practice questions

1. Explain what the study by Lord (1994) into motivating recycling behaviour tells us about how messages can impact on conservation behaviours. [10 marks]

2. Evaluate the usefulness of research into conservation behaviours. [15 marks]

3. A local authority wants to try different reward schemes to motivate people to increase their recycling.

   How could environmental psychologists assess the effectiveness of the different reward schemes? [10 marks]

Chapter 5

Sport and Exercise Psychology

Arousal and anxiety (Biological)

Having to perform in any setting, whether it is giving a presentation in class, performing on stage or performing in sports, will require us to be 'prepared' to perform. Physiologically this means being at a state of arousal that will enable us to do the task in hand. Arousal, then, is a physiological state, and it increases when the environment makes demands on us to do something. Our bodily responses include increased heart rate and increased respiration rate; the level of oxygen in our bloodstream increases and blood goes to our limbs. This increased arousal level prepares us for our most basic response to stress: the 'fight or flight' response. However, this heightened state of physiological alertness is also assumed to be necessary in order for us to meet challenges such as performing under pressure. As we shall see in this topic, researchers have tried to assess how much arousal we need in order to perform, and to outline what the optimal level of arousal for sports performance might be, and how to achieve this.

Anxiety is different from arousal, although the two are linked. Anxiety is a negative emotional state of apprehension that we experience when we perceive that a situation is threatening to us; for example, exam anxiety might arise from worrying that you haven't revised thoroughly enough and that, as a result, you will not do well. Anxiety, then, impairs performance, so in a sporting context it is necessary for athletes to control their anxiety to make sure that it does not interfere with their performance.

Arousal and performance

The earliest theory that tried to explain the relationship between arousal and performance was presented in 1908 and is based on the Yerkes–Dodson law, which predicts the relationship between levels of arousal and performance. It is called the inverted U hypothesis because, when presented on a graph, the pattern of the relationship between arousal and performance looks like an upside down letter U, as shown in Figure 5.1.

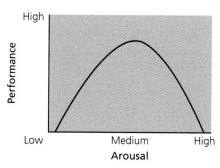

Figure 5.1 The relationship between arousal and performance according to the Yerkes–Dodson law

This model of arousal suggests that arousal steadily improves performance up to a point, but that too much arousal will lead to a steady decline in performance. The model suggests that the optimum level of arousal for best performance is a moderate level. The model also suggests that easy tasks are best performed when drive (arousal) is high, and complex tasks are best performed when drive is low.

 Stop and ask yourself…

● What is the difference between arousal and anxiety?

Links to
● Check your understanding

This model does not, however, account for individual differences in performance, or the fact that different types of skill require different levels of arousal to achieve optimal performance. In 1980 Oxendine extended the model to take these factors into account. Oxendine's research led him to suggest that the inverted U theory should be extended to include the following generalisations:

1. A high level of arousal is necessary for optimal performance in gross motor activities involving strength, endurance and speed.
2. A high level of arousal interferes with performance involving complex skills, fine muscle movements, co-ordination and concentration.
3. A slightly above average level of arousal is preferable to a normal or below average level of arousal for all motor tasks.

Oxendine's support for these proposals is based on largely anecdotal evidence; for example, in terms of his first proposal he suggests that someone being chased, for example by dogs, will experience high arousal and run faster, and claims that all runners will run faster and swimmers swim faster in a state of heightened arousal. He cites the mistakes that experienced athletes in sports such as basketball and gymnastics make in competition to support his second proposal as evidence that the high arousal experienced under the pressure of competition impedes tasks that require fine motor skills.

Figure 5.2 Oxendine suggests high arousal experienced under the pressure of competition impedes tasks that require fine motor skills and can account for the mistakes made in competition in sports such as gymnastics; this might explain this gymnast taking a tumble

There are problems with applying Oxendine's theory to real sports settings however, as the theory does not clearly define what 'complex' and 'simple' means in terms of tasks, nor what constitutes 'high', 'normal' and 'above average' arousal. Nonetheless, Oxendine concluded that there was evidence from research into sport for the application of the Yerkes–Dodson law in a sporting context. However, the optimal level of performance (the top of the U) would be on different points of the arousal axis, with sports that involve gross motor skills, strength, endurance and speed, such as tackling in football, having a high level of optimal arousal, and sports involving fine motor skills, co-ordination and concentration, such as putting in golf, requiring a lower level of arousal for optimum performance. Oxendine suggested different levels of optimal arousal required for different sports skills as follows:

Table 5.1 Optimal arousal levels for selected sports skills (Oxendine, 1980)

Arousal level	Sports skills
5 (extreme arousal)	American football tackling, doing sit-ups, weight-lifting
4	Long jump, running short and long distances, swimming races, wrestling
3	Basketball skills, boxing, high jump, gymnastic and soccer skills
2	Fencing, tennis, baseball (pitching and batting)
1 (slight arousal)	Archery, bowling, golf putting
0 (normal state)	

Have a go yourself

- On a graph, mark the horizontal axis 'level of arousal' and the vertical axis 'level of performance' and draw on a U-shaped curve to show the relationship between arousal and performance for archery skills, gymnastic skills and football tackling skills.
- How would the U-shaped graphs differ between a beginner and a professional in a sport? Sketch a further graph to show this

Both the inverted U theory and Oxendine's revision of it present difficulties in terms of measurement of variables but, nonetheless, they have proved useful in describing the effect of arousal on the performance of different skills in a variety of sporting contexts. However, more recent research has focused on studying the effects of anxiety on sporting performance.

Anxiety

Anxiety and arousal are related in that on sensing arousal someone might interpret this as indicating a challenge that they cannot rise to and will experience anxiety as a result. Anxiety in turn increases the person's arousal level; it is known as the anxiety/stress spiral and has a negative effect on performance.

Spielberger (1966) differentiated between trait and state anxiety:

- **trait anxiety** refers to the person's general personality or disposition to be anxious
- **state anxiety** refers to a person's level of anxiety experienced in a specific situation; for example, state anxiety might refer to the level of anxiety experienced when competing. State anxiety is further subdivided into:
  - **somatic state anxiety**: this refers to the person's physiological state at the time which is having a negative effect on their performance, such as feeling nauseous, breathing heavily or having your heart pounding in your chest
  - **cognitive state anxiety**: this refers to the person's negative thoughts and cognitive processes that are impeding their performance, such as lack of self-confidence and doubting whether they can do what is needed to perform well, fear of losing, or evaluation apprehension.

Figure 5.3 'If you don't have confidence, you'll always find a way not to win.' Quote from Carl Lewis, an international athlete who clearly understood the relationship between confidence and sporting performance.

Measuring anxiety

While it is normal for people to feel 'nervous' before a sporting performance, and indeed many athletes report that they use this feeling to help them optimise their arousal and ready themselves to play or compete, high levels of anxiety are not the norm. It is therefore useful for us to distinguish between a normal arousal reaction and a high anxiety reaction, and in order to do this we need be able to measure anxiety.

Rainer Martens has developed two scales to measure anxiety: the Sport Competition Anxiety Test, or SCAT, and the Competitive State Anxiety Inventory, or CSAI-2.

Sport Competition Anxiety Test (SCAT)

Martens' (1982) SCAT measures trait anxiety. It was designed to have an unambiguous procedure, so that respondents would be clear on what they had to do, would reduce the likelihood of response bias and would be easy to score. The test comprised of 15 items and was designed as a pen-and-paper test. For each of the 15 items the respondent had to select whether the item was true for them 'rarely', 'sometimes' or 'often'. The test categorised respondents as low, average or high in trait anxiety.

Some example items from the SCAT are shown in Table 5.2.

Table 5.2 Example items from the SCAT

Item	Rarely	Sometimes	Often
Items that were scored forwards to measure anxiety: 'rarely' was scored 1, 'sometimes' was scored 2 and 'often' was scored 3			
2. Before I compete I feel uneasy			
5. When I compete I worry about making mistakes			
Two items were scored backwards to measure anxiety (scoring some items backwards reduces response bias when completing the test)			
6. Before I compete I am calm			
11. Before I compete I feel relaxed			

Ten items out of the 15 test items were used to create a trait anxiety score out of 30.

Stop and ask yourself...

- Five 'spurious' items, not related to sport anxiety, were included in the SCAT. One example is 'Team sports are more exciting than individual sports'. Can you suggest why Martens included these in the SCAT test?

Links to methodological issues
- Validity of self-report measures

The first version was tested on a sample of 12–15-year-olds from schools in Chicago, from mainly white middle-class families. In establishing the test, Martens showed that the test was reliable (r = 0.77), and he conducted a further series of studies to confirm the construct validity of the test. Although originally designed for use with children Martens confirmed that it was valid for use with a range of clients.

Competitive State Anxiety Inventory (CSAI-2)

In 1990 Martens et al. presented a multi-dimensional model of sports state anxiety where:

1. somatic anxiety had a U-shaped relationship with performance
2. self-confidence had a positive linear relationship with performance

3. cognitive state anxiety had a negative linear relationship with performance.

A multi-dimensional model of state anxiety led to the development of a multi-dimensional test, which was specifically designed for use in a sporting context. The second test that Martens created was the Competitive State Anxiety Inventory (CSAI-2), designed, as its name suggests, as a measure of state anxiety and presented in its second version in 1990.

It is a pen-and-paper test consisting of 27 items, nine of which measure somatic state anxiety, nine measure cognitive state anxiety and nine measure self-confidence. Three scores on a scale from 9 (lowest) to 36 (highest) are obtained from the test, giving separate measures of cognitive anxiety, somatic anxiety and confidence.

Some example items from the CSAI-2 are shown in Table 5.3.

Table 5.3 Example items from the CSAI-2

Item	Not at all	Somewhat	Moderately so	Very much so
I feel tense in my stomach				
I am concerned that I may not do as well in this competition as I could				
I'm confident I can meet the challenge				
I feel self-confident				
I am concerned about choking under pressure				
I feel jittery				

The procedure for administering the test is to get a baseline test measure 48 hours before competition, then get the athlete to complete the test again 24 hours before, 2 hours before and 5 minutes before the competition. Martens et al. called this a time-to-event paradigm. Research results showed that cognitive anxiety decreases steadily in the run up to the event but increases rapidly just before the event, while somatic anxiety rises steadily up to the event and peaks dramatically just before the event.

 Stop and ask yourself ...

- For each of the six example items from the CSAI-2 in Table 5.3, can you work out which measure somatic anxiety, which measure cognitive anxiety and which measure self-confidence?

Links to
- Check your understanding

 Stop and ask yourself ...

- Draw up a table with two columns, one headed 'strengths of measuring anxiety using the CSAI-2' and one headed 'weaknesses of measuring anxiety using the CSAI-2'; list as many strengths and weaknesses as you can think of under the headings.

Links to methodological issues
- Validity
- Measurement of variables

Optimising arousal and controlling anxiety

From what you will have learned so far it will be clear to you that it is important that an athlete is aware of the possible effects of arousal and anxiety on their ability to perform. It is also important for them to practise and employ strategies that will help them to optimise their arousal and manage their anxiety. Suggestions for such strategies are included in the Applications section in this topic, after the key research by Fazey and Hardy.

Key research: Fazey and Hardy (1988) The inverted U hypothesis: A catastrophe for sport psychology

In this key research paper John Fazey and Lew Hardy are critical of the inverted U hypothesis as a full and convincing explanation of the relationship between arousal (stress) and performance. They make three main criticisms:

1. Research into the inverted U hypothesis has operationalised arousal, anxiety, stress and performance in a variety of ways, with much research treating arousal, anxiety and stress as if they were the same as each other, when they are not.
2. The research into the inverted U hypothesis does not provide convincing evidence for the validity of the predicted relationship between stress and performance.
3. There are difficulties in applying the model. Fazey and Hardy question the construct validity of the inverted U hypothesis in describing the effect of stress on performance. The inverted U hypothesis predicts that small increases in stress beyond the 'optimal' level lead to small decreases in the performance of an athlete. From their own research and observations of athletes, however, Fazey and Hardy suggest that when an athlete 'goes over the top' of the inverted U – that is, when they are over-aroused – small decreases in

performance did not happen. Instead they noted two things that did happen:

- far from steady and gradual, the drop off in performance was actually large and dramatic
- once this dramatic drop off in performance had occurred in competition, it was difficult for an athlete to regain even a mediocre level of performance, let alone get back to their performance level before the drop in performance occurred. This suggests that small decreases in arousal made little difference to performance once this stage had been reached (Hardy 1985).

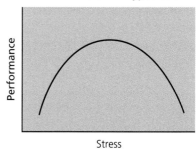

A traditional representation of the inverted U hypothesis

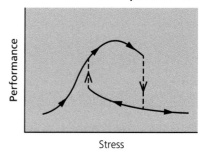

Hardy's (1985) model of the relationship between stress and performance

Figure 5.4 These two diagrams show the difference between the relationship between stress and performance as suggested by the inverted U theory, and what Hardy actually observed in athletes

According to Fazey and Hardy, then, the inverted U theory has 'a lack of predictive validity in practical situations'.

Instead Fazey and Hardy present their catastrophe model of anxiety and performance as an alternative to, or natural extension of, the inverted U hypothesis. This model assumes that an athlete's level of cognitive

> **Stop and ask yourself...**
>
> - What do Fazey and Hardy mean when they state that the inverted U theory has 'a lack of predictive validity in practical situations'? What evidence do they offer to support this criticism?

Links to methodological issues
- Predictive validity

anxiety determines whether the effect of physiological arousal is 'smooth and small, large and catastrophic, or somewhere between these two extremes'.

The model is quite complicated, and it is useful here to supplement Fazey and Hardy's research with a simplified version of the theory provided by Cox (2002). Cox uses three simple diagrams to explain the catastrophe model. The diagrams show the effect of low, moderate and high cognitive anxiety on physiological arousal and performance.

Figure 5.5 A simplified explanation of the catastrophe model adapted from Cox (2002)

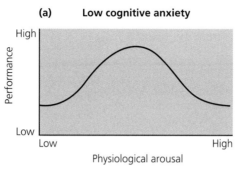

Low cognitive anxiety
When cognitive anxiety is low, a smooth, bell-shaped curve shows that as arousal increases so does performance and, as the athlete becomes over-aroused, a slow and steady decrease in performance occurs.

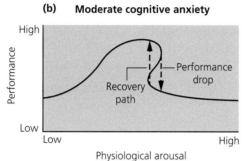

Moderate cognitive anxiety
When cognitive anxiety is at a moderate level, a somewhat distorted bell-shaped curve occurs, which shows that as the athlete 'goes over the top' of the curve, a fairly significant drop in performance happens; in order to return to optimal performance the athlete has to return to a lower level of arousal than that experienced just before the drop in performance (shown by the recovery path in the diagram).

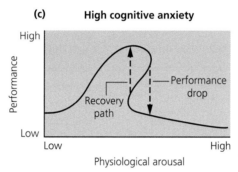

High cognitive anxiety
When cognitive anxiety is high, a very distorted bell-shaped curve pattern is seen. Very high arousal predicts very high performance but, as the athlete 'goes over the top', a very large or 'catastrophic' drop in performance occurs; in order to regain the level of performance that was reached pre-catastrophe, the athlete must return to an arousal level well below that experienced just prior to the catastrophe.

The catastrophe model shows that when cognitive anxiety is low, the inverted U hypothesis can be used to help explain the relationship between arousal and performance. However, the inverted U hypothesis does not predict the relationship between arousal and performance when the athlete is moderately or highly aroused.

Fazey and Hardy point out that their catastrophe model shows that cognitive anxiety influences performance, and that this begs the question of why this happens. In order to offer an explanation for this, Fazey and Hardy cite research by Parfitt and Hardy (1987). This research suggested that when performing a well-learned or easy task, an athlete has the capacity to control the adverse effects of physiological arousal on their performance and, indeed, will use the benefits of physiological arousal to improve their performance. Fazey and Hardy suggest that moderate to high cognitive anxiety serves as a distraction that interrupts the athlete's ability to monitor the effects of physiological arousal and impedes their ability to differentiate between what are helpful and what are unhelpful physiological effects and, as a result, arousal increases. In this way, moderate to high cognitive anxiety can have a negative effect on performance by leading to increased arousal, which in turn can have a negative effect on performance.

Fazey and Hardy suggest that their model presents a number of testable predictions, including that:
● physiological arousal is not necessarily detrimental to performance, however it will be detrimental to performance when cognitive anxiety is high

where cognitive anxiety is high *hysteresis* will occur; what this means is that performance will follow a different path as physiological arousal decreases from the path it follows as arousal increases.

A 1991 study by Hardy and Parfitt found empirical evidence for both of these predictions in an experiment involving eight experienced female basketball players aged between 18 and 23 who were from the North Wales University basketball team.

In their catastrophe model, Fazey and Hardy provide an alternative to the inverted U theory, or perhaps an extension of it, which offers a more comprehensive explanation of the relationship between anxiety, arousal and performance in terms of what athletes actually experience. They conclude their research paper with the hope that their model will generate future research and suggest that 'the real catastrophe would be for sport psychology to remain tied to the inverted U hypothesis as the only plausible model of the stress–performance relationship'.

Investigating the model, however, does present researchers with one main problem: that is, while it is possible, thanks to technology such as unobtrusive portable polygraph machines, to measure physiological arousal and to use behavioural methods to measure performance while an athlete is performing, it is not possible to measure their cognitive anxiety while they are actually performing. In addition, it is not clear at what point cognitive anxiety and arousal interact to lead to a catastrophic drop off in performance, nor what determines, or might influence, the rate of recovery from such a catastrophic drop off in performance.

Application: strategies for managing arousal and anxiety in sport

Any strategies used to optimise arousal and control anxiety must account for differences in type of sports and type of sporting skills, individual differences between athletes, and also differences in arousal in the same athlete in different sport settings and on different occasions. When it comes to optimising arousal and controlling anxiety in sports there is no 'one size fits all' method, and techniques need to be matched to the needs of the athlete. Coaches can help athletes to identify these needs and suggest appropriate strategies that the athlete might employ.

There are a number of strategies that can be used by athletes to reach their 'zone of optimal arousal'. These can be classified into two types of strategies. Firstly, there are techniques that can be used to energise the athlete and increase their arousal, commonly referred to as ways to 'psych up' the athlete in preparation for, and also during, performance. Secondly, there are strategies that are used to reduce arousal by controlling anxiety. We will consider examples of these in turn.

Energising strategies to increase arousal

Pep talks from the coach

A pep talk is a short five-to-ten-minute speech that is given by the coach or manager of a team either before a game, or at half-time, that is designed to energise, rouse, focus and inspire a team. Delivered with vigour, passion and integrity, a pep talk from the coach can raise arousal in the team. Pep talks include variations on 'go out there and show them what we can do', 'go out there and do your very best', 'go out there and bring back that trophy' type of messages, and might suggest that the team do it for themselves and each other, do it for their fans, or even for their country. Delivering an effective pep talk requires skill and practise. It is important that the coach doesn't simply reel off the same well-worn phrases – the team could become desensitised to them and the pep talk will not have the desired arousing effect.

Energising imagery

The athlete could be trained, as part of their training regimen, in the use of motivational imagery. This is a skill that has to be practised, just as physical skills have to be practised, possibly twice a day for 10 to 20 minutes over a period of several weeks. Motivational imagery might include using appropriate metaphors such as 'run as fast as a cheetah', or might

 Stop and ask yourself ...

- Why is it useful for Fazey and Hardy's model to 'present a number of testable predictions'?

Links to debates
- Psychology as science

involve mentally running through previous successful performance of a sporting skill, or previous wins, to recall and invoke the feeling that success arouses, or visualising what success will feel like – what it will be like to run a lap of honour with the crowd cheering, or to stand on the podium, or receive a trophy.

Energising self-talk

We all have an inner voice; a performer can control this inner voice and make sure that what it is saying is positive and motivating, for example 'I am going to reach my personal best', 'I can do this', or using verbal self-persuasion 'come on, you know you can do this'.

Rituals

Ritual behaviours prior to performance can motivate athletes, for example singing the national anthem, saying a team prayer or chanting a team motto can energise athletes. A well-known example of this is the use of the Maori 'Ka Mate' Haka by the New Zealand international rugby team. If you have not seen the Haka, look it up online and watch a video – it is a sight to behold! The Haka serves to 'psych up' the All Blacks ready for performance.

Figure 5.6 The All Blacks, the New Zealand international rugby team, have adopted the ritual of performing the 'Ka Mate' Haka before games

Methods for managing arousal and anxiety in sport

Diaphragmatic breathing techniques

Increased respiration rate is a symptom of heightened physiological arousal so, if an athlete learns a method for controlling their breathing, they can use it to reduce arousal and anxiety. A simple and effective way to control arousal

and manage anxiety is to practise diaphragmatic breathing techniques. Cox (2002) suggests that when practising deep breathing 'each expiration should be mentally linked with the feeling of expelling pent up tension and anxiety'.

Have a go yourself

- You might find this task easier lying down. Put one hand on your upper chest and one hand over your belly button, breathe out, then breathe in. Which hand raises first? If it was the hand on your chest then you, like most people, are chest breathing.
- Diaphragmatic breathing is breathing from your belly. Put your hands in the same place again. Breathe out again and this time when you breathe out try to make the hand over your belly button raise first. By doing this you are breathing deeply. Practising this for two minutes a day will help you to master deep breathing and will give you a simple and effective way to calm yourself down when you start to feel nervous – try it out just before that test or exam!

Woods (1998) suggests that using controlled breathing techniques to reduce anxiety in a sporting context has three advantages. Firstly, focusing on their breathing means the athlete is less likely to be distracted and can tune out irrelevant cues that could increase arousal; the technique is also simple and can be used in a wide variety of sports and sports settings; and, finally, focusing on breathing, literally taking a 'breathing space,' provides brief relief from the pressure of the situation in which the athlete can gather their thoughts and prepare themselves to perform.

Relaxation training programmes

In order to perform specific sporting skills, such as pitching or batting in baseball or cricket, or putting in golf or taking a football penalty, an athlete may need to find a way of 'turning down' their arousal in order to perform at their optimal level. A common relaxation technique is called progressive muscle relaxation, where the athlete is trained by a therapist in how to relax their whole body by being taught how to progressively relax all the different sets of muscles in the body. The athlete learns to do this a set of muscles at a time, by first tensing the muscles to be relaxed and then relaxing them.

Establishing and maintaining pre-competition routines and rituals

Pre-competition routines and rituals can be used to increase an athlete's sense of control and thus to manage their anxiety. Again this might include the use of music – Dame Kelly Holmes used ballads by Alicia Keys in her pre-event routine at the Athens Olympic Games in 2004 in which she was a double gold medal winner. Slow tempo music can be used to distract an athlete from worrying about their performance, and can help them feel calm and focused. Songs with meaningful lyrics or associations for the athlete would be useful. An athlete can prepare their own 'playlists' of both energising music to optimise their arousal (see above) and calming music to control their anxiety. Part of an athlete's routine might be to listen to their chosen music through headphones; keeping headphones on right up to just before they perform can help an athlete avoid the distracting and arousing effect of the crowd.

Figure 5.7 Dame Kelly Holmes used music to manage her arousal during the Olympic Games in Athens (2004)

As we have seen, there are a number of strategies that athletes can use to optimise their arousal and control their anxiety. It is apparent that athletes need to pay attention not only to their physical preparation and training for their sport, but also their psychological preparation and training if they are to reach their goal of performing 'in the zone'.

> ### ➡ Take it further
>
> - Create a mind map for revision of the different strategies that athletes can use to optimise their arousal.
> - Create a mind map for revision of the different strategies that athletes can use to control their anxiety.
> - To what extent are the techniques for optimising arousal and controlling anxiety useful in a sporting context? Write a 400-word response to this question.

Exercise and mental health (Biological)

While you will be familiar with the positive effects of exercise on physical health, you may not be as familiar with the positive effects of exercise and physical activity on mental health. While psychological well-being is often associated with 'happiness', this does not make it an easy variable to operationalise for research. Happiness is a vague and subjective experience. Psychological well-being is more complex than just 'feeling happy'. The World Health Organization (WHO) defines mental health as:

'a state of well-being in which every individual realises his or her own potential, can cope with the normal stresses of life, can work productively and fruitfully, and is able to make a contribution to her or his community'.

A range of factors, then, contribute to our sense of well-being. These include our sense of self-worth and self-acceptance, how positively we relate to others, our purposefulness and striving for personal growth, morale and life satisfaction. All of these factors are considered to contribute to our mood state, and mood state inventories are often used to operationalise psychological well-being and mental health in research; an example is the Profile of Mood State (POMS) inventory, which will be described in this chapter.

Threats to psychological well-being include negative affect (mood), stress and depression. In this section we will consider the positive effects of exercise on some of these factors and offer both biological and psychological explanations that may account for the positive effects of exercise on mental health and psychological well-being.

Figure 5.8 Exercise can contribute to good mental health

Benefits of exercise to mental health

Research has revealed that there are a number of psychological benefits of exercise on mental health. Exercise has been shown to improve moods, decrease depression, and reduce anxiety and stress.

Biological explanations of the positive effects of exercise on mental health

Biological explanations of this relationship began with the endorphin hypothesis. According to Steinberg and Sykes (1985), sustained physical activity such as aerobic exercise triggers the release of endorphins, a natural opioid or pain reliever in the brain, and that this produces a feel-good effect and leads to an improvement in mood. This is an attractive theory as it helps to explain the pleasurable experience that people report after exercising. However, apart from research on mice, there was little empirical evidence to support this hypothesis. This is due to the fact that endorphin release in humans is not easily measured. Endorphins released into the blood do not cross the blood–brain barrier easily. In order to test the endorphin hypothesis athletes would have had to have been given a spinal tap, an invasive and painful medical procedure, before and after exercise, and this would have been neither practical nor ethical to do in this type of research. As a result, some researchers cast doubt on the validity of the endorphin hypothesis. For example, Sparling et al. (2003) proposed that the endorphin hypothesis be rejected and suggested an alternative biological explanation of the positive effects of exercise on well-being. In a study of male students running for 50 minutes at 70 to 80 per cent of moderate heart rate, Sparling et al. found evidence that moderate exercise leads to activation of the endocannabinoid system. The research concluded that endocannibinoids might interact with other neurotransmitters, such as opioids or catecholamines, to provide an alternative biological explanation for the pain-reducing effects of exercise.

Other research suggested that BDNF (brain-derived neurotrophic factor), a brain-secreted protein that seems to have a role in neuron maintenance and may be linked to mood, might offer an alternative to the endorphin hypothesis as explanation for the positive effect of exercise on mood. Research in animals has confirmed that exercise increases BDNF, and also increases levels of serotonin and norepinephrine. A study by Heyman et al. (2012) confirmed that intense exercise increased BDNF in a study of 11 healthy male trained cyclists, suggesting that BDNF has a part to play in explaining the positive effects of exercise as a mood enhancer and antidepressant in humans.

In 2008, however, research at a German university led by Henning Boecker used brain scanning technology to provide evidence, at last, for the endorphin hypothesis in humans. Using positron emission tomography (PET) Boecker and his colleagues scanned the brains of ten distance runners before and after a two-hour run, and results from the scans confirmed that endorphins did indeed increase during the run. This research has renewed interest and credibility in the endorphin hypothesis as an explanation of the positive effect of exercise on mood state, and in particular of the post-exercise euphoric effect commonly referred to as the 'runners' high'.

Psychological explanations of the positive effects of exercise on mental health

There is a well-established relationship between exercise and psychological well-being and mental health. Penedo and Dahn (2005) conducted a review of the mental and physical health benefits of exercise. The studies in the review included diverse ethnic populations, including men and women, as well as several age groups. While concluding that much research supports the idea that exercise has the positive effect of reducing depression and improving mood, Penedo and Dahn point out that there are some weaknesses in the research. For example, many studies have a small sample size, are conducted in the short term with no long-term follow up, and also vary in the types of physical activity used.

The psychological benefits of exercise for decreasing anxiety and depression and improving mood have, then, been well supported by evidence.

 Stop and ask yourself…

- Using Penedo and Dahn's study, make a list of the factors that support the fact that exercise has a positive effect on depression and mood, and a list of reasons why we should be cautious about drawing these conclusions from this research.

Links to methodological issues
- Validity of psychological research

Woods (2001) suggests that explanations for these benefits include:

- increased self-efficacy
- increased opportunities for positive and pleasurable interactions with others – since exercise is often a social activity (an exercise class, dance class or one-to-one session with a trainer or teacher, for example) the psychological effects of exercise could be explained by greater social contact and improved social support
- distraction from other concerns – an opportunity, even if only temporary, to 'take your mind off' your worries
- production of neurotransmitters such as serotonin or dopamine while exercising may improve mood
- those suffering from anxiety or depression may benefit more from exercise than people who are already mentally healthy.

Measuring the benefits of exercise on mental health and psychological well-being

Research into the benefits of exercise on mental health usually employs self-report methods to measure these effects. One tool often used by psychologists is McNair *et al.*'s (1971) Profile of Mood States (POMS). The POMS measures six mood states, five of which are negative (tension, depression, anger, fatigue and confusion) and one positive (vigour). To complete the test, the respondent completes either a pencil-and-paper version or an online version. The test has 65 items, and for each item the respondent indicates on a five-point scale how they have been feeling in relation to the item for the past week including today. The scale goes from 'not at all' to 'a little' to 'moderately' to 'quite a lot' and ends with 'extremely'. Each item can therefore be given a quantitative value

and, when added up, the group of items that measure, for example, vigour ('lively', 'active', 'energetic', 'cheerful', 'alert', 'full of pep', 'carefree' and 'vigorous') a total score for that mood state can be calculated and a 'profile' plotted as a line graph. The advantage of an online version is that these calculations and graphs can be quickly created for the researcher. The POMS enables pre- and post-exercise activity/intervention mood scores to be compared either between individuals or between test conditions.

A useful element of the POMS test in terms of measuring mental health is that it offers a general measure of depression. In the key research for this topic by Lewis *et al.* (2014), the POMS was used to assess and compare mood states before and after a dance intervention with patients suffering from Parkinson's disease.

Key research: Lewis, Annett and Davenport *et al.* (2014) Mood changes following social dance sessions in people with Parkinson's disease

Background

Parkinson's disease (PD) is a neurodegenerative disease, and onset of the disease is usually over the age of 50. The major physical symptoms are to do with movement and include motor signs of tremor, bradykinesia (slow movement), muscle rigidity and postural instability. Symptoms are mild at first but worsen as the disease progresses.

The non-movement-related symptoms include mild cognitive impairment such as slight memory problems

 Stop and ask yourself ...

For Woods' five possible explanations of the benefits of exercise for people suffering from anxiety and depression, suggest:

- one of these which represents a social psychological explanation
- one of these which represents an individual differences explanation
- one of these which suggests a cognitive explanation
- one of these which suggests a biological explanation.

Links to
- Check your understanding

Stop and ask yourself ...

- Six of the items from the POMS test are 'worn out', 'muddled', 'grouchy', 'energetic', 'on edge' and 'miserable'. For each of these six items, can you suggest what mood state it contributes to measuring?

Links to
- Check your understanding

and problems with activities that require planning and organisation, insomnia (difficulties sleeping) and the most common psychological symptom altered mood, which usually manifests as depression and anxiety.

Lewis et al. point out that if depression is treated in PD sufferers it might help their cognitive function and improve their quality of life. They also point to the evidence that exercise is proposed to be effective in reducing anxiety and depression, the two most common psychological disorders both in PD and in the elderly in general. In addition, they quote research that suggests that dance has a positive effect on mood in the elderly, and increases both their sense of well-being and sense of belonging, even, according to Lima and Vieira (2007), leading some elderly dancers to report the feeling of 'being transported to a world of happiness' and 'being able to forget their problems'.

Figure 5.9 Elderly dancers report the feeling of 'being transported to a world of happiness' and 'being able to forget their problems'

Research into PD and dance had already shown that the movement symptoms of PD respond well to dance, but that the influence of dance on mood and depression in people with PD had not been fully reported. Similarly, no research existed before the present study that had considered whether dance classes can improve mood in people with PD in both the short term and longer term.

Aims

The aim of this study, then, was to examine the moderating effect of a dance intervention on mood in the elderly, specifically on a group of people with Parkinson's disease, across a long cycle of 12 weeks and a short cycle of one hour.

Participants

A total of 37 people aged 50 to 80 (mean age = 65.5 years) were recruited using local advertisements

and contact through a local support group for people with PD. Of these, 22 (12 male and 10 female) had been rated by a physiotherapist as having mild to moderate PD. The remaining 15 participants (7 male and 8 female) acted as an age-matched control group.

Method

Variables

The independent variables in the study were:

1. whether the participants had PD or not
2. the cycle time, with the participants being measured over the long cycle time (baseline test in week one and test to measure changes in mood in week 12) or short cycle time (test of mood before and after class on the ninth one-hour dance session).

The dependent variables were the participants' mood scores.

Measurement

Measurement of mood for the long cycle time was achieved using POMS. This gave six measures of the separate dimensions on the POMS:

- tension–anxiety
- vigour–activity
- depression–dejection
- anger–hostility
- fatigue–inertia
- confusion–bewilderment

The POMS score also enables a total mood disturbance (TMD) score to be calculated by subtracting the vigour score from the sum of the scores for the other five subscales.

To measure mood changes across the short time cycle the Brunel University Mood Scale (BRUMS) was used. This is based on POMS but is a short version, having only 24 items but still measuring all the same mood states as the full version of the POMS.

Procedure

After giving fully informed consent, participants completed the POMS for the past month and also completed a demographics questionnaire (week 1).

Participants then completed a weekly dance session run by a qualified dance instructor for ten weeks (weeks 2–11). Two identical sets of sessions were run, with each participant attending only one set. They were standardised as follows:

- all sessions lasted for 50 minutes, starting with a 10-minute warm-up followed by 30 minutes of dancing, a 5-minute break midway, and a 5-minute cool down

- each class was based on 'rhythmic dancing to a strong beat, designed to be appropriate for the age, mobility and constraints of people with mild to moderate PD'
- classes were designed to be taken standing up, but with an option to sit down if they liked
- the style of dancing changed every two weeks and included Bollywood, Tango, Cheerleading, Old Time Music Hall and Party dancing based on the Charleston and *Saturday Night Fever*.

Figure 5.10 Two of the dance sessions in the Lewis *et al.* study involved party dancing based on the charleston (left) and *Saturday Night Fever* (right); if you have never seen *Saturday Night Fever*, think 'enthusiastic dad at a wedding' and you'll have a close enough idea of what is involved

In the ninth week participants completed the BRUMS according to how they felt 'right now' before and after the dance session to provide the short cycle time data. A few days after the tenth dance session, participants were asked to complete the POMS for a second time (to provide the 'after' long cycle time data).

Results

Data from 30 participants were recorded (17 PD and 13 control). There were two drop-outs from the study, one from the PD group as a result of an unrelated medical issue and one from the control group who did not want to continue. Data from one further control subject was excluded, and five of the participants with PD could not attend the final test session (two were on holiday, two had other commitments and one was ill). The main results were that:
- Differences were found in the PD POMS baseline figures for tension, confusion, vigour and TMD from the POMS geriatric norms. Control subjects did not differ from the POMS geriatric norms.
- PD participants showed higher TMD scores than the control subjects throughout the study.
- Results showed a significant reduction in mood disturbance over the long cycle time in all participants. Anger in particular was reduced.

- The study did not find, as previous research had suggested, that those with PD scored higher on depression than control participants on their baseline measures.
- The researchers used the POMS scale to classify all participants as being low or high in depression using the POMS score of 7 as a cut-off point. Those high in depression reported less fatigue after the dance sessions.
- Using BRUMS, a reduction in TMD was shown in the short cycle time.

Conclusions

Based on this study the researchers suggest that taking part in a weekly dance class can significantly improve mood in the elderly, with and without PD. They suggest that there are two reasons why dance 'works' to improve mood in the elderly:
- dance steps and timing provide mental challenges (to memory, learning and spatial awareness)
- dance is a sociable form of exercise and, as the lack of sociability in the elderly is linked to depression, a social dance activity can help to improve their mood.

 Stop and ask yourself...

- Why do you think the researchers decided to wait until week nine of the dance sessions to collect the short cycle time data?
- Why did the researchers not get the participants to complete the POMS immediately after the tenth dance session?

Links to methodological issues
- Experimental procedures and controls

Discussion

To account for the fact that no initial difference in depression scores was shown between the PD participants and controls, the researchers suggest this may be because this was a self-selecting sample that would not attract people with PD with higher levels of depression, suggesting that volunteer PD participants do not represent the depression levels in the PD population in general. On the other hand, they point out that the control participants in this study was made up of carers/partners of the PD participants who may experience carer burden and therefore have higher levels of depression than a population of non-carers.

Another issue with the study's design is that as the control participants were the partners of the PD participants, any change in mood could be attributable to the social aspect of the dance sessions and having a positive experience with their partners rather than to the dance intervention itself. Other issues that the authors suggest would be useful to address in future research include testing a larger sample, as the small sample size in the present study might not enable generalisations to be made, and to consider the effects of the intensity of the exercise and the fact that the music used in the dance session could have accounted for the mood improvements.

Take it further

Using the suggestions for improvements that Lewis *et al.* suggest for future research, design a study that would address some of the challenges to the validity of their findings. For example:

- How could a larger and more representative sample be obtained?
- How could the control group be improved?
- How might including a no-exercise PD control group be useful?
- How could the effects of the level of intensity of the dance activity be tested?
- How could having a control group who danced alone to a training video be useful?
- How could a no-music exercise control condition be useful?

Explain how your proposed study would improve on the validity of Lewis *et al.*'s findings.

Application: exercise strategies

The key research by Lewis *et al.* leads us to conclude that a ten-week dance intervention in which people attend one hourly session a week can improve mood in the elderly. This shows how exercise, in the form of dance classes, has a benefit for mental health both in elderly clients in general and in clients with mild to moderate PD. It is feasible that such an intervention might be of benefit to other client groups, and therefore the study provides you with a suggested strategy for using dance to improve mental health.

A further study that showed the benefits of dance for mental health was conducted by Rosa Pinniger *et al.* (2012). This study was a randomised controlled trial designed to compare reduction in self-reported depression symptoms in a group who took tango lessons, a group who attended mindfulness meditation sessions and a control group who were told they were on a waiting list. Of the original 97 volunteers, 66 completed the study. Compared with waiting list controls, measures of depression were shown to be significantly lower in both the tango and mindfulness meditation groups. Stress was found to have been reduced in the tango condition but not in the mindfulness condition. Pinniger *et al.* conclude that this study shows that using tango classes or mindfulness meditation could both be considered to be effective strategies to help people overcome their depression, as complementary treatments alongside medical treatments, and that tango classes might be a useful adjunct to a stress-management programme.

The mental health benefits of yoga have also been investigated. Jeremy West *et al.* (2004) conducted a study that aimed to investigate the mental health benefits of yoga and dance. A sample of 69 healthy college students (47 female, 22 male, mean age 19, age range 17–24) participated in one of three 90-minute classes: a practical session learning African dance (N = 21); a session of hatha yoga (N = 18); or a biology lecture (N = 30), which acted as a control group.

The results showed a highly significant reduction in perceived stress in both treatment conditions ($p < 0.0001$), leading the authors to conclude that both yoga and dance are effective strategies for reducing stress and improving well-being.

In terms of strategies for improving mental health, it seems that mood, stress and depression can all be positively affected by interventions that involve exercise, for example using a series of general dance lessons, as used by Lewis *et al.* to improve mood, a series of Argentinean tango lessons to reduce symptoms of depression and stress, and African dance sessions or hatha yoga to help manage stress. In addition, mindfulness meditation sessions could also be used as strategy to reduce symptoms of depression and therefore improve mental health.

Figure 5.11 Pinniger *et al.* (2012) showed that taking Argentinean tango lessons could be an effective strategy for improving mental health by reducing symptoms of depression and stress

Motivation (Cognitive)

Motivation refers to what drives us to do particular things. In a sporting context, it might be what motivates an athlete to take up a particular athletic or sports activity, the motivation for them to continue, and the motivation to achieve their best and succeed in their chosen sport.

The OCR specification requires you to be able to describe how self-efficacy, sports confidence and sports orientation have an impact on an athletes' motivation, and also how imagery could be used to improve motivation by increasing self-efficacy and self-confidence.

Sports self-confidence

In 1986 Robin Vealey presented a model to explain self-confidence in a sporting context. Vealey's definition of sporting self-confidence was 'the belief or degree of certainty individuals possess about their ability to be successful in sport'.

Vealey's model suggests that there are two types of sport confidence. One of these is **trait sport confidence**, which is a relatively stable belief in your general level of sporting ability based on previous experiences. For example, if you have successful experience in a range of sports such as tennis, football, basketball and rugby, you will probably have a high level of trait sport confidence.

State sport confidence, on the other hand, is the level of confidence that can be changed quite quickly and relates to the athlete's confidence in their ability to perform in a particular sporting context at a given time. An example might be the level of self-confidence someone might have in scoring from a penalty in a football game.

Figure 5.12 An example of state sport confidence is the level of self-confidence a player might have in scoring from a penalty in a football game

A further feature of the model is the person's competitive orientation. This means how much they want to win in the given situation. For example, the drive to succeed would be higher if the penalty was likely to make the difference between your team reaching a final in a tournament or not than if your team was already 3–0 down in the game.

Vealey called the specific sporting performance, in this case the taking of a penalty shot, the objective sporting situation. Her theory suggests that the athlete's state sport confidence level in the context of the objective sporting situation would be affected by their level of trait sport confidence and their competitive orientation. The higher their trait sport confidence and the higher their drive to succeed, the higher their level of state sport confidence would be in this situation.

After the performance in the objective sporting situation, in this case after taking the penalty shot, the athlete makes a subjective assessment of the outcome. If this assessment is positive, that is they scored the goal, then this positive outcome will lead to an increase in trait sport confidence and in competitive orientation. Conversely, a negative assessment of the outcome, for example hitting the goalpost, will mean that the athlete will experience a decrease in both trait sport confidence and competitive orientation. In this way Vealey's theory operates on a 'loop' as, when facing a similar sporting challenge in future, the athlete's perceived success or

Stop and ask yourself…

- What is the difference between state sport confidence and trait sport confidence?

Links to
- Check your understanding

failure will have increased or decreased their trait sport confidence and competitive orientation, which in turn will increase or decrease their state sport confidence in a future similar sporting situation.

Vealey developed psychometric tests to measure the three features of her model. She developed a Trait Sport Confidence Inventory (TSCI), a State Sport Confidence Inventory (SSCI) and a Competitive Orientation Inventory (COI). These measures were tested and validated on a sample of 666 high school, college and adult sportspeople from a range of sports including track and field athletics, basketball, baseball, tennis, softball and gymnastics. The findings from these sports supported Vealey's theory.

Not all subsequent research has supported all elements of the theory, however. For example, an investigation by Martin and Gill (1991) found evidence that on the one hand supported Vealey's theory in that their sample(73 middle- and long-distance runners with a mean age of 16) state sport confidence and outcome self-efficacy were predicted by levels of trait sport confidence. However, they did not find that competitive orientation predicted state sport confidence, which contradicted Vealey's model.

Nonetheless, Vealey's model provided a useful framework for the understanding and assessment of sport confidence.

Figure 5.13 A diagram to show Vealey's Model of Sport Confidence

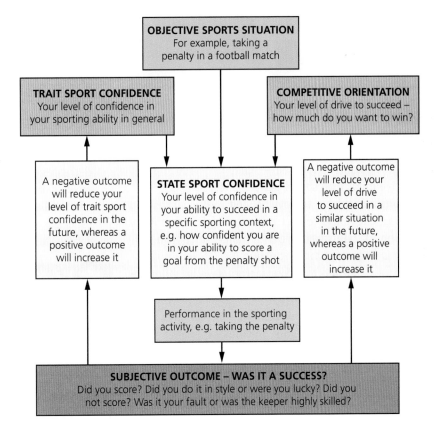

Self-efficacy

Albert Bandura first presented his model of self-efficacy in 1977. He believed that learning from consequences (either by direct or vicarious reinforcement) was a cognitive process that would lead to outcome expectancy. This means that a person could estimate the likely outcome of any behaviour they might do based on their own previous experience or their observations of others. In other words, people can see which actions lead to positive outcomes. In a sporting context, a person may know, for example, that training regularly and effectively will lead to success, as they have experienced this before.

Bandura also identified what he called efficacy expectations, by which he meant a person's belief about their personal ability to successfully achieve the desired outcome. A person may have high or low self-efficacy:

● **high self-efficacy** – we know what we need to do for success and are very confident that we can do it successfully

● **low self-efficacy** – we do not know what to do for success, or know what to do but lack the belief that we will be able to do it successfully.

Self-confidence and self-efficacy are not the same as each other. In a sporting context self-confidence is usually measured as trait self-confidence. For example, a gymnast may have a very high level of confidence in her level of skill on the beam. Self-efficacy, on the other hand, refers to an individual's belief that they can perform specific tasks or demonstrate skills in a specific context. So the gymnast may have high self-confidence but low self-efficacy in that she is unsure that she will be able to perform well in a particularly challenging competition.

Figure 5.14 While this gymnast may have high self-confidence in her ability on the beam, she may have low self-efficacy that she can demonstrate her skills in a challenging competition

In a sporting context, low self-efficacy will have a negative impact on sports performance, so it is important for athletes to develop, and their coaches and trainers to encourage them to develop, high self-efficacy in relation to their sporting performance, since high self-efficacy is important for motivation.

Bandura suggested that four factors have an influence on a person's self-efficacy.

1. **Previous personal achievement** – if you have been successful in the past your previous experience will act as a reinforcer that increases your self-efficacy and leads you to believe that you can succeed again in the future. If your team wins, then this increases your belief that they can win again. You think 'we have done it before, so we can do it again'. Of course, for novices or beginners, success in the form of 'winning' does not always come as easily as it might to elite or professional athletes, so coaches need to focus on small successes to encourage self-efficacy, such as a particularly good shot in tennis or an improvement in service technique.

2. **Vicarious experience** – Bandura suggests that we learn vicariously from the success of role models. If we see someone else demonstrating a sporting skill then their success can encourage us to think 'if they can do it, then so can I'. In a sporting context the model could be the trainer, a demonstration from a more advanced teammate or player, or perhaps a film clip of a sportsperson performing a particular skill. It is important in fostering self-efficacy that the skill being

modelled is not too advanced for the athlete being trained, as self-efficacy will only be increased with success in performing the modelled task. If the task is too hard and the attempt to perform it unsuccessful, this can lead to low self-efficacy.

3. **Verbal persuasion** – encouraging praise and positive feedback from the coach can act as effective verbal persuasion and increase self-efficacy. Similarly, encouraging talk from teammates or, in younger athletes, praise from parents could help to increase self-efficacy. Negative language should be avoided, as again this would be counterproductive and reduce efficacy beliefs, so it is important to model criticism carefully; for example, to a young golfer: 'It's a shame that you did not get the length on that shot that we were hoping for, but your grip on the club has really improved. Try again!'

4. Finally, **emotional arousal** has an impact on self-efficacy. It is important for an athlete to be fully focused on their performance and in order for this to happen they must be 'emotionally ready and optimally aroused' (Cox, 2002). Arousal must be carefully managed as over-arousal leads to anxiety and that decreases performance. An over-aroused, emotionally anxious athlete will lack self-efficacy, so these factors need to be taken into account by coaches and trainers, especially when preparing athletes for important competitions and performances.

Have a go yourself

- Imagine that you are a sports psychologist. Write a 250-word report to explain how a coach could increase young athletes' motivation in sport by increasing their self-efficacy.

Sports orientation

Diane Gill (1986) identified competitiveness as the key factor in explaining sports motivation, and that sport is a unique activity in this respect. She theorised that if we are to effectively measure motivation in a sporting context, then research tools from other fields, such as measures of academic achievement motivation or motivation at work, would not 'map on' easily. Consequently, in 1988, with her colleague Thomas Deeter, she created a measure of sports specific achievement motivation, which they called the Sports Orientation Questionnaire (SOQ). The SOQ is a 25-item questionnaire where the respondents indicate their responses to the items on a five-point scale (strongly agree to strongly disagree). The SOQ is a multi-dimensional measure of individual differences in sports achievement motivation. Woods (2001) identifies the three motivating factors for athletes identified by the SOQ:

- **Competitiveness** – where the motivation is to seek and strive for success. An example item on the SOQ that measures this is: 'I look forward to competing.'
- **Win orientation** – where the athlete judges their performance in comparison with others and has a strong desire to win when competing. Because competition is hard to control the athlete may fail to win and the impact of this may be that their motivation to compete will reduce, or they will restrict competing to events in which they believe they are bound to win or bound to lose. An example item from the SOQ that measures this is: 'The only time I am satisfied is when I win.'

Figure 5.15 Win orientation is one of the motivating factors for athletes, and for some athletes losing can have a very negative effect on their motivation to take part in future competitions

- **Goal orientation** – where the athlete's motivation to engage in sport is to set and achieve personal goals. The athlete compares their performance with their own previous performances and their goal is to keep improving on their own performance. The goal-orientated athlete is more likely to feel in control and to set themselves achievable targets. They are also less likely to see failure as a setback. An example from the SOQ that measures this is: 'Reaching personal performance goals is very important to me.'

Gill and Deeter tested the SOQ on a large group of athletes and non-athletes, both male and female. The findings showed interesting individual differences. For example, males scored higher on competitiveness and win orientation, whereas females scored higher on goal orientation. For athletes in general, goal orientation was more important than win orientation.

The key finding, however, was that the results confirmed that competitiveness did indeed have the strongest influence on the motivation to enter competitive sporting situations. Athletes who scored high on competitiveness might score high on goal or win orientation, or both, or indeed low on either or both of these measures. The important factor that discriminated the athletes from the non-athletes was competitiveness.

The sports-oriented participants scored consistently higher on the competitiveness scale than the non-sports-oriented participants. This provides evidence for the construct validity of the SOQ as a measure of sports-oriented motivation. Gill and Deeter also retested their participants on the scale and found that all three items – competitiveness, win and goal orientation – gave strong positive correlations on retest (0.89, 0.82 and 0.73, respectively), demonstrating that the scale was reliable.

Imagery

In a sporting context, the easiest way to define imagery is as mental practice or mental rehearsal, a process whereby the athlete thinks through or imagines themselves performing a particular skill or achieving a particular goal. They imagine themselves doing something and also imagine what it would or could feel like to experience it. In this way, imagery acts a mental 'run through' for the athlete.

Figure 5.16 If you want to achieve something, imagining yourself doing the activity can help you to achieve the desired outcome

Barbara Woods (2001) suggests that for the athlete imagery can perform various functions in addition to mental practice. For example, by performing a mental run though of achieving success, the athlete can improve their self-confidence. Combined with relaxation techniques, imagery can also be used to control arousal, to manage anxiety and to prevent over-arousal from impacting negatively on the athlete's sporting performance.

In terms of explaining why imagery is of benefit to sporting performance, Woods suggests six possible reasons for using imagery:

- Imagery enables the performer to try out different strategies, run through routines or correct faults. For example, a tennis player might replay a point in their head and replay it, correcting their fault, then play on mindful not to repeat the fault in the remainder of the match.
- The sports player is able to practise or run through routines privately, avoiding the arousal effects of an audience or the possibility of public failure.
- Imagery allows the athlete to suspend time and motion. For example, a tennis player can deconstruct the elements of their serve and mentally practise features that they want to improve. Then the whole sequence of the serve can be mentally rehearsed.
- Imagery enables the athlete to consolidate and rehearse newly acquired skills from a training session, either during rest breaks or between training sessions.
- Some researchers suggest that when we use imagery there is a slight activation of our muscles, and in this way imagery acts as a weak form of physical practice.
- Imagery enables an athlete who has an injury to practise skills mentally and enables them to retain their skills during periods of rest due to injury.

Imagery is used by many elite athletes, and research suggests it is of greater effectiveness in enhancing the performance of experienced athletes than of beginners or less-proficient performers.

Beginners or less-skilled players may not be able to use imagery effectively in terms of cognitive focused imagery – it is difficult to imagine the skill being correctly executed if you do not have a good understanding of what the correct procedure for the skill would be.

However, another function of imagery is focused on motivation. One type of motivational imagery is called Motivation General-Mastery (MG-M) imagery, and our key research on this topic shows that there are benefits for players of all ages and levels of using MG-M imagery, specifically in increasing a player's self efficacy and self-confidence, thereby increasing their motivation.

Brazilian footballer Ronaldinho employs imagery for game preparation and strategy purposes:

When I train, one of the things I concentrate on is creating a mental picture of how best to deliver the ball to a teammate, preferably leaving him alone in front of the rival goalkeeper. So what I do, always before a game, always, every night and every day, is try and think up things, imagine plays, which no one else will have thought of, and to do

so always bearing in mind the particular strength of each teammate to whom I am passing the ball. When I construct those plays in my mind, I take into account whether one teammate likes to receive the ball at his feet, or ahead of him; if he is good with his head, and how he prefers to head the ball; if he is stronger on his right or his left foot. That is my job. That is what I do. I imagine the game.

Figure 5.17 Ronaldinho employs imagery for game preparation and strategy purposes

Key research: Munroe-Chandler, Hall and Fishburne (2008) Playing with confidence: The relationship between imagery use and self-confidence and self-efficacy in youth soccer players

Within sport, Munroe-Chandler *et al.* note that research into imagery has been guided by Paivio's (1985) work, which suggested that imagery has both cognitive and motivational functions, and that these can both operate either on a specific or general level. Table 5.4 summarises these functions.

Table 5.4 Specific and general cognitive and motivational functions of imagery

Cognitive general (CG) function of imagery	Focus is on imagining general game strategies or routines
Cognitive specific (CS) function of imagery	Focus is on imaging specific sport skills, such as taking a free kick in football
Motivational specific (MS) function of imagery	Focus of imagery is on achieving specific goals, e.g. imagining yourself receiving a particular medal or trophy
Motivational general (MG) function of imagery	Includes imagining emotions and feelings, e.g. to get 'psyched up' for a race or game

The MG function has been refined to produce two sub-divisions:

- Motivational General-Arousal (MG-A) imagery, which focuses on mood regulation, such as staying calm under pressure, for example when taking a penalty shot in front of a large crowd.
- Motivational General-Mastery (MG-M) imagery, which consists of images related to mastery, self-confidence and 'mental toughness'.

The authors point out that the relationship between MG-M imagery and self-confidence has been well established in adult athletes. They cite a study by Callow, Hardy and Hall (2001) of three elite basketball players in which a 20-week imagery programme improved self-confidence significantly in two of the players and stabilised self-confidence in the third. In terms of self-efficacy, a study by Mills, Munroe and Hall (2001) showed adult individual sport athletes with high self-efficacy reported using more MG-M imagery than those with reported low self-efficacy. Other research links MG-M imagery to high sport confidence in 12–18-year-olds. Munroe-Chandler et al. suggest that the use of MG-M imagery should therefore be a good way for athletes to 'develop, maintain or reclaim' their sports confidence.

Figure 5.18 Canadian youth soccer

Aims

Munroe-Chandler et al. wanted to see if the relationship observed between MG-M imagery and increased self-confidence and self-efficacy for elite, adult and adolescent athletes would hold true for young athletes and recreational athletes. The aim of this study, then, was to investigate the relationship between MG-M imagery and self-confidence and self-efficacy in soccer players aged 11–14 years.

The authors predicted:

- MG-M imagery would be a predictor of both self-efficacy and self-confidence in young athletes.
- MG-M imagery would be a stronger predictor of self-efficacy and self-confidence in competitive rather than recreational athletes, since self-confidence and self-efficacy are important to success in competitive sport.

Soccer (football) was the chosen sport for this study. In Canada, where the study was conducted, soccer was the largest youth participation sport, played equally by both boys and girls. Soccer also had two levels: a 'house' league, which was recreational rather than competitive, with a focus on skills; and 'travel', where teams played against one another competitively in their league and a tournament to determine the league winners.

Sample

Data was reported from 122 male and female soccer athletes aged 11–14, a mix of boys and girls with a mean length of experience over six years, and who were recruited from both recreational and competitive soccer leagues in south-western Ontario, Canada.

Method

Three measures were taken: a measure of imagery use, a measure of self-confidence and a measure of self-efficacy.

To measure imagery, the Sport Imagery Questionnaire for Children (SIQ-C) was used. This is a 21-item questionnaire with statements measuring children's imagery use on a five-point scale from one (not at all) to five (very often). The participants were asked to circle the number that most applied to the statement. High scores on this scale would indicate a high use of imagery. The scale measures the five types of imagery.

Examples of scale items related to the types of imagery are included in Table 5.5.

Table 5.5 Examples of items in the Sport Imagery Questionnaire for Children (SIQ-C)

CS imagery	I can usually control how a skill looks in my head
CG imagery	I make up new game plans or routines in my head
MG-M imagery	I see myself being mentally strong
MG-A imagery	In my head, I imagine how calm I feel before I compete
MS imagery	I see myself doing my very best

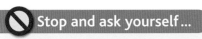 **Stop and ask yourself ...**

- What are the strengths and weaknesses of the sample used in this study?

Links to research methods

- Sampling and generalisability

To measure sport confidence, a trait sport scale was developed by the authors by adapting the confidence subscale from the Competitive State Anxiety Inventory-2 for Children, for example modifying 'I feel self-confident' to 'I usually feel self-confident'. This amended scale was called the Competitive Trait Anxiety Inventory-2 for Children, or CTAI-2C.

To measure self-efficacy, a soccer specific measure was available: the SEQ-S (Self-Efficacy Questionnaire for Soccer). The questionnaire asks participants to rate five items on a scale from 0 (no confidence) to 100 (complete confidence) in ten-unit intervals. The five items are:

- I am confident I can work through difficult situations.
- I am confident I can remain focused during a challenging situation.
- I am confident I can be mentally tough throughout a competition.
- I am confident I can remain in control in challenging situations.
- I am confident I can appear confident in front of others.

Procedure

Permission to conduct the study was obtained from the university's research ethics boards. Coaches were sent letters or emails outlining the study. Parental consent and player assent were obtained. The data was collected before practice at the players' usual practice fields. This was done over a two-week period in mid-soccer season. Participants completed a demographics questionnaire that asked for their age, gender, level and number of years playing. They then completed the three measures of imagery, self-confidence and self-efficacy in that order. The questionnaires took a total of approximately 15 minutes to complete.

Results

Pearson correlations were calculated for the five imagery subscales and self-efficacy, and the same for self-confidence. While all the imagery subscales correlated positively and strongly with both self-efficacy and confidence, as predicted the MG-M subscale of the SIQ-C yielded the strongest positive correlation with both the SEQ-S and CTAI-2C scores.

The data for recreational and competitive soccer players were separately analysed and the results showed that MG-M imagery was a significant predictor of both recreational and competitive soccer players.

Conclusions

This study confirmed the prediction that MG-M imagery (images related to mastery, self-confidence and mental toughness) is a strong predictor of self-efficacy and self-confidence not only in elite, adult and adolescent athletes, but also in young athletes, and regardless of whether they played recreationally or competitively. The authors suggest that this has implications for all athletes:

If an athlete wants to increase his/her self-confidence, or self-efficacy through the use of imagery, the MG-M function should be emphasised.

Application: strategies for motivating athletes

One strategy that could be used to motivate athletes might be for coaches to train athletes to use imagery techniques so that they can use mental practice alongside their physical practice. Cox (2002) suggests that it is useful for coaches to consider the where, what, when and why of imagery use. The 'where' and 'when' of imagery use refers to the situation in which the imagery is to be used (for example, if it will be during breaks in practice while waiting to perform, or between practice sessions). The 'why' of imagery is whether the purpose is motivational (for example, to increase self-confidence) or cognitive (to mentally rehearse skills). The 'what' of imagery refers to the nature and content of the imagery, for example suggesting an athlete use CS (cognitive-specific) imagery to run through what a skill looks like in their head.

Since MG-M imagery has been shown to predict both self-confidence and self-efficacy, if an athlete lacks or appears to have lost confidence the coach could suggest imagery training to the athlete. Imagery training using MG-M imagery would have the goal of increasing motivation by supporting the athlete in coping effectively, feeling confident and mentally tough. One way of using imagery is to construct an imagery script that would be audio recorded and which the athlete could listen to and work through twice a day. These are typically 10 to 15 minutes long and 'guide' the athlete through the imagery tasks, which would vary depending on the needs

🚫 **Stop and ask yourself…**

- Munroe-Chandler *et al.* point out that a limitation of their findings is that they are correlational. Can you explain why this is a limitation of the study's findings?

Links to research methods
- Correlational research

of the individual athlete. Nicholls and Jones (2013) suggest that it might be helpful for an athlete to be wearing their sports kit during imagery sessions, or holding an item related to their sport, such as a basketball, tennis racket or golf club. Nicholls and Jones also suggest a general imagery script for MG-M imagery that might begin:

Imagine you are about to perform a skill that is associated with your sport such as [insert skill here] ... Perform your skill in your mind, feeling confident and mentally tough as you do so ...

and might include such instructions as 'see and feel yourself performing successfully', as well as giving appropriate time within the script for the athlete to perform their mental practice.

Similar scripts could be devised and used daily over a number of weeks to increase either individual or collective self-efficacy using MG-M imagery.

Another strategy that can be used for motivating athletes would be to encourage them to develop and maintain high self-efficacy. Efficacy outcomes are a strong indicator of the amount of time and effort an athlete will put into their game. Psychological research has shown that perceived self-efficacy is an important cognitive factor that is closely related to success in a sporting context, so it is important for coaches, parents and trainers to encourage high self-efficacy in athletes by, for example:

- Setting achievable goals, especially in beginners, so that they can experience personal success that will increase their self-efficacy, and reminding athletes of their past successes to encourage them to believe that they will be successful again in the future.
- Using positive language, including encouragement and praise, and encouraging athletes to use positive self-talk to help them persuade themselves that they can achieve success.
- Presenting themselves as a positive model for the athlete, modelling not only the behaviour that will lead to success but also modelling confidence.

Find out more

- Find out what is meant by **intrinsic motivation** and **extrinsic motivation**, and suggest what a coach could do to offer both types of motivation. Is it better for an athlete to be intrinsically or extrinsically motivated? Give reasons for your answer.

Stop and ask yourself ...

- Can you apply the where, when, why and what of imagery use to the suggested application for using MG-M imagery?

Personality (Cognitive)

If you ask someone to describe the 'personality' of someone they know, they will probably describe them in terms of traits or characteristics, for example as a warm, friendly, sociable person who is the life and soul of any party, or can be counted on in a crisis to provide sympathy and a shoulder to cry on. They may even use psychological concepts that have become part of our common understanding, such as describing their friend as an extrovert, or an introvert.

What we mean in general by personality is that a person possesses a set of characteristics or traits, that these are relatively stable, and that these characteristics can be used to explain and predict their behaviour. As a definition, this is as good as any, since a definition of personality on which all psychologists agree does not exist, and this is an indication of how difficult personality is to operationalise as a variable. For our purposes, we will assume that personality refers to the set of consistent characteristics or traits that a person has and how people can differ in these traits. The study of personality is an example of research from the individual differences area of psychology.

In the background to this topic, the OCR specification requires you to give examples of personality, for example outlining theories of personality, to describe and evaluate different measures of personality, and to relate personality to a sporting context.

Personality, its measurement and its relationship to sport

Freud's psychodynamic theory of personality

One of the earliest, and most famous, theories of personality was the psychodynamic theory proposed by Freud. Freud proposed that the motivation for all behaviour came from our unconscious drives, and that our unconscious libidinal and aggressive drives have a strong influence on our behaviour. In order to spend the energy generated by our unconscious drives, Freud

Links to

- Check your understanding

suggested that we possess a tripartite personality consisting of the:

- **id**, which seeks to satisfy our drives in the way that generates the greatest pleasure
- **superego**, or moral element of our personality, which inhibits behaviour of which society would not approve
- **ego**, the part of the personality that has the task of expending the energy in conscious reality.

This model is essentially a conflict theory of personality, since it is the role of the ego to balance the demands of the id to satisfy the drives, against the demands of the superego to inhibit immoral behaviour. In order to resolve conflicts, the ego operates a number of defence mechanisms, which are essentially 'safe ways' to satisfy these conflicts. An example of a defence mechanism is displacement, where, for example, aggressive energy that the id demands is spent in overt aggression towards others in fights could be safely diverted from the unacceptable behaviour of getting involved in fights into the more acceptable solution of playing contact sports, such as rugby, or joining a boxing club.

Figure 5.19 Can you explain what Freud would mean by boxing having a 'cathartic function' for those engaged in the fight?

Freud considered that aggression is instinctual and innate but, as with any drive, the energy that is created can, and must, be spent. Following the chain of thought in Freud's theory, engaging in sports and games is a socially acceptable way of spending built-up aggressive energy. This is referred to as catharsis, which means a purging of the emotions. Psychodynamic theory relates to sport, then, in that it suggests that playing sports and games has a cathartic function.

Criticisms of the psychodynamic perspective can be applied to this theory. The unconscious drives and the tripartite personality are unfalsifiable and, as such,

Freud's theory is considered unscientific. Research also questions whether the catharsis effect actually works, or whether in fact aggression just leads to more aggression.

Trait theories of personality: Eysenck (1965)

Trait theories of personality are more commonly used in a sport context. Trait theories suggest that personality can be reduced to a number of traits or characteristics that we all share, but of which we have different amounts. Hans Eysenck proposed his trait theory in 1955. He proposed that there are two dimensions of personality: the extrovert–introvert dimension, and the emotionally stable–emotionally unstable (neurotic) dimension. According to Eysenck, personality is about 75 per cent nature and 25 per cent nurture.

Eysenck suggested that personality had a basis in biology, with the introversion–extroversion dimension being caused by the reticular activating system (RAS), which is the part of the brain that influences levels of arousal. Simply stated, the higher a person's 'set' level of cortical arousal, the more introverted a person will be as they try to avoid become over-aroused (stressed). Introverts are therefore stimulus avoidant and they avoid loud, crowded places, prefer to know what is going to happen, prefer order and are good at tasks that require them to focus and concentrate. On the other hand, extroverts have a low 'set' level of arousal, and are stimulus hungry, seeking out experiences that will increase their arousal levels. They tend to get bored easily, do not focus on tasks for long, prefer change, excitement and unpredictability. Extroverts are louder, more outgoing individuals than introverts.

The autonomic nervous system (ANS) responds to emotionally arousing events. Those who score at the neurotic (emotionally unstable) end of this dimension are likely to be quick to respond emotionally to a relatively minor stressful (negatively arousing) situation, as the fight or flight response kicks in quickly for them, whereas those who score towards the stable end on this dimension are more likely to remain calm and relaxed in the face of relatively minor stressors.

Later, Eysenck added a third dimension to his theory, psychoticism. This dimension, he suggested, was affected by the hormone testosterone and people high on this scale, which implies aggression, would be attracted to the competitive and arousing nature of sporting activity.

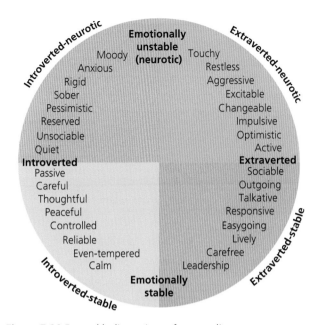

Figure 5.20 Eysenck's dimensions of personality

Eysenck *et al.* (1982) wrote a review article that linked Eysenck's personality theory to sport, suggesting that sportspeople would be extroverts, tend to be low in neuroticism (enabling elite sportspeople to manage their anxiety in high-pressure situations) and score high on psychoticism. Jarvis (2006) cites a study by Frances *et al.* (1998) which studied 133 female Irish university hockey players and compared them against a non-sporting control group. In support of Eysenck's theory, the hockey players scored significantly higher on both extroversion and psychoticism than the non-sporting controls. Similarly, McKelvie *et al.* (2003) conducted a study that compared 86 university athletes with a control group who did not play for their university and found that extroversion was higher in the athletes, although not significantly so, while athletes scored significantly lower on neuroticism. Again, this seems to support the idea that personality, specifically in terms of higher extroversion and lower neuroticism does have an influence on sports participation.

One question that arises from research into personality and sports participation, is whether the person chose to take part in sport because of their pre-existing personality traits (known as the gravitational hypothesis, as people with certain personalities gravitate towards sports) or whether it is taking part in the sport that has an influence on their personality. McKelvie *et al.*'s study suggests that there is support for the gravitational hypothesis since

they conducted their study over four years and found personality traits to be stable and consistent, suggesting they were pre-existing in the athletes, and it was therefore their personalities that influenced their involvement in sport and not the other way round.

Eysenck suggested that one factor that would influence the relationship between personality and sport would be the type of sport that a person participated in. Eysenck (1982) suggests that individualistic sports might attract introverts and, in support of this, Woods (1998) suggests that introversion has been found to be higher in distance runners, and that group or team sports such as ice hockey or football might attract extroverts. Even within a team, Eysenck continues, there may be variation, with a goalkeeper being more introverted than a forward, who may score higher on extroversion.

Figure 5.21 Research has shown that distance runners score high on introversion

Trait theories of personality: Cattell's 16 personality factors (1965)

Eysenck's dimensions can be criticised as being reductionist and lacking in detail. In addition, it could be argued that Eysenck's theory does not account enough for the effect of situation on personality.

Raymond Cattell proposed a trait theory of personality which, he argued, provides more detail than Eysenck's and which also gives more emphasis to situational factors. The basis for Cattell's theory was work by Allport and Odbert (1936) who had created a list of 4500 personality-related words by trawling through English dictionaries. Using factor analysis, a statistical process that identifies the most important factors, Cattell narrowed this down

---

🚫 **Stop and ask yourself...**

- For the studies by Frances *et al.* (1998) and McKelvie *et al.* (2003), suggest challenges to the validity of the research which might weaken their value as evidence to support the relationship between Eysenck's theory of personality and sports participation.

Links to methodological issues
- Sampling issues
- Measurement issues
- Validity

to 12 personality factors, to which he added four more in order to create his 16 personality factors (16PF). He proposed that these are the 16 factors that people use to describe themselves and others. Each of these factors represents a dimension on which people will all score, but on which there will be individual differences. The profile of their scores on these 16 dimensions represents their

'personality'. Cattell did not, however, expect people to score exactly the same each time they completed the 16PF questionnaire, as the responses on the questionnaire would be affected by situational factors such as their mood and level of motivation. Cattell's 16 primary personality factors and their dimensions are shown in Table 5.6.

Table 5.6 Cattell's 16 primary personality factors and their descriptions

		Primary factors	From ...	To ...
	A	Warmth	Reserved, cool	Easy-going, warm
	B	Reasoning	Concrete thinking	Abstract thinking
	C	Emotional stability	Easily upset	Emotionally stable
	E	Dominance	Submissive, accommodating	Assertive, opinionated
	F	Liveliness	Serious, prudent	Expressive, enthusiastic
	G	Rule consciousness	Expedient	Conforming, rule bound
	H	Social boldness	Shy, threat sensitive	Socially bold, unafraid
	I	Sensitivity	Tough-minded, rough	Tender-minded, refined
	L	Vigilance	Trusting, accepting	Suspicious, sceptical
	M	Abstractedness	Down-to-earth, conventional	Absent-minded, creative
	N	Privateness	Forthright, unpretentious, open	Polished, calculating
	O	Apprehension	Confident, complacent	Apprehensive, self-blaming
	Q1	Openness to change	Conservative, traditional	Liberal, innovative
	Q2	Self-reliance	Group-orientated, sociable	Resourceful, self-directed
	Q3	Perfectionism	Undisciplined, impulsive	Controlled, compulsive
	Q4	Tension	Relaxed, composed, low drive	Restless, high drive

According to Cattell, assessment of these 16 primary factors gives a detailed personality profile of an individual, and he also claimed that this profile could be used to predict behaviour. In order to measure personality, in 1965 Cattell presented the 16PF Questionnaire. This is described below as a measure of personality.

While Cattell's 16PF theory of personality is more holistic than Eysenck's theory, which describes personality in just three dimensions, both of these trait theories can be criticised for being reductionist. Whether in three dimensions or in a profile of 16 factors, both of these theories are limited in that they try to explain the complexity of human personality using a limited set of traits or factors, and so both theories fail to consider the whole person.

Kroll and Crenshaw (1970) used Cattell's 16PF to investigate personality in a variety of sports as we shall see in the key research below.

Measuring personality

The Rorschach Test

Devised in 1921 by Herman Rorschach, the 'ink blot' test is a projective test used to measure personality. Its use is most associated with the psychodynamic theory of personality. In this test participants are presented with ten cards with ink blots on, some in black and white, and some in colour. The participant is asked to say what he or she sees in each card. The tester makes notes on the responses and, after the test is complete, the examiner writes a report, or a Rorschach profile, based on the participant's responses. It has not been widely used in a sport setting since the test results require a level of subjective interpretation on the part of the examiner. The test assumes that the participant will 'project' their personality, including their unconscious motivations and

Stop and ask yourself ...

- How do theories of personality contribute to the nature–nurture debate in sport?
- How do theories of personality contribute to the individual–situational explanations of behaviour in sport?

Links to debates

- Nature–nurture
- Individual–situational

fears, on to the images and that these will be revealed to the examiner who is trained to identify features of the psychodynamic theory of personality. Questions of validity remain not only in terms of the test itself, but also of the theory that it claims to measure.

Eysenck's EPI, EPQ and EPQ-R

Structured questionnaires are the favoured method of measuring personality in psychology in general, and in sports psychology in particular. Eysenck designed the EPI (Eysenck Personality Inventory) and EPQ (Eysenck Personality Questionnaire) to measure the dimensions of his theory of personality. The test comprises of a number of questions that are answered either 'yes' or 'no'. The items correspond to the different dimensions; for example, to measure the E dimension (extroversion–introversion) items such as 'Are you a talkative person?' and 'Do you take the initiative when meeting new friends?' are used, and to measure the N dimension (neuroticism–stability) items such as 'Are your feelings easily hurt' and 'Are you a worrier?' are included.

The EPQ-R (revised version), was presented by Eysenck and Eysenck in 1985 and has two forms, a standard form consisting of 100 items and taking 20–35 minutes to fill in, and a short form that consists of 57 items and taking 10–25 minutes to complete. Both forms of the test have four scales, measuring extroversion–introversion, neuroticism, psychoticism and a scale for detecting lies. This test is intended for adults and is designed to be completed individually as a self-report test, either as a pen-and paper-test or on a computer.

Cattell's 16PF Questionnaire

Cattell amended and refined his 16PF Questionnaire over the decades; now in its fifth edition, it contains 185 items that ask simple questions about daily behaviour, preferences and attitudes. An example might be 'When I find myself in a boring situation, I usually "tune out" and daydream about things TRUE/FALSE.'

It is completed individually as a self-report test and takes 35–50 minutes to complete the paper form or about 30 minutes on a computer. The test results provide a personality profile comprising measures of each of the 16 primary factors.

In the key research for this topic, Kroll and Crenshaw (1970) used the 16PF to see if athletes involved in different types of sports would give different personality profiles.

What are psychometric tests?

Psychometric tests are instruments (for example, pen-and-paper tests, one-to-one tests) that have been developed to measure a range of mental characteristics, such as intelligence tests (IQ tests), brain damage/brain function (STM capabilities), creativity, personality, job attitudes, aptitude and skills, and, as we have seen in this section, psychometric tests are also used to measure personality.

The EPI/EPQ and Cattell's 16PF Questionnaire are both psychometric measures of personality. Psychometric measures provide quantitative measurements that are attractive to psychologists, as this makes comparison between participants/groups and analysis of data possible, and enables correlations between variables to be investigated. In addition, as psychometric tests are often administered as pen-and-paper tests, or as online tests, data can be collected relatively quickly, making research cost and time effective. Large samples can be used and this can increase the generalisability of the findings.

However, there are some problems associated with psychometric tests. They are often completed as self-reports, so data may be falsified. Participants may be affected by demand characteristics or social desirability bias and, if this happens, it affects the internal validity of the test. In an attempt to address social desirability issues, both the EPQ and the 16PF Questionnaire contain elements that are designed to detect lying, either to present oneself in a good or bad light, in an attempt to ensure the validity of participants' responses.

Construct validity is a problem in general for these tests. Are they really testing what they say they are testing? Do the EPI/EPQ and Cattell's 16PF questionnaire really measure 'personality'?

It is also very difficult to design a test that does not contain ethnocentric biases. Reliability is also important. If participants do not score significantly similar results on an equivalent test, or on retest, then the tests are not reliable and, if they are not reliable, they are not valid.

There are also ethical concerns associated with psychometric tests. They need to be administered and results analysed and interpreted by trained individuals. In the wrong hands they can be misinterpreted, for example low IQ scores used to 'label' someone as stupid, and treating them accordingly. Similarly, in a sporting context, Cox (2002) suggests that it would be inappropriate, and unethical, to use personality profiles alone to coerce athletes into deciding which sport would be the right one for them to focus on: 'If a young athlete with a tennis player's personality profile wants to be a golfer, then so be it.'

- The actual items for the Rorschach test, the items from the EPQ and for Cattell's 16PF are not in the public domain. Can you explain the advantage of this in terms of the validity of these tests?

- Validity of measurement

Key research: Kroll and Crenshaw (1970) Multivariate personality profiles analysis of four athletic groups

Background

Kroll and Crenshaw point out that previous studies into personality and sport used a range of measures that made comparisons between studies difficult. Similarly, the quality and the level of the players was varied, meaning that it would be difficult to generalise across a range of sports from the existing research.

In their study, Kroll and Crenshaw wanted to address both of these issues. They used a common assessment scale to measure personality across four different sports. They standardised the level of the participants by selecting athletes whose success in their sport was established since they played at either national or regional level.

Aim

The study aimed to investigate what differences, if any, there would be in the personality profiles of participants with a high level of skill in four different sports by using Cattell's 16PF.

Participants

A total of 387 male participants were studied from four different sports:
- 81 American football players (from three teams who were winners in their leagues)
- 141 gymnasts
- 94 wrestlers
- 71 participants in karate.

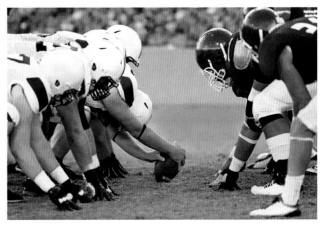

Figure 5.22 Kroll and Crenshaw studied personality profiles in a range of sports: American football, gymnastics, wrestling and karate

The quality of all these athletes was deemed to be of 'excellent or superior calibre'.

Procedure

All participants completed Cattell's 16PF. To control for falsification and ensure validity of responses, participants also completed a test that included the 15-item lie test from the MMPI (Minnesota Multiphasic Personality Inventory). Data were discarded for any participant who scored 7 or higher on this scale.

Comparisons between six pairs of sports were made to investigate the differences between the personality profiles for the different sports.

Results

With one exception, comparisons between all the sporting pairs showed significant differences in the personality profile of the sporting participants. The exception was football and wrestling where no differences were observed, suggesting that football and wrestling attracted and held on to men with

- What are the strengths and weaknesses of the sample in this study in terms of generalising the research findings about personality profiles of different sports to other athletes and other sporting situations?

- Sampling issues
- Generalisability

similar personality profiles. Table 5.7 summarises the differences observed.

Table 5.7 A table of the differences observed in the sporting profiles in six pairs of sports, using the components on the 16PF

Pair of sports compared	Components on the 16 PF where the major differences were observed
Football–wrestling	No differences
Football–gymnastics	H C J Q2
Football–karate	Q2 H L G
Wrestling–gymnastics	H B Q2 Q1
Wrestling–karate	Q2 Q4 N G
Gymnastics–karate	Q4 G F B

The results showed that high-level footballers and wrestlers had similar personality profiles, and that footballers' and wrestlers' profiles differed significantly from the profiles of participants in karate and gymnastics. Personality profiles also differed between participants in karate and gymnastics.

Footballers and wrestlers scored high on Q2 (group dependence versus self-sufficient). This was an exception to the general trend that suggested that participants in team sports scored higher on Q2 than participants in individual sports; Kroll and Crenshaw suggest that further research into this would be useful.

Conclusions

Kroll and Crenshaw's work leads to the conclusion that different personality profiles are related to participation at a level of high success in different sports.

Application: strategies for using knowledge of personality to improve sports performance

From the 1950s to the 1970s much research was done into the relationship between personality and sports. However, enthusiasm for research in this field waned as it became clear that personality was not a strong predictor of sporting performance. Cox (2002) cautions that if we are to consider the use of personality in sports that we bear in mind that:

no scientific study ... has shown a strong statistical relationship between personality and athletic ability.

This does not mean that personality does not have any influence on a person's decision to take up or maintain involvement in a particular sport, just that it is not a main factor. Indeed, Cox suggests that personality may account for just 10 to 15 per cent of the reasons for choosing a particular sport.

However, Cox does suggest that personality testing and its analysis might be useful in player development, especially as many athletes play a variety of sports. If they had come to a point in their career where they wanted to make a decision about which sport to choose to focus their efforts on, then the results of a psychometric test, such as the EPQ-R or Cattell's 16PF, might be used to help inform their decision.

On the other hand, Cox cautions against using tests to guide young athletes into particular sports or use personality tests for selecting team members. For example, it would not be an appropriate use of test results for a coach to say to a ten-year-old: 'Now I've tested all your personalities I have worked out you are the most introvert, Jill, so you are going in goal for this season.' Many successful athletes anecdotally report that before engaging in sport they were shy and introverted, but that participating in their sport gave them more confidence, so it is important not to use the personality of a young athlete as the sole predictor of the sport or team position in which they are likely to do best.

In terms of sports performance, particularly performance in an important competition, having tested athletes using the EPQ it might be useful to know which athletes score higher than average on the N dimension, since emotional stability is important to an athlete. An emotionally unstable athlete will find it difficult to control their over-arousal under pressure. If such athletes were identified, coaches could work with the athletes likely to succumb to pressure as suggested by their personality profile to help them to manage their anxiety. Athletes using a successful coping strategy to manage their arousal are more likely to perform better.

> **Have a go yourself**
>
> ● Imagine that you are the new coach of a volleyball team. How could you use knowledge of the personalities of your athletes in order to improve their sports performance?

> **Stop and ask yourself ...**
>
> ● Do you think that Kroll and Crenshaw's study can be considered to be useful? Explain your answer.

Links to debates
● Usefulness

Performing with others (Social)

Sports performance often takes place with athletes and sportspeople working together as a team. There are many interactive team sports, such as netball, hockey, rugby, basketball and football, that require athletes to perform with others as a team. In this section we will look at the formation of teams and the importance of group cohesion within sporting teams. This section will also explore the role of coaching and leadership in team sports. We will also look at factors that undermine team success and consider how coaches and sports leaders might try to prevent these.

Teams

Team formation and group cohesion

An important concept that contributes to the success of teams and satisfaction of team members is group cohesion. This concept is separated into two types of cohesion:

- **social cohesion**, which is the extent to which team members like one another and the degree of satisfaction they get from their team membership, and
- **task cohesion**, which is the extent to which team members work together to achieve shared and specific goals.

The development of group cohesion is described in a four-stage model proposed by Tuckman in 1965. For the team to emerge as a cohesive unit they must successfully pass through these stages. Tuckman called these stages forming, storming, norming and performing.

1. **Forming** – this is the coming together of group members; the excitement of meeting new team members is experienced and the members seek to accept and be accepted by the group.
2. **Storming** – as the name suggests, the 'storming' stage of team formation is one associated with conflict, typified by challenging, posturing and banter as team members vie for position in the group. The team members may feel frustrated at having to learn new team systems and making relationships with the other team members with whom they may not have much in common.

3. **Norming** – in terms of the development of group cohesion, the norming stage is most important. The team agrees it goals and what its standards for good performance are. Team members find their roles within the team, and individuals' opinions are adopted.
4. **Performing** – conflicts are resolved, which means the team can function effectively; in the performing stage the team becomes focused on performing the task in hand.

In terms of characteristics, cohesive teams have shared and clearly defined goals, a positive sense of team identity, shared respect and trust between team members, and good communication and co-operation.

Group cohesion has been shown in research to be important to a team's successful performance. For example, Carron *et al.* (2002) found a strong relationship between task cohesion and successful performance in a group of male and female basketball and club soccer team players. This suggests that task cohesion is a strong predictor of performance in interactive sports teams where team members are required to work together to achieve a shared goal. However, there is a problem with drawing this conclusion, since research in this area is correlational, so we cannot establish whether group cohesion leads to success, or if success leads to group cohesion. After all, it is much easier to like and support your team members after a win than after a defeat!

Leadership

The role of a leader is to direct the activities or behaviour of a group or team towards shared goals. In a sporting context leadership roles include team captain, coach and manager. National and international sports regulatory bodies, such as the International Olympics Committee or FIFA for football, offer leadership in terms of establishing rules, applying sanctions and setting up competitions.

Much research has been conducted into what makes a good leader. Early research focused on trait theories, assuming that some people possess certain characteristics or traits that predispose them to being appointed as leaders. An example of this is Stodgill's (1948) great man theory of leadership.

Stop and ask yourself ...

- Why is group cohesion important in a sporting team?

Links to
- Check your understanding

Stodgill's research involved a review of 124 articles that had researched traits and characteristics of leaders, covering a wide range of types of groups and settings. From this Stogdill identified differences in the physical, personality and cognitive traits between leaders and non-leaders. He considered a total of 24 features. His findings for many of the features were mixed; for example, in both weight and height leaders were mostly found to be taller and heavier, but there were contrary results in some studies for both of these findings. Nonetheless, Stogdill was confident enough in his results to suggest that a select number of stable traits exist in leaders in comparison with non-leaders, such as intelligence, both academic and athletic achievements, self-confidence and responsibility. However, the great man theory, while perhaps suggesting why leaders emerge, failed to account for which traits of leadership would be most effective in which setting and why.

In a sporting context, Stodgill's theory would suggest that those who become team captains, managers and other sports leaders do so because of they possess a universal set of personality characteristics that mean they would be successful leaders in any context, including in their involvement in sport.

Stodgill's study was, however, consequently considered not to have offered a credible theory of leadership, and the focus of research into leadership moved away from trait theories and instead began to focus on leadership behaviour. This shift in focus in leadership research resulted in a more holistic view of leadership. Rather than looking at the leader in isolation, an interactional approach was favoured where not only the leader but also the type of people being led and the situation in which they were being led were taken into account. In other words, effective leadership, it was theorised, arises from the appropriate leadership skills being employed in relationship to both the setting and characteristics and goals of those being led.

Work in this area began with Fiedler's (1967) contingency theory of leadership. Fiedler proposed that the success of a leader would be contingent upon (that is, would depend on) to what extent the style of leadership fits the situation. Fiedler's ideas were developed in a sporting context by Chelladurai (1978), who presented the multi-dimensional model of leadership. In this model Chelladurai suggests that the effectiveness of a team, both in terms of successful performance and team satisfaction, can be explained in terms of the interaction between three types of leader behaviour:

- **Prescribed leader behaviour** – this is the behaviour that the leader is required to perform.

For example abiding by the rules and expectations of the organisation overseeing their leadership. This behaviour is determined by the situation.
- **Preferred leader behaviour** – this is the type of behaviour that the team would choose for their leader to perform. For example, they might want a supportive leader who would offer praise and encouragement. Team satisfaction is one element of leader effectiveness, so whether or not the leader is behaving as the team would choose for them to behave will have an impact on the judgement of the leader's effectiveness.
- **Actual leader behaviour** – this is how the leader actually behaves and could be informed by both the prescribed and preferred behaviours in the given situation and is also influenced by the leader's own personality characteristics and traits.

According to Chelladurai's model, the combinations of prescribed, preferred and actual leadership behaviour have different predicted outcomes. These outcomes depend on whether or not the types of leadership are congruent (match up) with one another. For example, if the team wants a supporting leader who offers encouragement and praise, and the leader does not behave in this way, then the preferred and actual leadership behaviour would be incongruent as they do not match. If the leader was supportive and encouraging, however, then the preferred and actual behaviour would match and would therefore be congruent.

Table 5.8 Predicted outcomes from Chelladurai's multi-dimensional model of leadership

Type of leadership behaviour: congruent ☺ or incongruent ☹?			
Prescribed	Preferred	Actual	Outcome
☺	☺	☺	Ideal (high performance and high team satisfaction)
☺	☺	☹	Removal of leader
☹	☺	☺	Satisfaction
☺	☹	☺	Performance
☹	☹	☹	Laissez-faire

The model suggests that the ideal model for effective sports leadership is when predicted, preferred and actual behaviour are all congruent. This should lead to success in terms of both performance and team satisfaction.

Figure 5.23 When preferred and actual behaviour of the leader are congruent, both successful performance and team satisfaction are predicted

Conversely, when all three leader behaviours are incongruent, then this results in a laissez-faire leadership style. Lewin *et al.* (1939) identified this style of leadership as one where, in effect, there is no leadership and members of a group often argue among themselves and are not very productive. In a sporting context this would mean that this style of leadership would be unlikely to lead to high levels of performance nor high levels of team satisfaction.

When preferred and predicted behaviour are congruent, but the actual behaviour of the leader is incongruent to these – that is, the leader is doing neither what is required nor what would be preferred – the outcome is that the leader is likely to be removed; for example, if a football manager behaved in this way then they may well get the sack.

When the preferred and actual behaviour of the leader are congruent – that is, where the leader is behaving as the team would choose them to do, but this is incongruent with prescribed behaviour – the outcome of this is that the team may experience high satisfaction, but possibly at the expense of team performance.

When prescribed leadership and actual leadership are congruent, but what the team would prefer the leader to do is incongruent with these, the outcome would be

that the team would perform well but this might be at the expense of team satisfaction.

According to Chelladurai's model, a leader could and should be flexible in adapting their behaviour to meet the demands of a situation. This suggests that good leadership does not result from the exercise of a set of rigid traits or characteristics within the person, but rather that effective leadership involves the employment of a range of behavioural styles depending on what is required for success.

Coaching

The role of a sports coach is to help individual athletes, or teams of athletes, to reach their goals and fulfil their sporting potential. This includes instructing, demonstrating, mentoring, assessing and monitoring progress, creating the right conditions for learning and practise of skills to take place, and finding ways to maintain the motivation of the athletes they are working with. Having the right coach is important to the success of athletes.

Coaches can be professional or amateur. In the youth sports leagues in the USA many of the coaches of teams in sports such as baseball, basketball, volleyball, American football, soccer and rugby are non-professionals who coach in their spare time because of their enjoyment of the game.

In 2011 the Sports Fitness and Industry Association (SFIA, formerly the SGMA) reported that their research indicated that nearly 70 per cent of children aged 6–17 in the USA played team sports, and that three out of four teenagers played at least one team sport. 'The US is truly a team sports-driven society,' said SGMA President Tom Cove. 'While children represent the foundation and the roots of the team sports experience in the US, millions of Americans are also connected to team sports in a variety of ways – as athletes, coaches, parents, administrators, sponsors, and fans.'

Stop and ask yourself …

- What are three types of leader behaviour that Chelladurai identified in the multi-dimensional model of leadership?
- Explain what is meant by the terms 'congruent' and 'incongruent' in the context of this model.

Links to
- Check your understanding

Stop and ask yourself …

- Using Stodgill's great man theory and Chelludurai's multi-dimensional model of leadership, can you explain how leadership in a sporting context contributes to the nature–nurture debate in psychology?

Links to debates
- Nature–nurture

Often when we hear statistics about American children, it is about the rising levels of childhood obesity, so it is reassuring to hear that so many children are involved in team sports that have the potential to support them in living a healthy lifestyle. The benefits of sporting activity to levels of physical health are obvious and, therefore, it is to be hoped that the good start that so many American children are having in engaging with team sports will mean that they will continue to live active and healthy lives as adults, including continuing to engage in team sports. In order to make sure that this happens, a youngster's experience of involvement in team sports needs to be positive and to motivate them to continue to want to play. Youth sports programmes are often highly competitive; with coaches striving for success, there is the potential for the experience to be a negative one where the child is motivated by fear of failure, fear of the coach or their teammates' disapproval, or a positive one that rewards and motivates them and one in which they enjoy working with their coach and experience working in a team with strong social cohesion.

In our key research, Smith *et al.* (1979) recognised that the quality of coaches for youth teams is variable, and that their experience with working with children also varies, as do their abilities to form positive relationships with their teams and within their teams. They suggested that in order to ensure that youth sports participation had a positive effect on children's psychosocial development, so that it would be good for them psychologically as well as physically, one way would be to train coaches. In their 1979 study their focus was on the issue of 'how we can increase the likelihood that the outcome of participation [in youth sports programmes] will be favourable for children'.

Figure 5.24 How can the coaches of youth sports programmes be trained so that young people are encouraged to continue to participate in sports?

One of the findings of the 1979 study was that the training programme they designed, Coach Effectiveness

Training (CET) was shown to increase the self-esteem in children. In a study by Smoll *et al.* in 1993, CET was used with the baseball coaches of 152 boys. Boys with low self-esteem who played for coaches who undertook the CET programme showed more significant increases in self-esteem than boys with low self-esteem in a control condition in which the coaches did not take part in CET. A contribution of sports psychology to youth team sports, then, is the use of CET, which helps to support the psychosocial development of children, specifically in increasing self-esteem in low-esteem children. CET is described in the key research by Smith *et al.* (1979).

Key research: Smith, Smoll and Curtis (1979) Coach Effectiveness Training: A cognitive behavioural approach to enhancing relationship skills in youth sports coaches

Background

How can we make sure that the experience of engagement in youth sports is a positive one, one that supports the child's psychosocial development? Smith *et al.* theorised that one way to achieve this would be to focus on the behaviour of the adults who have the most control over the child's experience, namely the sports coaches. Smith *et al.* devised a training programme, which they called Coach Effectiveness Training (CET), with the aim of providing youngsters with good quality coaching. The programme was designed to help coaches 'relate more effectively' to their players and the aim was to change the behaviour of the coaches in order to improve the relationship between the players and their coach and teammates.

The programme developed out of a preliminary study that the authors had conducted in the previous year with 51 male Little League baseball coaches and the 542 boys that they coached. The coaches' behaviour was observed over four games and at the end of the season boys were interviewed in their homes about their coach's behaviour and asked to evaluate their coach and teammates.

Guidelines for good or bad practice were developed from the findings of this preliminary study.

Aims

The aims of the CET programme were to increase awareness in the coaches of what they did, what the likely outcomes of various coaching behaviours would be and to help them to develop or enhance their coaching skills in order to select and use behaviours that would have a positive outcome, and to avoid behaviours that could have a negative outcome.

- The authors predicted that CET would increase positive interactions between coaches and their players and positive interactions between teammates.
- The authors also predicted that young players with low self-esteem would give more pronounced differences in their perceptions of trained coaches and untrained coaches.

Participants

An initial sample of 34 male Little League baseball coaches was recruited from the sample of coaches who had taken part in the preliminary study. Their mean age was about 36 years old and they had a mean experience of just over eight years of coaching.

Of these, 18 were randomly allocated to be in the experimental condition, who would receive CET training, and 16 to the control condition who would receive no training (slightly more were allocated to the experimental condition in case some failed to turn up for the training sessions).

All 18 of the experimental condition attended the CET training session. Three of the control condition dropped out of the study, leaving 13 coaches in this condition and an overall sample size of 31.

Procedure

The experimental condition coaches were phoned and invited to an evening training session. They were told that during this session they would be informed of the results from the previous year's study and given coaching guidelines that had been formulated from the findings of that study. The authors conducted the training session, which lasted approximately two hours. In the session they described the relationships the previous study had found between coach attitudes and behaviours, and the boys' attitudes to their coach, to their teammates and to their sport. They were told that while liking the coach and wanting to play for him again in the future did not correlate highly with winning, the research had revealed that certain coach behaviours did correlate with winning and these behaviours had formed the basis for the guidelines for coach behaviours.

The guidelines:

- were presented verbally and in a written 'brochure' for the coaches to take away with them
- were modelled by the authors during the verbal presentation, demonstrating examples of both desirable and undesirable behaviours
- stressed the 'desirability of reinforcement, encouragement and technical instruction designed to elicit and strengthen desirable behaviours'

- were designed to achieve the goal of increasing positive relationships by increasing positive interactions, and decreasing negative interactions, between the coach and players, as well as between teammates, and to reduce fear of failure.

The guidelines gave examples of dos and don'ts for the coaches. For example, in response to player 'mistakes, screw-ups and bone-headed plays' the guidelines were as follows:

DO: *ENCOURAGE immediately after mistakes. That's when the kid needs encouragement most. Also, give corrective INSTRUCTION on how to do it right, but always do so in an encouraging manner. Do this by emphasising not the bad thing that just happened but the good things that will happen if the kid follows your instruction (the 'why' of it). This will make the player positively self-motivated to correct the mistake rather than negatively motivated to avoid failure and your disapproval.*

DON'T: *PUNISH when things are going wrong. Punishment isn't just yelling at kids; it can be any indication of disapproval. Fear of failure is reduced if you work to reduce fear of punishment.*

The written instructions in the brochure for coaches gave specific suggestions for communicating effectively with players, gaining respect from players and relating to parents.

Behavioural feedback was given after observing the experimental coaches in the first two weeks of the season, and for all coaches the feedback included the aim of raising their rate of reinforcement to 25 per cent of their responses. In addition, coaches self-monitored their behaviours. After each of the first ten matches of the season coaches completed a self-monitoring form indicating approximately what percentage of their time they spent using the desirable behaviours (the 'dos' from the guidelines). These were posted to the authors in stamped addressed envelopes provided for them.

The purpose of the behavioural measures and self-monitoring was to ensure that the coaches who were supposed to be using the guidelines were actually doing so, and these measures also reminded them to do so.

Measurement of variables

The experimental and control coaches were compared in terms of:

- **Observed behaviours during games** – these behavioural measures of the coaches were conducted by 16 undergraduates who had undergone four weeks' training and were deemed competent to observe using the CBAS (coaching and behavioural assessment system).
  Twelve categories of behaviour are observed for and coded when using the CBAS: reinforcement,

non-reinforcement, mistake-contingent encouragement, mistake-contingent technical instruction, punishment, punitive technical instruction, ignoring mistakes, keeping control, general technical instruction, general encouragement, organisation and general communication.

Each coach was observed covertly over four complete games, and the observers were blind to the condition each coach was in.

- **Player perception and attitudes** – these were assessed using structured interviews at the end of the season; 325 boys (82 per cent of all the total number of boys) were interviewed individually at home. They and their parents were assured that the data would remain confidential and that coaches would not be informed of any of their answers. To measure perception of coach behaviour the 12 items from the CBAS were used and boys were asked to rate their coach on each item using a 7-point scale in terms of how often they used them, ranging from 'never' to 'almost always'.

    The boys also responded to 11 items that measured their perception of their own ability, for example 'How good are you in baseball?'; their attitudes towards playing, for example 'How much do you like playing baseball?; and their attitudes to the coach, for example 'How good a baseball teacher is your coach?' These were completed on a clipboard so that the interviewer could not see the boy's responses.
- **Player self-esteem** – after the interview, boys completed a test of their general self-esteem.

Results

Observed behavioural differences

In general, the analysis of the findings from the CBAS showed no overall differences in behaviour between the experimental coaches and the control coaches. However, analysis of the individual items of the CBAS suggested that there was a significant difference in that the experimental coaches used reinforcement more frequently than the control coaches ($p < 0.05$).

Player perceptions and attitudes

The player perceptions revealed that the experimental coaches were using reinforcement, mistake-contingent encouragement and general technical instruction more, and using non-reinforcement, punishment and punitive technical instruction less than the control coaches. These findings are in line with the CET guidelines.

Player attitudes revealed that there was no difference between the two coach conditions for the liking of baseball. However, the boys in the experimental coach condition:

- enjoyed playing for their coaches more ($p < 0.001$)
- had a stronger desire to be coached by them in the future ($p < 0.001$)
- rated their coaches more highly as a teacher of baseball ($p < 0.01$)
- rated their relationship with their teammates more positively ($p < 0.01$).

Figure 5.25 How did the boys in the experimental coach condition differ from the other boys in their attitudes?

Player self-esteem

The authors had previous year self-esteem measures for 112 of the boys in the experimental condition and 75 in the control condition, allowing them to compare self-esteem pre and post coach training. The findings showed higher increased self-esteem in the experimental condition.

Stop and ask yourself...

- Can you identify five features of the way that data was gathered in this study that were put into place in order to ensure that the data that was gathered was valid?

Links to methodological issues
- Validity of data-gathering methods

Stop and ask yourself...

- What does 'p < 0.001' mean?
- Using examples from Smith *et al.*'s findings, explain what is meant by a type 1 error.

Links to methodological issues
- Inferential statistics – observed significance levels
- Type 1 error

The post-season self-esteem scores were used to classify the boys into three categories: high self-esteem, moderate self-esteem and low self-esteem. The researchers had predicted that the boys with low self-esteem would show greater attitudinal differences in the experimental coach condition, and analysis of the boys by self-esteem group showed that boys with low self-esteem did indeed rate the coaches who had received the CET programme more highly than the boys in the other self-esteem categories.

Effect on win–lose records

The authors compared the win and lose percentages for the experimental and control coaches. The mean wins for the experimental coaches was 54.5 (S.D. = 24.71) and for the control coaches the mean was 47.7 (S.D. = 26.91). Analysis failed to reach significance, and the authors point out that the large standard deviations show that both groups had their share of successful and unsuccessful coaches when it came to winning games.

Discussion

The researchers felt confident in concluding that the results they observed were caused by CET, since the two sets of coaches were highly comparable. They did not differ in age, gender, total years' coaching experience or number of years coaching baseball. They did not differ in performance based on previous season's CBAS assessments, nor in player attitude assessments from the previous season, and nor were they different in terms of their win–lose records. In other words, they were confident that they had isolated whether coaches received CET training or not as the independent variable in this study. Smith *et al.* conclude that:

- CET exerted a significant and positive influence on the overt coaching behaviours of those who undertook the training and that in the boys they coached this improved their attitudes to their coach, their teammates and to baseball.
- There was an increase in self-esteem in the boys coached by the coaches who received CET training.
- The 'positive' approach for coaches in relation to players as set out in the CET guidelines led to more positive interactions between team players. In other words, following the CET guidelines led to increased social cohesion in the baseball teams.

While the authors are cautious about making claims about the effectiveness of CET on the basis of one study and suggest that 'replication of these results is highly desirable', they conclude that the findings of this study suggest that 'training programmes designed to assist coaches, teachers and other adults occupying leadership roles in creating a positive and supportive environment can influence children's personality development in a positive manner'.

In addition, Smoll *et al.* (1993) suggest that their findings on the effects of the programme on boys with low self-esteem warrant further study, since 'it is the low self-esteem child who is probably in greatest need of a positive athletic experience and who appears to respond most favourably to desirable coaching practices'.

Application: strategies to improve team performance

There are a number of strategies coaches could employ in order to improve team performance. Since research has shown that group cohesion is important for success, it follows that coaches could improve team performance if they devise and employ strategies aimed at increasing group cohesion. Woods (1998) suggests some actions that coaches could take in order to develop strong group cohesion in their team. These include:

- get to know each player personally and devise ways of helping the other players to get to know each other
- encourage open and easy communication between players, emphasising tolerance, respect for differences and the importance of listening to others
- encourage group identity by developing group norms, wearing team T-shirts and clarifying group roles
- develop practice drills that emphasise not only individual but also interactive skills that require team members to work together to effectively achieve their goals

It is also important to emphasise areas of success, even when the team has not won. So, if a team has defended well even though they did not win the match, the coach should focus on this as an area of successful performance to celebrate, since successful performance affects group cohesion.

Another strategy that coaches could employ would be to ensure that they give feedback to each individual so they are aware that their effort, performance and contribution are being monitored and are valued, and that they make a contribution towards achieving the team's goals.

Figure 5.26 Coaches should give feedback to each individual so they know their performance is being monitored and that their contribution is valued

Take it further

- Read about Chelladurai's multi-dimensional model of leadership again in this section. If a leader wanted to improve team performance, how could they adapt their behaviour to bring this about according to Chelladurai's model?

Audience effects (Social)

What difference does an audience make to how well someone performs? This is an important question in a sporting context where athletes at all levels may be expected to play in front of spectators, whether it be playing to 20 or so enthusiastic and supportive parents at a Saturday morning football match for under 11s, or performing in front of a capacity crowd in a large stadium or arena. In this topic we will consider explanations of how and why performing in front of an audience enhances or inhibits sports performance, including the effects on sporting performance of a phenomenon known as home advantage.

How an audience can facilitate or inhibit sports performance

Psychologists use the term social facilitation to describe the positive effects other people present have on a person's performance of a task. Social facilitation suggests that when we are performing tasks that are easy, or at which we are highly skilled, then the presence of other people – that is, an audience – leads to an improvement in performance.

Theories to explain this phenomenon include Zajonc's drive theory (Zajonc is pronounced 'zi-ance' and sounds like 'science'). According to this theory, the effect of those present occurs as a result of increased arousal in the performer. However, Zajonc's theory suggests that arousal not only leads to task enhancement, where the presence of others improves performance, but can also lead to task impairment, where the presence of others has a negative effect on the person's performance. Zajonc suggests that it is arousal that explains why we perform differently on what he called a dominant task (tasks that are familiar, simple or well learned) and what he called non-dominant tasks (tasks that are unfamiliar, complex or novel). A

dominant task requires less arousal to be performed, so the arousing presence of an audience serves to improve the person's performance. On the other hand, if we are performing a non-dominant task, the level of arousal we need in order to perform this is already high. In this scenario, the arousal that is caused by the audience makes the performer over-aroused, in a state of arousal overload, and this is detrimental to their performance of a non-dominant task.

Our key research in this area is Zajonc et al.'s study on social facilitation and inhibition, which investigated drive theory on the performance of cockroaches (see below).

Support for drive theory in the context of a game was shown in a study by Michaels et al. (1982) who designed a study to test audience effects on pool players in a university bar. By observation, the researchers assessed the skill level of players, and then the four researchers approached tables where the players were firstly of below-average skill, and secondly of above-average skill. Their results were as predicted by drive theory: the presence of the audience improved the performance of the above-average players and impaired the performance of the below-average players.

Figure 5.27 Michaels et al. (1982) showed that when an audience was present the performance of above-average pool players improved, and the performance of below-average pool players was impaired, as suggested by drive theory

Zajonc's drive theory presents difficulties when applied to a sport setting, however. For example, in a sports setting how would we define a 'dominant' or 'non-dominant' task? Players are highly skilled when they are at the top end of their game, and Zajonc's theory fails to account for the poor performance in front of an audience these top athletes sometimes give. In addition, Zajonc suggested that it is just the presence of an audience that has an effect, but in a sporting context an audience is often loud, highly vocal and interactive with the performers, so in a sports context we have to consider not simply the presence of an audience but also the behaviour of the audience.

Stop and ask yourself...

Links to

- Can you explain the difference between 'dominant' and 'non-dominant' tasks in the context of Zajonc's drive theory?

- Check your understanding

Cottrell (1968) suggested that social inhibition effects could be explained by the level of anxiety experienced by the performer. Cottrell's evaluation apprehension theory suggests that the performer knows that the audience has the power to either reward them, to approve of them and praise them, or the power to punish them with their disapproval. According to this theory, the performer experiences a high level of anxiety as a result of evaluation apprehension – the fear of being judged negatively by the audience – and that this anxiety has a negative effect on their performance.

Cottrell's theory also suggests that the more expert an audience is then the greater the anxiety will be, and this could explain why the perfect performance of an athlete in training fails to be replicated when they are performing in front of judges in a competition. However, Cottrell's theory does not explain why audiences can sometimes improve an athlete's performance.

Another theory is Baron's (1986) distraction-conflict theory. This theory suggests that the audience distracts the attention of the performer, and they experience response conflict – they are conflicted about whether they should be attending to the audience or to the task in hand. Since we need little attention to perform dominant tasks, but much greater attention to perform non-dominant tasks, we experience greater conflict when performing non-dominant tasks and therefore our performance is more likely to be impaired by the presence of the audience. Response conflict leads to over-arousal, and this model explains the inhibiting effect of an audience on performance.

Have a go yourself

- In a critical game in a tennis match the crowd are excited and calling out support to the players they are supporting. Both players have highly vocal supporters urging them on to win. The server steps up to play and serves a double fault. Using what you have learned about social facilitation and inhibition, explain how the audience could have affected the player's performance.
- Now imagine that in the same scenario the server served an ace and dominates the game to win it easily. Again, explain how the audience could have had an effect on the tennis player's performance.

Home advantage

In a sporting context, much of the research into the social facilitation and inhibition effects of an audience has focused on home advantage. Home advantage simply suggests that if a team is playing 'at home' rather than 'away' that they have a greater chance of winning. This phenomenon is supported by research by Schwartz and Barsky (1977). They analysed data from:

- 1880 major league baseball games played in 1971
- the home team outcomes for all 182 football games played in 1971 in the National and American leagues
- the home team outcomes for the 910 games played by 182 college football teams in 1971
- data from the 542 hockey games played in both divisions of the National Hockey League in the 1971–2 season
- 15 years' worth of data from 1485 college basketball games played by the Philadelphia Big 5 teams for the years 1952–66

Thus, the study had large amounts of data from four different sports, baseball, basketball, (American) football and ice hockey. The results of the study were reported as the percentage of home wins, and showed that in all four sports this was over 50 per cent:

- baseball: 53 per cent
- ice hockey: 53 per cent
- football (professional): 55 per cent
- football (college): 59 per cent
- basketball: 82 per cent

The strongest effect was in basketball, as you can see, and Schwartz and Barsky suggested that the reason for this was attributable to teams playing better offensive rather than better defensive games on their home ground. Since basketball is an indoor sport, they suggest that it is not the size of the crowd that matters but factors such as crowd density and intimacy which may be important in contributing to the home advantage effect.

Figure 5.28 How might the Arsenal fans affect their team's performance when they are playing a home match at the Emirates Stadium?

The home advantage effect seems to offer support for arousal theories of social facilitation. Based on the assumption that the home team have the easier task and the away team have the harder task, drive theory would suggest that the home team would therefore perform better and the away team would perform worse. Indeed, it may not be home team advantage so much as away team disadvantage that accounts for the higher number of home team wins.

Home team advantage seems to be one variable that can have an effect on a team or athlete's performance. Of course, its influence must not be overstated. Team quality is a much more important factor in terms of team performance. Stronger teams playing at home to weaker teams may get the greatest benefit from home team advantage, but it might be argued that the stronger team does not really need it.

Home team disadvantage

It is important to point out that there is also a phenomenon called home team disadvantage, whereby the home team perform worse when playing at home. This may be because the expectations of the fans is that their team will win at home; a crowd can be very vocal in their support and encouragement, and

in the demands they may make of particular players, so much so that the home crowd could induce arousal overload in their home team players and thereby have a negative effect on their team's performance. In addition, Weinberg and Gould (2011) suggest that while home advantage might benefit teams in the regular games of a season, that the more important the game, the more home disadvantage might occur. They refer to this as 'championship choke'.

Key research: Zajonc, Heingartner and Herman (1969) Social enhancement and impairment of performance in the cockroach

Background

Zajonc et al. theorised that the presence of others is a source of general drive. Drive theory suggests that arousal increases in the presence of others, and that this affects performance. It improves performance for a well-learned or easy task, but impedes performance for a novel or complex task.

 Have a go yourself

- Conduct your own study into social facilitation. In their research, Zajonc et al. suggest that an easy task for human participants to be tested on might be crossing out vowels in a page of text. Design a study that would measure the effects of an audience on this task. Based on Zajonc et al.'s findings, what would your alternate hypothesis be?
- A more complicated task might be performing mental arithmetic tasks, such as adding 27 and 64 in your head. Design and conduct research that would show whether an audience would have an inhibiting effect on performance of this type of complex task.

 Stop and ask yourself...

- Look again at the results from Schwartz and Barsky's study. Do the results for football, ice hockey and baseball convince you that there is a general 'home advantage' in sport?

Links to research methods
- Validity of results
- Generalisability of findings

Stop and ask yourself...

- Can you explain how playing at home might have either a facilitating or inhibiting effect on a team or athlete's performance?

Links to
- Check your understanding

Aims

In this study the authors aimed to provide evidence for drive theory using cockroaches (*Blatte orientalis*).

Figure 5.29 Seventy-two female cockroaches were the sample for this study; why were cockroaches used?

Participants

Seventy-two adult female cockroaches were studied. For one week before the study they were kept individually in jars with screened lids, in the dark, at a relatively constant temperature of about 75 °F (24 °C). They were fed a diet of peeled and sliced apple.

Apparatus

The authors designed cockroach 'runs' that were set into a 20 × 20 × 20 inch Perspex cube. There were two types of 'run': one designed to be an easy task, and one designed to be a complex task. The easy task was a straight runway from a starting box on the outside of the cube to a goal box on the other side of the cube, again on the outside. The goal box had a dark interior designed to attract the cockroach. Both boxes had a sliding door that could be opened or closed to allow or cut off access to the runway or maze.

The complex task involved a 'maze', which was a cross of two paths across the cube; to reach the goal the cockroach would have to make a right turn.

The runway and maze both had a black Bakelite floor 2 inches wide, and had Perspex walls 1 inch high. A 150 watt floodlight was placed behind the start box.

Four triangular see-through Perspex boxes were arranged around the runway and the maze, and the purpose of these was to each hold a cockroach to provide an 'audience' for the cockroach(es) performing

the task. A diagram of the runway and maze apparatus can be seen in Figure 5.30.

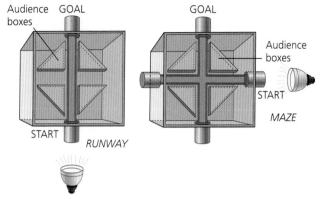

Figure 5.30 The apparatus used by Zajonc *et al.* in their cockroach studies; the 'runway' (easy task) is on the left and the 'maze' (complex task) is on the right

Procedure

Cockroaches are photophobic (afraid of light). It was because of their photophobia that cockroaches were used in this study as their scuttling away from a floodlight gave a predictable and specific 'performance' to measure in these insects. The task they were being tested on was, in response to the floodlight being turned on, to run from the start box to the goal box, and their performance on this task was timed. The floodlight provided the only light source while the tests were being run.

Some of the cockroaches ran the maze alone, and this gave a baseline measure of task performance. To test drive theory, some of the cockroaches were tested in pairs (the 'co-action' condition). The authors predicted that this would increase performance in the runway (easy) task but impede performance in the complex (maze) task.

However, a possible confounding variable could be that, instead of increased arousal affecting their task performance, an alternative explanation would be that the cockroaches did better because they copied each other. To control for this variable, a third condition was introduced. In this condition, four cockroaches from the sample of 72 were placed in the 'audience boxes'. In this condition, then, any difference in performance would be due to the presence of others and not their behaviour. This was called the 'audience condition'.

 Stop and ask yourself ...

- Can you explain why Zajonc *et al.* kept the cockroaches in the conditions they describe for a week before the study?

Links to research methods
- Experimental controls

In each trial, the cockroach(es) were placed in the start box. The light was turned on and the start box sliding door opened. The cockroaches were then timed on how long they took to reach the goal box.

The boxes and runs were cleaned with alcohol between trials.

Results

In the runway condition (the simple task), Zajonc *et al.* found that the co-acting cockroaches completed the task in the fastest time, followed by the cockroaches who ran with a passive 'audience' of four cockroaches, and slowest in this task condition were the cockroaches who ran alone with no audience.

In the maze condition (the complex task), the findings were the reverse of the runway task findings. In the maze, the lone cockroaches ran faster, followed by the cockroaches with an audience and the co-acting cockroaches ran the slowest.

Conclusions

In the co-action and audience conditions, arousal was increased in the test subject cockroaches and this facilitated their performance on the easy (runway) task and inhibited their performance on the complex (maze) task. Zajonc *et al.* conclude that the presence of others, including the presence of a passive 'audience', increases arousal and has an impact on performance, and that this study therefore provides empirical support for Zajonc's drive theory.

Application: strategies for training for and playing spectator sports

In training, Woods (1998) suggests that it would be advisable for coaches to be aware of the social facilitation and inhibition effects on performance, and to be aware that when an athlete is learning a new skill, it is best for them not to be observed by others.

Home advantage is just one factor that might impact on a team or athlete's performance. What seems to matter more to their success in terms of their performance on the field or court is not how familiar they are with their changing rooms or their home field, or whether the crowd is large, or even if the crowd is partisan in their favour, but the quality of the team or athlete's sporting skills. A coach might therefore be best to focus training on developing sporting skills, which through preparation and practice the coach and athlete can gain some control over, and worry less about factors such as audience effects, which are beyond their control and may only contribute in a minor way to the team's likelihood of success.

The theories of social facilitation described at the beginning of this topic all have one thing in common: they all suggest that sporting crowds increase arousal. From the topic on arousal and anxiety, you will recall that anxiety is the psychological response to over-arousal. In order to help athletes to train and prepare for spectator sports it would be useful, then, for them to employ strategies to manage arousal and control anxiety in order to optimise their performance in front of spectators.

For examples of strategies to optimise arousal and control anxiety, see the Applications section of the topic on arousal and anxiety.

Take it further

- Make a list of five strategies that an athlete could develop and use in training and preparation for playing spectator sports.
- For each strategy suggest a sporting example to explain how using the strategy would help prepare an athlete for performing in front of spectators.

IN THE NEWS

A newspaper article written by Jerome Taylor appeared in the *Independent on Sunday* on 29 July 2012, during the London Olympics. The article suggested that fans at the Olympic Games were unhappy about the athletes wearing headphones. This was especially true of swimmers wearing headphones as they entered the aquatics centre to compete. Taylor noted that: 'British swimmer Ellen Gandy was one of the few athletes who removed her headphones to soak up the thunderous applause from the gathered crowd. But many more barely acknowledged their fans.' The fans seemed to be surprised and upset – they had paid a lot of money for their tickets and were there to support the athletes, but the athletes seemed to be ignoring them and not acknowledging their support while wearing their headphones.

Some spectators considered that the athletes were being rude, and Taylor quoted Philippa Perry, author and wife of British artist Grayson Perry, who was equally unimpressed and said: 'Those headphones the swimmers wear when they come out: at best toss potty, at worst rude,' she said. 'Or maybe they didn't have a 20p for the lockers.'

A spokesperson for team GB defended the swimmers' rights to prepare for the races in the way that put them in the mindset in which they would be able to perform best in the pool. Taylor quotes him as saying: 'All the athletes have their own way of getting into the zone before a race. Some prefer to listen to music so they can block out the noise of the crowd, others feed off the audience. But either way it's their choice.'

Taylor points out that the trend for wearing headphones was not just in the aquatics centre but also prevalent in other sports. He describes how a huge crowd of fans had turned up at Heathrow to greet the Brazilian football team coming to compete in the Olympics, but were walked past by the players who were mostly wearing headphones.

Back at the aquatics centre, some spectators defended the swimmers use of headphones and seemed to understand that they played an important part in the athletes' preparation for their races. One said: 'They train hard 364 days of the year. If they want to use music to stay calm as they get ready to race then they should.' The father of a Canadian competitor supported his son wearing headphones and Taylor quotes him as saying: 'He's been training for the last six years … This is his day. Listening to music helps him stay in the zone.'

Figure 5.31 The Chinese Olympic gold medallist Sun Yang wore 'Beats by Dr Dre' headphones at the 2012 Olympics, which are designed to cut out all background noise

Questions

1. Using your knowledge of sport psychology, give two reasons why it might be of benefit for the Olympic swimmers to wear headphones in the aquatic centre.
2. Summarise the different attitudes from spectators, team representatives and the swimmers' families to the swimmers wearing headphones presented in this article.
3. Why were the Brazilian football team members wearing headphones, and why might the fans waiting to see them be more annoyed by them wearing the headphones than by the use of headphones described by the Olympic swimmers?
4. If you were the coach for an elite swimmer, what would you advise them about using their headphones in the aquatic centre? Use psychological evidence to support your answer.

📑 Practice questions

1. Outline the research by Kroll and Crenshaw (1970) into multivariate personality profile analysis of four athletic groups, and what it tells us about personality and sport.   [10 marks]
2. Assess the validity of measuring personality in sport.   [15 marks]
3. Pop up velodromes (cycle tracks) have been used to identify people with the physical strength to partake in cycling, but sports psychologists also want to assess the personality of applicants.

    Evaluate the usefulness of using knowledge of personality to improve sports performance.   [10 marks]

Chapter 6

Exam Guidance for Component 3

Unit 3 is worth 35 per cent of the full A Level. There is one exam, which will be two hours long, and there are 105 marks available for the exam paper as a whole. It is divided into three equal sections as shown in the table below.

Section	Format	Content
Section A (35 marks)	Several (approximately five or six) questions ranging from a mark allocation of 2 marks for short-answer questions and 10 marks for longer answers	This section will cover the Issues in mental health chapter. You can expect to be asked questions across the whole of this section on the specification: • the historical context of mental health • biological explanations of mental illness • non-biological explanations of mental illness.
Section B (2 × 35 marks)	Four questions, each with three parts, from which you will choose two to answer based on the options you have studied. The question will be from one topic per option, for example intelligence (child), impact of prison (crime), recycling (environmental) and personality in sport (sport and exercise). You will need to answer every part of the question.	Each question will have three parts. Part A will be worth 10 marks. • It will ask you about the background of the topic and/or the key research. Part B will be worth 15 marks. • It will ask you to evaluate either the background or key research. • You will often be given a specific evaluation point to consider, such as a methodological issue, debate or area. Part C will be worth 10 marks. • It will ask about an application to a specific scenario. • It may ask for a suggested strategy – as defined in the specification – or consideration of how this application might be researched, the problems of the application or researching the application. • This problem might be a specified or general problem.

Guidance about how to approach exam questions

The advice below has been provided by the authors, not OCR. It will help you to approach exam questions with confidence.

Section A

This section will contain several short-answer questions as well as some long-answer questions.

Here is an example of what the questions might look like.

The key points to look for here are how many marks are being awarded, to ensure you have enough but not too much detail.

Question 1 is only worth 2 marks and only asks for **one** historical view, not the whole history of mental

Example questions

1. Give one historical view of mental illness. [2 marks]

2. How might psychologists categorise psychological disorders? [3 marks]

3. With reference to Rosenhan's (1973) study, discuss the validity of diagnosing mental illness. [5 marks]

4. Outline one non-biological explanation of mental illness. [5 marks]

5. Compare the biological treatment with the non-biological treatment of mental illness. [10 marks]

6. Discuss the issue of determinism in explaining mental illness. [10 marks]

illness, so pick one era that you know and write two concise, accurate sentences about the views of mental illness in that era. You cannot be asked about any specific era as there are none stated on the specification.

Question 2 is worth 3 marks and asks about categorising disorders. You will probably have studied DSM-5 and/or ICD-10, so you need to consider describing these. There is a depth–breadth trade off: you could write about one in a bit more detail, or both of them in slightly less detail. A good rule of thumb is to allow 1 mark per minute on this paper, which gives you some planning and reading time, so don't spend too long answering these short-answer questions.

Question 3 specifically states you have to refer to Rosenhan (the key research) so, if you wrote about the validity of diagnosing mental illness without mentioning Rosenhan's study appropriately, you would not be able to gain full marks. Make sure you clearly write about validity and not reliability. It might be worth one sentence defining validity and then making two good points about whether Rosenhan says diagnosing is or isn't valid. Don't be lured into writing about the ecological validity of the study – it is the validity of diagnosing that is the key to the answer.

Question 4 asks for an outline of an explanation, and you have a choice here. The question could have specified behaviourist or cognitive but can't ask specifically about humanistic, psychodynamic or cognitive neuroscience as these are options. Again, you do not need to evaluate this explanation, just show your knowledge and understanding. You might show understanding by using examples or defining key terms.

Question 5 asks for a comparison of two treatments. The points to consider are practical, ethical and theoretical (remember PET):
- practical, such as effectiveness and side effects
- ethical, such as needing consent, or causing distress
- theoretical, for example whether they are based on reductionist or deterministic theories.

Comparing can consist of similarities or differences, so you could choose two similar points, or two different points. Make sure you explain the point and relate it to each of the two treatments you are using. You could compare one biological treatment or biological treatments as a whole with one non-biological treatment or non-biological treatments as a whole. It is worth planning some comparison points for both treatments and explanations when you are revising.

Question 6 asks for the discussion of determinism in relation to mental illness. This gives you the chance to show your knowledge of determinism and to relate it to some different explanations. Are they deterministic or is there a small or a large element of free will? Most explanations will fall towards one or other end of the continuum, but there is always discussion, such as why concordance rates are not 100 per cent or why not everyone has the same reaction to trauma. Could this be free will or is it just down to temperament? As the question doesn't explicitly say you have to consider explanations, you could also include treatments. This might be more appropriate if any of the other debates or issues are used, such as ethics or individual–situational. Any debate could be used here so have a look at how you would consider explanations or treatments in relation to the debates.

Section B
Part A

This question will ask you to show knowledge and understanding of the background or the key research in relation to the topic. There will be no marks on the mark scheme for evaluation; this is purely knowledge and understanding. For full marks, the mark scheme says:
- Response demonstrates good relevant knowledge and understanding.
- Accurate and reasonably detailed description.
- There is an appropriate selection of material to address the question.
- Response demonstrates a good application of psychological knowledge and understanding of the question.
- Application will be explicit, accurate and relevant to the question.
- There is a well-developed line of reasoning, which is clear and logically structured.
- The information presented is relevant and substantiated.

🗒️ Example questions

1. Using the research by Ainsworth and Bell (1970), outline the types of attachment a child may have with their caregiver. [10 marks]
2. Outline what psychologists mean by cognitive overload. [10 marks]
3. Using research by Zajonc *et al.* (1969), explain how an audience might impact on a sports person's performance. [10 marks]
4. Describe how a zero-tolerance policy can influence crime. [10 marks]

Using the mark scheme you can see that it is important to make sure you answer the question; for example, questions 2 and 4 are not asking for the key research but for the background knowledge. This might include some research (and occasionally even the key research; for example intelligence, where genes – identified in the key research – are a biological factor influencing intelligence) but it won't have to. What it does need is psychological (not anecdotal, newspaper-type assumptions) knowledge about the topic. It is worth 10 marks, so you should aim to write for about ten minutes or just over. The mark scheme asks for 'reasonable detail', and reasonable is what we could expect from a notional 18-year-old student in exam conditions.

Part B

This question will ask you to evaluate using one of the issues from Component 1 and Component 2. It might be a debate or consideration of a psychological area in light of the topic, such as the biological area in relation to intelligence or the social area reflected in the prison situation. You need to make sure whether you should be evaluating the key research or the background knowledge of the topic. For full marks, the mark scheme says you need to include:
- Good relevant knowledge and understanding.
- Many points of analysis, interpretation and evaluation covering a range of issues.
- Material explicitly related to the context of the question.
- Effective use of examples where appropriate.
- Valid conclusions, effective summaries of issues, highly-skilled argument with good understanding.
- A well-developed line of reasoning with a clear and logical structure.

Example questions

1. Assess the usefulness of research into leadership in sports teams. [15 marks]
2. Assess the individual and situational debate in relation to how juries can be persuaded by the characteristics of witnesses. [15 marks]
3. Evaluate the methodology used by Raine *et al.* (1997) in the study 'Brain abnormalities in murderers indicated by positron emission tomography'. [15 marks]
4. Consider the problems of social sensitivity in the study by Dixon *et al.* (2002) 'Accents of guilt? Effects of regional accent, race, and crime type on attributions of guilt'. [15 marks]

Using the mark scheme you can see that your answer has to explicitly relate to the question. Don't just evaluate using points you know – are they relevant, and have you made them explicitly relevant to the question? Examples may be from research or may be psychological concepts, or may be examples from everyday life that show your understanding of psychology.

The mark scheme asks for many points, but examiners know that you only have about 15 minutes to write this answer so won't expect a huge number. The valid conclusions, arguments and so on can be comments that extend the point your have made, either defending a negative point or linking the point to another issue or debate (for example, the lack of ecological validity impacting on usefulness).

Part C

This question will ask you about the application of the topic. There will be a scenario that you will have to refer to, and you could be asked to suggest a strategy to be used. If you don't refer to the scenario you will not be able to gain full marks. This makes it difficult to plan an answer, as it will need to be customised to the question, but you can certainly plan the points you want to put across in a generic sense. You might find the information from the background or key research helpful in addition to the preparation you have done for this part of the specification. You must refer to the scenario to contextualise your answer. You could also be asked to consider the implications for the strategy, or how to research the effectiveness of a strategy or to evaluate the problems of the strategy. You won't always be asked just to suggest a strategy. You could use a single strategy or adopt an eclectic approach and combine several strategies into one. Make sure you know what it is you are meant to be considering in the application section. For full marks, the mark scheme says:
- Response demonstrates a good application of psychological knowledge and understanding to the question.
- Application will be explicit, accurate and relevant to the question.
- There is a well-developed line of reasoning, which is clear and logically structured.
- The information presented is relevant and substantiated.

Example questions

1. Suggest one strategy that psychologists could use for police interviews. [10 marks]

2. How could psychologists investigate the effectiveness of play strategies to develop perception in young children? [10 marks]

3. Discuss the issues with researching techniques used to increase recycling or other conservation behaviours. [10 marks]

4. Assess the ethical problems of researching exercise strategies to improve mental health. [10 marks]

The mark scheme for this section is all about relevance to the question with the appropriate psychological knowledge to underpin suggestions you make about either the strategy or the research into the strategy. Again, for 10 marks you should be writing for about ten minutes. It is important to plan what you are going to say, and then double check with the question that you have actually answered with what they have asked for. It is too easy to make a mistake at the end of an exam when you are tired and miss a word which completely changes the focus of the question.

References

Acking and Kuller (1972). Referred to in Bell, P.A., Greene, T.C., Fisher, J.D. and Baum, A. (1996) *Environmental Psychology* (4th edition). Orlando, FL: Harcourt Brace. (page 427)

Adler, A. (1943). Referred to in Bell, P.A., Greene, T.C., Fisher, J.D. and Baum, A. (1996) *Environmental Psychology* (4th edition). Orlando, FL: Harcourt Brace. (page 248)

Adler, A. (1943). Neuropsychiatric complications in victims of Boston's Coconut Grove disaster. *Journal of the American Medical Association*, 17, 1098–1101.

Aiello (1987). Referred to in Bell, P.A., Greene, T.C., Fisher, J.D. and Baum, A. (1996) *Environmental Psychology* (4th edition). Orlando, FL: Harcourt Brace. (page 285)

Aiello (1987). Referred to in Cave, S. (1998) Applying Psychology to the Environment. London: Hodder & Stoughton. (page 71)

Allport, G.W. and Odbert, H.S. (1936). Trait names: a psycho-lexical study. *Psychological Monographs*, 47(211).

Altman (1975). Referred to in Bell, P.A., Greene, T.C., Fisher, J.D. and Baum, A. (1996) *Environmental Psychology* (4th edition). Orlando, FL: Harcourt Brace. (pages 304–305)

Altman (1975). Referred to in Veitch, R. and Arkkelin, D. (1995) *Environmental Psychology – an interdisciplinary perspective*. Upper Saddle River, NJ: Prentice-Hall Inc. (page 267)

Armitage, R. (2011). The impact of connectivity and through-movements within residential developments on levels of crime and anti-social behaviour. University of Huddersfield repository (unpublished).

Atkinson and Shiffrin (1968). Referred to in Kellogg, R.T. (2007) Fundamentals of Cognitive Psychology. Thousand Oaks, CA: Sage Publications Inc. (pages 95–101; page 108)

Atkinson and Shiffrin (1968). Referred to in Moxon, D. (2000) Memory. Oxford: Heinemann. (pages 16–17)

Baca-Motes et al (2013). Baca-Motes, K., Brown, A., Gneezy, A., Keenan, E.A. and Nelson, L.D. (2013) Commitment and behaviour change: evidence from the field. *Journal of Consumer Research,* 39, 1070–1084.

Bandura, A. (1997b). Self-efficacy: Toward a unifying Theory of Behavioral Change. *Psychological Review*, 84, 191–215.

Banyard, P. (2002). Psychology in Practice: Health. London: Hodder & Stoughton. (pages 77–78, 118–119)

Baron, R.S. (1986). Distraction-conflict theory: Progress and problems. In Berkowitz, L. (ed) *Advances in Experimental Social Psychology*, Vol 19. New York: Academic Press.

Baum and Davies (1976). Referred to in Bell, P.A., Greene, T.C., Fisher, J.D. and Baum, A. (1996) *Environmental Psychology* (4th edition). Orlando, FL: Harcourt Brace. (page 427)

Belenky, G., Wesensten, N.J., Thorne, D.R., Thomas, M.L., Sing, H.C., Redmond, D.P., Russo, M.B. and Balkin, T.J. (2003). Patterns of performance degradation and restoration during sleep restriction and subsequent recovery: a sleep dose-response study. *Journal of Sleep Research,* 12(1), 1–12.

Bell, P.A., Greene, T.C., Fisher, J.D. and Baum, A. (1996). *Environmental Psychology* (4th edition). Orlando, FL: Harcourt Brace. (page 535)

Bell, P.A., Greene, T.C., Fisher, J.D. and Baum, A. (1996). *Environmental Psychology* (4th edition). Orlando, FL: Harcourt Brace. (pages 117–119, 153, 226, 248, 275, 305–306, 326–327, 377–378, 384, 399–401, 416, 438–442, 520, 525–526, 535, 548)

Bennet et al (1991). Referred to in Cassidy, T. (1997) *Environmental Psychology – behaviour and experience in context.* Hove: Psychology Press Ltd. (page 84)

Bickman et al (1973). Referred to in Bell, P.A., Greene, T.C., Fisher, J.D. and Baum, A. (1996) *Environmental Psychology* (4th edition). Orlando, FL: Harcourt Brace. (page 342)

Black, D.A., Black, J.A., Issarayangyun, T. and Samuels, S.E. (2007). Aircraft noise exposure and residents' stress and hypertension: a public health perspective for airport environmental management. *Journal of Air Transport Management,* 13(5), 264–276.

Boecker, H., Sprenger, T. and Spilker, M.E. et al (2008). The runner's High: opioidergic mechanisms. *Cerb Cortex,* 18, 2523–2531.

Brehm (1972). Referred to in Steg, L., Van Den Berg, A. and De Groot, J.I.M. and contributors (2013) *Environmental Psychology – an introduction.* Chichester: the British Psychological Society and John Wiley & Sons Ltd. (page 239)

Brehm (1972). Referred to in Veitch, R. and Arkkelin, D. (1995) *Environmental Psychology – an interdisciplinary perspective.* Upper Saddle River, NJ: Prentice-Hall Inc. (page 434)

Bronzaft et al (1998). Referred to in Black, D.A., Black, J.A., Issarayangyun, T. and Samuels, S.E. (2007) Aircraft noise exposure and residents' stress and hypertension: a public health perspective for airport environmental management. *Journal of Air Transport Management,* 13(5), 264–276.

Brown and Poulton (1961). Referred to in Bell, P.A., Greene, T.C., Fisher, J.D. and Baum, A. (1996) *Environmental Psychology* (4th edition). Orlando, FL: Harcourt Brace. (page 119)

Brown, B. (1995). Closed Circuit Television in Town Centres: Three case studies. Crime Prevention and Detection Series Paper 73, Home Office London.

Browne, B. (1998). Gender Stereotypes in Advertising on Children's Television in the 1990s: A Cross-National Analysis. *Journal of Advertising.* Vol 27 Issue 1, 1998. Pages 456–470.

Brown, I.D. and Poulton, E.C. (1961). Measuring the spare "mental capacity" of car drivers by a subsidiary task. *Ergonomics,* 4, 35–40.

Brunner, H.G., Nelen, H., Breakefield, X.O., Ropers, H.H. and van Oost, B.A. (1993). Abnormal behaviour associated with a point mutation in the structural gene for monoamine oxidase A. *Science,* 262(S133), 578–80.

Buijzen, M. and Valkenburg, P. (2000). The Impact of Television Advertising on Children's Christmas Wishes. *Journal of Broadcasting & Electronic Media.* Pages 456–470.

Buijzen, M. and Valkenburg, P. (2005). Parental Mediation of Undesired Advertising Effects. *Journal of Broadcasting & Electronic Media.* Volume 49, Issue 2, 2005. Pages 153–165.

Bushnell, I.W., Sai, F. and Mullin, J.T. (2011). Neonatal recognition of the mother's face. British Journal of Developmental Psychology, Vol 7(1), Mar 1989, 3–15.

Callow, N., Hardy, L. and Hall, C. (2001). The effects of a motivational general-mastery imagery intervention on the sport confidence of high-level badminton players *Research Quarterly for Exercise and Sport,* 72, 389–400.

Campos, J.J., Langer, A. and Krowitz, A. (1970). Cardiac responses on the visual cliff in prelocomotor human infants. Science, 170, 196.

Carron, A.V., Bray, S.R. and Eys, M.A. (2002). Team cohesion and success in sport. *Journal of Sports Science,* 20, 2: 119–126.

Cases, Olivier et al (1995). Aggressive Behaviour and Altered Amounts of brain Serotonin and Norepinephrine in Mice lacking MAOA, Science. (New York, N.Y.) 268(5218), 1763–66.

Casey, B.J., Somerville, L.H., Gotlib, I.H., Ayduk, O., Franklin, N.T., Askren, M.K., Jonides, J., Berman, M., Wilson, N., Teslovich, T., Glover, G., Zayas, V., Mischel, W. and Shoda, Y. (2011). Behavioural and neural correlates of delay of gratification 40 years later. *Proceedings of the National Academy of Sciences of the United States of America,* 108(36), 14998–15003.

Caspi, Avshalom et al (2002). Role of genotype in the cycle of violence in maltreated children. *Science,* 297, 5582, 851–4.

Cassidy, T. (1997). *Environmental Psychology – behaviour and experience in context.* Hove: Psychology Press Ltd. (pages 125, 136–137, 157, 194–196, 202)

Cattell, R.B. (1965). The scientific analysis of personality, Hammondsworth: Penguin Books.

Cave, S. (1998). Applying Psychology to the Environment. London: Hodder & Stoughton. (pages 68–69, 85, 137, 141–142)

Chandler, D. and Griffiths, M. (2000). 'Gender-Differentiated Production Features in Toy Commercials', *Journal of Broadcasting & Electronic Media.* Volume 44, Issue 3, 2000. Pages 503–520.

Chaney, G., Clements, B., Landau, L., Bulsara, M. and Watt, P. (2004). A new asthma spacer device to improve compliance in children: a pilot study. *Respirology,* 9, 499–506.

Chelladurai, P. (1978). A multidimensional model of leadership, Unpublished doctoral dissertation, University of Waterloo, Waterloo, Ontario.

Christian, J.J., Flyger, V. and Davis, P.C. (1960). Factors in the mass mortality of a herd of Sika deer, Cervus Nippon. *Chesapeake Science,* 1, 79–95.

Clarke R.V. (1992). Situational Crime Prevention: Successful Case Studies. New York: Harrow and Heston.

Cockett M. and Tripp J.H. (1994). Exeter family study. (Exeter University Press, Exeter).

Cohen et al (1973). Referred to in Oliver, K. (2002) Psychology in Practice: Environment. London: Hodder & Stoughton. (page 20)

Cohen, S., Glass, D.C. and Singer, J.E. (1973). Apartment noise, auditory discrimination and reading ability in children. *Journal of Experimental Social Psychology,* 9, 407–422.

Cook (1970). Referred to in Bell, P.A., Greene, T.C., Fisher, J.D. and Baum, A. (1996) *Environmental Psychology* (4th edition). Orlando, FL: Harcourt Brace. (page 285)

Cottrell, N.B. (1968). 'Performance in the presence of other human beings:mere presence, audience and affiliation effects'. In Simmel, E.C., Hoppe, R.A. and Milton, G.A. (eds), *Social Facilitation And Imitative Behaviour.* Boston: Allyn and Bacon.

Cox (2002). *Sport Psychology: Concepts and Applications.* 5th edition. McGraw-Hill.

Czeisler, C.A., Moore-Ede, M.C. and Coleman, R.M. (1982). Rotating shift work schedules that disrupt sleep are improved by applying circadian principles. *Science,* 217(4558), 460–463.

Damasio, A. (1985). The frontal lobes. In Heilman K.M., Valenstein, E. (eds), *Clinical Neuropsychology.* New York: Oxford University Press, pp. 339–375.

Dando, C., Wilcock, R. and Milne, R. (2009). The cognitive interview: the efficacy of a modified mental reinstatement of context procedure for frontline police investigators. *Appl. Cognit. Psychol.,* 23: 138–147. doi: 10.1002/acp.1451

Davis, S. (2003). 'Sex stereotypes in commercials targeted toward children: a content analysis'. *Sociological Spectrum: Mid-South Sociological Association*, Volume 23, Issue 4, 2003.

De Leon and Fuqua (1995). Referred to in De Leon, I.G. and R.W. Fuqua (1995) The effects of public commitment and group feedback on curbside recycling. *Environment and Behaviour,* 27(2), 233–250.

DeCoursey, P.J., Krulas, J.R., Mele, G. and Holley, D.C. (1997). Circadian performance of suprachiasmatic nuclei (SCN)-lesioned antelope ground squirrels in a desert enclosure. *Physiological Behaviour,* 62, 1099–1108.

Diener, E., Fraser, S.C., Beaman, A.L. and Kelem, R.T. (1976). Effects of deindividuation variables on stealing among Halloween trick-or-treaters. *Journal of Personality and Social Psychology,* 33(2), 178–183.

Dion, K.K., Berscheid, E. and Walster, E. (1972). What is beautiful is good. *Journal of Personality and Social Psychology,* 24, 285–290.

Ditchburn (2014). *The rise and fall of the hot desk: say hello to activity-based working*, 'The Conversation', London. Available online at http://theconversation.com/the-rise-and-fall-of-the-hot-desk-say-hello-to-activity-based-working-26622

Dixon, J.A., Mahoney, B. and Cocks, R. (2002). Accents of Guilt Effects of Regional Accent, race and Crime Type on Attributions of Guilt. *Journal of Language and Social.*

Dooley, E. (1990a). Prison suicide in England and Wales 1972–1987. *British Journal of Psychiatry*, 156, 40–45.

Drews, F.A. and Doig, A. (2013). Evaluation of a configural vital signs display for intensive care unit nurses. *Human Factors: the Journal of the Human Factors and Ergonomics Society,* 56(3), 569–580.

Dror, I.E. (2012). Cognitive bias in forensic science. In The 2012 yearbook of science & technology. New York: McGraw-Hill, pp. 43–45.

Dror, I.E., Charlton, D. and Peron, A. (2006). Contextual information renders experts vulnerable to making erroneous identifications. Forensic Science International, 156, 174–178. http://dx.doi.org/10.1016/j.forsciint.2005.10.017

Dwyer, D. (2001). Angles on Criminal Psychology. Nelson Thornes.

Edwards (1972). Referred to in Bell, P.A., Greene, T.C., Fisher, J.D. and Baum, A. (1996) *Environmental Psychology* (4th edition). Orlando, FL: Harcourt Brace. (page 280)

Ellis (1977). Referred to in Sarafino, E.P. (1998) *Health Psychology – biopsychosocial interactions* (3rd edition). New York: John Wiley & Sons, Inc. (pages 149–150)

Eshel, N., Nelson, E.E., Blair, R.J., Pine, D.S. and Ernst, M. (2007). Neural substrates of choice selection in adults and adolescents: Development of the ventrolateral prefrontal and anterior cingulate cortices. Neuropsychologia. 2007; 45: 1270–1279.

Evans (1979). Referred to in Bell, P.A., Greene, T.C., Fisher, J.D. and Baum, A. (1996) *Environmental Psychology* (4th edition). Orlando, FL: Harcourt Brace. (page 345)

Eysenck, H.J. (1965). Fact and Fiction in Psychology, Harmondsworth, Penguin.

Eysenck, H.J., Nias, K.B.D. and Cox, D.N. (1982). Sport and Psychology. *Advances in Behavioral Research and Therapy*, 4, 1: 1–56.

Eysenck, H.J. and Eysenck, M.W. (1985). Personality and individual differences. New York: Plenum Press.

Farrington, David P. CAMBRIDGE STUDY IN DELINQUENT DEVELOPMENT [GREAT BRITAIN], 1961–1981 [Computer file]. Conducted by David P. Farrington, Cambridge University. 2nd ICPSR ed. Ann Arbor, MI: Interuniversity Consortium for Political and Social Research [producer and distributor], 1994.

Fazey, J. and Hardy, L. (1988). The inverted-U hypothesis: A catastrophe for sport psychology. British Association of Sports Sciences Monograph, No. 1, Leeds: The National Coaching Foundation.

Festinger (1957). Referred to in Gross, R. (1996) *Psychology – the science of mind and behaviour* (3rd edition). London: Hodder & Stoughton. (pages 450–451)

Festinger (1957). Referred to in Roberts, C. and Russell, J. (2002) Angles on Environmental Psychology. Cheltenham: Nelson Thornes Ltd. (page 119)

Festinger (1957). Referred to in Steg, L., Van Den Berg, A. and De Groot, J.I.M. and contributors (2013) *Environmental Psychology – an introduction.* Chichester: the British Psychological Society and John Wiley & Sons Ltd. (page 227)

Fiedler, F.E. (1967). A Theory of Leadership Effectiveness, New York: McGraw Hill.

Fisher, R.P. (2010). Interviewing cooperative witnesses. *Legal and Criminological Psychology*, 15, 25–38. doi: 10.1348/135532509X441891.

Fisher, R.P. and Geiselman, R.E. (1992). *Memory enhancing techniques for investigative interviewing: The Cognitive Interview.* Springfield 111: Charles C. Thomas.

Fisher, R.P., Geiselman, R.E. and Amador, M. (1989). Field test of the cognitive interview: Enhancing the recollection of the actual victims and witnesses of crime. *Journal of Applied Psychology*, 74(5), 722.

Frances, L.J., Kelly, P. and Jones, S.J. (1998). The personality profile of female students who play hockey. *Irish Journal of Psychology*, 19: 394–9.

Frederick Windlow Taylor (1911). Referred to in Steptoe-Warren, G. (2013) *Occupational Psychology – an applied approach.* Harlow: Pearson. (pages 3 and 150)

Freud, S. (1953–74). The Standard Edition of the Complete Works (24 Vols) trans. And ed. J. Strachey with A. Freud, assisted by A. Strachey and A. Tyson. London: Hogarth.

Geiselman, R.E., Fisher, R.P., Firstenberg, I., Hutton, L.A., Sullivan, S., Avetissian, I. and Prosk, A. (1984). Enhancement of eyewitness memory: An empirical evaluation of the cognitive interview. *Journal of Police.*

Geiselman, R.E. and Callot, R. (1990). Reverse versus forward order recall of script based texts, *Applied Cognitive Psychology,* 4, 141–4.

Gergen et al (1973). Referred to in Bell, P.A., Greene, T.C., Fisher, J.D. and Baum, A. (1996) *Environmental Psychology* (4th edition). Orlando, FL: Harcourt Brace. (page 286)

Gergen et al (1973). Referred to in Cave, S. (1998) Applying Psychology to the Environment. London: Hodder & Stoughton. (page 53)

Gilbreth, F.B. (1911). Motion Study – a method for increasing the efficiency of the workman. New York: D. Van Nostrand Company.

Gill, D. and Deeter, T. (1988). Development of the sport orientation questionnaire. *Research Quarterly for Exercise and Sport*, 59(3), 191–202.

Gill, D.L. (1986). Psychological Dynamics of Sport, Champaign, IL: Human Kinetics Publishers.

Gilliam (1991). Referred to in Cassidy, T. (1997) *Environmental Psychology – behaviour and experience in context.* Hove: Psychology Press Ltd. (page 84)

Gilliam, J.E. (1991). The effects of Baker-Miller pink on physiological and cognitive behaviour of emotionally disturbed and regular education students. *Behavioural Disorders,* 17(1), 47–55.

Glass, D.C. and Singer, J.E. (1972). *Urban Stress – Experiments on Noise and Social Stressors.* New York: Academic Press, Inc. (pages 45–67)

Gneezy and Rustichini (2000). Referred to in Gneezy, U. and Rustichini, A. (2000) A fine is a price. *The Journal of Legal Studies,* 29(1), 1–17.

Gneezy and Rustichini (2000). Referred to in Sandel, M.J. (2012) What Money Can't Buy. London: Allen Lane. (pages 64–65)

Gneezy and Rustichini (2000). Referred to in Steg, L., Van Den Berg, A. and De Groot, J.I.M. and contributors (2013) *Environmental Psychology – an introduction*. Chichester: the British Psychological Society and John Wiley & Sons Ltd. (page 240)

Gottesman, I., Laursen, T., Bertelsen, A. and Mortensen, P. (2010). Severe mental disorders in offspring with 2 psychiatrically ill parents. *Archives of General Psychiatry*, 67 (3).

Grierson, J. (2013). Reoffending Rate Increases. *The Independent*, 31 January.

Gross, R. (1996). *Psychology – the science of mind and behaviour* (3rd edition). London: Hodder & Stoughton. (pages 78, 138, 142–143, 162, 164, 166, 285, 293–295, 440–448)

Gross, R. and Kinnison, N. (2007). Psychology for nurses and allied health professionals. London: Hodder Arnold. (pages 71–72, 186–187)

Gudjonsson, G.G. (2003). The Psychology of Interrogations and Confessions: A Handbook, John Wiley and sons.

Haber (1980). Referred to in Bell, P.A., Greene, T.C., Fisher, J.D. and Baum, A. (1996) *Environmental Psychology* (4th edition). Orlando, FL: Harcourt Brace. (page 311)

Hall (1963). Referred to in Bell, P.A., Greene, T.C., Fisher, J.D. and Baum, A. (1996) *Environmental Psychology* (4th edition). Orlando, FL: Harcourt Brace. (pages 278–279, 283–284)

Hall (1963). Referred to in Cave, S. (1998) Applying Psychology to the Environment. London: Hodder & Stoughton. (page 69)

Hall, L.J. and Player, E. (2008). Will the introduction of an emotional context affect fingerprint analysis and decision-making? *Forensic Science International*, 181, 36–39.

Hampikian, G., West, E. and Akselrod, O. (2011). The genetics of innocence: Analysis of 194 U.S. DNA exonerations. *Annual Review of Genomics and Human Genetics*, 12, 97–120.

Haney, C., Banks, W.C. and Zimbardo, P.G. (1973). A study of prisoners and guards in a simulated prison. *Naval Research Review*, 30, 4–17.

Hanley, P. (2000). Copycat Kids? The Influence of Television Advertising on Children and Teenagers. Independent Television Commission.

Harari, P. and Legge, K. (2001). Psychology and Health. Oxford: Heinemann. (page 15)

Hardin, G. (1968). The tragedy of the commons. *Science*, 162(3859), 1243–1248.

Hardy, L. and Parfitt, G. (1991). A catastrophe model of anxiety and performance. *British Journal of Psychology*, 82, 163–178

Hardy, L. (1985). *Factors Affecting Performance: Resource Pack 9*. Leeds: The National Coaching Foundation.

Hayduk (1983). Referred to in Bell, P.A., Greene, T.C., Fisher, J.D. and Baum, A. (1996) *Environmental Psychology* (4th edition). Orlando, FL: Harcourt Brace. (page 285)

Heberlein (1975). Referred to in Bell, P.A., Greene, T.C., Fisher, J.D. and Baum, A. (1996) *Environmental Psychology* (4th edition). Orlando, FL: Harcourt Brace. (pages 535–552)

Heshka and Nelson (1972). Referred to in Bell, P.A., Greene, T.C., Fisher, J.D. and Baum, A. (1996) *Environmental Psychology* (4th edition). Orlando, FL: Harcourt Brace. (pages 280–281)

Heyman, E., Gamelin, F.X., Goekint, M., Piscitelli, F., Roelands, B., Leclair, E., Di Marzo, V. and Meeusen, R. 'Intense exercise increases circulating endocannabinoid and BDNF levels in humans – possible implications for reward and depression'. Psychoneuroendocrinology. 2012 Jun; 37(6):844–51. doi: 10.1016/j.psyneuen.2011.09.017. Epub 2011 Oct 24.

Hirst, A. (2011). Settlers, vagrants and mutual indifference: unintended consequences of hot-desking. *Journal of Organisational Change Management*, 24(6), 767–788. http://psychology.jrank.org/pages/549/Rosenzweig-Picture-Frustration-Study.html

Huey and McNulty (1995). Referred to in Huey, M.P. and McNulty, T.L. (2005) Institutional conditions and prison suicide: conditional effects of deprivation and overcrowding. *The Prison Journal*, 85(4), 490–514.

Dror, I.E., Peron, A.E., Hind, S. and Charlton, D. (2005). When emotions get the better of us: the effect of contextual top-down processing on matching fingerprints. *Applied Cognitive Psychology*, 19(6), 799–809.

Inbau, Reid (1962). Criminal Interrogation and Confessions, Inbau, Reid, Buckley and Jayne 5th ed, 2011 Jones and Bartlett, Burlington, MA.

Jacoby et al (1980). Referred to in Roberts, C. and Russell, J. (2002) Angles on Environmental Psychology. Cheltenham: Nelson Thornes Ltd. (pages 124–129)

Janis and Feshbach (1953). Referred to in Roberts, C. and Russell, J. (2002) Angles on Environmental Psychology. Cheltenham: Nelson Thornes Ltd. (pages 131–135)

Janis, I.L. and Feshbach, S. (1953). Effects of fear-arousing communications. *Journal of Abnormal and Social Psychology*, 48, 78–92.

Jarvis, M. (2006). *Sport psychology: a student handbook.* London, Routledge.

Joseph, S. (2011). *What doesn't kill us.* London: Piatkus. (pages 38–41)

Kahn-Greene, E.T., Lipizzi, E.L., Conrad, A.K., Kamimori, G.H. and Killgore, W.D.S. (2006). Sleep deprivation adversely affects interpersonal responses to frustration. *Personality and Individual Differences,* 41(8), 1433–1443.

Kassin, S., Dror, I. and Kukucka, J. (2013). The forensic confirmation bias: Problems, perspectives and proposed solutions. *Journal of Applied Research in Memory and Cognition,* 2, 27–37. http://dx.doi.org/10.1016/j.jarmac.2013.01.001

Kassin, S.M., Appleby, S.C. and Perillo, J.T. (2010). Interviewing suspects: Practice, science and future directions. *Legal and Criminological Psychology*, 15, 39–55.

Kellogg, R.T. (2007). Fundamentals of Cognitive Psychology. Thousand Oaks, CA: Sage Publications Inc. (pages 107, 117–120)

Kenrick, D.T. and MacFarlane, S.W. (1986). Ambient temperature and horn honking: a field study of the heat/aggression relationship. *Environment and Behaviour,* 18, 179–191.

Kent (1991). Referred to in Bell, P.A., Greene, T.C., Fisher, J.D. and Baum, A. (1996) *Environmental Psychology* (4th edition). Orlando, FL: Harcourt Brace. (pages 457–458)

Koriat, A. and Goldsmith, M. (1994). Memory in naturalistic and laboratory contexts: Distinguishing the accuracy-oriented and quantity-oriented approaches to memory assessment. *Journal of Experimental Psychology: General*, 123, 297–316.

Kroll, W. and Crenshaw, W. (1970). Multivariate personality profile analysis of four athletic groups. *Contemporary psychology of sport*, 97–106.

Larson, M. (2001). Interactions, Activities and Gender in Children's Television Commercials: A Content Analysis. *Journal of Broadcasting & Electronic Media*. Volume 45, Issue 1, 2001. Pages 41–56.

Lewin, K., Lippitt, R. and White, R.K. (1939). Patterns of aggressive behaviour in experimentally created "social climates". *Journal of Social psychology,* 10, 271–299.

Lewis, C., Annett, L., Davenport, S., Hall, A. and Lovatt, P. (2014). Mood changes following social dance sessions in people with Parkinson's Disease. *Journal of Health Psychology*, 19(4).

Lima, M.M.S. and Vieira, A.P. (2007). Ballroom dance as therapy for the elderly in Brazil. *American Journal of Dance Therapy* 29(2), 129–142.

Loftus, E.F. and Palmer, J.C. (1974). Reconstruction of automobile destruction: An example of the interaction between language and memory. *Journal of Verbal Learning and Verbal Behavior*, 13(5), 585–589.

Lombroso, C. (1876). L'Uomo delinquent. Milan, Italy, Torin.

Lord, K.R. (1994). Motivating recycling behaviour: a quasi-experimental investigation of message and source strategies. *Psychology & Marketing,* 11(4), 341–358.

Luyben and Bailey (1979). Referred to in Roberts, C. and Russell, J. (2002) Angles on Environmental Psychology. Cheltenham: Nelson Thornes Ltd. (page 117)

Martens, R., Burton, D., Vealey, R., Bump, L. and Smith, D. (1990). The development of the Competitive State Anxiety Inventory-2 (CSAI-2), in Martens, R., Vealey, R.S. and Burton, D. (eds), *Competitive Anxiety in Sport*. Champaign IL: Human Kinetics, pp. 117–190.

Main, M. and Solomon J. (1986). "Discovery of an insecure disoriented attachment pattern: procedures, findings and implications for the classification of behaviour". In Brazelton T, Youngman M. Affective Development in Infancy. Norwood, NJ: Ablex. ISBN 0-89391-345-6.

Martens, R. (1982). Sport competition anxiety test Champaign, IL: Human Kinetics.

Martin, J.J. and Gill, D.L. (1991). The relationships among competitive orientation, sport-confidence, self-efficacy, anxiety and performance. *Journal of Sport and Exercise Psychology*, 13(2), 149–159.

Martin, P. (2003). Counting sheep – the science and pleasures of sleep and dreams. London: Flamingo. (pages 69–70, 114–116, 123–124)

Mazzella, R. and Feingold, A. (1994). The effects of physical attractiveness, race, socio-economic status and gender of defendants and victims on judgments of mock jurors: A meta-analysis. *Journal of Applied Social Psychology*, 24, pp. 1315–1344.

McCartt, A.T., Shabanova, V.I. and Leaf, W.A. (2003). Driving Experience, Crashes, and Traffic Citations of Teenage Beginning Drivers. *Accid Anal Prev*. 2003; 35:311–20.

McKelvie, S., Lemieux, P. and Stout, D. (2003). Extraversion and neuroticism in contact athletes, no contact athletes and nonathletes: a research note. *Athletic Insight* 5.

McNair, D., Lorr, M. and Droppleman, L. (1971). *POMS: Profile of Mood States*. San Diego, CA: Educational and Industrial Testing.

Medin, D.L., Ross, B.H. and Markman, A.B. (2001). *Cognitive Psychology* (3rd edition). Orlando, FL: Harcourt Brace. (pages 158–163)

Meister and Donatelle (2000). Referred to in Black, D.A., Black, J.A., Issarayangyun, T. and Samuels, S.E. (2007) Aircraft noise exposure and residents' stress and hypertension: a public health perspective for airport environmental management. *Journal of Air Transport Management,* 13(5), 264–276.

Memon, A. and Higham, P.A. (1999). A review of the cognitive interview. *Psychology, Crime & Law*, 5: 1–2, 177–196.

Memon, A., Wark, L., Bull, R. and Koehnken, G. (1997a). Isolating the effects of the cognitive interview techniques. *British Journal of Psychology*, 88(2), 179–198.

Memon, A., Wark, L., Holley, A., Bull, R. and Koehnken, G. (1996b). Reducing suggestibility in child witness interviews. *Applied Cognitive Psychology,* 10, 503–18.

Memon, A., Milne, R., Holley, A., Bull, R. and Koehnken, G. (1994). Towards understanding the effects of interviewer training in evaluating the cognitive interview. *Applied Cognitive Psychology*, 8, 641–59.

Michaels, J.W., Blommel, J.M., Brocato, R.M., Linkous, R.A. and Rowe, J.S. (1982). 'Social facilitation and inhibition in a natural setting'. *Replications in Social Psychology*, 2: 21–4.

Middlemist et al (1976). Referred to in Bell, P.A., Greene, T.C., Fisher, J.D. and Baum, A. (1996) *Environmental Psychology* (4th edition). Orlando, FL: Harcourt Brace. (pages 296–297)

Middlemist, R.D., Knowles, E.S. and Matter, C.F. (1976). Personal space invasions in the lavatory: suggestive evidence for arousal. *Journal of Personality and Social Psychology,* 33(5), 541–546.

Miller (1956). Referred to in Gross, R. (1996) *Psychology – the science of mind and behaviour* (3rd edition). London: Hodder & Stoughton. (page 280)

Miller (1956). Referred to in Kellogg, R.T. (2007) Fundamentals of Cognitive Psychology. Thousand Oaks, CA: Sage Publications Inc. (pages 106–107)

Miller, L.S. (1987). Procedural bias in forensic science examinations of human hair. *Law and Human Behavior*, 11, 157–163. http://dx.doi.org/10.1007/BF01040448

Mills, K.D., Munroe, K.J. and Hall, C.R. (2001). The relationship between imagery and self-efficacy in competitive athletes. *Imagination Cognition and Personality*, 20(1), 33–40.

Milne, R. (1997). *Application and Analysis of the Cognitive Interview* Doctorat Dissertation. University of Portsmouth.

Milne, R. (2004). *The Enhanced Cognitive Interview. A step-by-step guide*.

Miyakita et al (2002). Referred to in Black, D.A., Black, J.A., Issarayangyun, T. and Samuels, S.E. (2007) Aircraft noise exposure and residents' stress and hypertension: a public health perspective for airport environmental management. *Journal of Air Transport Management,* 13(5), 264–276.

Munroe-Chandler, K., Hall, C. and Fishburne, G. (2008). Playing with confidence: the relationship between imagery use and self-confidence and self-efficacy in youth soccer players. *Journal of Sports Science*, 26(14), 1539–1546.

Moxon, D. (2000). Memory. Oxford: Heinemann. (pages 9, 19–20)

Newman and McCauley (1977). Referred to in Bell, P.A., Greene, T.C., Fisher, J.D. and Baum, A. (1996) *Environmental Psychology* (4th edition). Orlando, FL: Harcourt Brace. (page 379)

Newman, O. (1996). Creating Defensible Space. Publisher: Diane Pub Co.

Nicholls, A.R. and Jones, L. (2013). Psychology in Sports Coaching – Theory and Practice. Routledge.

Olds, D. cited in Raine (2013). The Anatomy of Violence: The biological roots of crime, Penguin books, p. 277.

Oliver, K. (2002). Psychology in Practice: Environment. London: Hodder & Stoughton. (pages 2–3, 4–7, 50, 53–54, 68–69, 94, 140–141, 157–159, 172)

Oxendine, J.B. Emotional arousal and motor performance, *Quest*, 13, 23–30.

Paivio, A. (1985). Cognitive and motivational Functions of Imagery in human performance *Canadian Journal of Applied Sport Sciences,* 10, 22–28.

231

Pakes, F. and Pakes, S. (2009). Criminal Psychology, Willan publishing Gillis, C.A. and Nafekh, M. (2005) The impact of community-based employment on offender reintegration *The Forum For Corrections,* 17(1), 10–15.

Palmer, E.J. and Hollin, C.R. (1998). A comparison of patterns of moral development in young offenders and non-offenders. *Legal and Criminological Psychology,* 3: 225–235. doi: 10.1111/j.2044–8333.1998.tb00363.x

Parfitt, C.G. and Hardy, L. (1987). 'Further evidence for the differential effects of competitive anxiety upon a number of cognitive and motor sub-components'. *Journal of Sports Science,* 5, 62–72.

Patterson and Holmes (1966). Referred to in Bell, P.A., Greene, T.C., Fisher, J.D. and Baum, A. (1996) *Environmental Psychology* (4th edition). Orlando, FL: Harcourt Brace. (page 285)

Penedo F.J. and Dahn J.R. (2005). Exercise and well-being a review of mental and physical health benefits associated with physical activity, *Current opinion in psychology,* 18, 189–193.

Pennington, N. and Hastie, R. (1988). Explanation-based decision-making: effects of memory structure on judgement. *Journal of Experimental Psychology, Learning and Memory and Cognition,* 14(3), 521–533.

Penrod, S. and Cutler, B. (1995). Witness confidence and witness accuracy: assessing their forensic relation. *Psychology, Public Policy and Law,* 1(4), 817–845.

Peterson and Peterson (1959). Referred to in Medin, D.L., Ross, B.H. and Markman, A.B. (2001) Cognitive Psychology (3rd edition). Orlando, FL: Harcourt Brace. (page 155)

Pike, J. and Jennings, N. (2005). 'The Effects of Commercials on Children's Perceptions of Gender Appropriate Toy Use'. *Sex Roles,* Vol. 52, Nos. 1/2, January 2005 1,2,3.

Pine, K. and Nash, A. (2002). Dear Santa: The effects of television advertising on young children. *International Journal of Behavioral Development* 2002; 26: 529.

Porteus (1977). Referred to in Bell, P.A., Greene, T.C., Fisher, J.D. and Baum, A. (1996) *Environmental Psychology* (4th edition). Orlando, FL: Harcourt Brace. (page 394)

Pratt, T.C., Gau, J.M. and Franklin, T.W. (2010). *Key ideas in criminology and criminal justice.* Sage.

Preckel, F., Lipnevich, A.A., Boehme, K., Brandner, L., Georgi, K., Könen, T., Mursin, K. and Roberts, R.D. (2013). Morningness-eveningness and educational outcomes: the lark has an advantage over the owl at high school. *British Journal of Educational Psychology,* 83(1), 114–134.

Raine (2013). The Anatomy of Violence: The biological roots of crime, Penguin books.

Raine, A., Buchsbaum, M. and Lacasse, L. (1997a). Brain abnormalities in murderers indicated by positron emission tomography. *Biological Psychiatry,* 1997, 42, 495–508.

Recht et al (1995). Referred to in Wiseman, R. (2014) Night school. London: Macmillan. (page 45)

Recht, L.D., Lew, R.A. and Schwartz, W.J. (1995). Baseball teams beaten by jet lag. *Nature,* 377, 583.

Rechtschaffen and Bergmann (1995). Referred to in Wiseman, R. (2014) Night school. London: Macmillan. (page 57)

Rechtschaffen, A. and Bergmann, B.M. (1995). Sleep deprivation in the rat by the disk-over-water method. *Behavioural Brain Research,* 69(1–2), 55–63.

Reich and Robertson (1979). Referred to in Veitch, R. and Arkkelin, D. (1995) *Environmental Psychology – an interdisciplinary perspective.* Upper Saddle River, NJ: Prentice-Hall Inc. (pages 434–435)

Roberts, C. and Russell, J. (2002). Angles on Environmental Psychology. Cheltenham: Nelson Thornes Ltd. (pages 3–4, 39–43, 124, 126)

Romer, D. (2010). Adolescent Risk Taking, Impulsivity, and Brain Development: Implications for Prevention. Developmental Psychobiology, 52(3), 263–276. doi:10.1002/dev.20442

Rorschach, H. (1942). *Psychodiagnostics: A Diagnostic Test Based On Perception* (4th ed). New York: Grune and Stratton (originally published in 1921)

Sarafino, E.P. (1998). *Health Psychology – biopsychosocial interactions* (3rd edition). New York: John Wiley & Sons, Inc. (pages 134–135)

Scholl et al (2003). Referred to in Chabris, C. and Simons, D. (2010) The invisible gorilla and other ways our intuition deceives us. London: Harper Collins. (page 25)

Scholl, B.J., Noles, N.S., Pasheva, V. and Sussman, R. (2003). Talking on a cellular telephone dramatically increases 'sustained inattentional blindness'. Talk given at the annual meeting of the Vision Sciences Society, 5/13/03, Sarasota, FL. [*Abstract published in Journal of Vision,* 3(9), article 156]

Schwartz, B. and Barsky (1977). 'The Home Advantage'. *Social Forces,* 55, 641–661 *Science and Administration,* 12, 74–80.

Scoville and Milner (1957). Referred to in Gross, R. (1996) *Psychology – the science of mind and behaviour* (3rd edition). London: Hodder & Stoughton. (page 287)

Scoville and Milner (1957). Referred to in Kellogg, R.T. (2007) Fundamentals of Cognitive Psychology. Thousand Oaks, CA: Sage Publications Inc. (pages 102–106)

Seggie, I. (1983). Attribution of guilt as a function of ethnic attitude and type of crime. *Journal of Multicultural and Multilingual Development, 4,* 197–206.

Sherif, M. (1956). Experiments in group conflict. *Scientific American,* 195(5), 54–8.

Sherman, L.W. and Strang, H. (2007). *Restorative justice: The evidence.* London: Smith Institute.

Sigall, H. and Ostrove, N. (1975). Beautiful but dangerous: Effects of offender attractiveness and nature of crime on juridic judgment. *Journal of Personality and Social Psychology, 31,* pp. 410–414.

Smith (1981). Referred to in Oliver, K. (2002) Psychology in Practice: Environment. London: Hodder & Stoughton. (page 153)

Smith, H.W. (1981). Territorial spacing on a beach revisited: a cross-national exploration. *Social Psychology Quarterly,* 44(2), 132–137.

Smith, R.E., Smoll, F.L. and Curtis, B. (1979). Coach effectiveness training: a cognitive-behavioral approach to enhancing relationship skills in youth sports coaches. *Journal of Sport Psychology*, 1(1), 59–75.

Smoll, F.L., Smith, R.E., Barnett, N.P. and Everett, J.J. (1993). Enhancement of Children's Self-Esteem Through Social Support Training for Youth Sport Coaches. *Journal of Applied Psychology, 78,* 602–610.

Sommer (1969). Referred to in Bell, P.A., Greene, T.C., Fisher, J.D. and Baum, A. (1996) *Environmental Psychology* (4th edition). Orlando, FL: Harcourt Brace. (pages 303, 310–311)

Sparling, P., Guirida, A., Piomelli, D., Rosskopf, L. and Dietrich, A. (2003). Exercise activates the endocannabinoid system. *Neuroreport*, 14(17), 2209–11.

Sperry, R.W. (1974). Lateral specialization in the surgically separated hemispheres. In Schmitt F.O., Worden F.G. (eds), *The Neurosciences: Third Study Program*. Cambridge, MA: MIT Press.

Spielberger, C.D. (1966). Anxiety and Behavior, New York: Academic press.

Spillman, L. and Werner, J.S. (Eds.) (1990). Visual perception: The neurophysiological foundations. San Diego, CA: Academic Press.

Sporting Goods Manufacturers Association's (SGMA, 2011). *U.S. Trends in Team Sports* (2011 edition) – www.sfia.org/press/369_State-of-Team-Sports-in-America

Sprafkin, J.N., Liebert, R.M. and Poulos, R.W. (1975). Effects of a prosocial televised example on children's helping. *Journal of Experimental Child Psychology*, 20, 119–126.

Steg, L., Van Den Berg, A. and De Groot, J.I.M. and contributors (2013). *Environmental Psychology – an introduction*. Chichester: the British Psychological Society and John Wiley & Sons Ltd. (pages 186–188, 225, 234–241)

Steinberg, H. and Sykes, E.A. (1985). Introduction to symposium on endorphins and behavioural processes: a review of literature on endorphins and exercise. *Pharmacology, Biochemistry and Behaviour* 23, 857–62.

Steptoe-Warren, G. (2013). Occupational Psychology – an applied approach. Harlow: Pearson. (pages 150–152, 278)

Stewart, J.E. (1985). 'Appearance and punishment: The Attraction-leniency effect in the courtroom'. *The Journal of Social Psychology,* 125, 373–378.

Stodgill, R.M. (1948). Personal factors associated with leadership: survey of literature, *Journal of Psychology,* 25, 35–71.

Sutherland, E.H. (1934). *Principles of criminology*. Chicago: Lippincott.

Taylor, F.W. (1911). Principles of Scientific Management. New York: Harper & Brothers.

Thukral, A., Sankar, M.J., Agarwal, R., Gupta, N., Deorari, A.K. and Paul, V.K. (2012). *Neonatology*. 2012; 102(2):114–9. doi: 10.1159/000337839. Epub 2012 Jun 14.Early skin-to-skin contact and breast-feeding behavior in term neonates: a randomized controlled trial. Jonathan Green and Ruth Goldwynjhu Annotation: Attachment disorganisation and psychopathology: new findings in attachment research and their potential implications for developmental psychopathology in childhood. Vol. 43 Issue 7, October 2002. Pages 833–970.

Tuckman, B.W. (1965). Developmental sequences in small groups. *Psychological Bulletin*, 63, 384–389.

Ulrich, R.S. (1984). View through a window may influence recovery from surgery. *Science,* 224(4647), 420–421.

Van Leeuwen, M., Van Den Berg, S. and Boomsma, D. (2008). A Twin-family study of general IQ. *Learning and Individual Differences,* vol. 18, no. 1. Amsterdam: Elsevier.

Vealey, R.S. (1986). Conceptualization of sport-confidence and competitive orientation: preliminary investigation and instrument development. *Journal of Sport Psychology,* 8, 221–246.

Veitch, R. and Arkkelin, D. (1995). *Environmental Psychology – an interdisciplinary perspective.* Upper Saddle River, NJ: Prentice-Hall Inc. (pages 266–272, 434–438).

Warr, P. and contributors (2002). *Psychology at work* (5th edition). London: Penguin. (pages 35–36)

Weinberg, R. and Gould, D. (2011). *Foundations of Sport and Exercise Psychology.* 5th ed. Champaign, IL: Human Kinetics.

Welch, R., Huston-Stein, A., Wright, J. and Plehal, R. (1979). 'Subtle Sex-Role Cues in Children's Commercials'. *Journal of Communication,* 29(3), 202–9.

Wells, M.M. (2000). Office clutter or meaningful personal displays: the role of office personalisation in employee and organisational well-being. *Journal of Environmental Psychology,* 20(3), 239–255.

Wheeler, G. and Almeida, A. (2006). These four walls: the real British office. In Clements-Croome, D. (2006) *Creating the productive workplace* (2nd edition). Abingdon: Taylor & Francis.

White et al (2013). Referred to in White, M.P., Alcock, I., Wheeler, B.W. and Depledge, M.H. (2013) Would you be happier living in a greener urban area? *A fixed-effects analysis of panel data. Psychological Science,* 24(6), 920–8.

Wilson, J.Q. and Kelling, G.L. (1982). Broken Windows Theory: Police and neighbourhood safety. *Atlantic Monthly* 249 (March), pp. 29–38.

Wiseman, R. (2014). Night school. London: Macmillan. (pages 33–39, 40, 42–47, 58–60, 66–67)

Woods, B. (1998). 'Applying Psychology to Sport'. London: Hodder and Stoughton.

Woods, B. (2001). Psychology in Practice: Sport. London: Hodder and Stoughton.

Yerkes, R.M. and Dodson, J.D. (1908). "The relation of strength of stimulus to rapidity of habit-formation". *Journal of Comparative Neurology and Psychology,* 18, 459–482.

Zajonc, R.B., Heingartner, A. and Herman, E.M. (1969). Social enhancement and impairment of performance in the cockroach. *Journal of Personality and Social Psychology,* 13(2), 83–92.

Zajonc, R.B. (1965). 'Social facilitation'. *Science,* 149, 269–274.

Glossary

Actual leader behaviour how a leader actually behaves

Adolescence the period between puberty and adulthood, often understood to be the teenage years

Affectionless psychopathy tendency to display a lack of affection to others, lack of guilt or shame and lack of empathy for one's victims

Amniotic fluid the fluid surrounding a fetus in the womb

Antecedent strategies strategies that occur before the behaviour they are attempting to change has occurred

Anterograde amnesia the inability to create new memories after the event which has caused amnesia

Anxiety negative emotional state of apprehension that we experience when we perceive that a situation is threatening to us

Arousal physiological state that enables us to complete required tasks

Attachment "an affectional tie that one person or animal forms between himself and another specific one" (Ainsworth, 1967)

Autonomic nervous system part of the peripheral nervous system which controls such processes as respiration, heart rate and salivation

Baron's distraction-conflict theory theory which suggests that where an audience distracts the attention of a performer the performer experiences a response conflict – they are conflicted about whether they should be attending to the audience or to the task in hand

Brain-derived neurotropic factor (BDNF) one of the most common proteins in the adult brain

Broken windows theory theory which suggests that disorderly neighbourhoods lead to serious crimes

Brown-Peterson technique task used to test the capacity of short-term memory

Brunel University Mood Scale (BRUMS) scale used to measure mood changes across a short time cycle, based on POMS

Cattell's 16PF Questionnaire psychometric test that asks questions about daily life

Central nervous system comprises the brain and spinal cord

CET (coach effectiveness training) coaching technique designed increase self-esteem in low-esteem children

Chronotype combination of factors which determine whether a person is more alert in the morning or evening

Chunking process of grouping information together into units that mean something to us

Circadian rhythms biological changes that occur on a roughly 24 hour cycle, for example the sleep awake cycle

Closed-plan office office in which employees have their own individual room to work or share a room with a few people

Cognitive deficits impairments which act as a barrier to mental abilities or processes

Cognitive interview (CI) technique framework which police use when interviewing witnesses

Cognitive neuroscience scientific field concerned with biological factors which have an impact on cognition

Cognitive overload a situation where our capacity to process information is exceeded by the amount of information making a claim on our attention

Cognitive state anxiety negative thoughts and cognitive processes that impede performance

Competitive orientation how much a competitor wants to win in a given situation

Confirmation bias tendency to interpret or seek data that confirm preconceptions

Consequent strategies strategies that occur after a particular behaviour has taken place

Conservation (cognitive development) ability to determine that changes in shape are not necessarily being accompanied by changes in size or mass

Constancy tendency to see familiar objects as being the same size, shape, colour etc., irrespective of distance, lighting or the angle from which it is viewed

Corpus callosum bundle of nerve fibres which joins the two hemispheres of the brain

Cortex (brain) largest part of the human brain which is associated with higher level processes such as thought and action

Cottrell's evaluation apprehension theory theory that suggests that a performer knows that the audience has the power to either reward them, to approve of them and praise them, or the power to punish them with their disapproval

Crystallised intelligence (gc) knowledge and language skills

Defensible space crime-prevention theory operates by subdividing large portions of public spaces and assigning them to individuals and small groups to use and control as their own private areas

Deindividuation where a person undergoes a change of awareness, a change of personal identity, which leads to a reduced sense of personal agency (that is, they do not feel responsible for their behaviour)

Deprivation (maternal) where a bond between child and carer has been formed but broken, possibly due to separation

Detachment where a child avoids their carer emotionally when united after a period of separation

Differential association hypothesis theory which states that the more contact someone has with attitudes favourable to criminal activity, and the more exposure they have to criminal behaviour in their family and friends, the more criminal behaviour they will themselves come to commit

Dispositional hypothesis theory that the brutality in prisons is due to the nature of those who administer it or to the nature of those who populate prisons

Dizygotic twins genetically unidentical twins (dizygotic - two eggs)

Dominant tasks tasks that are familiar, simple or well learned

Dreamwork the process by which latent content becomes manifest content

Drive theory Zajonc's (1969) theory, which suggests that the presence of others is a source of general drive

ECI technique (enhanced cognitive interview technique) a revision of the cognitive interview technique which involves training police interviewers not only how to employ memory-retrieval techniques and mnemonic cues, but also how to set up and manage an interview that will put the interviewee at their ease and enable the most detailed and accurate account to be given

Ego defence mechanism mechanism employed by our ego to prevent our conflicts from damaging ourselves

Endorphin hypothesis explanation for the positive benefits of exercise that suggests that sustained physical activity such as aerobic exercise triggers the release of endorphins, a natural opioid or pain reliever in the brain, and that this produces a feel-good effect and leads to an improvement in mood

EPQ Eysenck Personality Questionnaire, a structured questionnaire used to measure personality

Ergonomics user-focused design

Extravert/extrovert a person who has a law 'set' level of arousal and therefore seeks out experiences or activities that will increase arousal

Fluid intelligence (gf) problem solving and logic ability

Forensic science the collection and analysis of information, often from a crime scene, which can be presented as evidence in a court of law

General Adaptation Syndrome (GAS) the body's response to stress, which is the same whatever the stimulus is, as defined by Hans Selye (1956)

Gravitational hypothesis the suggestion that people with certain personalities gravitate towards activities such as sports because of their pre-existing personality traits

Habituation immunity to the effect of a stimulus after repeated presentation of that stimulus

Hawthorne studies research undertaken by Elton Mayo in the 1920s and 30s, the aim of which was to investigate the impact of the physical environment on the productivity levels of the workers

High and low self-efficacy the strong (high) or weak (low) belief that we can succeed at something we want to do

Home advantage when a team is playing 'at home' rather than 'away' they have a greater chance of winning

Home disadvantage where the home team performs worse when playing at home

Hot-desking in the context of office work, where workers are permitted to use any desk that happens to be available at a given time

Humours according to Hippocrates: blood, phlegm, yellow bile and black bile - the imbalance of which was thought to cause madness

Imagery (in sporting context) mental practice or mental rehearsal, a process whereby the athlete thinks through or imagines themselves performing a particular skill or achieving a particular goal

Infradian rhythm a biological rhythm, longer than a circadian rhythm, which last for more than 24 hours (for example the menstrual cycle)

Interrogation a questioning technique that differs from interviews primarily in the fact that interrogation is guilt presumptive and accusatory

Introvert a person who has a high 'set' level of arousal and therefore avoids situations or activities that increase arousal

Kappa a measure of the extent of agreement between two clinicians diagnosing the same patients

Latent fingerprint a fingerprint created by sweat and left behind at a crime scene, often without the perpetrator realising

Limbic system the emotional centre of the brain

MAOA gene gene is responsible for the enzyme monoamine oxidase-A (MAOA), the function of which is to breakdown (or metabolise) excess serotonin in the brain, thus helping to control the levels of serotonin available for take-up by the brain; also known as the 'Warrior Gene', it is thought to be related to aggressive and violent criminal behaviour

Melatonin a hormone that makes us feel drowsy and tired

Mental health psychological wellbeing

MG-M Imagery Motivation General-Mastery imagery: a type of motivational imagery which is specifically beneficial in increasing a player's self-efficacy and self-confidence, thereby increasing their motivation

Mnemonic a memory improvement technique

Mock trial method method adopted in many psychological studies of jury decision making and persuasion in which participants play the role of jurors

Monozygotic twins genetically identical twins (monozygotic - one egg)

Motion studies studies investigating movements made by workers in order to identify ways of improving efficiency in the workplace

Multi-store model of memory model of memory put forward by Atkinson and Shiffrin (1968), in which they suggested the existence of three distinct memory stores: sensory, short-term and long-term memory

Myelination a stage of brain development in which neurons in the brain develop myelin sheaths that insulate them and allow them to send messages along the appropriate pathways

Negative cognitive triad according to Aaron Beck (1961), the three main dysfunctional belief themes in people with depression: 'I am worthless or flawed'; 'everything I do results in failure'; 'the future is hopeless'. It is the negative view of self, world and future

Negative punishment punishment which involves the removal of something pleasant

Negative reinforcement the removal of something unpleasant following desired behaviour

Negatively framed message message which describe the risks of undesirable behaviour

Nondominant tasks tasks that are unfamiliar, complex or novel

Open-plan office office in which employees share a large open space in which to work

Parkinson's disease neurodegenerative disease, the major physical symptoms of which include motor signs of tremor, bradykinesia (slow movement), muscle rigidity and postural instability

Peers people who are in the same social group, which may be determined due to factors such as age, class, interests or educational status

Peripheral nervous system comprises the parts of the body which are not part of the central nervous system, including all our vital organs such as the heart and lungs, kidneys, liver and stomach

Personal space the physical space around us which if encroached makes us feel uncomfortable

Personality the set of characteristics or traits which a person has and which can be used to predict their behaviour

PET scan positron emission tomography scan, which shows 2D images from within a person's body and which can highlight brain activity

Phase advance a forward shift in the sleep wake cycle, i.e. when a person brings forward when they go to sleep, for example when adjusting to a new time zone

Phase delay a backward shift in the sleep wake cycle, i.e. when a person holds back when they go to sleep, for example when adjusting to a new time zone

Physical disorder (in the context of criminal psychology) disorders which physically affect the environment, such as graffiti, littering, vandalism, untidiness

Physical disorder (in the context of medicine) Disorder which affects the body rather than the mind

Pineal gland part of the brain that seems to be involved in maintaining our sleep–wake cycle by producing melatonin, a hormone that makes us feel drowsy and tired

Population density how many people there are in a given area

Positive punishment punishment which involves the presentation of something unpleasant

Positive reinforcement receiving something pleasant following desired behaviour

Positively framed message message which describes the benefits of desirable behaviour

post-traumatic stress disorder (PTSD) psychological disorder that may be present after a traumatic event and is characterised by three clusters of symptoms: persistent re-experiencing of the traumatic event, avoidance of stimuli that act as reminders of the event and emotional numbing

Preferred leader behaviour the type of behaviour that the team would choose for their leader to perform

Prefrontal cortex part of the brain above the eyes and just behind the forehead which is involved in planning and regulating behaviour and focusing attention

Prescribed leader behaviour behaviour that the leader is required to perform

Primary reinforcers things that are naturally reinforcing in themselves, such as food, water or sex

Privacy according to Irwin Altman (1975): 'the selective control of access to the self or to one's group'

Privation where no bond has been formed between child and caregiver

Profile of Mood States (POMS) tool used by psychologists to measure six mood states, five of which are negative (tension, depression, anger, fatigue and confusion) and one positive (vigour)

Pseudopatients people pretending to be mentally ill

Psychometric tests instruments that have been developed to measure a range of mental characteristics

Recidivism reoffending

Restorative justice a process that tries to recognise the needs of the victim of a crime

Scaffolding (cognitive development) process which involves structured support between a more knowledgeable person and a child which aims to help the child learn

Schema mental organisations with which we make sense of the world and which direct our actions

Secondary reinforcers things that are not reinforcing in themselves but which become reinforcing because of their association with primary reinforcers, such as money which enables us to buy food

Secondary task performance method which aims to assess cognitive overload by seeing how much spare 'mental capacity' is left over for subsidiary tasks

Self-actualisation the reaching of one's potential

Self-efficacy belief that we can succeed at something we want to do

Self-esteem how much a person values him- or herself

Sequential unmasking a method of controlling examiner bias in forensic analysis by ensuring that irrelevant information that could bias the examiner's decision is filtered out of the process of analysing the evidence

Social cohesion (in the context of sports psychology) the extent to which team members like one another and the degree of satisfaction they get from their team membership

Social density the number of people in a set amount of space

Social disorder (in the context of criminal psychology) disorders which affect society, such as sales of drugs, drugs abuse, prostitution, begging

Somatic state anxiety this refers to the person's physiological state at the time which is having a negative effect on their performance, such as feeling nauseous, breathing heavily or having your heart pounding in your chest

Spatial density the amount of space that a set number of people occupy

Sporting self-confidence according to Robin Vealey (1986): 'the belief or degree of certainty individuals possess about their ability to be successful in sport'

State anxiety a person's level of anxiety experienced in a specific situation

State sport confidence a person's level of confidence in their ability to succeed in a specific sporting context

Stereotyping an attitude which suggests that all people who share one particular characteristic share other similar characteristics

Stigma a mark of disgrace associated with a particular circumstance or characteristic

suprachiasmatic nucleus (SCN) one part of the brain, located deep in the centre of the brain, that seems to be involved in controlling the circadian rhythms of humans and other animals by acting acts as an internal clock and controlling our daily rhythms including sleep, physical activity, hormone levels, body temperature and digestive activity

Task cohesion the extent to which team members work together to achieve shared and specific goals

Territory a particular location which a person or group regards as their own

Theory of Planned Behaviour theory put forward by Ajzen and colleagues in the 1980s which proposed that behaviours flow from behavioural intentions which, in turn, arise from three influencing factors: attitudes towards the behaviour, subjective norms and perceived behavioural control

Time studies studies in which the main focus is on the length of time it should take to complete a given task

tragedy of the commons Hardin's (1968) theory, in which it was argued that an individual farmer will always be likely to add an extra cow to common grazing land to add to his or her profits but, because this will be true of other farmers too, the individual actions that they each take will eventually lead to the overgrazing and ruination of the common land

Trait anxiety general personality or disposition to be anxious

Trait sport confidence one's level of confidence in one's own sporting ability in general

Trait theories of personality theories which suggest that personality can be reduced to a number of traits or characteristics that we all share, but of which we have different amounts

Trial by jury trial in which guilty/not guilty verdict is decided by a jury

Ultradian rhythm (ultra-rapid) biological rhythms which occur in cycles of less than 24 hours

Urban renewal according to Porteus (1977): an integrated series of steps taken to maintain and upgrade the environmental, economic and social health of an urban area

Working Memory model Baddeley and Hitch's (2001) reworking of the multi-store model of memory, which suggested that STM consists of different subsystems co-ordinated by a central executive that work together to temporarily maintain mental representations of relevance to the performance of a cognitive task in an activated state

Yale Model of Persuasion model, first developed by Hovland and colleagues at Yale University in the 1950s, which can be used as the basis for attempts to change attitudes towards the environment

Zeitgeber 'time giver' in German - an external cue, such as light, which influences internal biological rhythms

Zero tolerance policy policy used in policing in which the priority to crackdown on minor offences is increased so that disorder is decreased and in turn serious crime is reduced

Zone of proximal development (ZPD) the area of cognitive skills a child can reach with the help of a more-knowledgeable other

Index